Gendering Knowledge in A the African Diaspora

CW00497401

Gendering Knowledge in Africa and the African Diaspora addresses the question of to what extent the history of gender in Africa is appropriately inscribed in narratives of power, patriarchy, migration, identity and women and men's subjection, emasculation and empowerment. The book weaves together compelling narratives about women, men and gender relations in Africa and the African Diaspora from multidisciplinary perspectives, with a view to advancing original ways of understanding these subjects.

The chapters achieve three things: first, they deliberately target long-held but erroneous notions about patriarchy, power, gender, migration and masculinity in Africa and of the African Diaspora, vigorously contesting these, and debunking them; second, they unearth previously marginalized and little known his/herstories, depicting the dynamics of gender and power in places ranging from Angola to Arabia to America, and in different time periods, decidedly gendering the previously male-dominated discourse; and third, they ultimately aim to re-write the stories of women and gender relations in Africa and in the African Diaspora. As such, this work is an important read for scholars of African history, gender and the African Diaspora.

This book will be of interest to students and scholars of African Studies, Diaspora Studies, Gender and History.

Toyin Falola is the Jacob and Frances Sanger Mossiker Chair in the Humanities, and a Distinguished Teaching Professor at the University of Texas at Austin, USA.

Olajumoke Yacob-Haliso is Senior Lecturer in Political Science at Babcock University in Nigeria.

Global Africa
Series Editors: Toyin Falola and Roy Doron

Gendering Knowledge in Africa and the African Diaspora

Contesting History and Power

Edited by Toyin Falola and Olajumoke Yacob-Haliso

Routledge
Taylor & Francis Group

LONDON AND NEW YORK

First published 2017
by Routledge

2 Park Square, Milton Park, Abingdon, Oxfordshire OX14 4RN
52 Vanderbilt Avenue, New York, NY 10017

Routledge is an imprint of the Taylor & Francis Group, an informa business

First issued in paperback 2019

British Library Cataloguing in Publication Data
A catalogue record for this book is available from the British Library

Library of Congress Cataloging in Publication Data
Names: Falola, Toyin, editor. | Yacob-Haliso, Olajumoke, editor.
Title: Gendering knowledge in Africa and the African diaspora : contesting history and power / edited by Toyin Falola and Olajumoke Yacob-Haliso.
Other titles: Global Africa ; 5.
Description: New York, NY : Routledge, 2018. | Series: Global Africa ; 5 | Includes bibliographical references and index.
Identifiers: LCCN 2017006083 | ISBN 9781138037700 (hardback) | ISBN 9781315177717 (ebook)
Subjects: LCSH: Women–Africa–History. | Women–Africa–Social conditions. | Sex role–Africa–History. | Africa–Social life and customs. | African diaspora–Social conditions.
Classification: LCC HQ1787 .G458 2018 | DDC 305.42096–dc23
LC record available at https://lccn.loc.gov/2017006083

ISBN: 978-1-138-03770-0 (hbk)
ISBN: 978-0-367-88845-9 (pbk)

Typeset in Times New Roman
by Wearset Ltd, Boldon, Tyne and Wear

For Ashenaffi and Betsega, with love.

Contents

PART II
Gender, migration and identity   85

PART III
Gender, subjection and power   141

Illustrations

Figures

Tables

Contributors

Dotun Ayobade broadly situates his research at the intersection of performance, identity and postcolonialism in twentieth century West Africa. He earned his PhD from the Department of Theatre and Dance at the University of Texas at Austin. He also obtained portfolio certificates in African and African Diaspora Studies (AADS) and in Women and Gender Studies (WGS). He is currently working on his first book manuscript tentatively titled *Women That Danced the Fire Dance: Fela Kuti's Queens and the Postcolonial Politics of Play*. This work examines the shifting notions of power and agency that Fela's wives (famously known as Afrobeat Queens) embodied through Afrobeat performance, and within the context of postcolonial Nigeria. Ayobade's research earned him the University of Texas at Austin's Graduate School Named/Endowed Continuing Fellowship for 2014–2015. He currently teaches courses in Yoruba language, history and culture, as well as in West African popular culture in the Department of African and African Diaspora Studies (AADS) at the University of Texas at Austin.

Leamon Bazil is a post-doctoral fellow in the Philosophy Department at Saint Louis University. His areas of specialization include social political philosophy and ethics. His areas of competency are Africana studies and contemporary critical theory. Leamon Bazil has experience teaching ethics, applied ethics and Ancient Greek philosophy. Also, because he has completed a substantive amount of coursework that examines the history of philosophy, he is qualified to teach other subjects from a historical point of view. Leamon can be reached at: lbazil@slu.edu.

Elias K. Bongmba is the Harry and Hazel Chair in Christian Theology and Professor of Religion at Rice University. He is the current President of the African Association for the Study of Religion. His book, *The Dialectics of Transformation in Africa*, won the Franz Fanon Prize in Caribbean Thought in 2007. He is also author of *Facing a Pandemic: The African Church and Crisis of AIDS* and editor of *The Routledge Companion to Christianity in Africa*.

Toyin Falola is the Jacob and Frances Sanger Mossiker Chair in the Humanities and University Distinguished Teaching Professor at the University of Texas at Austin. He has authored/edited or co-authored/edited over 140 books on Africa and the African Diaspora. He is the recipient of seven honorary doctorates from universities in the United States and Nigeria, as well as of dozens of other academic honors, awards and fellowships. Falola is currently (2016) the Kluge Chair in Countries and Cultures of the South at the Library of Congress in Washington, DC.

Tiffany N. Florvil is Assistant Professor of Twentieth-Century European Women's and Gender History at the University of New Mexico, where she specializes in the African Diaspora in Europe, gender and sexuality, and emotions. She received her PhD from the University of South Carolina in 2013 and her MA from the University of Wisconsin-Madison in 2007. She is the Co-Chair of the Black Diaspora Studies Network at the German Studies Association, an advisory board member and a network editor for H-Black Europe and a network editor for H-Emotions. Florvil has received fellowships from the American Council on Germany, the German Academic Exchange Service (DAAD) and the Feminist Research Institute at the University of New Mexico. She is co-editing a volume entitled *New Perspectives in Black German Studies* with Peter Lang, and is co-editing a special issue on transnational civil rights and anti-racist activism for the *Journal of Civil and Human Rights*. She has published a chapter in the volume *Audre Lorde's Transnational Legacies* and has a forthcoming chapter in *To Turn This Whole World Over: Black Women's Internationalism during the Twentieth Century*. She is currently revising her manuscript entitled *Making a Movement: A History of Black Germans, Gender, and Belonging.*

Catherine Cymone Fourshey is Associate Professor of History and International Relations at Bucknell University. Fourshey's published research focuses on agriculture, hospitality, migration, and the intersections of environment, economy and politics in precolonial Tanzania. She has conducted research and published on gender in Africa both in precolonial and colonial spaces. She has published articles in the *African Historical Review*, *International Journal of African Historical Studies*, *JENdA* and *Ufahamu*. Fourshey recently completed a co-authored manuscript entitled *Bantu Africa*, which is being published by Oxford University Press. She is completing a book manuscript titled *Strangers, Immigrants and the Established: Hospitality as State Building Mechanism in Southwest Tanzania 300–1900 CE*. Additionally, Fourshey has been conducting research on the history of immigrants/refugees in Tanzania who are known in international aid and development circles as "the Bantu Somali." She has been a recipient of research grants and fellowships from the American Association of University Women, Fulbright, The National Endowment for the Humanities and Notre Dame University. Her email is ccf014@Bucknell.edu.

Rhonda M. Gonzales is Associate Professor of African and African Diaspora History and Director of *PIVOT for Academic Success* at the University of

Texas at San Antonio. The National Endowment for the Humanities, Andrew Mellon Foundation, Ford Foundation and The American Historical Association have supported her research on women and their roles in sustaining and transforming society through religion, medicine and economy in both precolonial Africa and in the African Diaspora in Mexico. She is author of *Societies, Religion, and History: Central East Tanzanians and the World They Created*, c.*200 BCE to 1800 CE*. *Bantu Africa, 3500 BCE–1500 CE*, a co-authored title, is forthcoming with Oxford University Press. Gonzales is an American Council on Education Fellow. As a first-generation college graduate, she is passionate about envisioning and implementing programming and best practices that support first-generation, transition, low SES and STEM student retention through graduation. In late 2015 she was awarded a $3.25 million Department of Education Title-V Grant to build four student success programs at UTSA: F2G&G, RTE, Alamo Runners and Math Matters. Gonzales is from Long Beach, California. She holds a BA in Sociology and an MA and PhD in History from UCLA.

Alaine S. Hutson is a full professor currently at Huston-Tillotson University in Austin, Texas. She has also taught at Missouri State University, Michigan State University and Houston Community College. Dr. Hutson specializes in African and Middle East history with an emphasis on slavery and gender in Islamic societies. Dr. Hutson's research is currently surrounding the larger question: Is there an African Diaspora in the Middle East? In pursuit of that research she has recently traveled to seminars and conferences in Cape Town, South Africa; Amman, Jordan; and Salzburg, Austria. Dr. Hutson is a research affiliate at the University of Texas at Austin, has been a Henry C. McBay Fellow and a UNCF/Mellon Faculty Fellow resident at the James Weldon Johnson Institute at Emory University. While resident at JWJI, Dr. Hutson built and published the REMAP database website (www.remapdatabase.org). She also received grants from the Sam Taylor Fellowship from the United Methodist Church. Dr. Hutson's academic publications include: "REMAPping the African Diaspora: Place, Gender and Negotiation in Arabian Slavery" in Olajumoke Yacob-Haliso and Toyin Falola (eds.), *Gendering Knowledge in Africa and the African Diaspora*, London: Routledge (2017). "Enslavement and Manumission of Africans and Yemenis in Saudi Arabia, 1926–1938" in *Critique: Critical Middle Eastern Studies*; "African Sufi Women and Ritual Change" in the *Journal of Ritual Studies*; and "Gender, Mobility, and Sharia Law in Northern Nigeria" in *International Institute for the Study of Islam in the Modern World (ISIM) Newsletter*. She will be on sabbatical for 2016–2017 working on a manuscript entitled *I Now Pray for My Freedom* on slavery on the Arabian Peninsula in the early twentieth century.

Omotola Adeyoju Ilesanmi is a research fellow in the Division of International Law and Organisations of the Research and Studies Department at the Nigerian Institute of International Affairs (NIIA), Lagos, Nigeria. She holds both

Bachelor's and Master's degrees in Political Science from the University of Lagos, Nigeria. She is currently pursuing a PhD in the Department of Political Science and Public Administration at Babcock University, Ogun State, Nigeria. Her areas of research interest include gender, foreign policy, security and peacebuilding. She has several publications including book chapters and journal articles in reputable journals.

Rachael Oluseye Iyanda is of the Department of Political Science and Public Administration, Veronica Adeleke School of Social Sciences, Babcock University, where she has been a faculty member since 2008 and from 1997–2008 she also served in various administrative capacities. She completed her PhD at Babcock University, her MA at the University of Ibadan and her BSc was from Babcock University. Her research interests lie in the areas of policy design and analysis; comparative politics and gender studies; human development and trafficking in persons; and international conflict, peace and security. She is a member of the International Political Science Association (IPSA), West African Political Science Association (WAPSA), Society for Peace Studies and Practice (SPSP) and the Liberian Studies Association. She was the recipient of several awards as an undergraduate student and produced one of the best PhD dissertations in her department for 2014. Rachael is married and blessed with four beautiful daughters born between November 1993 and June 2008. Rachael enjoys fashion, traveling, reading novels, and counseling.

Francis O. Jegede is a poet, journalist and seasoned literary artist with a rare passion for orature and community theatre. He has authored many books and collections of poems. He currently teaches literature in the English Department, School of Languages, Adeniran Ogunsanya College of Education, Otto/Ijanikin, Lagos, Nigeria.

Methuselah Jeremiah holds a PhD in Theatre Arts. He is a lecturer in the Department of English and Drama, Kaduna State University, Kaduna, Nigeria. Apart from documenting aspects of Akurmi history and culture in *The Akurmi People of Central Nigeria: Their Heritage and Hope* (a book he co-edited with Elisha Madaki) and *Snapshots of the Female Ethos: Essays on Women in Drama and Culture in Africa* (a book he co-edited with Professor Mabel Evwhierhoma), Jeremiah has also published book chapters and journal articles both locally and internationally. His areas of research include gender studies in drama, culture and development with a special emphasis on women.

Gift U. Ntiwunka (PhD) is a senior lecturer in the Department of Political Science and Public Administration, Babcock University, Ilisan-Remo, Ogun State Nigeria. She holds a BA in Religion/Business Administration from Andrews University, Berrien Springs, Michigan, an MA in Public Administration from Onabisi Onabanjo University, Ogun State, Nigeria and a PhD in Political Science with specialization in public administration. Dr. Ntiwunka has published a number of articles in local and international journal and has

also contributed book chapters. Her areas of interest include public administration, gender and development studies.

Senayon Olaoluwa is of the Institute of African Studies at the University of
Ibadan where he coordinates a postgraduate program in Diaspora and Trans-
national Studies. Some of his reviews and essays have appeared in *African
Affairs, Journal of Contemporary African Studies, English Studies, English
Studies in Africa, Okike, Current Writing, Critique: Studies in Contemporary
Fiction* and the *Journal of Film and Video*, among others.

Sharon Adetutu Omotoso taught politics and philosophy and was formerly
Acting Head of Department, Politics and International Relations, Lead City
University, Ibadan. She is currently with the Gender Studies Program at the
Institute of African Studies, University of Ibadan, Nigeria. As a member of
the Nigerian Philosophical Association (NPA), an Associate Registered Prac-
titioner in the Advertising Practitioners Council of Nigeria (APCON), an
associate member of the Council for Research in Values and Philosophy and
Member (CRVP) and the Association of Communication Scholars and Professional of Nigeria (ACSPN), she has consulted for international organizations
such as the UNESCO. Dr. Omotoso attends and participates at local and international academic conferences and workshops. Her areas of research interest
include applied ethics, media and gender studies, political communications,
philosophy of education, socio-political philosophy and African philosophy
where she has published extensively.

Christine Saidi is Associate Professor of African History at Kutztown Univer-
sity (a state university serving first-generation students). Saidi is the recipient
of three prestigious Fulbright Fellowships, a Social Science Research Council
Grant and a Woodrow Wilson Women's Studies Grant. She was instrumental
in establishing the Center for the Study of Gender in Africa at the African
Studies Center at UCLA. She conducted research in Somalia and in The
White Fathers' Archive, Rome, and later in Zambia and the Democratic
Republic of the Congo as a Senior Fulbright Scholar. She has authored a
book, *Women's Authority and Society in Early East-African History*, several
scholarly articles and is completing a co-authored a book. She and her two
colleagues have just won a $200,000 National Endowment for the Humanities
Grant to research on gender in Africa and entitled "Expressions and Transformations of Gender, Family, and Status in Eastern and Central Africa,
500–1800 CE."

Mobolanle E. Sotunsa is Professor of African Oral Literature and Gender
Studies in the Department of Languages and Literary Studies, Babcock University, Nigeria. She holds a Doctorate degree from the Department of
English, University of Ibadan, Nigeria. Her areas of specializations are
African oral literatures, African women writings, literary theories and African
literature. She has authored, edited or co-edited ten books in addition to
several scholarly articles and book chapters in learned journals and

peer-reviewed books both nationally and internationally. Mobolanle Sotunsa was the Head of Department of Languages and Literary Studies Department at Babcock University from 2006 to 2009. She was a visiting scholar at School of African and Oriental Studies (SOAS) at the University of London in 2009. She was also a visiting professor/scholar in residence at the African Studies Institute, University of Georgia, USA in 2013. Mobolanle Sotunsa is the Coordinator of Gender and African Studies Group at Babcock University (BUGAS). She is also the Deputy Director of the Centre for Open, Distance and e-learning (CODeL) at Babcock University.

Olajumoke Yacob-Haliso is Senior Lecturer in the Department of Political Science and Public Administration at Babcock University, Nigeria. Olajumoke's research has focused on women in peace, conflict and security as well as on comparative African politics. Her essays have been published in *Wagadu: The Journal of Transnational Women's Studies*, the *Liberian Studies Journal*, the *Africa Peace and Conflict Journal* and elsewhere. She is co-editor of *Women in Africa: Contexts, Rights, Hegemonies*, as well as of three other forthcoming titles and is also editor of the *Journal of International Politics and Development*. Olajumoke has held fellowships and grants from the Harry Frank Guggenheim Foundation, the University for Peace Africa Program, the International Development Research Centre, amongst others. In 2012, she was (post-doctoral) Global South Scholar-in-Residence at the Graduate Institute of International and Development Studies, Geneva, Switzerland. She is currently a post-doctoral fellow of the American Council of Learned Societies (ACLS)'s African Humanities Program (AHP), 2016–2017.

Preface

The core objective of *Gendering Knowledge in Africa and the African Diaspora: Contesting History and Power* is to vigorously contest and possibly invert commonly held notions about gender in Africa and the African Diaspora worldwide, while also presenting more accurate information intended to contribute to re-writing the history of gendered power about Africans everywhere. As Africans on the continent and elsewhere take advantage of the forces of globalization, modernity and postmodernism, transcending borders in space and time, they are constantly confronted with a Conradian view of African history and culture that has become difficult to dislodge. When this reality is further extended to an exploration of gender relations among the various groups of Africans, the situation is even worse, leading to the call among Black and African feminist scholars for a re-construction of the history of the continent that both includes and uplifts women's contributions to history and the inscription of power in knowledge. Indeed, those who write history, write power into history and can apportion it as they deem fit. This volume seeks to write gender into the history of Africa and the African Diaspora where conspicuously missing or in some cases "deleted," or to re/interpret the accounts that have been passed down for decades, even centuries. In so doing, perhaps, this volume could bequeath to posterity important "knowledges" able to transform the present and the future of Africa and the African Diaspora.

To achieve these ends, the book is divided into three major parts. The first part contains three chapters which explicitly embark on the task of re/writing the history of gender in the Bantu-speaking region of the continent, in the African Diaspora in Saudi Arabia and, more contemporarily, in the history being written every day on various New Media platforms. The second part through three piquant essays turns to the pervasive influence of migration in moulding the identity of Africans and the African Diaspora. Here, a young slave girl representing millions of silent other ones unsung bravely resists the forces of patriarchy, exploitation, slavery and colonization, and becomes a metaphor for a continent bound, but free. Black German women find their voice and reclaim their identity and their place in a nation that wishes to forget they exist. And an American Diaspora woman returns to the continent to reclaim her identity and sense of belonging, claiming back the forced migration of her forbears with the voluntary reverse migration to Africa. In six unique essays, the third part confronts the trenchant dynamics of power and subjection often to be found in gender narratives of society. While Fela Kuti's Queens take flight and re-appear in the Diaspora in an empowering manner, women in Wimbum land in Cameroon cannot escape the disempowering accusations of witchcraft that seeks to entrench their subservience to patriarchal norms, as women in Jos attempt the very opposite to produce peace in their land. Further away, in the United States, Black men and women are shackled with stereotypes that literally kill them, mirroring similar subjections occasioning silence and a lack of development in African spaces explored, while back in a fictional political party in Nigeria women break free from male domination, with the unintended consequence of emasculation of their male counterparts.

Thus, from historical, literary, anthropological, linguistic, sociological, feminist and other perspectives, the authors of *Gendering Knowledge* explode for the reader worlds unsung and inherently captivating in their variegated dynamics. This rich multidisciplinary volume will be of interest to scholars, students, policy makers, activists and others interested in the various themes covered.

We wish to acknowledge and appreciate the patience and the efforts of the authors featured in this volume who entrusted us with their intellectual effluence and trusted that we would acquit our task judiciously. The journey through repeated reviews and re-submissions was long, but they stayed the course. We thank our publishers and editors for their interest in getting this book to the public. Of course, we take all responsibility for any shortcomings of the book. Thank you.

Toyin Falola, *University of Texas at Austin*
Olajumoke Yacob-Haliso, *Babcock University*
September 2016

Introduction

Gendering knowledge in Africa and the African Diaspora

Olajumoke Yacob-Haliso and Toyin Falola

This book weaves together compelling narratives about women, men and gender relations in Africa and the African Diaspora from multidisciplinary perspectives, with a view to advancing original and nascent ways of knowing and understanding women, gender and society in Africa and the African Diaspora. Explorations of landscapes ranging from ancient Arabia to modern day Africa and America in this volume demonstrate the possibilities of gendering knowledge about Africa and the African Diaspora by superseding existing frameworks to unearth marginal narratives, centering them within respective knowledge modes in order to bring fresh perspectives that might otherwise have been unknown or overlooked. The Africa that is portrayed is multi-colored and fascinating, escaping the single-dimensional picture often given by extant scholarship undertaken about the continent—indeed, a 7-D Africa is here presented. Likewise, the Diaspora that we explore in this book, *Gendering Knowledge*, is a boundless one, exceeding the geographically defined. Toyin Falola has opined, and we aver that:

> What we characterize as a diaspora cannot be limited to one event or an episode (as in that of slavery), to ties created by the transatlantic slave trade, and to a time in the past. Scholars of the African diaspora deal with movements in various eras … the creation and continuity of cultures, the survival and repackaging of traditions to meet new challenges, the creation of identities that do not respect boundaries, the linkages between power and representation … between and within diasporic identities.[1]

Women's experiences came to be the focus of academic research as a product of the feminist movements of the last century, and, by vigorous theorizing as well as by vibrant activism, women and gender studies have gained space as a legitimate subject of history, philosophy, science and the arts. Indeed, an "international consensus" has developed around certain norms with respect to women's rights.[2] However, the journey to this acceptance was not an easy one as feminist scholarship suffered challenges from without and from within, and a brief historical excursion here is indicative and necessary.

The feminist movement of the 1960s and 1970s (referred to as second-wave feminism in the literature) was focused on challenging patriarchy not only in the public sphere but even more so in the 'private' sphere of the family and work environment. This feminist movement was characterized by a close link between activist and academic feminists, resulting in a movement that prioritized research and was highly critical of existing ways of *knowing* reality. This strand of feminism thus bequeathed important legacies for subsequent decades of feminist activism. However, one important shortcoming of the feminist expression of that time is that there was the assumption that one *essential* woman existed, needing liberation from one common enemy—the male man. It is this assumption that birthed the criticism by feminist scholars of color who rejected the notion of a universal experience for all women, declaring instead that in many ways they (Third World and African American women) had more in common with their own men than with white women. In the words of Mohanty,[3] "Sisterhood cannot be assumed on the basis of gender; it must be forged in concrete historical and political practice."

Throughout the 1970s, 80s and 90s, feminists from the Global South (and some from the North too) built up the argument for a gender analysis that rejects all essentialism and recognizes difference to go beyond sex difference. Entering into the debate, third world women's organizations such as the Association of African Women for Research and Development (AAWORD) and the Development Alternatives for Women in a New Era (DAWN) challenged the Eurocentric approach to studying gender and adopted a critical gender research agenda.[4]

The challenge of this strand of feminism is fundamental to our understanding of gender as social process, social stratification and social structure. If gender is social structure, then any investigation of gender must take into account how it intersects with other pertinent structures of social differentiation. The insistence on difference recognizes that social location in terms of race, ethnicity, status, class and access to power and privilege can significantly alter the meaning of gender as these other factors confer power on some women and men at the expense of others.[5] Many Black (American) feminist scholars have critiqued feminist articulations of gender as it applies to their own situation, insisting that in the United States there is no way gender can be considered outside of race and class and feminists must theorize multiple forms of oppression wherever these exist in society.[6] In other places, scholars critical of the prevailing Western explanation of gender insist on the need to theorize the impact of imperialism, colonialism, globalization, 'modernization,' the Washington Consensus, and other local and global forms of social stratification on women and men.[7]

In studies of Africa and the African Diaspora, therefore, gender becomes a highly contested concept, subject to different interpretations within different contexts since the fundamental implication of power differentiation and subordination does not hold the same meaning in every African society and culture. For example, two Nigerian scholars, Ifi Amadiume and Oyeronke Oyewumi[8] in their respective seminal works *Male Daughters, Female Husbands* and *The Invention of Women* have sought to demonstrate that the gender discourses of the West might not have any relevance at all to the Nigerian socio-cultural context on the basis of the underlying assumptions and internal logic that drive Western feminism. Gender identities must be seen as culturally and historically specific and holding social meaning for individual cultures. Thus, the recognition that gender is a socially constructed identity and structure, "historically grounded and culturally bound" implies that

> gender cannot behave the same way across time and space. If gender is a social construction, then we must examine the various cultural/architectural sites where it was constructed, and we must acknowledge that variously located actors ... were part of the construction.[9]

How do we achieve this nuanced exploration of gender in different social contexts? From a feminist standpoint, research is power, and the epistemologies we use signify power and hierarchies of power. Jane Bennett, in her editorial for a 2008 special edition of *Feminist Africa* themed *Researching for Life: Paradigms and Power*, explicates this dimension of research thus:

> *Researchers* constitute a large and complicated congregation, but one riven with differentiation not only of discipline but much more powerfully of status and privilege (medical is more valuable than historical, pure is better than applied, quantitative is stronger than qualitative; positivist is more credible than feminist/indigenous/post-anything). The cultural habits of hierarchization extend to the notion of what is "non-research"[10] (emphasis in original).

Thus, *gendering knowledge* is an enterprise in according power and status to traditionally snubbed subjects, modes, methods and methodologies of research and their productions, which have had deleterious consequences for the empowering of women and other marginalized subjects. Furthermore, Sylvia Tamale warns that African feminists (and African Diaspora feminists by extension to this book) must remain aware of the "dangers associated with the uncritical application of Western theories to non-Western contexts."[11] Western theories inevitably are outgrowths of the history, culture, language, politics and experiences of Western peoples, applied to their own circumstances to provide solutions to their own problems primarily. An uncritical application to non-Western societies and social relations such as gender would be inapposite.

The caution, however, is not only with regard to the contextual concerns and subjects central to Western theories and theorizing. Also important are the subjects and topics and ways of knowing that are excluded from the study and made invisible in the academy, and therefore shielded from the notice of policy makers and change-makers. One of the triumphs of the second wave of Western feminism was precisely that it brought to the public agenda the discourse on women's rights, reproductive health issues, the critique of patriarchy, women's oppression and other women-focused issues. In keeping with this tradition, gendering knowledge must involve uncovering 'marginal' and marginalized narratives for study by feminist scholars. The fact is that all "theoretical frames

... border and exclude. Our concern should be less with what is framed in and more with what is framed out, what is silenced."[12]

In order to achieve this objective, "we must interrogate feminist scholarship not only on theoretical grounds, but also on epistemological grounds."[13] Indeed, the knowledge examined is neither singular nor linear nor knowable in a fixed fashion; thus, to use the term 'knowledges' is by no means inappropriate. Feminist scholarship has as one of its hallmarks this questioning of existing modes of knowledge production—theoretical and epistemological—seen as one of the elements by which women's subordination has been historically produced in both Western and African spaces.

Intervention

This volume, *Gendering Knowledge in Africa and the African Diaspora: Contesting History and Power*, makes a solid contribution to the feminist aspirations enunciated above. Each chapter brings to the fore previously neglected or marginalized knowledges about women and men and their social relationships in Africa and the African Diaspora. They highlight and question the position accorded to women in specific contexts as well as in relation to existing knowledge and the literature. The chapters provoke us to see the ways in which gender is being daily constructed and re-constructed in the activities of the state and state institutions, non-governmental organizations, male men, by women themselves and by the larger society. Each chapter boldly makes claims that push the frontiers of knowledge about women and gender in Africa and the African Diaspora. Ultimately, this book makes important connections: between women and men; between experience and/or empiricism and epistemology; between Africa and the Diaspora; between the Old and the New Diaspora; between objective realities and subjective ideas; between humanistic and social scientific epistemologies; and between gendered knowledge and the larger body of scholarship on the subjects treated.

The book is organized into three parts, following this introductory chapter. The first part, titled "(Re-)Writing Gender in African and African Diaspora History," houses three important chapters. These chapters have in common the explicit objective of (re-)writing the history of women in Africa and the African Diaspora, and show how to do this using the cases of matrilineality in the Bantu Belt of Africa, of slavery and the Arabian African Diaspora, while the third prescribes a project for infusing feminist ethics into the narratives being spawned by new media in contemporary Africa.

The second part of the book, "Gender, Migration and Identity," explores questions of identity, migration and resistance in the experiences of very different women, located in different times and spaces: German Diaspora Black women in post-Unification Germany; women disabled both physically and emotionally by trans-Saharan and trans-Atlantic slavery; and Diaspora Black American women who choose reverse migration to Africa.

The third part, "Gender, Subjection and Power," contains six essays that analyze women in relation to subjective ideas, imaginations and manifestations of power and subjection: Fela Kuti's "Queens" are depicted to be in transcendence, appearing in various contemporary women artistes in the Diaspora; women in a Cameroonian community are disproportionately accused of diabolical witchcraft; in Jos, Nigeria, women defy conflict to perform peacebuilding roles, thereby prolonging the survival of their communities; subjective portrayals of black women and men by the media, politicians, social workers and the welfare system is shown as keeping them perpetually in the role of the subjected and oppressed, decades after the official end of slavery in the United States; Silence is explored as a consequence and a cause of women's inability to contribute to development agendas on the African continent; and the final essay in the volume spotlights the psychological anxieties and emasculation experienced by men and masculinity in patriarchal settings when women are politically empowered.

Outline

In Chapter 1 the authors of "The Bantu Matrilineal Belt: Reframing African women's history" provide a deliberate challenge to various false notions that have bedeviled the writing of African women's history. This is pertinent because, while Bolanle Awe[14] has rightly observed that, "compared with the history of many other parts of the world, the writing of the history of Africa itself is a fairly recent development," the writing of the history of African women in particular lagged even further behind. In an assessment of gender biases in African historiography, Paul Zeleza has asserted that "women remain largely invisible or misrepresented in mainstream, or rather 'malestream' African history. They are either not present at all, or they are depicted as naturally inferior and subordinate, as eternal victims of male oppression."[15] In Chapter 1 of this book, Rhonda M. Gonzales, Christine Saidi and Catherine Cymone Fourshey argue against the tendency by which African women's history is "commonly reduced to a 'single story' characterized by victimization, marginalization, and, most significantly, silence"; the notion that African women's history cannot be known, or that African men have always held more power and authority than women; or that the relationship between African women and men in history was linear and oppositional.

This lead chapter sets out to vigorously debunk these widely perpetuated notions by marshalling an enormous amount of carefully selected historical, linguistic and ethnographic data, covering a historical period of over 5,000 years, and a geographic region of Africa spanning Angola in the West, through Central Africa to Tanzania, and to Mozambique in the East. The authors propose the concept of a "Bantu Matrilineal Belt" to describe this region comprising over 450 Bantu-descended languages, of which at least 100 are matrilineal. Furthermore, the chapter makes the important suggestion that, rather than a hierarchy of gendered power and authority in this region, what existed was a *heterarchy*, diffuse power among several loci of authority, rather than vertically related centers of power. Gender is therefore identified as just one in a multiplicity of salient factors that shape social relations in these societies. For these authors, matrilineality is an approach for re-imagining, re-thinking and re-constructing the history of the people of the region under study, and especially with reference to the key themes of heterarchy, matrilineality, sororal groups, bride-service and life-stages. This chapter provides the kind of nuanced analysis of gendered power relations that makes it possible to re-write the history of Africa and Africans.

Chapter 2 similarly attempts a bold re-writing, this time of African Diaspora history, by considering the role of place, gender and Africanness in the experience of African slaves in Arabia. "REMAPping the African Diaspora" is an extensive project that confronts the previously held notions that so-called Islamic slavery was so much more benign than trans-Atlantic slavery, and that when freed, former slaves were absorbed into the society and did not stand apart as a Diaspora. Also, Arabian historiography 'deleted' the domestic and agricultural work of slaves from the record, constituting a huge gap in the account that recent scholarship is only beginning to pay attention to. This chapter makes a significant contribution to re-writing this history by confronting these notions using a quantitative analysis of the historical record, while also drawing important parallels with Atlantic slavery. The chapter is based on a publicly accessible, searchable and invaluable online database created by the author, Alaine S. Hutson, and called the Runaways Enslaved and Manumitted on the Arabian Peninsula (REMAP) database (www.REMAPdatabase.org). The details of the lives of enslaved Africans are found in the records of the British Legation in Jeddah, Saudi Arabia from 1926 to 1938, made up of a total of Foreign Office files on 263 people, including the narratives of runaway slaves about their lives in servitude. The chapter suggests that when made to do similar work, particularly rural agricultural or urban domestic work, slaves in Saudi Arabia experienced patterns of subordination similar to the slaves in the Americas. Furthermore, urban and rural contexts of slavery produced significant differences in slaveholding patterns within both Arabia and the Americas, and also revealed the gendered nature of power in those societies. Religion and gender also shaped the slave family units. Ultimately, these varied factors determined where the Atlantic Diaspora settled; and, as Hutson argues here, because the same patterns existed in Arabia, certainly, an Arabic Diaspora also exists, not absorbed and assimilated and erased, refuting the history projected by the Ottoman Empire, and ambitiously attempting to re-write that history of this portion of the African Diaspora.

The third chapter in this signal first part turns our attention to a contemporary project in re-writing African women's stories. Sharon Omotoso in her chapter unpacks the concepts of new media and feminist ethics, while adopting communications analysis for making a proposal toward linking these two concepts for the empowerment of African women and feminist narratives in Africa. The author points out that so-called new media has been a primary vehicle for the sustenance of globalization, a process flagged as having bequeathed negative consequences for women, "denying them of identity and autonomy within hegemonic global cultures." The chapter reflects on the impact of new media on

African societies that have neither reflected upon, nor anticipated or prepared for the onslaught of new images, values and ideas that come with the use of these media, including the heightened exposure to ideas and images of women that further objectify, demean and violate women, thereby contributing to women's victimization, oppression and the perpetuation of patriarchy in the lives of African women. The author argues that ethics and responsibility must be central to the use of new media in Africa as the latter has liberatory and other potentials if properly harnessed for feminist objectives. The chapter embarks on a critique of the treatment of women on five new media platforms: the news, advertisements, photographs, anti-feminist websites and blogs, and the fashion world. Omotoso then assesses the relevance of the ethics of care and of risk proposed by other scholars and calls for a deconstruction of gender prejudices peddled by new media and the decolonization of feminist ethics. The chapter then proposes the adoption of a feminist "ethic of vigor" which is designed to be more contextually sensitive and relevant to African values and therefore more suited to the emancipation of African women and the achievement of gender justice and equity. By thus infusing new media with feminist concerns and feminist ethics, this chapter closes the first part of the book on the hopeful note that we can re-write the present and the future of the African woman, even if we cannot erase the past.

The three chapters in Part II are descriptive of the experiences of women in three different kinds of migration scenarios, linking these women's experiences with broader macro-perspective questions of national/state aggression, state capacity and even state complicity in the challenges besetting the lived experiences of women of African descent. In Chapter 4, Tiffany N. Florvil brings to light the unique situation of Black/Afro-German women in Germany in the years following the reunification of Germany, a period in which neo-conservative public and political opinions resulted in a hostile environment for migrants and immigrants to Germany. The women spotlighted in this chapter banded together around the Fifth Cross-Cultural Black Women's Studies Summer Institute held in Germany from August 2, 1991, hosting over 130 women of color from six continents. It was an occasion for the Black German women, many of whom were second generation progeny of immigrant Africans, Asians and other people of color, to experience transnational solidarity, an affirmation of their identity, for community building and affective connections. This chapter explicates how these Black German women's involvement in the Institute was an opportunity for them to obtain recognition of their identities as fully German too in "a nation that still considered itself to be homogenously white." The Institute also provided a platform for them to engage and strategize with activist, academic and other women from other places to combat the racism, xenophobia and other socio-economic and political conditions they faced. Such a forum was also an opportunity for the women participants to seek the transformation of society through their writing: documenting common challenges, affirming the value of diversity and difference, calling governments to responsibility for women's conditions both in Germany as well as in other countries of the South, and re-interpreting history and politics from multiple feminist standpoints. This chapter makes a unique contribution to this book on *Gendering Knowledge* as it focuses on African Diaspora women in Germany, a little-studied segment of the Diaspora as the vast majority of studies focus on African American and other Diasporas. Thus, the authors interpret the involvement of Black German women in the Institutes and in building bridges with other Diaspora women of color as a critical moment for enhancing their identities and even for provoking broader social change.

The two remaining chapters in Part II utilize literary depictions and literary analysis to explicate the decisions and trajectories of women migrants in two different time periods. Chapter 5 embarks on achieving the objectives of *Gendering Knowledge* similarly as Chapter 1: In Chapter 5, Senayon Olaoluwa employs Manu Herbstein's *Ama* to challenge the paucity of women heroes in the narratives of resistance to trans-Atlantic slavery. The chapter explicitly asserts that "the history of resistance to slavery cannot be fully accounted for without mainstreaming the role of women." Herbstein's *Ama* is reminiscent of the acclaimed work of Yvette Christiansë, Unconfessed,[16] and Andrea Levy's *The Long Song*[17] both of which celebrated slave resistance and assigned agency to the slaves themselves in their emancipation as opposed to elevating the efforts of the white abolitionists. Herbstein's *Ama* depicts a young woman who, from the beginning of her story shows tremendous courage in resisting all the manifestations of patriarchy, enslavement, oppression and victimization that a woman in her circumstance came to expect. Furthermore, in adopting the metaphor of disability, Olaoluwa effectively links the slave girl's story with the larger story of a continent, Africa—a continent exploited, raped and pillaged and perpetually underdeveloped, but which, like Ama in Herbstein's novel, has the capacity to transcend and resist and triumph in the face of immense structural and systemic obstacles to her emancipation. Ama's story, while showing the continuous and nearly universal tendency of patriarchy across spaces and time to desire to subjugate the female body, also shows quite spectacularly that the female body can also be the site of the struggle against patriarchy and is resilient. In echoing Ojwang below, Olaoluwa captures the essence of this book on the gendering of knowledge about Africa and the African Diaspora thus:

> Women's agency ... exceed the strictures of patriarchal culture, for the historicity of their participation cannot be completely written out by a stilted historiography. [The] absence or silences of historiographical practice in regard to women does not change the intrinsic historical importance of their immersion in society.[18]

In Chapter 6, which analyzes Tess Akaeke Onwueme's play, *Legacies*, the central character, Mimi, embarks on a different kind of migration journey from Herbstein's Ama: Mimi's journey is a voluntary one, and it is in the opposite direction from Ama's as Mimi, a Diaspora African woman in the US, returns to the African 'homeland' in search of her runaway husband, and in search of a 'true identity.' In this chapter, Methuselah Jeremiah confronts the crisis of identity migrants undergo on three distinct levels, in the case of a reverse migration. The first crisis is occasioned by undemocratic politics, poverty and the failure of the postcolonial state in Africa which then propels the efflux of migrants from Africa to the West in search of so-called 'greener pastures' where their needs and desires have a better chance of being met. However, on a second level, the crisis of identity intensifies for these migrants when they realize that their new homes in the West foster loneliness and a longing for an African home where they mostly did not have to deal with the hostility, racism, discrimination and intolerance of a hostile host population. A return migration, Onwueme's *Legacies* shows, is merely an invitation for a third crisis of identity as vividly shown in the reaction of Mimi's son to Africa: as a second generation Diaspora, he cannot accept the strange land. The question then remains: if the crisis of identity remains unresolved by repeated migration, where lies the remedy? Jeremiah proposes an enlightened decision making process that balances expectations with reality and may guarantee the achievement of the migrant's desire for a 'home.'

Part III contains six chapters that expertly explore the intertwining of gender aspirations with subjective claims upon African people on the continent and in the Diaspora, as well as the subtle and often unrecognized ways in which gender confronts power, either performatively or discursively. In Chapter 7, Dotun Ayobade probes the "flight" of Fela's Queens from the recent past in Nigeria to their appearance in contemporary Diaspora artistes Aya Yem and Wunmi Olaiya, as well as in the photographs of Alim Mohammed. While acknowledging that the figure of the Queens represents a paradox of power and subjection at the same time, this chapter suggests that "the aesthetic and affective connection between the figure of the Queen … and women in the black Diaspora provides a basis for imagining a 'black' feminist Diaspora." Ayobade argues that the adoption of the Queens by these three contemporary artistes "forcefully gender[s] Afrobeat history"—a significant contribution to the gendering of knowledge about how performance creates its own unique Diaspora. Furthermore, while Fela and patriarchy used the erotic power of the Queen to maximum effect in the past, the Queens have transcended this identity by their appearance in other artists who adopt their dress, make-up and persona as symbols of power and of beauty, and an inspiration. For though the Queen derives her power from the black woman's body, her flight, transcending space and time to appear in the Diaspora further challenges our thinking about a Diaspora defined by place and emplacement, by location and geography, by physical movement and rooting. The flight of the Queen is phantasmal, and defies space and geography, to create a different kind of Diaspora.

Another kind of women subjection is discussed in Chapter 8, one also involving the transcendental "flight" of women, as Cameroonians in Wimbum Community struggle with the burden of tradition and superstitious beliefs as they accuse and punish suspected witchcraft (*tfu*) practitioners, mainly female members of their community. This chapter, based on Elias K. Bongmba's in-depth case study of one community with a disproportionately high number of witchcraft accusations, explores the gender dimensions of these accusations, linking the explanations with modernity and religion. Gender is depicted here as intersecting with patriarchy as many of the women accused of *tfu* are picked upon following the death of their husbands, and following the invocation of traditional ceremonies conducted as inquisitions. This chapter is also unique in its weaving of African narratives with Diaspora perspectives to give a holistic and wholly African interpretation to the events in Wimbum Community. Eventually, it is modernity, through the medium of the mass media and the internet, that makes it possible for the story of *tfu* in Wimbum Community to be extrapolated into a conversation that stretches across the Cameroonian nation, reaching into the Diaspora and back again to determine the lives of women (and men) accused of witchcraft in an African community.

Chapter 9 is another case study in how women navigate gender norms in their community with consequences for life and death. Omotola Adeyoju Ilesanmi brings to the fore the ways in which women in Jos City, Nigeria, rendered prostrate by an internecine conflict that defied solution for over a decade, refused to remain prostrate for long. Instead, they organized, and they marched, and they lobbied and they spoke out, and they worked for the return of peace to their communities. Whereas the literature overwhelmingly portrays women in conflict as helpless victims, Ilesanmi provides a refreshing alternative portrayal that centers the empowered initiatives of women in the narrative of the conflict, foregrounding women's agency as a veritable form of political activism for peace studies practitioners to embrace.

Subjectivity and subjection once again come into play in Chapter 10 as Leamon Bazil confronts the stereotypical labels assigned to black men and women by the American 'System' and the consequences of these, mainly death at the hands of the System. This chapter explores police violence in the United States as both a tool and strategy for maintaining racial segregation, following Hirshfield's schema,[19] and also examines how the imagery of black men as "thugs" and of black women as "welfare queens" contributes to the disproportionate killing of blacks by American police. Bazil argues that these stereotypes are labels for black bodies which both mark them out as the Other and also renders them invisible, *à la* Iris Young.[20] The chapter scrutinizes the evolution of black gender and sex roles in the US within the context of "institutionalized white supremacy" in society, manifested in ghettoization, the prison and welfare systems. The author asserts that "thug and welfare queen iconographies are derisive conceptualizations designed to cut off empathy for black men and women, such that their violent deaths and constant disparagement are unproblematic." The vibrant analysis in this chapter is concluded with a proposal for a program of Pan-African education that could equip Blacks in the Diaspora to protest and resist and overcome the oppression of the System.

In Chapter 11, we confront further how women's subjection, by retrogressive traditional ideas and practices, contributes to the elusiveness of development goals. Gift U. Ntiwunka and Rachael Oluseye Iyanda successfully link the private sphere of women's marginalization and discrimination with the public sphere of policy and law, linking also the local with the international through an examination of how international law seeks to attenuate women's subjection to harmful domestic and cultural mores. Silence is explored in this chapter as both a consequence and a cause of women's inability to contribute to development efforts, and to make significant progress toward their emancipation from misogynistic cultural norms and practices. However, these authors assert quite startlingly that women adopt silence also as a coping strategy against impregnable customs and disadvantages, with the unintended consequence of the perpetuation of their sufferings in the African states examined.

What happens when it is men confronted with disempowerment and forced to accept the leadership of women in a political landscape designed by men for men? This is the dilemma highlighted in the final chapter of this book on *Gendering Knowledge*, further extending the boundaries of the variegated ways in which power and subjection are gendered and complicated by many variables. The metaphor of dancing is apposite to depict the marginalization and frivolization of women's work and worth that is often the result of dominant patriarchal attitudes that en-fringe women, giving them little to pacify their anxieties and needs, while barring them from decision-making positons that have the potential to transform their lives and that of the nation too. The men in Irene's *More Than Dancing* learn that masculine privilege can be reversed, that the construction of masculinity as always strong, powerful and independent is not guaranteed in all spaces, at all times. The result for these characters, mirroring many African political spaces, is social humiliation and a sense of emasculation. Gendering knowledge, as the central aim of this book, requires us to invert knowledge in this way and probe the tropes that are considered given, and subvert them, in order to better understand society.

Moving forward, scholars and students of gender in Africa and the African Diaspora would do well to take on the challenge identified by Jane Bennett:

> A key challenge for African feminists remains the need to create knowledges which both emerge from the diverse and complex contexts in which we live and work and speak to such contexts with sufficient resonance to sustain innovative and transformative action. Designing research methodologies capable of addressing the questions which compel us constitutes a politics in its own right, demanding a re-evaluation of received approaches and sophisticated reflection on the intersections of theory and practice as researchers and writers.[21]

This is an imperative that will serve to advance the objective and subjective aims of feminist and gender scholarship and activism in and about Africa and the African Diaspora.

Notes

1 Toyin Falola, *The African Diaspora: Slavery, Modernity and Globalization* (New York: University of Rochester Press, 2013), 236.

2 Aili Mari Tripp, "The Evolution of Transnational Feminisms: Consensus, Conflict and New Dynamics," in *Global Feminism: Transnational Women's Activism, Organising and Human Rights*, edited by Myra Marx Ferree and Aili Mari Tripp (New York and London: New York University Press, 2006), 51.

3 Chandra Talpade Mohanty, "Under Western Eyes," in *Third World Women and the Politics of Feminism*, edited by C. Mohanty, D. Russo and L. Torres (Bloomington, IN: Indiana University Press, 1991), 58.

4 Filomena C. Steady, "An Investigative Framework for Gender Research in Africa in the New Millennium." Paper presented at the CODESRIA Conference on African Gender in the New Millennium, held in Cairo, April 7–10, 2002, available at www. codesria.org/links/conferences/gender/STEADY.pdf; Samuel Egwu, "Setting the Context: Global and Domestic Imperatives of Affirmative Action," in *Affirmative Action Strategies: Perspectives and Lessons from around the Globe*, edited by S. Egwu and O. Nwankwo (Enugu: Fourth Dimension Publishing/ Civil Resource Development and Documentation Centre, 2003).

5 Chandra Talpade Mohanty, *Feminism Without Borders: Decolonizing Theory, Practicing Solidarity* (Durham, NC and London: Duke University Press, 2003); Chandra Talpade Mohanty, "Under Western Eyes"; Filomena C. Steady, "An Investigative Framework"; Filomina C. Steady, ed., *The Black Woman Cross-Culturally* (Cambridge: Schenkman Publishing Co., 1981); Ayesha Imam, Amina Mama and Fatou Sow, eds, *Engendering African Social Sciences* (Dakar: CODESRIA, 1997).

6 Patricia Hill Collins, *Black Feminist Thought: Knowledge, Consciousness and the Politics of Empowerment*, 2nd ed. (New York: Routledge, 2000); Kimberlé Crenshaw, "Demarginalizing the Intersection of Race and Sex: A Black Feminist Critique of Antidiscrimination Doctrine, Feminist Theory and Antiracist Politics," *University of Chicago Legal Forum* 1(8) (1989): 139–167; Kimberlé Crenshaw, "Mapping the Margins: Intersectionality, Identity Politics and Violence Against Women of Color," *Stanford Law Review* 43(6) (1991): 1241–1299; Oyèrónkẹ́ Oyěwùmí, "Conceptualizing Gender: the Eurocentric Foundations of Feminist Concepts and the Challenge of African Epistemologies." Paper presented at CODESRIA Conference on African Gender in the New Millennium held in Cairo, April 7–10, 2002, available at www. codesria.org/links/conferences/gender/OYEWUMI.pdf.

7 Amina Mama, "Challenging Subjects: Gender and Power in African Contexts," in *Identity and Beyond: Rethinking Africanity*, edited by Suleymane B. Diagne, Amina Mama, Henning Melber and Francis Nyamnjoh (Uppsala: Nordic Africa Institute, 2001).

8 Ifi Amadiume, *Male Daughters, Female Husbands: Gender and Sex in an African Society* (London: Zed Books, 1987); Oyèrónkẹ́ Oyěwùmí, *The Invention of Women: Making an African Sense of Western Gender Discourses* (Minnesota: University of Minnesota Press, 1997).

9 Oyèrónkẹ́ Oyěwùmí, *The Invention of Women*, 10.

10 Jane Bennett, "Editorial: Researching for Life: Paradigms and Power," *Feminist Africa* 11 (December 2008): 1–12, 2.

11 Sylvia Tamale, "Introduction," in *African Sexualities: A Reader*, edited by Sylvia Tamale (Cape Town: Pambazuka Press, 2011), 3; cf. Akosua Adomako Ampofo and S. Arnfred, eds, *African Feminist Politics of Knowledge: Tensions, Challenges, Possibilities* (Uppsala: The Nordic Africa Institute, 2010).

12 Obioma Nnaemeka, "Bringing African Women into the Classroom: Rethinking Pedagogy and Epistemology," in *African Gender Studies: A Reader*, edited by Oyèrónkẹ́ Oyěwùmí (New York: Palgrave Macmillan, 2005), 53.

13 Ibid., 54.
14 Bolanle Awe, cited in Paul T. Zeleza, "Gender Biases in African Historiography," in *African Gender Studies: A Reader*, edited by Oyèrónkẹ́ Oyěwùmí (New York: Palgrave Macmillan, 2005), 217.
15 Ibid., 207.
16 Yvette Christiansë, *Unconfessed* (Cape Town: Kwela, 2007).
17 Andrea Levy, *The Long Song* (New York: Farrar, Straus and Giroux, 2010).
18 Dan Ojwang, *Reading Migration and Culture: The World of East African Indian Literature* (Basingstoke: Palgrave, 2013), 106.
19 Paul J. Hirschfield, "Lethal Policing: Making Sense of American Exceptionalism," *Sociological Forum* 30 (4) (December 2015).
20 Iris Marion Young, *Justice and the Politics of Difference* (Princeton, NJ: Princeton University Press, 1990).
21 Jane Bennett, "Editorial," 1; cf. Oyèrónkẹ́ Oyěwùmí, ed., *Gender Epistemologies in Africa: Gendering Traditions, Spaces, Social Institutions, and Identities* (New York: Palgrave Macmillan, 2010); Toyin Falola and Wanjala S. Nasong'o, eds, *Gendering African Social Spaces: Women, Power and Cultural Expressions* (Durham, NC: Carolina Academic Press, 2016); Toyin Falola and Nana Amponsah, eds, *Women, Gender and Sexualities in Africa* (Durham, NC: Carolina Academic Press, 2013); Toyin Falola and Bridget Teboh, eds, *The Power of Gender and the Gender of Power: Women's Labor, Rights and Responsibilities in Africa* (Trenton, NJ: Africa World Press, 2013).

Bibliography

Amadiume, Ifi. *Male Daughters, Female Husbands: Gender and Sex in an African Society*. London: Zed Books, 1987.
Ampofo, Akosua Adomako and S. Arnfred, eds. *African Feminist Politics of Knowledge: Tensions, Challenges, Possibilities*. Uppsala: The Nordic Africa Institute, 2010.
Arthur, John A. *African Diaspora Identities: Negotiating Culture in Transnational Migration*. Lanham, MD: Lexington Books, 2010.
Ball, Erica, Melina Pappademos and Michelle Ann Stephens. *Reconceptualizations of the African Diaspora*. Durham, NC: Duke University Press, 2009.
Bennett, Jane. "Editorial: Researching for Life: Paradigms and Power," *Feminist Africa* 11 (December 2008): 1–12.
Byfield, Judith A., LaRay Denzer, and Anthea Morrison. *Gendering the African Diaspora: Women, Culture, and Historical Change in the Caribbean and Nigerian Hinterland*. Bloomington, IN: Indiana University Press, 2010.
Christiansë, Yvette. *Unconfessed*. Cape Town: Kwela, 2007.
Collins, Patricia Hill. *Black Feminist Thought: Knowledge, Consciousness and the Politics of Empowerment*, 2nd ed. New York: Routledge, 2000.
Collins, Patricia Hill. *Black Sexual Politics: African Americans, Gender, and the New Racism*. New York: Routledge, 2004.
Cornwall, Andrea. *Readings in Gender in Africa*. Bloomington, IN: Indiana University Press, 2005.
Crenshaw, Kimberlé. "Demarginalizing the Intersection of Race and Sex: A Black Feminist Critique of Antidiscrimination Doctrine, Feminist Theory and Antiracist Politics," *University of Chicago Legal Forum* 1(8) (1989): 139–167.
Crenshaw, Kimberlé. "Mapping the Margins: Intersectionality, Identity Politics and Violence Against Women of Color," *Stanford Law Review* 43(6) (1991): 1241–1299.

Egwu, Samuel. "Setting the Context: Global and Domestic Imperatives of Affirmative Action," in *Affirmative Action Strategies: Perspectives and Lessons from Around the Globe*, edited by S. Egwu and O. Nwankwo, 1–21. Enugu: Fourth Dimension Publishing/Civil Resource Development and Documentation Centre, 2003.

Falola, Toyin. *The African Diaspora: Slavery, Modernity and Globalization*. New York: University of Rochester Press, 2013.

Falola, Toyin, and Nana Amponsah, eds. *Women, Gender and Sexualities in Africa*. Durham, NC: Carolina Academic Press, 2013.

Falola, Toyin, and Christian Jennings, eds. *Africanizing Knowledge: African Studies Across the Disciplines*. London: Transaction, 2002.

Falola, Toyin, and Wanjala S. Nasong'o, eds. *Gendering African Social Spaces: Women, Power and Cultural Expressions*. Durham, NC: Carolina Academic Press, 2016.

Falola, Toyin, and Bridget Teboh, eds. *The Power of Gender and the Gender of Power Women's Labor, Rights and Responsibilities in Africa*. Trenton, NJ: Africa World Press, 2013.

Grewal, Inderpal. "Women's Rights as Human Rights: Feminist Practices, Global Feminism and Human Rights Regimes in Transnationality," *Citizenship Studies* 3(3) (1999): 337–354.

Hirschfield, Paul J. "Lethal Policing: Making Sense of American Exceptionalism," *Sociological Forum* 30(4) (December 2015): 1109–1117.

Imam, Ayesha, Amina Mama and Fatou Sow, eds. *Engendering African Social Sciences*. Dakar: CODESRIA, 1997.

Levy, Andrea. *The Long Song*. New York: Farrar, Straus and Giroux, 2010.

Mama, Amina. "Challenging Subjects: Gender and Power in African Contexts," in *Identity and Beyond: Rethinking Africanity*, edited by Suleymane B. Diagne, Amina Mama, Henning Melber and Francis Nyamnjoh, 9–18. Uppsala: Nordic Africa Institute, 2001.

Mohanty, Chandra Talpade. "Under Western Eyes," in *Third World Women and the Politics of Feminism*, edited by C. Mohanty, D. Russo and L. Torres, 51–80. Bloomington, IN: Indiana University Press, 1991.

Mohanty, Chandra Talpade. *Feminism Without Borders: Decolonizing Theory, Practicing Solidarity*. Durham, NC and London: Duke University Press, 2003.

Nnaemeka, Obioma. "Bringing African Women into the Classroom: Rethinking Pedagogy and Epistemology," in *African Gender Studies: A Reader*, edited by Oyěwùmí, Oyèrónkẹ́, 51–65. New York: Palgrave Macmillan, 2005.

Ojwang, Dan. *Reading Migration and Culture: The World of East African Indian Literature*. Basingstoke: Palgrave, 2013.

Oyěwùmí, Oyèrónkẹ́. *The Invention of Women: Making an African Sense of Western Gender Discourses*. Minnesota: University of Minnesota Press, 1997.

Oyěwùmí, Oyèrónkẹ́. "Conceptualizing Gender: the Eurocentric Foundations of Feminist Concepts and the Challenge of African Epistemologies." Paper presented at CODESRIA Conference on African Gender in the New Millennium held in Cairo, April 7–10, 2002. Available at www.codesria.org/links/conferences/gender/OYEWUMI.pdf.

Oyewumi, Oyeronke, ed. *Gender Epistemologies in Africa: Gendering Traditions, Spaces, Social Institutions, and Identities*. New York: Palgrave Macmillan, 2010.

Pietila, Hilkka. *Engendering the Global Agenda: The Story of Women and the United Nations*. Development Dossier, UN/Non-Government Liaison Service, Geneva, 2002.

Steady, Filomina C., ed. *The Black Woman Cross-Culturally*. Cambridge: Schenkman Publishing Co., 1981.

Steady, Filomena C. "An Investigative Framework for Gender Research in Africa in the New Millennium." Paper presented at the CODESRIA Conference on African Gender in the New Millennium, held in Cairo, April 7–10, 2002. Available at www.codesria.org/links/conferences/gender/STEADY.pdf.

Tamale, Sylvia. "Introduction," in *African Sexualities: A Reader*, edited by Sylvia Tamale, 1–8. Cape Town: Pambazuka Press, 2011.

Tripp, Aili Mari. "The Evolution of Transnational Feminisms: Consensus, Conflict and New Dynamics," in *Global Feminism: Transnational Women's Activism, Organising and Human Rights*, edited by Myra Marx Ferree and Aili Mari Tripp, 51–78. New York and London: New York University Press, 2006.

Young, Iris Marion. *Justice and the Politics of Difference*, Princeton, NJ: Princeton University Press, 1990.

Zeleza, Paul Tiyambe. "Gender Biases in African Historiography," in *African Gender Studies: A Reader*, edited by Oyèrónkẹ́ Oyěwùmí, 207–232. New York: Palgrave Macmillan, 2005.

Zeleza, Paul Tiyambe. *In Search of African Diasporas: Testimonies and Encounters*. Durham, NC: Carolina Academic Press, 2012.

Part I

(Re-)writing gender in African and African Diaspora history

1 The Bantu Matrilineal Belt

Reframing African women's history

*Rhonda M. Gonzales, Christine Saidi and
Catherine Cymone Fourshey*

Introduction

Historian Paul Tiyambe Zeleza's quantitative analysis of African history texts demonstrates that African women and issues of gender are rarely a subject of study. He documents that women "are either not present at all, or they are depicted as unnaturally inferior and subordinate, as eternal victims of male oppression."[1] The current authors have noticed that African women's history is commonly reduced to a single story characterized by victimization, marginalization, and, most significantly, silence.[2] This story and the omissions are upheld both in Western media representations of African women and scholarship. There are occasional powerful though aberrant women, such as Queen Nzinga, Queen Amina, Queen of Sheba and the celebrated military force known as the Dahomey Amazon, who are celebrated for their exceptional status or "improbable" feats for African women. The challengers to the critiques of these stereotypes claim that there is no way to know the earlier history of women or gender in Africa. The silences and the circular arguments continue. The role of gender and the history of African women cannot be known; therefore, it is excluded from the histories of Africa, which leads to a continuation of the "African woman as victim" myth. And since this silence perpetuates the image of African women as powerless, it reinforces yet another widely accepted belief that African men have always held more authority and power than women. This is a problematic starting point for understanding African gender history, because it works within a binary that depends on a hierarchical relationship between African women's suppression and men's domination. It rests on an inherent opposition between women and men with regard to authority and power that is not questioned, not investigated nor verified within historical context. Moreover, a new understanding of the past can transform thinking about the present and possibilities for the future. While there are notable monographs on women and gender relations in African history, these histories are primarily from the colonial era or later. And as Zeleza noted they are rarely cited in the general African history texts or the popular media.[3]

This chapter presents an alternative to silence and the single story with an introduction to a deeper historical vision of women and gender relations, over

5,000 years, in a region of sub-Saharan Africa that stretches from Angola in the West, through Central Africa to Tanzania, and to Mozambique in the East. Contributing to the aims of *Gendering Knowledge in Africa and the African Diaspora*, it introduces the concept of the Bantu Matrilineal Belt as a fruitful region for researching and understanding the histories of women and gender in precolonial Africa. While many of the individual histories of African women may be lost to history, much of the bigger picture is recoverable. Additionally, this chapter questions and reframes historical assumption of female subjugation and male dominance, and it proposes that it is worthwhile for scholars to revisit and reinterpret previously published data. At the same time, it recommends that we consider an alternate analytic framework for gender studies in pre- and post-colonial Africa.

Based on our research on precolonial histories of Bantu-speaking communities, we posit that authority and power are best analyzed and understood when they are thought of as *heterarchical* rather than solely hierarchical concepts. Heterarchy provides an avenue to analyze authority and power in ways that are dynamic and nimble. It acknowledges that multiple historical actors may hold horizontal rather than vertical social, political, economic, religious or other relevant relationships. And they may contest, check and wield authority that influences the decisions and effectual power that leaders might leverage. Recently, historian Kathleen Smythe, among others, has suggested that heterarchy is "about power and authority across and among social groups, institutions, and people. It implies diffuse, independent sources of power, rather than concentrated, vertical power."[4] Such people can represent independent, shared and sometimes competing interests that can be brought to the attention of and sway the single or collective body of powerbrokers. In this way, historian Holly Hansen explains, "[h]eterarchical strategies become part of a hierarchical polity."[5] Applied to studies of gender, heterarchy requires that scholars pay attention to the nuances of gender status, gender concepts, gender dynamics, gendered lifestages and the transformations of these within their historical contexts. Thus gender, where relevant, is only one variable among many possible social identifiers at play when authority and power holders are interacting and negotiating. Heterarchy suggests that power emerges at intersections of integrated and negotiated social status considered in deciding what is best for the collective. Within systems of heterarchy, social positions related to lineage, ancestors, age, clan, land and maternal/paternal fertility, are each salient. We suggest that one must intentionally set aside accepted narratives that assume authority and power are imbedded in firm hierarchies that require rigid categories and practices of exclusion based primarily on gender.

Focused on a region of Bantu-speaking Africa known as the Bantu Matrilineal Belt, a goal is to raise questions, provide examples and suggest ways for thinking about gender, authority and power as robust and dynamic categories and paradigms that might renew our ability to reconstruct African women's and gender history. It revisits select published research on twentieth century societies in East and Central Africa to suggest ways that we might pinpoint the heterarchical nature of authority and power that may have gone unrecognized at the time earlier research was conducted. We build on recent works demonstrating that in early Bantu societies a person's or a collective's power and authority depended on a multitude of socially relevant factors.[6] This methodology is also useful for reconsidering unconscious biases that project present-day power relations, categories, practices and situations onto the past. Moreover, it permits us to interrogate the ways in which gender interacted with authority and power in Bantu-speaking Africa. This is a vast area where, today, speakers of more than 450 Bantu-descended languages and dialects comprise diverse communities. Of those, approximately 100 are identified as matrilineal, in a region that extends from the Atlantic Ocean to the Indian Ocean through the center of sub-Saharan Africa.[7]

Linguistic and genetic evidence supports the theory that Bantu-descended people, who migrated and settled across the mentioned regions, historically shared a variety of common elements in their institutions, practices and worldviews. They often traced inheritance and identity through the mother's lineage.[8] In the twentieth century, anthropologists Audrey Richards, Mary Douglas and George Murdock termed the region the "Matrilineal Belt." We refer to this as the Bantu Matrilineal Belt.[9] This large area, though linguistically similar and having matrilineal institutions, is in fact composed of people living in varied environments and with diverse political organizations, religious beliefs and economic systems. While there are societies that are defined as patrilineal in this region, most of them demonstrate features of matrilineal institutions that are seeming retentions from an early time in their history or may be borrowed elements from neighbors. The most important point here is that over time many of these communities upheld matrilineal institutions and forms of organizing, which is a testament to the importance of looking beyond patrilineality. This also brings into question theories about patriarchy and male domination as the only way communities approached their worlds.

It is important to state that authority and power in Bantu societies are not assigned according to gender or sex. Furthermore, matrilineality does not assume that women dominate in all spheres of society nor do patrilineal societies only maintain the rule of men. Exclusion from and inclusion in various social spheres is based on a variety of factors. Karen Brodkin-Sacks argues in her foundational work, *Sisters and Wives*, that to understand the status or authority of a person is more dependent on variable positions within that society than just their gender. Based on her in-depth study of various ethnographies from patrilineal Bantu-speaking peoples of East and Southern Africa, she shows that young women may have lost power as wives, but maintained authority as sisters within their own patriclan.[10] Brodkin-Sacks notes that women have a great deal of status, power and authority within patrilineal societies when there is a nuanced examination of their varied roles.

However, within matrilineal societies mothers and grandmothers are central to social, cultural, economic and political institutions. One should not imagine patrilineal and matrilineal societies as mirror images or polar opposites. Lineage systems are dynamic, complex and varied. What one should contemplate are the ways in which matrilineal and patrilineal systems are embedded in heterarchical networks of simultaneous relationships among historical actors wielding and leveraging coterminous authority and power.[11] Studying matrilineality within the context of diverse societies in the Bantu Matrilineal Belt reveals a great deal about gender and the complexity of gender history. The works of scholars Nwando Achebe, Cynthia Brantley, Karen Brodkin-Sacks, Christopher Ehret, Rhonda Gonzales, Kairn Klieman, Onaiwu Ogbomo, Oyeronke Oyewumi, Karla Poewe, Christine Saidi, David Lee Schoenbrun and Rhiannon Stephens on African history reveal that women have not always held less power and status relative to men, even in societies that are patrilineal.

The following section is a discussion centered on matrilineality as an approach to reconstructing the *longue durée* history of the Bantu Matrilineal Belt. It employs five themes that include concepts that are familiar to readers such as economics, technology, religion, worldview and politics. This chapter also considers key ideas and practices that may be less familiar, including heterarchy, matrilineality, sororal groups, brideservice and life stages. Together, the themes are intended to show by way of select examples useful ways in which scholars might imagine rethinking and reconstructing early African women and gender histories.

Matrilineality, heterarchy and social organizing

Nineteenth century anthropologists coined the term *matrilineality* to characterize societies that practice inheritance and ways of forming identity that follow a maternal bloodline.[12] Anthropologists like Karla Poewe[13] and historians Saidi and Gonzales[14] suggested that matrilineality is more comprehensive in scope than inheritance and identity. In their studies matrilineality informs a worldview. That worldview emphasizes the importance of safeguarding matrilineal cohesiveness and community sustainability, and it is a worldview that makes strong use of metaphors. For example, in matrilineal societies metaphors that connect the idea of a womb with how lineages are politically, socially and economically organized are pervasive in oral traditions.[15]

Poewe's study of the matrilineal societies in the Luapula Province, Zambia, located at the center of the Bantu Matrilineal Belt, sheds light on how matrilineality functioned more than forty years ago. In the 1970s she observed that people described their communities as being united within one womb. In their worldview, their shared metaphorical womb symbolized a well-protected community that would always have enough nourishment and food to feed the lineage. Members comprising the matrilineage embodied a communal-based economy established on the philosophical tenets of dispersing or sharing, so that within matrilineal societies individuals rarely accumulated surplus, but in fact distributed surplus widely to relatives.[16] Some of these very concepts can be tied to deeper historical elements represented in archaeology and linguistic data.

The worldview and practice of dispersal as a tenet of matrilineality helps us understand what may have made matrilineality a viable and enduring approach to organizing. While many matrilineal societies are located in less agriculturally productive regions of the Bantu Matrilineal Belt, the belief that the womb or matrilineage will provide enough sustenance for all persists. This perspective does not stem from an abundance of natural resources, but, rather, faith in the human resources that form the lineage and their philosophy of networking and redistribution of resources within the community.

In the 1970s, when Poewe was working in Zambia's Luapula Province, it was a time of tremendous change and economic challenge. In the latter 1960s, the state had begun transitioning from British colonialism. After independence there was an economic push for the creation of locally owned small businesses. In the Luapula Province, Poewe noted that this resulted in two types of business models in the decade after independence. Generally, those people who had converted to Protestant Christianity under the colonial regime created nuclear-family-owned businesses. On the other hand, those who gave primacy to their matrilineal history and worldview created collective enterprises based on lineage membership. While both embraced new capitalist, market-based economics, the former employed a vertical, linear hierarchical model, while the latter, based on matrilineal ideology, utilized a horizontal, heterarchical strategy toward its management.[17]

Poewe's work allows us to view recent manifestations of matrilineality, but how early in Bantu history was matrilineality relevant? The first Bantu-speaking peoples lived in the borderlands regions of modern Nigeria and Cameroon more than 5,000 years ago. Historians Christopher Ehret and Kairn Klieman suggest that linguistic and historical evidence support the theory that matrilineality was the earliest form of lineal reckoning. Linguistic evidence reveals a proto-Bantu word for matriclan, *-ganda*, which was present in those earliest communities. Though the word root *-ganda* is found in many modern-day Bantu languages, the meanings have morphed over time. When historians analyze those new meanings, they range in meaning, yet they still pertain to the locus of the lineage. Some examples of its meanings include "village," "house," and "hearth." In a majority of the languages *-ganda* means, "camp," "quarter of a village," or "chief's compound." This may have represented the matrilineages that comprised the matriclan. The transformation of *-ganda* from "matriclan" to areas of a village reflects how in later historical periods and contexts villages may have been comprised of numerous matriclans.[18]

Today, *-ganda* is a widely distributed word root. It is present in vocabularies throughout Bantu-speaking Africa, from the forested regions of Gabon south to Namibia and northeast to the Great Lakes. This distribution suggests that it is a proto-Bantu-era word that has endured in new forms across the *longue durée* of history. As Bantu-speaking people expanded and migrated, for more than 5,000 years, they carried ideas of matriclans and matrilineages with them in their worldviews and practices.[19]

Linguistic evidence indicates that Bantu-speaking peoples were matrilineal in the past and that Bantu Matrilineal Belt societies retained this form of social organization for a wide variety of reasons.[20] Historians Jane Guyer and Samuel

Belinga have theorized that kinship and lineage are prominent in the historical record because they were among the few pre-colonial systems of organization and affiliation that survived colonial structures and hegemony.[21] Indeed, it is very likely that crosscutting practices and associations existed alongside lineage as one of several affiliations people maintained. Yet, we contend that matriclans and matrilineages were resilient because of their deep, though not uniform or unbroken, histories, and because of their effectiveness in sustaining and provisioning societies.

Linguistic analysis correlates well with the field of genetic studies to provide another set of evidence that supports the theory that early Bantu-speaking people were matrilineal. Mitochondrial DNA (mtDNA) can be used to trace the migration of people. As mtDNA is passed down, minute mutations occur, and if these mutations persist, they become genetic markers that help scientists distinguish one maternal line from another. Recent studies of both fathers' and mothers' genetic histories have shown that in early Bantu societies daughters remained with their families while sons moved away. This type of exogamous marriage of sons indicates kinship patterns most closely aligned with matrilineality.[22]

There is widespread and multidisciplinary evidence that Bantu-speaking people were matrilineal when they began their expansions that eventually populated two-thirds of sub-Saharan Africa. But to understand how Bantu speakers conceptualized and implemented matrilineal social organization, especially in the Bantu Matrilineal Belt, historians need more than just a word for matriclan and genetic evidence, they need to understand how matrilineality played out. The next themes will look at the linguistic, oral tradition and comparative ethnographic evidence to do just that.

Life stages, motherhood and sororal groups

Since the earliest Bantu period of more than 5,000 years ago, matrilineal societies have paid close attention to their children, particularly their daughters. Within their societies there were prevalent roles and traditions associated with life stages that considered a person's age and seniority. And there were processes followed pertaining to workforce, marriage and producing children. With regard to each of these interconnected and intersectional positions and experiences, there were holders of heterarchical authority and power who would have looked out for, particularly, lineage daughters.

Daughters represented security. When they birthed children and secured hardworking sons-in-law, they added laborers to the lineage. When it came to a girl's education and initiation into young-adult status, her mother, backed by women from her lineage, determined when the girl would be allowed to establish her own home and grind her own grain, thus becoming independent.

Linguistic evidence helps reconstruct one female life stage to the proto-Bantu era of more than 5,000 years ago, permitting us an opportunity to further understand early Bantu matrilineal societies. One such word is the root *-yadi*, a life stage that includes young women from the time of their first menstruation to first

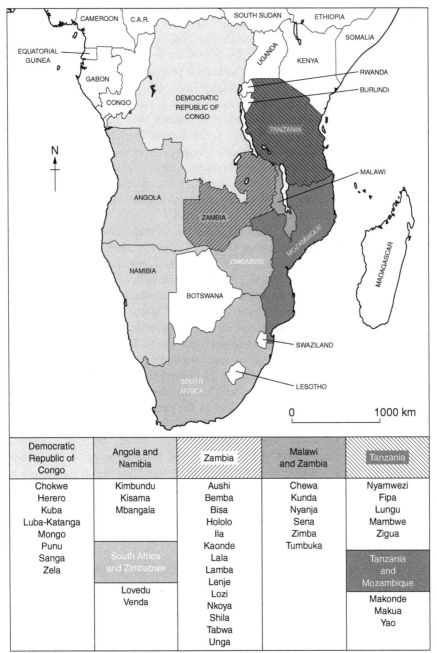

Democratic Republic of Congo	Angola and Namibia	Zambia	Malawi and Zambia	Tanzania
Chokwe	Kimbundu	Aushi	Chewa	Nyamwezi
Herero	Kisama	Bemba	Kunda	Fipa
Kuba	Mbangala	Bisa	Nyanja	Lungu
Luba-Katanga		Hololo	Sena	Mambwe
Mongo		Ila	Zimba	Zigua
Punu	**South Africa and Zimbabwe**	Kaonde	Tumbuka	
Sanga		Lala		**Tanzania and Mozambique**
Zela		Lamba		
		Lenje		Makonde
	Lovedu	Lozi		Makua
	Venda	Nkoya		Yao
		Shila		
		Tabwa		
		Unga		

The groups listed under each country can be found within the boundaries of that country but this should not be taken to imply that each group was spread or scattered throughout the territory.

Figure 1.1 Ethnolinguistic groups making up the Bantu Matrilineal Belt.

pregnancy. *-Yadi* is still attested in widespread modern Bantu languages in the rain forested areas, Southwest, Central, Southern and throughout East Africa. According to ethnographic and written missionary accounts from the early twentieth century, *-yadi* signified a female life stage from her first menstrual period to her first successful pregnancy. The significance of *-yadi* is that it indicates the importance of marking motherhood as a process from the life stage of the first period to the birth of the first child. This widely distributed life stage term raises interesting questions since it implies that a young woman's elevation in status occurred with the first successful pregnancy she carried for her lineage. Though this term for such a life stage is not attested in all Bantu-speaking societies today, the idea persists throughout large parts of the Matrilineal Belt. In some areas the term is not used, but in recent times female initiation ceremonies started at a young girl's first menstruation and a final ceremony was celebrated when she felt the movement of her first child, which indicates this life stage was honored even if the term used for it has changed.[23]

The significance of the *-yadi* life stage is twofold. First, it illustrates that marriage is not the most important ritual or institution, since the transformative event for a young woman is that of motherhood, not marriage. Second, the *-yadi* life stage reinforces the significance of the birth of the first child, which not only made the mother an adult, but also earned the father adulthood status. Throughout Bantu-speaking Africa, the birth of a first child appears to have made parents full-fledged adults and transformed grandparents into elders.[24]

Another term, *-gole*,[25] appears to have had a more limited geographic distribution, but is significant because it is used among Bantu speaking peoples whose social organizations are quite different. In Central-East Tanzania, among matrilineal peoples *-gole* means "a girl who has just developed breasts," a life stage that preceded the *-yadi* life stage. Yet in the patrilineal and more centralized Bantu-speaking regions around the East African region of the Great Lakes, the meaning of the life stage *-gole*, was narrowed to mean "bride or newlywed woman with maternal potential."[26] As the change in the meaning of *-gole* indicates, in the Great Lakes from 700 CE to 1900, motherhood transformed from an important multi-staged position to a subset of wifehood. While motherhood in its various manifestations in the Great Lakes was still important, it no longer wielded the authority it once did and does in the Matrilineal Belt. The matrilineal people of Tanzania named each stage of a young girl's development toward motherhood and this suggests its significance.

As daughters moved toward adulthood, the next step was becoming a mother. To do this the young women would participate in a processional marriage based on brideservice. A young man seeking a wife would be required to do brideservice, which involved working for the wife's mother and her closest relatives within the matrilineage to prove himself worthy. He had to remain in his wife/prospective wife's village for several years performing any labor required by his mother-in-law and produce children.[27] For older women within the matrilineages who had daughters old enough for marriage, this meant that through the institution of brideservice, they controlled the labor of young prospective husbands as well as that of their daughters. In subsistence agricultural economies, control of young labor brought the older women of the matrilineage a great deal of economic power and prestige.[28] Only the mother-in-law in consultation with the other older women could determine whether the young man had completed his brideservice. If he was considered lazy, or he could not father children, the brideservice would be terminated and the young man would have to look for a new wife. Once brideservice was completed successfully he could then move with his wife and children to his own maternal village, or alternatively, the couple might choose to begin their own village.[29] A young woman went through a marriage ceremony, but both she and the young man had to show they could work hard and produce children over a long period of time, to be allowed to have their own house and some independence. In the 1950s in East-Central Africa, brideservice lasted at least seven years.[30] Often the colonial anthropologists and missionaries did not understand this concept of processional marriage and just described it as a "trial marriage," a term that does not describe the complex social relations involved in marriage by brideservice.

The various ethnographies from East and East-Central Africa indicate that there was one other element of the institution of brideservice that gave older women real authority, both socially and religiously.[31] That was mother-in-law avoidance. In many matrilineal Bantu societies a son-in-law was not allowed to speak directly to his mother-in-law or even look at her. To quote the observations of one White Father missionary writing about East-Central African mothers-in-law, "For the least little thing, she will flay the young man with the whiplash of her gross, insulting tongue, while he is powerless to answer."[32] To answer back was an unpardonable insult. More than that, to break this prohibition could invoke immense ritual danger. The young man was forbidden to confront his mother-in-law.[33] When the mother-in-law deemed that the young man has proven to be good husband and father "material" she would then perform a ceremony that would begin to lessen the avoidance rules.[34]

The use of historical linguistic and ethnographic data has allowed the authors to discuss some of the major ways matrilineality operated within the Bantu Matrilineal Belt. Another important matrilineal institution was the sororal group or the *-bumba*, which gave women power within their matrilineages. We theorize that across the Bantu Matrilineal Belt and within matrilineal societies there were sororal groups. The sororal group is a subset of a matrilineage. It comprises grandmothers, their sisters, their daughters and young grandchildren regardless of gender.[35] Saidi's research has shown that in precolonial East and East-Central Africa female lineage members, who were accorded status as mothers and grandmothers, led sororal groups. These related women presided over important sociocultural and religious institutions, as well as ceremonies that were critical to socializing and educating youth in practical and intellectual skills. For example, among the Bemba, Ila, Chewa and many other Bantu language speakers in East and Central Africa, there is a word to name the sororal group: *-bumba*.[36] This distribution of the term within the Bantu Matrilineal Belt suggests that *-bumba* may have been in use among the forbearers of these Bantu-speaking peoples at early as 2,000 years ago and perhaps even earlier. In Tanzania, anthropologist T. O. Beidelman recorded an interesting additional attestation of *cibumba* among the matrilineal Kaguru people. According to him, it names a "secret meeting" associated with the end of a boy's initiation.[37] But identifying the earliest meaning and history of the words pertaining to the concept of sororal groups will require additional research.

Matrilineal political institutions

The linguistic evidence for female political leadership is oblique, yet the complexities suggest that power and authority were very much both male and female purviews. Bantu terms for leadership positions are rarely marked for gender. In Bantu languages nouns, both proper and common, did not indicate gender. To convey gender, one must choose to add a female or male marker; therefore, it is difficult to determine with evidence from nouns alone the role of women in political leadership within Bantu-speaking societies. Unlike the distinct English words for male and female rulers "king" and "queen," for example, titles for leaders typically were not inherently gendered in Bantu languages.

Analyzing language data, it appears that both women and men could serve as political leaders. There is an early Bantu term for a clan ritual chief, *-kụmu*, a position that even until recent times was unrestricted by gender.[38] In the 1950s colonial records available for two Matrilineal Belt regions, the Katanga Province of the Congo (now the DRC) and Northern Rhodesia (now Zambia), documented that more than 25 percent of the *Mufumu* (chiefs) were women. *Mufumu* derives from the root, *-kụmu*.[39] Belgian colonial officials, shocked and dismayed by women holding positions of power, wrote memos on how best to eliminate women serving in the position of chief.[40] Likewise, British and German colonists, who had to contend with female rulers, looked for ways to remove them from power.

An interesting contrast to *-kụmu* is found among Bantu societies in both Eastern and Central Africa whose political systems centralized.[41] As some lineages became patrilineal and more stratified, the authority of women and men also took on new configurations. The prefix *na-* derives from the old Bantu root *-ina* "mother." Reduced in shape to a single syllable, as commonly happens in prefixes or suffixes, it can be used to gauge some of these transformations in gendered authority. The *na-* prefix is found among diverse Bantu speaking peoples and was probably used by Bantu-speaking peoples at least 5,000 years ago. Among the matrilineal, decentralized people of East-Central Africa the *na-* prefix is used to emphasize whether a leader is male or female, since the leadership term is non-gendered. A leader who happens to be female is *namfumu*.[42]

Conversely, *na-* is used differently among various centralized, patrilineal Bantu-speaking societies. For example, the Kanyok and Lunda, who reside today in central and southern DRC, created centralized government institutions approximately 600 years ago. The Lunda, in particular, consolidated a massive empire that stretched from modern Angola in the west to the Luapula Province, Zambia in the east. Both the Kanyok and Lunda were agricultural people composed of communities where some lineages had become more powerful than others. The women of the royal or chiefly lineage had specific titles, and the *na-* prefix became part of them. Some of those titles included *Inanbanz* [mother of the enclosure]; *Inamwan* [mother of the chief and most powerful female elder]; *Inabanz* [leading maternal aunt or sister of the chief] and *Nambaz* [official sister of the chief].[43] The *na-*prefix in these situations was not just indicating that the non-gendered important title was at this time filled by a woman, but that these were positions and titles created exclusively for women. The male titles had no prefix. Thus there appears to have been an ideological shift in the conception of who could be a leader. The belief that leaders could come from either gender was replaced by the new view that the normal position of leader is male and the few exceptions when a leader is female her title would be distinguished by the addition of a female prefix. These positions could only be held by women of leading lineages, a practice that contrasts with the broad application of *na-* among de-centralized matrilineal people. This may add evidence to the historical theories that within Bantu-speaking Africa, elite women from important lineages maintained their authority and status during at least the early stages of centralization, while women of lesser means held less favorable positions.[44]

Ethnographic and oral traditions from many communities with large numbers of Bantu speakers help shed light on the historical role of women within matrilineal societies. In the 1500s, *Nyendwa* became the name, chiefly, of clans among several matrilineal ethnic groups in East-Central Africa. They claimed origins from the patrilineal Luba,[45] but they also remained matrilineal, as their name, *Nyendwa*, a term for female genitalia, implies.[46] In our analysis, this title was not about fertility, but rather it was a metaphor for the power of matrilineality as the *Nyendwa* oral tradition indicates. The origin myth of the Nyendwa clan holds that there was a group of chiefs whose members negotiated collaboration. They wanted to settle their disagreements by drinking water out of a common gourd cup, but they did not feel they had enough unity to do this. A woman then squatted over the water pot and urine descended from her loins, after which the chiefs said, "This is what we have been waiting for." They then bent over the water pot and sucked all the water up. Afterwards they changed the name of their clans to "Nyendwa," because they drank "water" that had come from the loins of a woman.[47] The metaphor within this tradition suggests political unity was based on honoring women's authority.

A number of scholars have assumed that centralization reinforces patrilineality and that once a society becomes patrilineal it will persist as such. Historical evidence from the Kongo Kingdom shows that this is not necessarily so. From 1500 to 1650, the once matrilineal Kingdom of the Kongo, under the influence of Portugal and the Catholic Church, took on a patrilineal system. But even in this context, elite women retained a relatively high status, while common women faced greater hardships due to diminished status.[48] Elite women of a matrilineage, the *kanda*, could still broker power, but within a patrilineal context. As the other states in the region eclipsed the Kingdom of the Kongo, the *kanda* returned to their previous status, and the matrilineal worldview is still influential among modern people of the Kongo.[49]

There are other examples where political centralization did not lead to the decline of matrilineality. For example, during the creation of the Malawi Empire, the Chewa Phiri clan leadership remained matrilineal, even though their oral tradition and their use of the borrowed Luba word for tribute, *musonko*,[50] offer evidence that the patrilineal East Luba Empire influenced Phiri notions of strong leadership. In this case centralization and pressure from a neighboring Empire did not sway them enough to result in change in their matrilineal form of organization.[51]

The effects of political centralization had yet another kind of result in the Luba Empire of the eastern area of the modern Democratic Republic of the Congo. As they centralized, women's positions did not change in the same way as in the Kongo Kingdom. Among the Eastern Luba, the ruling lineages shifted to patrilineal descent and identity and women lost status. However, the vestiges of their matrilineal past can still be seen in their naming and conceptualizing of people and their origins. For instance, when the Luba refer to people they employ the title prefix *Bena*, meaning "people of the mother," a decidedly matrilineal way to view communities especially for patrilineal people.[52] Additionally, symbols of chiefly rule included the use of spears, statues and bow stands with a woman holding onto her breast or her navel while seated in the birthing position, which is suggestive of the centrality of motherhood and matrilineages.[53] Among the Luba centralization and the transition to patrilineality occurred while they still maintained matricentric signs of mothers and matrilineages having been central figures of prominence.

Women and men's authority within lineage systems changed under such conditions as political centralization and economic diversification. Social stratification and cattle as the economic and wealth base typically led to transitioning to patrilineality, which was accompanied by patrilocal settlement, or living among a father's lineage. But this was not necessarily true within the Matrilineal Belt. The Ila of Zambia based their economy on cattle, yet remained matrilineal. In Namibia, the Herero, a unique cattle-keeping Bantu-speaking people, who have both strong patriclans and matriclans, determine cattle inheritance through the mother's line. For most of the twentieth century, anthropologists of Africa believed that matrilineality would die out as Africans "modernized." Clearly this is not what happened.

Until recently a tenet of anthropology was that transformation of lineage type were unidirectional, from matrilineal to patrilineal. However, there are examples that are contrary to this theory. Some Bantu communities have over time shifted in either direction—matrilineal to patrilineal and patrilineal to matrilineal. One example can be found in Eastern Zambia where 150 years ago the southern African patrilineal and militarized Ngoni moved into this region where the local communities followed matrilineal institutions and practices. In accordance with the precepts of anthropology, the powerful Ngoni should have forced patrilineal organizing on conquered populations. Yet historians in the 1980s discovered that the Ngoni instead had become matrilineal.[54] This was a process that likely parallels what occurred in other societies as well.

While there is great diversity in terms of lineage structure among Bantu-speaking people, the linguistic evidence indicates that matrilineality was probably the dominant model in the earlier history. It is significant that there are still so many Bantu matrilineal societies today, even in the midst of many patrilineal influences such as Islam, Christianity, colonialism and modern African nation states, all of which opposed matrilineality. This suggests that Bantu-speaking peoples continued to find matrilineal organization a beneficial approach to their lives.

Matrilineage and religion

As early as 3500 BCE, the earliest Bantu speaker's worldview included the idea of a Creator or Force responsible for establishing the cosmos.[55] That force was genderless, neither female nor male in nature, whether a society was matrilineal or patrilineal. However, there were ways in which the Creator might be imbued with attributes that gave it a stronger presence.[56] One example of this comes from the Matrilineal Belt region in the DRC's Katanga Province, in Zambia, and in parts of Malawi. There, as early as 2,000 years ago, matrilineal people innovated a new word for the Creator: *Leza. Leza*'s essence involved a significant and innovative shift in the proto-Bantu Creator, who was thought to be distant or removed from people. In contrast, *Leza* derived from an old Bantu verb root meaning "to nurture."[57] By the turn of the second millennium CE, this word and concept for God was in use among more than fifteen ethno-linguistic groups. These included Bantu languages belonging to three Bantu subgroups, the Eastern Luba, all of the Sabi (Bemba and related peoples) and the Botatwe (the Ila, Tonga, Lenje, Soli and others) of Zambia as well as the Chewa, Fipa and Lungu. These communities located today in Zambia and Southern Tanzania and squarely within the Matrilineal Belt mostly maintained matrilineal organizational structures.[58] But the Eastern Luba in the last 500 years had become patrilineal, yet they still use *Leza* for "God." Interestingly, the Eastern Luba adapted this word and concept of the Creator God from the matrilineal peoples they encountered as they settled what is today, Katanga Province.

The essence of *Leza* appears to be linked with motherhood, since the concept of nurturing usually implies a mother's relationship with her child or children. But these religious beliefs were more complex, since *Leza* appears to have attributes of all genders and sexes. While most of the attributes of the Creator God are feminine, there are also male attributes, such as *buta bwa Leeza*, a term for rainbow, which means literally, "the bow [as in a bow and arrow] of God/ rain," among the Ila of Zambia.[59] The bow indicates hunting and implies a masculine attribute for the Creator God.

For the early Sabi peoples about 2,000 years ago, *Leza* was a new conceptualization of the Creator. *Leza* retained the monotheism of the ancient Bantu Creator God. They innovated a new way of viewing God. God was no longer an

Ancient Creator who was distant from people's everyday life. Through the *Leza* conceptualization, God became a much closer and nurturing Creator God. The various elements hint at ways *Leza* was being associated with the roles of motherhood and the matrilineages.

In terms of gendered elements, it seems older women have long been central to religion within Bantu societies. In those that became patrilineal and/or central-ized, this religious role may be the one area where women often retained author-ity and status. Among various centralized Bantu-speaking societies from Great Lakes to Cameroon or Southern Africa, it was primarily women who mediated spiritually between the ruler, the ancestors and the Creator. For example, among the Bangwa of Western Cameroon, a centralized and patrilineal agricultural people, the Queen Mother, *Mafwa*, has the major religious position within *Ndem Bo*, the ancestor-honoring religious ceremonies. The *Mafwa* has her own ancestor altars, but all other Bangwa women must worship at their father's altar.[60] In Bangwa societies, the matriclans maintain their authority through the Mafwa, since her role is essential in maintaining the power of or creating a new male ruler. Further south within the Swazi kingdom, a cattle-keeping patrilineal society, the role of the Queen Mother is similar. She is considered essential to the survival of the Swazi nation, since she is the custodian of the sacred national rituals. The Queen Mother is also the only one able to communicate with the important ancestors and advise the current king as to the ancestors' desires.[61] Her role strongly contrasts with the role of other Swazi women, who are excluded from major religious activities. The wide geographical distribution of these tra-ditions may indicate a long-term tendency for women, especially royal women, to maintain the matriclans' power base through their roles as intermediaries between living people, ancestors and God.

Among the centralized Buganda of East Africa and the Nguni of South Africa, women, supported by their matriclans, play a substantial role in the reli-gious practices that maintain the rule of male leaders. In recent times, the Cwezi-Kubandwa, has been an important religious organization dominated by older women within the patrilineal Great Lakes Baganda Empire. The older women participating in the Cwezi-Kubandwa's religious activities provided the link between the people and the ancestors and have created a place for prestige and standing for many women, not just the elite.[62] In southern Africa, the Nguni, a patrilineal cattle-keeping people, have powerful patriclans, yet women played crucial roles in the religious life. Only women serve as spirit mediums and are the only means for people to communicate with their ancestors. In contrast, other societies of the region have weaker patriclan institutions and the spirit mediums are both male and female. It appears that older women within both the Baganda and Nguni societies maintained some religious authority and status within their societies to preserve a gender balance, or heterarchy, among political and reli-gious realms and across male and female gender.

The Eastern Luba Empire always had a royal woman as the medium between the current leader and the ancestor leaders. Her role was crucial to maintaining the Luba Empire since she was the only one who could communicate with previous leaders and thus inform the new ruler of the wants and demands of the ancestors. But the religious theology of the Luba religion involved more than just royal women, since it was believed that only women could communicate with God.[63] The Luba claim, "Luba men are chiefs in the daytime, but women are the chiefs at night."[64] This saying eloquently presents the dual nature of authority among the Luba. The men rule in the political realm, and the women have a major influence in the spiritual world. In the Luba world the heterarchy is clearly defined.

In Bantu Africa, women, especially older women, played crucial religious roles within their societies. In the more patrilineal and centralized societies, either individual elite women or older women in general were the link between the political world and the ancestors. This ability to communicate with the ancestors produced a form of "checks and balances" on the political authority. Thus religion within the Matrilineal Belt and in the broader Bantu world reflected a heterarchy of authority as well as the ethos of matrilineal ideology.

Matrilineality, economy and technology

As in all areas of the lives of the people of the Matrilineal Belt, the matrilineal worldview shapes and is shaped by economic and technological innovations. In areas of subsistence agriculture, matrilineality does seem to flourish. As discussed above, matrilineal societies likely favored a wide distribution of surplus goods. This might be because an expansive distribution of surplus supports survival in a limited agricultural area and, since food is distributed widely, it means that if there are limited agricultural disasters, those who are not affected can assist those that are. This communal view of the world is also part of the complex social institutions of hospitality. Most matrilineal societies believe that there are resources for everyone to survive—much like how the mother nurtures the child within the womb.

An example of matrilineal persistence is found in the history of the Yao, a matrilineal Bantu-speaking people from Mozambique. In the nineteenth century, the Yao participated in the East African long-distance trade that connected economies of the central African interior with the Indian Ocean. The movement of ivory and enslaved people was at the heart of this economic relationship. Male Yao traders active in this economy become quite rich in this trade. Over time those traders became reluctant to redistribute their wealth to their matriclans. Some of the most successful Yao traders turned toward marrying enslaved women in an attempt to avoid having to accommodate Yao brideservice. Their unions with enslaved women would produce children that did not belong to the matriclan, but to the trader's father, thus creating a patrilineage within the broader Yao matrilineal society. During this period many Yao also converted to Islam. This persisted to the colonial period. However, once colonialism ended, the African long-distance trade and the former Yao traders had to return to farming, they once again embraced matrilineality, but this time as matrilineal Muslims.

The research on technological innovations within the Bantu Matrilineal Belt also reflects a female-centered emphasis to varying degrees. Ceramic production, a technology that can be traced back nearly 6,000 years to the Proto-Bantu period, is much more than just a technology. It embodies elements of religion, initiation and other social institutions. For example, while Leza indicated the Creator God among the Sabi, *Nakabumba* was an alternate name for the Creator God. The na- prefix indicates female, the -ka- is an honorific and -*bumba*[65] is a potter, thus God in this case is an "Honored Female Potter." While Leza, Creator God, had male and female attributes, Nakabumba clearly also was tied to the maternal ability to create creating/creation/creator of people and things.

With the exception of tobacco pipes, women in Bantu Africa did nearly all the potting. In matrilineal societies ceramic production and potters were important, because they amplified women's status. Conversely, within the Matrilineal Belt, the equivalent male technology, iron smelting, did lend status to men, but it is clear that technology also honored mothers and matrilineality. The iron smelter and the process of producing iron became a metaphor for a woman giving birth. These smelters—smelting ovens—referred to as "gynecomorphic" in form by anthropologists, represented a pregnant woman, and the process of smelting iron symbolized a woman giving birth. While women did contribute to setting up the smelt, collecting the raw materials and in many places singing to provide energy to the smelt, women were excluded from the actual smelting process. Yet in a large section of the Matrilineal Belt, the smelting oven and the process were homages to motherhood. Anthropologist Eugenia Herbert's research shows that the Chokwe, Lunda, Lucazi, Yeke and Luyana (Lozi), the Bena and Kinga of the southern highlands of Tanzania, the Fipa and Lungu of the border areas between Tanzania and Zambia, the Chewa of Malawi, the Sabi-speaking peoples, the Botatwe, the Kaonde and the Luba of southeastern Congo all shaped their smelting furnaces in the nineteenth century and earlier—based on archaeological evidence—so as to convey the image of a woman giving birth and/or used the same terminology—based on linguistic evidence—in the smelting process as was used in childbirth. These structures are suggestive of the significant meaning and power that members of a matrilineage and motherhood held in the success of technological endeavors.

In the twentieth century, oral tradition and linguistic evidence supports an example from more recent history, showing that Bantu-speaking Chewa of Zambia and Malawi were particular about the naming of technological processes involved in iron smelting. While a furnace was being built it was called a pot, but once its basic structure was completed it was called *mwali*, who was a female initiate at the *-yadi* life stage. It can be considered a pregnant woman. Some societies place breasts on the smelter, and others use terminology for a woman in labor and view the interior of the furnace as the stomach or womb. It can be inferred from this that, wherever and however far back in time this furnace type is found in the archaeology, the application of birthing terminology, the accompanying rituals invoking birth and the respect shown to women's reproductive powers likely would have been essential elements in the smelters' activities and related technologies. It could be referred to as a form of male reproduction.

Conclusion

Recent historical changes have brought patrilineal practices into greater focus in the last 200 years in Africa, yet deeper historical analysis reveals that the ideologies of patrilineality are not the exclusive ways in which people organized from the beginning of time. Indeed, the evidence reveals that, in fact, matrilineages and matrilocal settlements were the norm in certain regions like the Bantu Matrilineal Belt and these coexisted with patrilineal systems within and in neighboring areas. Deconstructing externally-imposed values of gender reveals that women have held positions of power and wielded authority regardless of the lineage system in greater and lesser degrees. The goal is not to contend that women dominated in some places, but rather to demonstrate that within matrilineal societies, women were not powerless or oppressed and gender alone was not the determining factor for power and authority. Matrilineal societies probably were always heterarchical and power was shared in various ways among men and women, mothers and fathers, iron producers and potters, religious experts and political leaders.

It is imperative that Africanist scholars rethink the conventional narratives to better understand and better explain the nuances of gender and history. This is important because it will provide credible evidence to refute unsubstantiated claims about women's perpetual gender-based subordination. This broad survey of the Matrilineal Belt shows more varied and comprehensive patterns and understandings of gendered power, dynamics and hierarchies. The larger research takes a comprehensive look at the Bantu Matrilineal Belt. That work will provide other scholars both new theoretical structure for thinking about gender constructs and power. Further researching the Matrilineal Belt will furnish more than enough evidence to open a wide debate among historians of Africa and should ignite new debates on the diversity of gendered authority in African and World history. This chapter and the entire text of *Gendering Knowledge in Africa and the African Diaspora* collectively contribute to addressing the dynamic and often misunderstood topic of gender status and authority in Africa.

Notes

1 Paul Tiyambe Zeleza, "Gender Biases in African Historiography," in *African Gender Studies: Theoretical Questions and Conceptual Issues,* edited by Oyèrónké̩ Oyěwùmí (Basingstoke and New York: Palgrave Macmillan, 2005), 207. See also Akosua Adomako Ampofo, Josephine Beoku-Betts and Wairimu Ngaruiya Njambi "Women's and Gender Studies in English-Speaking Sub-Saharan Africa: A Review of Research in the Social Sciences," *Gender & Society* 18(6) (December 2004): 685–714.

2 The authors adapted the idea of a single story from TED Talks: Chimamanda Adichie, "The Danger of a Single Story." *Films on Demand*, Films Media Group, 2009. Accessed May 30, 2014. http://digital.films.com.libweb.lib.utsa.edu/PortalPlaylists. aspx?aid=2478&xtid=48462.

3 In the major general texts used to teach African history, written by both Africans and non-Africans, rarely if ever are women mentioned. In Bill Freund's *The Making of*

Contemporary Africa (London: Macmillan, 1984), "Almost invariably, they [women] are mentioned as 'dependents' together with youth, clients and slaves whether in the pre-colonial period (63) or the colonial period" (129, 131, 134); see also Paul Tiyambe Zeleza (2005), 210, 211.

4 Kathleen R. Smythe, *Africa's Past, Our Future* (Bloomington, IN: Indiana University Press, 2015), 103.

5 Holly Hanson, "Mapping Conflict: Heterarchy and Accountability in the Ancient Capital of Buganda," *The Journal of African History* 50(2) (2009): 202.

6 David Lee Schoenbrun, *A Green Place, a Good Place: Agrarian Change, Gender, and Social Identity in the Great Lakes Region to the 15th Century* (Portsmouth, NH: Heinemann, 1998); Christopher Ehret, *An African Classical Age: Eastern and Southern Africa in World History, 1000 B.C. to 400 A.D.* (Charlottesville, VA: University Press of Virginia, 1998); Jeff Marck and Koen Bostoen, "Proto-Bantu Descent Groups," in *Kinship, Language, and Prehistory: Per Hage and the Renaissance in Kinship Studies*, edited by Doug Jones and Bojka Milicic, 1st ed. (Salt Lake City, UT: University of Utah Press, 2010); Marcia Wright, *Strategies of Slaves & Women: Life-Stories from East/Central Africa* (New York: Lilian Barber Press, 1993); Edward A. Alpers, *Ivory and Slaves in East Central Africa* (Portsmouth, NH: Heinemann Educational Publishers, 1975); Christine Saidi, *Women's Authority and Society in Early East-Central Africa* (Rochester, NY: University of Rochester Press, 2010); Marja-Liisa Swantz, *Ritual and Symbol in Transitional Zaramo Society, with Special Reference to Women* (Uppsala; Stockholm: Scandinavian Institute of African Studies; distributed by Almqvist & Wiksell International, 1986), www.diva-portal.org/smash/get/diva2:277677/FULLTEXT01.pdf; Audrey Richards, *Chisungu: A Girl's Initiation Ceremony Among the Bemba of Zambia*, 2nd ed. (New York and London: Routledge, 1982).

7 For a history of the Bantu Expansions across sub-Saharan Africa, see, for example, Christopher Ehret, (1998); Kairn Klieman, *The Pygmies Were Our Compass* (Portsmouth, NH: Heinemann, 2003). An important note about Bantu languages is that they are not gendered and as such gender should not be read into them. This was a mistake in interpretation and translation that outsiders such as missionaries and colonial officials sometimes made in writing about Bantu-speaking peoples. For example, where colonial officials learned about chiefs, they would assume that they were male.

8 See Jeff Marck and Koen Bostoen (2010).

9 G. P. Murdock, *Africa: Its Peoples and Their Culture History* (New York: McGraw-Hill, 1959); G. P. Murdock, *Social Structure* (New York: Macmillan, 1949); Audrey Richards, "Mother-Rite Among the Central Bantu," in *Essays Presented to C. G. Seligman*, edited by E. E. Evans-Pritchard, Raymond Firth, Bronislaw Malinowski and Isaac Schapera (London: Kegan Paul, 1934), http://uuair.lib.utsunomiya-u.ac.jp/dspace/bitstream/10241/6358/1/kokusai26-002.pdf; Mary Douglas, "Matriliny and Pawnship in Central Africa," *Africa: Journal of the International African Institute* 3(4) (1964): 301–313, doi:10.2307/1157471.

10 Karen Sacks, *Sisters and Wives: The Past and Future of Sexual Equality*, Contributions in Women's Studies no. 10 (Westport, CT: Greenwood Press, 1979).

11 Jean Comaroff, *Body of Power, Spirit of Resistance: The Culture and History of a South African People* (Chicago, IL: University of Chicago Press, 1985), 140–141.

12 See Mathias E. Mnyampala, *The Gogo: History, Customs, and Traditions*, trans. Gregory H. Maddox (Armonk, NY: M. E. Sharpe Inc, 1995).

13 Karla O. Poewe, *Matrilineal Ideology: Male-Female Dynamics in Luapula, Zambia*, 1st ed. (London: New York: Academic Press, 1981).

14 Christine Saidi (2010); Rhonda M. Gonzales, *Societies, Religion, and History: Central-East Tanzanians and the World They Created, c.200 BCE to 1800 CE* (New York: Columbia University Press, 2009), www.gutenberg-e.org/gonzales/index.html.

15 As we will examine a bit more closely later, the word for matrilineage often has a reference to mothering in many Bantu languages spoken in Luapula Province, Zambia.

The simile is quite obvious; a mother feeds the child in her womb, as the matrilineage cares for those within the community. Karla Poewe, "Matriliny in the Throes of Change: Kinship, Descent and Marriage in Luapula," *Africa: Journal of the International African Institute* 48(3) (1978).

16 Karla Poewe, "Matrilineal Ideology: The Economic Role of Women in Luapula, Zambia," in *The Versatility of Kinship*, edited Linda Cordell and Stephen Beckerman (New York: Academic Press, 1980), 334.

17 See Karla Poewe, *Matrilineal Ideology: Male–Female Dynamics in Luapula, Zambia* (London: International African Institute, 1981) Chapter 1; Pauline Peters "Revisiting the Puzzle of Matriliny in South-Central Africa," *Critique of Anthropology* 17(2) (1997): 125–146.

18 Christopher Ehret (1998), 151–155.

19 For an example of an additional widespread word for matriclan, *-cuka* see Kairn Klieman (2003), 69–70.

20 For a more in depth discussion see Chapter 2 in Christine Saidi, Catherine Cymone Fourshey, Rhonda Gonzales, *Bantu Africa* (Oxford University Press, forthcoming).

21 Jane Guyer and S. E. Belinga, "Wealth in People as Wealth in Knowledge: Accumulation and Composition in Equatorial Africa," *Journal of African History* 36 (1995): 91–120.

22 Sen Li, Carina Schlebusch and Mattias Jakobsson, "Genetic Variation Reveals Large-Scale Population Expansion and Migration during the Expansion of Bantu-Speaking Peoples," Proceedings of the Royal Society, September 10, 2014. doi: 10.1098/rspb.2014.1448.

23 Christine Saidi (2010), 103–136.

24 Rhonda Gonzales (2009), 147–152.

25 Ibid., 145, 146.

26 Rhiannon Stephens. *A History of African Motherhood: The Case of Uganda, 700–1900* (Cambridge: Cambridge University Press 2013), 48, 49.

27 As recently as 2010 this type of brideservice was still important for any marriage, Saidi fieldwork, Mbala, Zambia, June 2010.

28 Christine Saidi (2010), 76.

29 Frank Marlowe, "Male Contribution to Diet and Female Reproductive Success among Foragers," *Current Anthropology* 42 (2004): 277–284; Interestingly for what it shows us about the imposition of Western presumptions even when inappropriate, Richards writes about this period of life as if the husband were working for his father-in-law, when in fact the man's duties were to his wife's matrikin, to which his wife's father did not belong; Christine Saidi (2010), 76.

30 Audrey Richards, "The Bemba of North-Eastern Rhodesia," in *Seven Tribes of British Central Africa*, edited by Elizabeth Colson and Max Gluckman, 126. (Oxford: Oxford University Press, 1951): 126.

31 Ibid. Richards remarked that if a young husband wanted to move his family out of his wife's village, the result was often divorce, since most women did not want to leave their mother's village.

32 L. Etienne, 1962, White Father Archive, Lusaka, Zambia, Section 111/14.

33 Christine Saidi (2010), 78.

34 Ibid. Among the Bemba there is a term for the ceremony for ending mother-in-law avoidance.

35 Bruce Kapferer, "Co-operation Leadership and Village Structure: A Preliminary Economic and Political Study of Ten Bisa Villages in the Northern Province of Zambia," Zambian Papers, No. 1 (University of Zambia Institute for Social Research, 1967), 75; Christine Saidi (2010), 75–80.

36 Saidi (2010), 91–94. The comparative ethnographic record of the Sabi (Bemba related) and Botatwe peoples describes the *-bumba* as the arbiter of the fundamental relations that reproduced the society; initiation, marriage, childbirth. The same root

word, *-bumba,* named the sororal group is found in two branches of the Nyasa branch of the Mashariki Bantu. In Nyanja-Cewa, the term was transformed during the past few centuries to mean "the people of the chief" co-opting the older legitimizing idiom of women's authority into the support for the larger scale of political authority that developed under the Phiri rule in the Malawi Empire of the 1400s. In the Ruvuma branch of Eastern Bantu as well as Matengo and Ngindo of the Mbinga Branch, *-bumba* is used as term for "adult woman." The connecting semantic link between this meaning and the meaning of "sororal group" is that the Sabi used it to represent mature women of the same matriclan. Most probably the other Bantu groups shifted the meaning to just an adult woman when the sororal groups were replaced with other forms of social organization. These three diverse branches of Bantu languages indicate that this word for sororal group probably dates back at least to 2000 BCE.

37 T. O. Beidelman, *Kaguru: A Matrilineal People of East Africa* (New York: Holt, Rinehart and Winston, Inc., 1971), 157.
38 Christopher Ehret (1998), 146–149.
39 Christine Saidi (2010), 81–83.
40 Tervuren Museum, Ethnographic Section, Tervuren, Belgium, housing the Belgian colonial archives. Province Katanga/District Haut-Katanga/Territoire Sakania.
41 In this example, /k/ followed by the super high closed vowel /μ/ becomes /f/. This is a regular sound change in a number of Bantu languages.
42 Christine Saidi (2010), 95.
43 John Yoder, *The Kanyok of Zaire* (Cambridge: Cambridge University Press, 1992), 20–21. The Lunda or Ruund Kingdom borrowed these terms from the Kanyok, see James Hoover, "The Seduction of Ruweji: Reconstructing Ruund History." PhD Dissertation, Yale University, 1978, 201.
44 Iris Berger and E. Frances White, *Women in Sub-Saharan Africa* (Bloomington, IN: Indiana University Press, 1999), 21–27, 73.
45 The main evidence that the new concept of chiefly clans was from the Luba region is that the word they used for "tribute," *munsoko* is a loan from the Luba language. Christine Saidi (2010), 87.
46 Ibid., 89.
47 Thomas Munday, "Some Traditions of the Nyendwa Clan of Northern Rhodesia," *Bantu Studies* 14 (1940): 449.
48 See Anne Hilton, "Family and Kinship among the Kongo South of the Zaire River from the Sixteenth to the Nineteenth Centuries," *The Journal of African History* 24(2) (1983): 189–206.
49 Ibid., 199–201.
50 Christine Saidi (2010), 86.
51 Ibid., 87, 89.
52 Harry Johnston, *Comparative Study of Bantu and Semi-Bantu Languages* (Oxford, UK: OUP, Clarendon, 1919), 19.
53 Mary Nooter Roberts, *Memory: Luba Art and the Making of History* (New York: Museum for African Art and Munich: Prestel, 1996), 21, 42–43, 169, 205.
54 Cynthia Brantley, "Through Ngoni Eyes: Margaret Read's Matrilineal Interpretations from Nyasaland," *Critique of Anthropology* 17(2) (June 1997).
55 See Christopher Ehret, *The Civilizations of Africa: A History to 1800* (Charlottesville, VA: University of Virginia Press, 2002).
56 Christine Saidi (2010), 92, 93.
57 Ibid.
58 Ibid., 93–94.
59 Ibid.
60 Robert Brain, "The Bangwa of West Cameroon," (1967). www.lebialem.info/The%20Bangwa%20of%20West%20Cameroon.pdf: 32, 33.

61 Rita Astuti, "Ritual, History and the Swazi Ncwala. Sacred Kingship and the Origin of the State," *Africa: Rivista Trimestrale Di Studi e Documentazione Dell'Istituto Italiano per L'Africa e L'Oriente* 43(4) (1988): 603–620. For women in religious ritual in other parts of Bantu Speaking Africa see, Shane Doyle, "The Cwezi-Kubandwa Debate: Gender, Hegemony and Pre-Colonial Religion in Bunyoro, Western Uganda," *Africa: Journal of the International African Institute* 77(4) (2007): 559–581; John K. Thornton, "Elite Women in the Kingdom of Kongo: Historical Perspectives on Women's Political Power," *The Journal of African History* 47(3) (2006): 437–460; Beverley Haddad, "The Manyano Movement in South Africa: Site of Struggle, Survival, and Resistance," *Agenda: Empowering Women for Gender Equity* 61 (2004): 4–13; Isabel Phiri, "African Women's Theologies in the New Millennium," *Agenda: Empowering Women for Gender Equity* 61 (2004): 16–24; Laurence D. Schiller, "The Royal Women of Buganda," *The International Journal of African Historical Studies* 23(3) (1990): 455–473; Edward A. Alpers, "'Ordinary Household Chores': Ritual and Power in a 19th-Century Swahili Women's Spirit Possession Cult," *The International Journal of African Historical Studies* 17(4) (1984): 677–702; Marion Kilson, "Women in African Traditional Religions," *Journal of Religion in Africa* 8(2) (1976): 133–143.

62 Doyle (2007), 525.

63 Mary Nooter Roberts (1996) 86, 91 Cat 35.

64 Ibid., 122 Cat 48.

65 This *bumba* has a different root from **-bumba*, the sororal group. There may be a connection between the two meanings, but presently there needs to be more research before such a link can be made.

Bibliography

Alpers, Edward A. "Trade, State, and Society among the Yao in the Nineteenth Century," *The Journal of African History* 10(3) (1969): 405–420. doi: www.jstor.org/stable/179674.

Alpers, Edward A. *Ivory and Slaves in East Central Africa*. Portsmouth, NH: Heinemann Educational Publishers, 1975.

Alpers, Edward A. "'Ordinary Household Chores': Ritual and Power in a 19th-Century Swahili Women's Spirit Possession Cult," *The International Journal of African Historical Studies* 17(4) (1984): 677–702.

Ampofo, Akosua Adomako, Josephine Beoku-Betts and Wairimu Ngaruiya Njambi. "Women's and Gender Studies in English-Speaking Sub-Saharan Africa: A Review of Research in the Social Sciences," *Gender & Society* 18(6) (December 2004): 685–714.

Astuti, Rita. "Ritual, History and the Swazi Ncwala. Sacred Kingship and the Origin of the State," *Africa: Rivista Trimestrale di Studi e Documentazione Dell'Istituto Italiano per L'Africa e L'Oriente* 43(4) (1988): 603–620.

Beidelman, T. O. *Kaguru: A Matrilineal People of East Africa*. New York: Holt, Rinehart and Winston, Inc., 1971.

Berger, Iris, and E. Frances White. *Women in Sub-Saharan Africa*. Bloomington, IN: Indiana University Press, 1999.

Brain, Robert. "The Bangwa of West Cameroon," (1967). www.lebialem.info/The%20 Bangwa%20of%20West%20Cameroon.pdf.

Brantley, Cynthia. "Through Ngoni Eyes; Margaret Read's Matrilineal Interpretations from Nyasaland," *Critique of Anthropology* 17(2) (1997): 147–169.

Comaroff, Jean. *Body of Power, Spirit of Resistance: The Culture and History of a South African People*. Chicago, IL: University of Chicago Press, 1985.

Douglas, Mary. "Matriliny and Pawnship in Central Africa," *Africa: Journal of the International African Institute* 34(4) (1964): 301–313. doi:10.2307/1157471.

Doyle, Shane. "The Cwezi-Kubandwa Debate: Gender, Hegemony and Pre-Colonial Religion in Bunyoro, Western Uganda," *Africa: Journal of the International African Institute* 77(4) (2007): 559–581.

Ehret, Christopher. *An African Classical Age: Eastern and Southern Africa in World History, 1000 B.C. to 400 A.D.* Charlottesville, VA: University Press of Virginia, 1998.

Ehret, Christopher. *The Civilizations of Africa: A History to 1800.* Charlottesville, VA: University Press of Virginia, 2002.

Fields-Black, Edda L. *Deep Roots: Rice Farmers in West Africa and the African Diaspora.* Bloomingdale and Indianapolis, IN: Indiana University Press, 2008.

Freund, Bill. *The Making of Contemporary Africa.* London: Macmillan, 1984.

Gonzales, Rhonda M. *Societies, Religion, and History: Central-East Tanzanians and the World They Created, c.200 BCE to 1800 CE.* New York: Columbia University Press, 2009. www.gutenberg-e.org/gonzales/index.html.

Guyer, Jane, and S. E. Belinga, "Wealth in People as Wealth in Knowledge: Accumulation and Composition in Equatorial Africa," *Journal of African History* 36 (1995): 91–120.

Haddad, Beverley. "The Manyano Movement in South Africa: Site of Struggle, Survival, and Resistance," *Agenda: Empowering Women for Gender Equity* 61 (2004): 4–13.

Hansen, Karen Tranberg, ed. *African Encounters with Domesticity.* New Brunswick, NJ: Rutgers University Press, 1992.

Hanson, Holly. "Mapping Conflict: Heterarchy and Accountability in the Ancient Capital of Buganda," *The Journal of African History* 50(2) (2009): 179–202.

Herbert, Eugenia W. *Iron, Gender, and Power: Rituals of Transformation in African Societies.* Bloomington, IN: Indiana University Press, 1994.

Hilton, Anne. "Family and Kinship among the Kongo South of the Zaire River from the Sixteenth to the Nineteenth Centuries," *The Journal of African History* 24(2) (1983): 189–206.

Hodgson, Dorothy Louise, and Sheryl McCurdy. *"Wicked" Women and the Reconfiguration of Gender in Africa.* Social History of Africa. Portsmouth, NH: Heinemann, 2001.

Hoover, James. "The Seduction of Ruweji: Reconstructing Ruund History." PhD Dissertation, Yale University, 1978.

Johnston, Harry. *Comparative Study of Bantu and Semi-Bantu Languages.* Oxford, England: OUP: Clarendon, 1919.

Jones, Doug, and Bojka Milicic, eds. *Kinship, Language, and Prehistory: Per Hage and the Renaissance in Kinship Studies,* 1st ed. Salt Lake City, UT: University of Utah Press, 2010.

Kapferer, Bruce. "Co-operation Leadership and Village Structure: A Preliminary Economic and Political Study of Ten Bisa Villages in the Northern Province of Zambia." Zambian Papers, No. 1: University of Zambia Institute for Social Research, 1967.

Kilson, Marion. "Women in African Traditional Religions," *Journal of Religion in Africa* 8(2) (1976): 133–143.

Klieman, Kairn. *The Pygmies Were Our Compass.* Portsmouth, NH: Heinemann, 2003.

Li, Sen, Carina Schlebusch and Mattias Jakobsson, "Genetic variation reveals large-scale population expansion and migration during the expansion of Bantu-speaking peoples," *Proceedings of the Royal Society,* September 10, 2014. doi: 10.1098/rspb.2014.1448.

Marlowe, Frank. "Male Contribution to Diet and Female Reproductive Success among Foragers," *Current Anthropology* 42 (2004): 277–284.

Marck, Jeff, and Koen Bostoen. "Proto-Bantu Descent Groups," in *Kinship, Language, and Prehistory: Per Hage and the Renaissance in Kinship Studies*, edited by Doug Jones and Bojka Milicic, 1st ed., 75–78. Salt Lake City, UT: University of Utah Press, 2010.

Marck, Jeff, and Koen Bostoen. "Proto-Oceanic Society (Austronesian) and Proto-East Bantu Society (Niger-Congo)," in *Kinship, Language, and Prehistory: Per Hage and the Renaissance in Kinship Studies*, edited by Doug Jones and Bojka Milicic, 1st ed., 83–94. Salt Lake City, UT: University of Utah Press, 2010.

Mnyampala, Mathias E. *The Gogo: History, Customs, and Traditions*, trans. Gregory H. Maddox. Armonk, NY: M. E. Sharpe Inc., 1995.

Munday, Thomas. "Some Traditions of the Nyendwa Clan of Northern Rhodesia," *Bantu Studies* 14 (1940): 435–454.

Murdock, G. P. *Africa: Its Peoples and Their Culture History*. New York: McGraw-Hill, 1959.

Murdock, G. P. *Social Structure*. New York: Macmillan, 1949.

Ogbomo, Onaiwu. *When Men and Women Mattered: A History of Gender Relations Among the Owan of Nigeria*. Rochester, NY: University of Rochester Press, 1997.

Oyěwùmí, Oyèrónké. *Gender Epistemologies in Africa: Gendering Traditions, Spaces, Social Institutions, and Identities*. New York: Palgrave Macmillan, 2010.

Peters, Pauline. "Revisiting the Puzzle of Matriliny in South-Central Africa," *Critique of Anthropology* 17(2) (1997): 125–146.

Phiri, Isabel. "African Women's Theologies in the New Millennium," *Agenda: Empowering Women for Gender Equity* 61 (2004): 16–24.

Poewe, Karla O. "Matriliny in the Throes of Change: Kinship, Descent and Marriage in Luapula," *Africa: Journal of the International African Institute* 48(3) (1978): 353–367.

Poewe, Karla O. "Matrilineal Ideology: The Economic Role of Women in Luapula, Zambia," in *The Versatility of Kinship*, edited by Linda Cordell and Stephen Beckerman, 333–355. New York: Academic Press, 1980.

Poewe, Karla O. *Matrilineal Ideology: Male-Female Dynamics in Luapula, Zambia*, 1st ed. London: International African Institute, 1981.

Poewe, Karla O. *Religion, Kinship and Economy in Luapula, Zambia*. Lewiston, NY: Edwin Mellen Press, 1989.

Richards, Audrey. "Mother-Rite Among the Central Bantu," in *Essays Presented to C. G. Seligman*, edited by E. E. Evans-Pritchard, Raymond Firth, Bronislaw Malinowski and Isaac Schapera. London: Kegan Paul, 1934. http://uuair.lib.utsunomiya-u.ac.jp/dspace/bitstream/10241/6358/1/kokusai26-002.pdf.

Richards, Audrey. "The Bemba of North-Eastern Rhodesia," in *Seven Tribes of British Central Africa*, edited by Elizabeth Colson and Max Gluckman, 164–193. Oxford: Oxford University Press, 1951.

Richards, Audrey. *Chisungu: A Girl's Initiation Ceremony Among the Bemba of Zambia*, 2nd ed. London: Routledge, 1982.

Roberts, Andrew. *A History of Zambia*. New York: Africana Pub. Co., 1976.

Roberts, Mary Nooter. *Memory: Luba Art and the Making of History*. Munich and New York: Prestel, 1996.

Sacks, Karen. *Sisters and Wives: The Past and Future of Sexual Equality*. Contributions in Women's Studies, no. 10. Westport, CT: Greenwood Press, 1979.

Saidi, Christine. *Women's Authority and Society in Early East-Central Africa*. Rochester, NY: University of Rochester Press, 2010.

Saidi, Christine, Catherine Cymone Fourshey and Rhonda Gonzales. *Bantu Africa* (Oxford University Press, forthcoming).

Schiller, Laurence D. "The Royal Women of Buganda," *The International Journal of African Historical Studies* 23(3) (1990): 455–73.

Schoenbrun, David Lee. *A Green Place, a Good Place: Agrarian Change, Gender, and Social Identity in the Great Lakes Region to the 15th Century.* Portsmouth, NH: Heinemann, 1998.

Smythe, Kathleen R. *Africa's Past, Our Future.* Bloomington, IN: Indiana University Press, 2015.

Stephens, Rhiannon. *A History of African Motherhood: The Case of Uganda, 700–1900.* New York: Cambridge University Press, 2013.

Swantz, Marja-Liisa. *Ritual and Symbol in Transitional Zaramo Society, with Special Reference to Women.* Uppsala; Stockholm: Scandinavian Institute of African Studies; Distributed by Almqvist & Wiksell International, 1986. www.diva-portal.org/smash/get/diva2:277677/FULLTEXT01.pdf.

Swantz, Marja-Liisa. *Blood, Milk, and Death: Body Symbols and the Power of Regeneration among the Zaramo of Tanzania.* Westport, CT: Bergin & Garvey, 1995.

Thornton, John K. "Elite Women in the Kingdom of Kongo: Historical Perspectives on Women's Political Power," *The Journal of African History* 47(3) (2006): 437–460.

Turner, Victor. *The Ritual Process: Structure and Anti-Structure (Lewis Henry Morgan Lectures).* Reprint. New York: Aldine Transaction, 1995.

Vansina, Jan M. *Paths in the Rainforests: Toward a History of Political Tradition in Equatorial Africa.* Madison, WI: University of Wisconsin Press, 1990.

Wright, Marcia. *Strategies of Slaves & Women: Life-Stories from East/Central Africa.* New York: Lilian Barber Press, 1993.

Yoder, John. *The Kanyok of Zaire.* Cambridge, UK: Cambridge University Press, 1992.

Zeleza, Paul Tiyambe. "Gender Biases in African Historiography," in *African Gender Studies: Theoretical Questions and Conceptual Issues*, edited by Oyèrónké Oyěwùmí, 207–232. Basingstoke and New York: Palgrave Macmillan, 2005.

2 REMAPping the African Diaspora

Place, gender and negotiation in Arabian slavery

Alaine S. Hutson

Introduction

The primary vehicle for the making and expansion of the African Diaspora before the twentieth century was the slave trade from the continent. The Atlantic slave trade and the Diaspora it birthed in the western hemisphere have the oldest and most mature scholarship dedicated to their study. The trade between Africa and Arabia was a substantial and much older slave trade but is a relatively "new" site for Diaspora studies or more diverse, nuanced research about the bulk of those enslaved men and women on the Arabian Peninsula. Using chi-square statistical tests of variable pairs from Arabian slavery data and theoretical frameworks from Atlantic slavery scholarship, this chapter shows that Arabian and Atlantic slavery had some similar patterns of slave life and slave-holder's practices. This research makes clear that slavery in this region was not a single benign, cosmopolitan, humane system, just as Atlantic slavery was not monolithic in its brutality, economic role or relationships between masters and slaves.

Currently much of the scholarship on so-called Islamic slavery comes from or feels the need to reference the portrait of "benign," "non-productive" harem slavery Ottoman officials painted in the mid-nineteenth century and assumes that when freed, slaves were absorbed into slaveholder's society rather than stood apart as a Diaspora. Ehud Toledano described the Ottoman strategy in creating this image as an "amplification" of the role of the empire's military, administrative and harem slaves in more benign slavery, and a "deletion" of domestic and agricultural slavery, even though the bulk of slaves did domestic and agricultural work.[1] Some scholars have started to reveal the inadequacies of Arabian slavery historiography. Benjamin Reilly has written on why African slaves were used for labor-intensive agriculture in Arabia.[2] Matthew Hopper has written on "productive use" of slaves in the palm date and pearl industries of Arabia.[3] Toledano has called for scholars to "reexamine the argument that Islamic slavery was so much milder than its counterparts" and suggested six criteria as the framework for that reexamination: work of the enslaved, social status of the slaveholder, location in the core or periphery of the empire, habitat (urban, rural or nomadic), gender and African or not.[4] The last three criteria are analyzed in this chapter. Reilly suggests that Africans were specifically used on the peninsula for agricultural slavery that had harsh and unhealthy labor conditions. Toledano states outright that slaves of African descent were treated more harshly than others throughout the empire. This chapter shows that Africanness was important. Africanness was a determinant for how slave holders utilized slaves at work and this chapter also provides evidence that African culture and notions of gender were central to the ways enslaved women and men imagined and reimagined their lives, families and strategies for surviving slavery.

This chapter engages the lives and work of slaves, most engaged in domestic and manual labor in close proximity to their Arab owners and all their owners' demands, control and negotiation. I concentrate on Saudi Arabia in an attempt to reveal the lived rules of slavery in a Middle East context. I am trying to undelete domestic and agricultural slaves' lives by offering up sharper pictures of the lives of Africans enslaved in twentieth-century Saudi Arabia as extracted from the narratives of runaways.[5] These pictures suggest that when made to do similar work (rural agricultural or urban domestic) slaves in Saudi Arabia experienced patterns of subordination similar to the enslaved in the Americas. The chapter compares the official image of slavery projected by the Ottomans with the lived experiences that can be extracted from the narratives of runaways. All of the chapter's findings point to further comparative research and that the benign quality of Middle Eastern slavery may be more "amplification" by slave holders and other elites than the lived experience of the enslaved. These findings support Toledano's framework and also bring into question the validity of claims that African slaves were absorbed into Middle Eastern societies instead of establishing distinct African Diaspora communities.[6]

The details of the lives of enslaved Africans are found in the records of the British Legation in Jeddah, Saudi Arabia from 1926 to 1938.[7] During this time, Jeddah was the destination of hundreds of runaway slaves because the British were freeing and repatriating these runaways as stipulated in Article 7 of the 1927 Treaty of Jeddah.[8] All together the Foreign Office files give information on 263 people.[9] For sixty fugitives there are brief but detailed hand-written narratives or typed questionnaires. I have compiled and coded the data from these documents into a free, online searchable database for researchers—Runaways Enslaved and Manumitted on the Arabian Peninsula (REMAP) www.REMAP-database.org. The database contains the dataset of direct and imputed variables, high-resolution images of the archival documents from which the information came and full citation of the archival source. When citing information from individual runaways I will be using their REMAP database ID number.

Analyzing data from the Saudi Arabian narratives and questionnaires using theoretical concepts from Atlantic scholarship provides information that parallels New World slavery in several areas. Using Gabriel Debien's framework to analyze and categorize runaway slaves on the data, this chapter shows that slaves used "petit marronage" to negotiate with owners for better labor and living conditions.[10] Scholars like Goldin and Wade have shown that urban and rural contexts of slavery produce significant differences in Atlantic slave holding patterns and those differences hold true for the Saudi Arabian data. These issues are squarely in the categories of owners' cultural and labor practices. These parallels not only tell historians about the conditions of Middle Eastern and Atlantic slavery, they also reveal insights about the gendered nature of power in slave societies;[11] how power and its maintenance result in owners' attempts to control most aspects of slaves' lives and identities and how owners often used similar gendered patterns to do so.

Arabs, Americans and Europeans tried to domesticate slaves, especially African men, in order to stave off escapes—at times by negotiating with individual fugitive slaves. Where slave owners lived helped determine the economics of slave labor; locale and cultural norms of religion and gender helped shape the structure of slave family units. All of these practices and norms in the Americas helped determine where African Diaspora communities would live after the abolition of slavery and helped distinguish Diaspora family unit structures from their majority communities. The existence of these practices in Saudi Arabia may indicate that a similarly situated African Diaspora exists on the Arabian Peninsula as well.

Marronage in Arabia

The narratives of runaways in combination with statistical tests indicate that both women and men slaves in Saudi Arabia engaged in what Gabriel Debien described as "petit marronage"[12]—that is, they used running away as a strategy to negotiate better treatment within Saudi Arabia, and ran away to get permanently out of slavery. Scholars have compared the two forms of running away and found that the diverse patterns of subordination that slaves labored under, in part dictated by demographics such as age, status and gender, helped determine which form slaves chose. Here I will discuss petit marronage.

Patterns of subordination by labor assignment

Statistical analysis[13] of data in the REMAP database gives us insight into how the jobs African slaves worked in Saudi Arabian towns and rural areas led to diverse patterns of subordination: agricultural slaves in rural areas were enslaved longer than other slaves and ill treated, but they were more likely to have one owner; commercial male workers, usually enslaved in urban areas, appeared to have more skills than other slaves, to be more viable as free people and to be most threatened by sale to another owner; women in urban areas were overwhelmingly likely to be domestics (some of them engaged in sex work as well) and often opted for local manumission instead of repatriation. Despite the fact that they appeared to be property whom owners valued highly and kept for longer periods than others, agricultural slaves' value did not improve the treatment they received.[14] In fact Table 2.1 shows that 93 percent of runaway slaves in agricultural work cited ill treatment as the reason they had fled.

Table 2.1 Labor assignment and reason for running away[15]

Type of labor	Agricultural		Commercial		Domestic		Total	
	n=	%	n=	%	n=	%	n=	%
Family reasons	0	0	4	16	2	8	6	9
Free, status threatened	1	7	4	16	4	16	9	14
Ill treatment	14	93	7	28	13	52	34	52
Sale	0	0	10	40	6	24	16	25
Total	15	100	25	100	25	100	65	100

The chi-square tests also showed that those born to slave parents in Saudi Arabia were enslaved on average longer than others—a median of thirty years. Abdul Kheyr Ibn Faraj was a twenty-five-year-old man whose slave parents, a Sudanese father and Yemeni mother, had both died.[16] Ibn Faraj was then raised by another slave woman and continued to serve his owner as an agricultural worker. Ibn Faraj ran away because his owner was feeding him poorly. Ibn Faraj only reported having the one owner, probably that of his parents. His story illustrates the chi-square test which found that those born a slave outside the five major urban areas of Saudi Arabia—Mecca, Medina, Jeddah, Tayf and Riyadh—were 4.1 times more likely to have one owner than those captured for the Saudi market.[17]

On a comparative basis, agricultural laborers were 3.7 times more likely than commercially utilized slaves to give ill treatment as a reason for running away. Commercial workers were more likely than domestic or agricultural workers to leave their owners because of an impending sale. Abdullah Ahmed ibn Bashir, a forty-five-year-old water carrier, ran away from his owner in 1931.[18] Abdullah had been sold twice, his wife and child were sold with him each time at his request. The third time he was threatened with sale he ran. Abdullah's story shows that sale was a gamble for commercial slaves; their circumstances, family status and treatment would change with their new owners, perhaps for the worse. His commercial skills may have emboldened him, and his actions may denote that commercial slaves knew they had skills that made their freedom viable.

Patterns of subordination by gender

Women's viability in freedom in Saudi Arabia or Africa was more in doubt. Living in a patriarchal, family-oriented society as a single woman with no patron or family and only domestic experience was not ideal for Saudi Arabia and not realistic for repatriation to Africa; most of these women only had a knowledge of Arabic and their owner's families. These doubts and societal conditions may have limited the number of women who sought refuge at the legation and led many runaway women without husbands or adult children to request local manumission.[19] Children, the natural results of concubinage, also limited and shaped domestically employed women's choices. Table 2.2 shows that although women were only 37 percent of the table,[20] they represented 75 percent of those locally manumitted.

Table 2.2 Gender and result of bid for freedom[21]

	Women			Men			Total	
	n=	% of women	% of result	n=	% of men	% of result	n=	% of total
Free person with safety issues	1	3	33	2	3	67	3	3
Left without manumission	2	5	25	6	9.25	75	8	8
Local manumission	18	47	75	6	9.25	25	24	23
Manumitted and repatriated	17	45	25	51	78.5	75	68	66
Total # (% of total)	38	100	(37)	65	100	(63)	103	100

Petit marronage

Like slaves in the Americas, slaves in Saudi Arabia often voiced their resistance to owners' work demands with their feet but never intended to leave their owners' employ or slavery completely. Debien called this temporary running away and the negotiation that took place upon the runaway's return as petit marronage. Some slaves simply left the legation without manumission: some stated their intention to go back to their owners and the British made educated guesses for some of the others and, based on interaction with them individually, concluded that the slaves ran in "the heat of the moment" and they had returned to slavery as well.[22] In the Saudi case petit marronage also includes slaves who ran away to the British Legation and later asked to be locally manumitted. These runaways usually indicated a preference or expressed no objection to returning to the employ of their former owners. Even though officially and legally classified as manumitted persons no longer slaves, Islamic law and Arab culture would have required these freed people to continue to live in subordinate client–patron relationships with their old owners. Their former owners were entitled under *Shari'ah* law to portions of former slaves' earnings, had to serve as guardians/ witnesses for former slaves' marriages to be legal and were heirs to former slaves' estates.[23] The first of these former Saudi owners' entitlements was an enduring source of income for owners in the Americas and was a prime motivation for the continued presence of slaves in American cities.[24] It appears to have been an important source of income for poorer Saudi owners as well.[25] The Saudi narratives and British reports also make it clear that locally manumitted persons were still open to "conditional difficulties," no doubt including ex-owners' ill treatment (e.g., beatings, confiscating of property and rendering sexual services), re-enslavement and neglect. The British themselves recognized that manumitted women were in "danger of … occupying a position in the actual household hardly distinguishable from that of a slave."[26]

John Thornton has analyzed class as a dominant force in the petit form of running away in the Americas.[27] In Saudi Arabia the determining factor for petit marronage appears to be gender and to some degree age. The Saudi data indicates that women, older bondmen and women, and domestic workers were the most likely to engage in some form of petit marronage. Diba was a slave woman who ran away and requested local manumission.[28] Diba was found to be about three months pregnant and claimed the child belonged to her owner's son. The owner's family was "Sherifian [sic] ... of some consequence" so repatriation would have been problematic as "a Sherif [sic] ... should not be sent out of the country under foreign and non-Moslem [sic] auspices." This was the case even though the Sharifian[29] family had "caused a miscarriage" during a previous pregnancy. Diba's occupation was not listed, so concubinage may not have been her only work in her owner's house. Diba was housed with a relative of her owner for the duration of her pregnancy and visited by the Legation doctor.

In another instance a slave woman named Halima who was seeking manumission first claimed her child, Zahra, was fathered by a fellow slave only to later reveal it was by her owner.[30] Halima's initial pretense was warranted because unlike the Americas, Islamic codes of law recognized children of a slave mother and a free Muslim father as members of the father's family and free. Shari'ah law also only allowed slave women to keep their children with them until the age of seven, at the latest. While these women who bore their owners children could not be sold or given away, Islamic law mandated their manumission only upon the death of their owners and if one of their children was still alive.[31] Halima's negotiation was for immediate manumission for herself and in the process obtained witnessed acknowledgment of paternity for Zahra. When she received both, she and Zahra returned to her owner's house. Scholars point to this aspect of Islamic law as pivotal in the absorption of slaves into slaveholders' families and the absence of African Diaspora in the Ottoman and Arab worlds. Diba and Halima's experiences show that slaveholders were not always willing to absorb the children of slave women into their families. Besides forced abortion and silence, slaveholders used other tactics to deny free status and paternity to slave women's children. Arab slaveholding families would sell slave women impregnated by their male kin or marry them to a male slave and assign paternity to him.[32] Sometimes enslaved women had to insist and strategize to gain Shari'ah rights for themselves and their children.[33]

The Saudi government acted several times throughout this period to stop the British from removing children of free Saudi fathers from Arabia. In one case, it appears a Saudi owner falsely claimed a slave was his son in order to stop his repatriation and newly captured slaves were imported into Saudi Arabia by slavers claiming them as their children.[34] Because free Arab fathers had the over-riding power in these relationships, a power granted to them by Shari'ah law and the Saudi Government, women domestics like Diba often chose local manumission; it was the only option they had to retain contact with their children.

In fact Table 2.2 shows that gender significantly affected how slaves acted once they reached the legation. Women were 5.13 times more likely to be locally manumitted than men, and men were 1.75 times more likely to leave the legation without manumission or to be manumitted and repatriated than women. In combination, Table 2.2 and the narratives clearly attest to women's use of running away as a tool of negotiation, especially for resolving family matters. Runaway women who gave birth to owners' children did not appear to want to leave owners' homes permanently: rather, they were establishing their worth and the free status of their children within owners' families. These women who opted for local manumission were able to have the free status of their children, and sometimes their own manumission and, for a few, sanctified Muslim marriages recorded in a Saudi *Shari'ah* court. Other women were like Mubaraka, who ran away from her owner once, but the Saudi official to whom she applied for freedom returned her. Thereafter she appears to have snuck away from her owner's place in the countryside several times to visit relatives in Jeddah (a two-day walk) until she realized she might have better luck getting local manumission from the British Legation.[35] Peter Wood notes that women in South Carolina practiced petit marronage for family reasons as well; like Mubaraka they ran in order to visit relatives and friends and then returned voluntarily.[36] Many of the runaways who left the legation or who successfully negotiated local manumission at one point stated an intention, nay a threat, to choose repatriation. The all too real possibility of repatriation may have been an important mediation tool for slaves introducing more dialog over treatment, resale or family matters into their relationships with slaveholders.

The British retained copies of all local manumission certificates issued by the *Shari'ah* court in Jeddah. That way if ex-slaves later faced personal safety issues, such as being threatened physically or with resale by ex-owners and patrons, they would have recourse. From the data emerge two sets of strategies used by locally manumitted Africans: those who ran because of ill treatment and required British intervention in their petit marronage negotiations over their circumstances with patrons, and those who were threatened with sale and becoming slaves again in name as well as circumstance and who felt their only choice was repatriation.

Some manumitted slaves found that freedom in Saudi Arabia with their former owners was not all they had hoped, either because of an inability to fend for themselves or because little had changed in the client–patron relationship with, and treatment from, former slaveholders. In these cases, the former slaves first stated the wish to be repatriated. A Sudanese man with the slave name of Faraj provides an illustration. Originally named Bilal, this Sudanese domestic had been freed six years before in 1929 and had since been working for his ex-owner, who said he "paid [Faraj] a few riyals as his monthly wages."[37] In "the heat of the moment" Faraj ran to the legation after his ex-owner struck him and told the British he would consider repatriation. Faraj cooled his heels at the legation for two months as the British tried to process his case. It turned out that Faraj's assailant was Indian Vice-Consul Munshi Ihsanullah's "dearest friend." Ihsanullah spoke with his friend about the case and confirmed that Faraj's freedom had been registered "in the Municipal Office." Faraj's owner had other connections at the legation and was visiting on business when Faraj saw and left with him. Ex-owners were usually not allowed to see runaways in order to avoid any coercion and one British official feared Faraj had been the victim of "enticement." However, after examining the circumstances another official (not the dear friend) reckoned Faraj had grown weary of his prolonged stay at the legation and had reportedly initiated the contact with his former owner. Like Faraj, other recently freed refugees who were treated poorly ran and threatened to leave Saudi Arabia, but none actually chose repatriation.

Other locally manumitted slaves faced a worse scenario—being sold. These ex-slaves reported having been freed by deathbed manumissions (some were even witnessed) only to be threatened with sale by the deceased's heirs and fewer were freed by owners who showed signs of reneging after a financial turn for the worse. Most of these cases involved informal or witnessed but unregistered local manumissions. In these circumstances of impending or completed sale and formal re-enslavement, most of the ex-slaves were like the thirty-year-old Sudanese water carrier who had been manumitted once only to be re-enslaved. He had an "exciting passage to Agency, being arrested at Bahra," but eventually had his manumission confirmed by the British process and was repatriated.[38] In New World slavery, sale and marronage were also intimately linked, and the pairing was also made up of several issues; Wood writes about slaves running to prompt sale, but his work also holds documentation of owners selling slaves to curb a tendency toward petit marronage. Others write of slaves running to prevent sale.

The British saw enough of these cases to know that certification of the manumission in *Shari'ah* court and sustained documentation of the ex-slave's status were necessities. To prevent more cases occurring, the British held the certificates of freedom as a way for ex-slaves to reassert their free status and garner another chance to flee the kingdom through repatriation. Having the British involved as safe keepers was apparently effective; not one runaway during the tenure of the Treaty of Jeddah who was manumitted by an owner—with the encouragement of the British—and whose *Shari'ah* certificate was kept at the British Legation returned for repatriation or in "the heat of the moment." Without knowledge and documentation of other destinations and strategies for Saudi runaways it is hard to measure whether petit marronage and negotiation was only possible with British intervention, but British mediation in the process was certainly valuable for slaves.

While those locally manumitted after 1926 were not seen again at the legation, it is clear from the records that, as in the Americas, both free Africans with slave origins and freed Africans had several security concerns in and around Arabia. A free Nigerian man serves as an illustration. No doubt he earned money to start a coffee shop as a soldier in the Turkish army during the Medina War. Though he had at least enough means to be a small business owner in 1930, his status did not seem sufficient protection to him; when another West African threatened to sell him he sought to leave Saudi Arabia via a British ship.[39]

In the few cases when runaway slaves left the legation without a resolution to their case, their narratives and British officials' notes again reinforce the pattern that women and older slaves participated in petit marronage and that family issues may have stopped these groups from completing the emancipation process. Scholars of slavery in the Americas have posited that one reason owners encouraged the building of slave families was to domesticate slave men; having a wife and children was to keep slave men from running and revolting by giving them ties to plantations or local counties.[40] Faraj ibn Murjan illustrates the pull of family for men and also the problems older slaves faced. Faraj was a Sudanese slave born to slave parents. Like his parents, he married a fellow slave who gave birth to a second-generation *muwallid* or person born a slave; they had a daughter. Once Faraj had worked as a slave for sixty years and was too old to work, his owner, Hazza bin Hamid, stopped feeding him. Old and neglected, Faraj was faced with the choice of staying with his family and starving or leaving behind his wife and daughter in order to seek manumission and repatriation at the British Legation. Faraj told his family to follow as soon as they could. After two weeks, Faraj left the legation without manumission.[41]

Itir, a woman from an emir's palace, sought refuge with the British. After a long stay at the legation, the British were still trying but had not been able to get the Saudi government's clearance for her to be manumitted and repatriated because she was a royal slave. Itir had also left behind a husband at her owner's house. She left without manumission.[42] In her case the British surmised, and one cannot completely discount their claims, that factors other than family influenced her decision to leave: she saw how she would be treated outside the palace—the legation had poor housing for temporary guests, especially women whom they couldn't dorm with unrelated men.

The full gender implications of petit marronage appear when Tables 2.2, 2.3 and 2.4 are considered together. Ethiopian women who were most likely domestic slaves, chose to be locally manumitted and were engaging in petit marronage. Even in dire circumstances this pattern held true.

Take for example the distressing case of twenty-three-year-old Ghuzlan, an Ethiopian slave woman involved in sexual work. Ghuzlan was first the slave of a

Table 2.3 Country of origin and result of bid for freedom[43]

	Free person with safety issues		Left without manumission		Local manumission		Manumitted and repatriated		Total	
	n=	%	n=	%	n=	%	n=	%	n=	%
Ethiopia	0	0	4	50	13	62	20	29.5	37	37.5
French Eq. Africa	0	0	0	0	0	0	1	1.5	1	1
Nigeria	1	50	2	25	0	0	8	12	11	11
Sudan	0	0	2	25	5	24	39	57	46	46.5
Yemen	1	50	0	0	3	14	0	0	4	4
Total	2	100	8	100	21	100	68	100	99	100

Table 2.4 Women's labor assignments and country of origin[44]

Type of labor	Agricultural		Commercial		Domestic		Total	
	n=	%	n=	%	n=	%	n=	%
Ethiopia	0	0	2	40	14	35	16	33
French Eq. Africa	1	25	1	20	2	5	4	8
Nigeria	0	0	2	40	2	5	4	8
Sudan	3	75	0	0	20	50	23	47
Yemen	0	0	0	0	2	5	2	4
Total	4	100	5	100	40	100	49	100

woman, Aziza; after five years she was sold to Aziza's brother. The available documentation does not list Ghuzlan's occupation, so there is no way of knowing if she only served as a concubine in her owner's house, but it is most likely that in order to have sexual access to her, her owner probably employed her in domestic labor and not agricultural or commercial work. Ghuzlan was in the possession of the brother for eleven years, during which time she became pregnant by him on three occasions and three times he "caused abortion to her." He then told her that she would leave his house by being sold, manumitted by the British, or any other manner she wished. To add insult to grievous injury he took most of her jewelry and her clothes before she left. Ghuzlan obviously chose to take refuge at the British Legation, but did not want repatriation "because she does not know any body [*sic*] in her country."[45] Despite this harrowing tale of seeming sexual exploitation, forced abortion and theft, Ghuzlan left the legation three weeks later with her manumission papers and her former owner. Though he had driven her from his home, he subsequently freed Ghuzlan in *Shari'ah* court and escorted her back to his house. Ghuzlan's example shows that these women had very few safe options for living as freed or slave women. Single women domestics' vulnerability made them more subject to petit marronage than repatriation.

In the Saudi Arabian slave market women and children had similar positions, and this market preferred women and children to adult male slaves. Yet, these two groups' manumissions did not follow the same patterns. Only one unaccompanied child under the age of fifteen was locally manumitted—Faraj, a Yemeni boy who had been captured at only age four with his older brother in Yemen. They were sold in Jeddah to separate owners. At age eleven Faraj ran away from his owner after hearing from a fellow Yemeni that he had other relatives in the area and because his owner was beating him. Faraj sought local manumission, no doubt because he could not remember even the name of his home town but did have relatives in Saudi Arabia. Faraj had "no objection to return[ing] to his master after he is emancipated, but if his master beats him again he will then apply to the Legation [for repatriation]."[46] Faraj was locally manumitted and his manumission papers kept by the British. It appears that Faraj's family connections in Saudi may have qualified him for local manumission, but curiously a twelve-year-old born to Sudanese slave parents and emancipated by his owner is not listed as locally manumitted, the pattern of child repatriation indicates his fate was not petit marronage.[47]

Does woman domestic slave equal harem concubine?

Woman slave and harem concubine were not synonymous. In the data, only two Abyssinian women had concubine listed as their job in slavery. While many more women domestic slaves reported sexual contact with members of their owners' families, not all of them were concubines that were specifically bought for and employed in sexual and reproductive roles with the privilege of having other women domestic slaves employed for their care and feeding. Hunwick describes how Abyssinian women (from modern day Ethiopia) were preferred as concubines for their beauty and "cool" bodies whereas Sudanese women were good as wet nurses, not concubines.[48] As noted above, most women who reported sexual contact with their owners or other males of their families didn't report occupations. However, their situations can indicate whether they were the elite slaves within the harem or the domestic slaves who cared for owners and elite concubines.

The documents for the three women in this chapter who had sexual relations with owners or owner's family members serve to show what the documents do and do not say about this subject. For Diba the documents are silent on her occupation and report the "impossibility of determining with any certainty" her ethnic origins and "whose physical appearance afforded no definite clue."[49] Halima's narrative gives an indication that she was a domestic working slave and not a concubine. She was born to slave parents, a Sudanese father and an Abyssinian mother, so she may have been seen as Sudanese or Abyssinian, but she complained of being overworked by more than one member of the household. This complaint points toward her being a domestic slave working for the comfort of others.[50] Ghuzlan appears to have been a concubine. According to her narrative timeline her owner caused her first abortion around the age of twelve or thirteen. He apparently gave her jewelry over the years and then took it back when he ran her out of his house at age twenty-three. She did manage to keep a gold chain and buttons which would seem a possession out of reach of most working domestic women.[51]

This data shows that woman slave usually did not equal elite harem slave. The women described here were not all harem slaves but they were having sex with slaveholding, mostly Arab, men which can be described as one of the jobs they could not refuse to do. Therefore, not all sexual work of slaves was performed by pampered concubines. Far from being pampered, forced abortion, unacknowledged paternity and threats of being turned out onto the streets were sometimes the wages of concubines or women domestic slaves who performed sex work.

Urban vs rural slavery

Bernard Lewis and David Barry Gaspar suggest that different economic conditions would bring differences in the use of slaves.[52] The conventional wisdom
being those differences would account for the variation between slaves' lives in
the Middle East and the Americas. Instead the Saudi data makes clear more
similarities. This data suggests that the difference in some "patterns of subordination" for slaves are less striking between one side of Africa and the other, than
between cities and countryside on either side of the continent.

In the Saudi data the urban–rural divide influenced the jobs enslaved Africans
worked, how long these people were enslaved, how often they were sold and if
and how their cases were resolved. It also was affected by their country of origin
and whether they were enslaved as children or adults. Here I will discuss how
the urban–rural divide affected frequency of sale and slave family structure
which parallel Atlantic slavery patterns.

For the Americas, historians agree that this urban–rural difference affected
how often slaves were sold; Americanists debate how it affected slave family
structure. Richard Wade notes that US owners in urban areas of the South frequently sold slaves and Claire Robertson reports "some evidence that women
may have been sold more frequently" and more repeatedly than men in cities.[53]
Slaves in the five major urban areas in Saudi Arabia were also subject to sale
more often than slaves from villages and other rural areas, especially women
slaves, and slave family structure varied the further one traveled from cities like
Jeddah.

For sale in the city

In the case of Saudi Arabia, the majority of slaves who had only one owner
escaped from the countryside (55.5 percent); an overwhelming majority of slaves
who had more than two slave owners lived in the five major cities (70.5 percent).
These statistics do not support the picture of benign slavery painted by Ottoman
amplification in which slaves are cherished beloved junior family members frequently manumitted and absorbed into the dominant Arab society; instead, the
slaves in the Saudi countryside ran because of ill-treatment and were born into
slavery as their parents were un-manumitted slaves and the urban slaves who
changed hands through buying, selling, gifting and inheriting support Marmon's
argument that slaves were commodities.[54] As in the Americas these exchanges
often centered on a traumatic turn of events in owners' lives—a bankruptcy, war
or death.

Khadija bint Hasanin serves as an example of the kinds of events that could
befall a slave and result in changes in owner. By 1930 Khadija had had three
owners, survived two wars and had been inherited once.[55] Born in the Sudan
around 1905, Khadija was stolen at age six and sold to Medina. Her owner took
her to Syria during World War I. When that owner died, Khadija was not manumitted but inherited by his daughter. Having moved back to Medina, Khadija

was swept up in the war waged by Ibn Saud to win the Hijaz from the Hashemite ruling family. She was captured by the Hashemite Amir of Medina; he was then forced to flee the area with the takeover by the House of Saud. Slaves could be exchanged as a gift, captured as a spoil of war, used as a debt payment, or inherited as an asset; they were vulnerable because of their value.

The picture sharpens even more if the numbers of the sale of men and women slaves are analyzed separately. There is no correlation between number of owners and the place fled from for men but for women the correlation is significant.[56] The literature often describes African Muslim slaves as "traveler's checks" for their African owners on pilgrimage.[57] Women slaves were equally negotiable in the hands of urban Saudi slaveholders.

The ties that bind

Scholars of slavery in the Americas have studied slave family structure at various times and in various locales and their analysis reflects varied thinking on the subject. Some scholars insist that the slave family was surprisingly intact and nuclear.[58] Others, like Brenda Stevenson in her study of Loudon County Virginia slave families, show that slaves' patterns of residence and marriage were varied, but find a common thread in matrifocality.[59] Here I use matrifocality in the way Stevenson and Raymond Smith define it—households that have "women in their role as mothers who come to be the focus of relationships, rather than head of the household as such."[60] An African example is how children in many polygynous societies eat in their mother's rooms, get access to school fees, etc. from

Table 2.5 Number of owners and place fled from[61]

	Five major cities		Other places		Total (% of total)	
	n =	%	n =	%	n =	%
One owner	10	44.5	12	55.5	22	20.5
Two owners	12	50	12	50	24	22.5
More than two owners	43	70.5	18	29.5	61	57
Total # (% of total)	65	(61)	42	(39)	107	100

Table 2.6 Women—number of owners and place fled from[62]

	Five major cities		Other places		Total (% of total)	
	n =	%	n =	%	n =	%
One owner	3	13.5	5	62.5	8	27
Two owners	5	23	1	12.5	6	20
More than two owners	14	63.5	2	25	16	53
Total # (% of total)	22	(73)	8	(27)	30	100

their mother's intervention even if the household is patrilocal or headed and primarily financed by a male. Stevenson argues that most households were matrifocal even when a male and female couple and their children could be identified, because most men did not live in the actual house with their families but were "abroad husbands" (living on another plantation, etc.). Still others see matrifocality as an issue in slave families but analyze it as stemming from the rural–urban divide. Robertson writes that "Nuclear families were most common in rural areas and mother-child units in towns."[63] While Stevenson argues that matrifocal slave residence is a result of both slaves' African cultures and the circumstances of abroad slave marriage, her data does suggest that in rural areas slave families had a better chance of having a consistent coupling of slave mother and slave father, even if he lived abroad; whereas in cities, despite the frequency of women's sale, it is slave fathers who were absent from slave families.[64]

Table 2.7 indicates the family status of slaves when they reached the Jeddah legation and suggests that in Saudi Arabia slave family structures varied based on differences in urban and rural slavery, as in Robertson's analysis of the Americas. It seems that Saudi rural slavery had a tendency toward stable conditions of servitude: slaves labored for owners longer than those from urban areas and more slaves who resided outside of urban areas had only one owner. This relative stability would have made it easier for slaves outside of the cities to maintain marriages and families. Though Table 2.7 reports marital/family status at the time of running away, 64 percent reported living for some period of time as a couple or a nuclear family outside of a city. The Saudi data is not as specific as the Virginia data; it does not always identify to whom these mothers and fathers were enslaved or if their owners had more than one property on which the bondmen and women worked and lived. Saudi data indicates that some

Table 2.7 Runaway slave family types and the place fled from

	Five major cities	Other places	Unrecorded
Nuclear[1]	0	3	1
Couple	1	1	2
Husband, left wife and children behind	0	3	1
Wife, runaway husband	0	2	0
Single mother, children	1	1	0
Newly Single man[2]	1	1	0
Wife, left husband behind	2	0	0
Wife of owner, children	0	0	0
Wife of owner	0	0	1
Mother of owner's children[3]	5	0	1

Notes
1 This includes a family REMAP ID#221-223 with one child, the woman's son and man's stepson.
2 One man from the city of Tayf REMAP ID#232 had divorced his wife before running away.
3 Included in this number are two women who gave birth to children of one owner's nephew and one owner's son.

couples belonged to different owners and therefore may have had abroad marriages. However, as Saudi land holdings were not on the same scale as American plantations and counties and Saudi laws controlling slaves' movements with passes etc. were not developed, even these abroad couples and their children were probably living closer together if not in strictly nuclear families. The smaller scale of most slave holding in Saudi Arabia probably helped limit slave family structure possibilities.

Moreover, Islamic law and Muslim owners did not make divorce difficult or stigmatized, and when selling a slave an owner might force divorce and remarriage upon slaves, no doubt to encourage new slave couplings and families. Jamila bint Abdullah is an example of this phenomenon and a possible abroad marriage. Jamila and her husband Salem, a Sudanese slave soldier, ran away because their family was threatened. Originally they had different owners: his owner had threatened to sell Salem unless he divorced her, perhaps to encourage Salem to marry a younger slave woman with more childbearing potential (Jamila was in her late forties) or to make Salem more mobile and saleable as a single man.[65] Jamila was herself a freed slave, but her deceased owner's son was also trying to sell her. Jamila already had lost a husband and a daughter when she was captured in the Sudan and sold into slavery.[66] Being enslaved meant her previous marriage was nullified.[67] Jamila and Salem saved their family by running away. They were manumitted and repatriated to the Sudan together. Jamila's case suggests that Saudi owners used divorce to clear the way for resale and remarriage so that new owners could reap the benefits of slave marriage. American slave holders who favored slave marriages believed these marriages domesticated slaves, provided an economic unit that performed subsistence tasks like cooking and handing out rations. Some authors have noted slave families and days off were ways for owners to require slaves to provide food for themselves and to reproduce more slaves for more slave labor.[68] While there is no direct evidence in the data of Saudi slaves in their prime being responsible for providing their own food rations, there is some indirect evidence that they were separate economic units. Some slaves reported living in different locales than their owners and being responsible for sending money to owners from their earnings. Also the British reported that "many of the Arabs let their slave & female slave live together & [illegible] their children as slaves too."[69]

The relative stability of slave families for the reproduction of labor was especially important in agricultural areas where child slave labor was not only employed but seemingly preferred and where labor was utilized over a longer period. *Shari'ah* dictated that children inherit their father's status, and this legal principle apparently made the domestication of male slaves and building of slave families even more important in agricultural Arabia because otherwise owners would lose the children's labor as slave labor.

On the other hand, the cities of Saudi Arabia and the Americas were places where women were sold more frequently and child labor was less important. Of the seven women who reported marrying or giving birth to children fathered by free Arab Muslim men five were from the five major cities and the others were unreported. This implies that in the wider slave population more urban women had relationships with owners. Add to that the chance for repatriation in the city of Jeddah and we see the many pressures brought to bear on urban slave families that could turn a nuclear family into a matrifocal one.

The overwhelming majority of fugitives did not mention children and spouses. Again, slave family structure was not one of the British officials' concerns in the slavery issue and so no space in the questionnaire was accorded to marital status or number of children, although there was a specific place to record accompanying minor children. Because of this silence the questionnaires' data may underrepresent marriage and child bearing rates in Saudi slavery. Few marriages and children and frequent divorce is a very different family structure from the one traditionally associated with twentieth century Arab families, indicating a distinct feature within the community of African descent, possibly a branch of the African Diaspora.

Conclusion

A slave society existed where owners negotiated with valued individual slaves during the process of recovering runaways and tried to domesticate agricultural men slaves through marriage and women slaves through childbearing. In this society slaves had long-term relationships with owners outside cities and African influenced matrifocal family structures, especially in urban areas where slave–owner relationships were of shorter duration with frequent selling of slaves. This description could apply to African slaves and their owners in many places and times in the Americas; instead, it is the picture of slave life in early twentieth century Saudi Arabia painted by the words of those enslaved. This chapter has shown that African culture and notions of gender were also central to the ways enslaved women and men negotiated their subordination within slavery.

It is a picture of Middle Eastern slavery much different than previous historians' writings have drawn, by showing that woman slave did not always equal harem concubine and not all sexual work of slaves was performed by concubines. These women's lives also attest to the fact that if a woman slave at times performed sex work it did not secure for her a pampered "benign" lifestyle. Nor were women slaves so completely absorbed into or adapted to Arab culture and social norms that they forgot African ways of constructing matrifocal families.

Instead, the chapter's findings are that the patterns of subordination for slaves varied by place and gender and were subject to gendered negotiation. When made to do similar work (rural agricultural or urban domestic) slaves in Saudi Arabia experienced gendered patterns of subordination similar to the enslaved in the Americas. In the gap between the two pictures of Arabian slavery there may be a new branch of the African Diaspora yet to be identified on the Arabian Peninsula.

Notes

1 Ehud Toledano, "Late Ottoman Concepts of Slavery (1830s–1880s)," *Poetics Today* 14 (Autumn, 1993): 477–506.
2 Benjamin Reilly, *Slavery, Agriculture, and Malaria in the Arabian Peninsula* (Athens, OH: Ohio University Press, 2015).
3 Matthew Hopper, *Slaves of One Master: Globalization and Slavery in Arabia in the Age of Empire* (New Haven, CT: Yale University Press, 2015).
4 Toledano.
5 This is part of larger research that compares runaways' narratives from Saudi Arabia, Oman and Bahrain in the early twentieth century. Here I do not use the term "voice" in a conscious effort not to engage in what Gayatri Spivak terms "the ventriloquism of the speaking subaltern," in " 'Can the Subaltern Speak?' revised edition, from the 'History' chapter of Critique of Postcolonial Reason," in *Can the Subaltern Speak?: Reflections of the History of an Idea*, edited by Rosalind C. Morris (New York: Columbia University Press, 2010), 27.
6 Ronald Segal, *Islam's Black Slaves* (New York: Farrar, Straus and Giroux, 2001), 9.
7 Eve Troutt Powell, "Will the Subaltern Ever Speak? Finding African Slaves in the Historiography of the Middle East," in *Middle East Historiographies: Narrating the Twentieth Century*, edited by I. Gershoni, Amy Singer and Y. Hakan Erdem (Seattle, WA: University of Washington Press, 2006), 254. Powell has stated that "a detailed understanding of the lives of African slaves does not emerge in the archives of the Public Record Office." I argue that it hasn't yet but that data does exist there from which historians can tease out many details for a sharper, well-defined picture of many different slaves' lives.
8 Britain relinquished this right in 1936, the same year King Ibn Saud decreed the Saudi Arabian slave regulations. See Suzanne Miers, "Diplomacy versus Humanitarianism: Britain and Consular Manumission in Hijaz, 1921–1936," *Slavery and Abolition* 10 (December 1989): 102–128, for more on the provisions of the slave regulations and their relationship to the renunciation. Two years later, fugitive slaves continued to seek manumission from the British. These slaves were turned away, but the British did record the incidents and they were included in the data set and statistical tests.
9 There are both summarized reports and individual documents for the former slaves. F.O. 905/11, Embassy and Legation, Saudi Arabia: General Correspondence. Slaves: General Question. 1934 contains one of the reports (206 are listed in the report, seven of whom have individual documents: six in F.O. 967/1 Legation, Hejaz: Various Papers. Slave traffic. 1926 and one in F.O. 905/62 Embassy and Legation, Saudi Arabia: General Correspondence. Slaves, Slavery and slave trade: Gabor Ahmed. 1938); F.O. 905/28, Embassy and Legation, Saudi Arabia: General Correspondence. Slaves: Manumission: Individual cases. 1935 contains updated reports of manumissions from 1930–1935 (fifty-three listed in the updates, fifty-one of whom have individual documents); F.O. 905/61, Embassy and Legation, Saudi Arabia: General Correspondence. Slaves, Slavery and Slave Trade: General. 1938 contains the narratives from the two 1938 runaways.
10 Gabriel Debien, "Le marronage aux Antilles française au XVIIIᵉ siècle," *Caribbean Studies* 6 (1966): 3–44.
11 Saadi Simawi, "Color and Race in the Poetry of Black Poets in Arabic: A Comparative Study of Images of Blackness and Africanness in Arabic and African American Literature." Paper presentation at "Slavery and the African Diaspora in the Lands of Islam," Northwestern University April 30–May 2, 1999.
12 Debien, 3–44.
13 For this chapter, chi-square statistical tests were performed on all variable pairs in the data, for example labor assignment (commercial, agricultural or domestic) paired with years enslaved; number of owners paired with place fled from (rural or urban);

reasons for running away with labor assignment; and result of bid for freedom (local manumission, left without manumission or manumitted and repatriated) or gender and country of origin. Chi-square analysis tests the standard statistical probability of variable pairs distribution to their actual distribution. If the difference is significant (reported as $p<0.05$ or less) it indicates that one variable is most likely influencing the other. The test cannot explain the nature of that influence. Chi-square tests can only test pairs so those tests that showed significance were sometimes separated into tables by gender, country of origin, etc. for further analysis. Chi-square tests are most suitable for variables with few categories so variables like labor assignment which had nineteen different directly report responses were condensed into three imputed categories.

14 See Alaine S. Hutson, "Enslavement and Manumission in Saudi Arabia," *Critique* 11 (Spring 2002): 49–70, 65, for more on the value of agricultural slaves in Saudi Arabia.

15 This table originally appeared in Hutson 2002, 66.

16 REMAP ID #233.

17 ($n=146, X^2=28.97$, df=4, $p<0.001$).

18 REMAP ID#156.

19 Most scholarship on slavery indicates that more African women than men were sold into the trans-Saharan and other slave trades bound for the Arab Muslim world; see Ralph Austen, "The Trans-Saharan Slave Trade: A Tentative Census," in *The Uncommon Market: Essays in the Economic History of the Atlantic Slave Trade*, edited by Henry A. Gemery and Jan S. Hogendorn (New York: Academic Press, 1979), 44; and Claire Robertson and Martin Klein, *Women and Slavery in Africa* (Madison, WI: University of Wisconsin Press, 1983), 4. Yet, in the Saudi Arabian statistics, men outnumbered women 2.64 to 1. Women accounted for 27.5 percent of those who sought refuge at the British Legation ($n=72$), whereas men were 72.5 percent ($n=190$). While women appear to be underrepresented, the number of women who ran away is a significant one and gives a female perspective on slavery.

20 The table has statistics for the 103 runaways for whom there is documentation of the outcome of their bid for freedom.

21 ($n=103, X^2=19.34$, df=3, $p<0.001$). Free person with safety issues indicates exslaves whose lives or freedom were threatened by their owners or others.

22 F.O. 403/460, 11.

23 Shaun Marmon, ed., *Slavery in the Islamic Middle East* (Princeton, NJ: Markus Weiner, 1999), 3, and I. P. Petrushevsky, *Islam in Iran*, trans. by Hubert Evans (London: Athlone Press, 1985), 155.

24 Claudia Dale Goldin, *Urban Slavery in the American South 1820–1860: A Quantitative History* (Chicago, IL: The University of Chicago Press, 1976), 28–30, 38. Slave hiring in cities was important enough to owners' and users' bottom lines that they resisted laws, usually bought by white artisans and skilled workers, that sought to restrict slaves' use. Slaves were hired through agencies and self-hire. Self-hire cut out the agent's fees and was more profitable for owners.

25 F.O. 403/460, 12.

26 REMAP ID #257.

27 John Thornton, *Africa and Africans in the Making of the Atlantic World, 1400–1800* (Cambridge: Cambridge University Press, 1998), 273.

28 REMAP ID#263.

29 *Sharif* indicates a family who claims blood ties to the family of the Prophet Muhammad.

30 REMAP ID#253, her daughter Zahra is REMAP ID#252. Their stories are further reported in Hutson, 54.

31 Petrushevsky, 156–157.

32 Hopper, 129–130.

33 There are cases in Jeddah Legation reports of other women slaves who bore owners' children and who had to flee to the British to initiate their own free status: REMAP ID#183 and 189.

34 REMAP ID#170, Jabir ibn Abdullah from French Ouaddaï was brought through the Sudan port of Suakin by a Nigerian who claimed him as his son. REMAP ID#217 Abdullah ibn Muhammad, who is listed under his slave name Saleh, was prevented from being manumitted and repatriated because his apparent owners posed as his parents and managed to enter the legation and take him away. They were met by the Saudi police who took him to jail.

35 REMAP ID#8.

36 Peter Wood, *Black Majority: Negroes in Colonial South Carolina from 1670 Through the Stono Rebellion* (New York: W.W. Norton and Company, 1996), 241.

37 REMAP ID#259.

38 REMAP ID#103.

39 REMAP ID#119. Though later the British clearly refused to deal with and repatriate free Africans, it appears they helped to repatriate this free Nigerian man because an appendix to the report states that all but 8 were repatriated. As his narrative does not indicate that he was ever a slave, he would not have been classified as locally manumitted, but neither was any note made to indicate he was dealt with in any special way or stayed on in Saudi Arabia.

40 L. Virginia Gould, "Urban Slavery—Urban Freedom: The Manumission of Jacqueline Lemelle," in *More Than Chattel: Black Women and Slavery in the Americas*, edited by David Barry Gaspar and Darlene Clark Hine (Bloomington, IN: Indiana University Press, 1996), 300.

41 REMAP ID#240. Faraj's story also appears in Hutson, 59.

42 REMAP ID#210, she reported that her husband had given her the money to hire the donkey she rode to the legation. Unlike Faraj, there is no mention of a plan for him to join Itir, but perhaps she waited for his arrival or tested the waters for escape from a royal household for both of them and returned when their plans appeared to fail.

43 ($n=99$, $X^2=33.65$, df=12, $p<0.001$).

44 ($n=49$, $X^2=15.37$, df=8, $p<0.05$)

45 REMAP ID#239.

46 REMAP ID#227.

47 F.O. 905/11 report 1934. The report indicates that all but 8 runaways were repatriated and those 8 are noted as locally manumitted in the report. This boy does not have such a note on his case. However, I did find one woman who married her ex-owner but was not listed as locally manumitted. It seems unlikely this married woman was repatriated and perhaps the boy was not either.

48 John Hunwick, "Black Africans in the Islamic World," *Tarikh* 5(4) (1978): 20–40, 27.

49 REMAP ID#263.

50 REMAP ID#252.

51 REMAP ID#239.

52 Bernard Lewis, *Race and Slavery in the Middle East* (New York: Oxford University Press, 1990), 99–102; and David Barry Gaspar, *Bondmen and Rebels: A Study of Master-Slave Relations in Antigua* (Baltimore: The Johns Hopkins University Press, 1985), 93.

53 Richard Wade, *Slavery in the Cities: The South 1820–1860*, (New York: Oxford University Press 1964), 197 notes that all slaves could be expected to be sold at least once and that for urban slaves the possibility of sale was much higher. See also Claire Robertson, "Africa into the Americas?" in *More Than Chattel: Black Women and Slavery in the Americas*, edited by David Barry Gaspar and Darlene Clark Hine (Bloomington, IN: Indiana University Press, 1996), 13.

54 Marmon (*Slavery in the Islamic Middle East*, 5) argues that slaves were considered commodities in Islamic law as well as Saudi Arabian practice.

55 REMAP ID#121.
56 The chi-square test for men slaves was ($n=77$, $X^2=3.65$, df=2, $p<0.16$).
57 Toyin Falola and Aribidesi Usman, eds. *Movement, Borders, and Identities in Africa* (Rochester, NY: University of Rochester Press, 2009), 6.
58 For an example of this kind of analysis see John W. Blassingame, *The Slave Community: Plantation Life in the Antebellum South* (New York: Oxford University Press, 1972).
59 Brenda Stevenson, *Life in Black and White: Family and Community in the Slave South* (New York: Oxford University Press, 1996), 211–213.
60 Raymond T. Smith, *The Matrifocal Family: Power, Pluralism, and Politics* (New York: Routledge, 1996), 43.
61 ($n=107$, $X^2=5.75$, df=2, $p.<0.056$) The five major cities included in this table are: Jeddah, Mecca, Medina, Tayf and Riyadh.
62 The chi-square test for women slaves was ($n=30$, $X^2=6.75$, df=2, $p<0.034$).
63 Robertson, 19.
64 Stevenson, 220–221.
65 Jamila's story is an example of a Muslim owner exercising the right to force a slave to divorce his wife; Petrushevsky, 156 reports this right.
66 REMAP ID#242, Jamila and Salem's story is also found in Hutson, 54.
67 Petrushevsky, 156 and Imam Muslim, #3432 chronicled by Muslim and related by Abu Sa'id al-Khudri, both discuss the nullification of a slave woman's marriage in the context of being captured as a prisoner of war. Despite the fact that Jamila and other slaves were not pagan prisoners of war, their original families were discarded in the same way and perhaps justified by *hadith*.
68 Robertson, 14.
69 REMAP ID#8.

Bibliography

Austen, Ralph. "The Trans-Saharan Slave Trade: A Tentative Census," in *The Uncommon Market: Essays in the Economic History of the Atlantic Slave Trade*, edited by Henry A. Gemery and Jan S. Hogendorn, 23–76. New York: Academic Press, 1979.

Blassingame, John W. *The Slave Community: Plantation Life in the Antebellum South.* New York: Oxford University Press, 1972.

Debien, Gabriel. "Le marronage aux Antilles française au XVIIIᵉ siècle," *Caribbean Studies* 6 (1966): 3–44.

Falola, Toyin and Aribidesi Usman, eds. *Movement, Borders, and Identities in Africa.* Rochester, NY: University of Rochester Press, 2009.

Gaspar, David Barry. *Bondmen and Rebels: A Study of Master-Slave Relations in Antigua.* Baltimore, MD: The Johns Hopkins University Press, 1985.

Goldin, Claudia Dale. *Urban Slavery in the American South 1820–1860: A Quantitative History.* Chicago, IL: The University of Chicago Press, 1976.

Gould, L. Virginia. "Urban Slavery—Urban Freedom: The Manumission of Jacqueline Lemelle," in *More Than Chattel: Black Women and Slavery in the Americas*, edited by David Barry Gaspar and Darlene Clark Hine, 298–314. Bloomington, IN: Indiana University Press, 1996.

Hopper, Matthew. *Slaves of One Master: Globalization and Slavery in Arabia in the Age of Empire.* New Haven, CT: Yale University Press, 2015.

Hunwick, John. "Black Africans in the Islamic World," *Tarikh* 5(4) (1978): 20–40.

Hutson, Alaine S. "Enslavement and Manumission in Saudi Arabia.," *Critique* 11 (Spring 2002): 49–70.

Lewis, Bernard. *Race and Slavery in the Middle East*. New York: Oxford University Press, 1990.

Marmon, Shaun, ed. *Slavery in the Islamic Middle East*. Princeton, NJ: Markus Weiner, 1999.

Miers, Suzanne. "Diplomacy versus Humanitarianism: Britain and Consular Manumission in Hijaz, 1921–1936," *Slavery and Abolition* 10 (December 1989): 102–128.

Al-Nawawi, Muhyiddin. *Gardens of the Righteous*. Trans. Muhammad Zafrulla Khan. London: Curzon Press, 1975.

Petrushevsky, I. P. *Islam in Iran*. Trans. Hubert Evans. London: Athlone Press, 1985.

Powell, Eve Troutt. "Will the Subaltern Ever Speak? Finding African Slaves in the Historiography of the Middle East," in *Middle East Historiographies: Narrating the Twentieth Century*, edited by I. Gershoni, Amy Singer and Y. Hakan Erdem, 242–261. Seattle, WA: University of Washington Press, 2006.

Reilly, Benjamin. *Slavery, Agriculture, and Malaria in the Arabian Peninsula*. Athens, OH: Ohio University Press, 2015.

Robertson, Claire. and Martin Klein. *Women and Slavery in Africa*. Madison, WI: University of Wisconsin Press, 1983.

Robertson, Claire. "Africa into the Americas?" in *More Than Chattel: Black Women and Slavery in the Americas*, edited by David Barry Gaspar and Darlene Clark Hine, 3–40. Bloomington, IN: Indiana University Press, 1996.

Segal, Ronald. *Islam's Black Slaves*. New York: Farrar, Straus and Giroux, 2001.

Simawe, Saadi. "Color and Race in the Poetry of Black Poets in Arabic: A Comparative Study of Images of Blackness and Africanness in Arabic and African American Literature." Paper presentation at "Slavery and the African Diaspora in the Lands of Islam," Northwestern University April 30–May 2, 1999.

Smith, Raymond T. *The Matrifocal Family: Power, Pluralism, and Politics*. New York: Routledge, 1996.

Spivak, Gayatri. "'Can the Subaltern Speak?' revised edition, from the 'History' chapter of Critique of Postcolonial Reason," in *Can the Subaltern Speak?: Reflections of the History of an Idea*, edited by Rosalind C. Morris, 21–80. New York: Columbia University Press, 2010.

Stevenson, Brenda. *Life in Black and White: Family and Community in the Slave South*. New York: Oxford University Press, 1996.

Thornton, John. *Africa and Africans in the Making of the Atlantic World, 1400–1800*. Cambridge: Cambridge University Press, 1999.

Toledano, Ehud. "Late Ottoman Concepts of Slavery (1830s-1880s)," *Poetics Today* 14 (Autumn, 1993): 477–506.

Toledano, Ehud. *As if Silent and Absent: Bonds of Enslavement in the Islamic Middle East*. New Haven, CT: Yale University Press, 2007.

Wade, Richard. *Slavery in the Cities: The South 1820–1860*. New York: Oxford University Press, 1964.

Wood, Peter. *Black Majority: Negroes in Colonial South Carolina from 1670 Through the Stono Rebellion*. New York: W.W. Norton and Company, 1996.

3 Communicating feminist ethics in the age of New Media in Africa

Sharon Adetutu Omotoso

Introduction

This chapter examines the connection between moral orientation and gender and therefore sets out to scrutinize the origin and nature of women oppression created by New Media technologies, ethical issues emanating therefrom and how these are and can be more effectively communicated in various parts of Africa. Using methods of critical analysis, deconstructive and reconstructive argumentations, the chapter examines the impact of such communications and considers what New Media, if consciously and critically approached, can contribute to the development of gender sensitive societies in Africa.

New Media is a generic term for the many different forms of electronic communication that are made possible through the use of computer technology. The term is in relation to 'old' media forms such as print (mostly newspapers and magazines) that are static representations of text and graphics.[1] Described as the technology that supports the activities involving the creation of information, together with their related method, management and application,[2] New Media consists of a wide range of technological, textual, conventional and cultural changes in media production, distribution and use, characterized by digital, interactive, hypertextual, virtual networked and simulated attributes.[3] For Bello,[4] "these new technologies of obtaining, storing, editing, retrieving, packaging and communicating information relies on scientific means and are quite fast as they are mostly computer driven." On their functions, Bello adds that;

> they aid the transmission and reception of knowledge for decision making by individuals, corporate organizations and even government. They enhance the amalgamation of data images, texts, documents, voice and many other items intelligently to make meaning in the process of communication.[5]

Thus, New Media include, though are not restricted to, the media of communication which have been introduced across the globe to either complement or totally replace conventional media. These include email, chat rooms, avatar-based communication forums, voice image transmissions, the World Wide Web, blogs, computer multimedia, computer games, CD-ROMs and DVD, virtual reality, social networking sites and mobile telephony, among others. New Media are in different forms ranging from Blogs, Social Networking, Social Bookmarking, Wikis, People to People (P2P) File sharing and Video Clips to Virtual Worlds.[6] More prominent among these are social media, which Kaplan and Haenlein[7] categorized into six groups: Content Communities e.g., YouTube; Blogs and Microblogs e.g., Twitter; Collaborating Projects, e.g., Wikipedia; Virtual Game Worlds, e.g., World of Warcraft; Virtual Social Worlds, e.g., Second Life; and Social Networking Sites, e.g., Facebook. From this categorization, social media are deemed most prominent because of how they cut across other media forms in their operations and usage.

Although New Media evolves and morphs continuously due largely to the fact that what was tagged 'new' some years back is already becoming old, thus paving the way for changing definitions, we may surmise that New Media consists of a wide range of information and communication technologies which are digital, linked and crosslinked and used in processing, transforming, storing, retrieving and accessing information for the achievement of pre-defined objectives. The introduction of New Media is justified with a major argument that they make communication faster, easier and, in most cases, personal, while also possessing the ability to reach a wider and heterogeneous audience. However, ambiguity and relativity come to play largely because of the global attributes of New Media.[8] Arguments arise concerning the 'newness' of a medium, for what may be tagged 'new' in a particular society might have become old or even obsolete in another society. For instance, the appearance of the World Wide Web in the early 1990s did not gain recognition in Africa until later years and so was described as 'new' despite its existence several years before in some parts of the world. In order to downplay such ambiguities and relativities, we shall, in this chapter, take as New Media newly explored communication technologies in Africa, such as the Internet, recent android and windows telephony technology, blogspots and social media among others. The majority of the issues will be drawn from social media, although the work considers New Media in a general and holistic form, arguing that whether built to serve social, economic, communication, health or security functions, they all have particular ways of impacting societies.

Gender is a social and cultural construction that assigns different roles to members of a society; these constructions have been founded on basic and unchanged principles over time. Noting that discrimination against women is profoundly manifested through gender and class, Chakravarty observes that "Gender is not fixed. It is fluid and unstable. Historically, attempts have been made to define, delimit, and stabilize gender for purposes of social control and maintenance of the heteropatriarchal social order."[9] Accordingly, gender constructions by ruling masculinities have kept women repressed despite intellectual and technological developments over the ages. Suffice to say that most globally celebrated developments are also built to extol and validate patriarchy at the expense of respect for women's images and identities. One major system that has nurtured women oppression is globalization, an objective which has been achieved largely through the media and is in fact being sustained by New Media. Perceived as a negative word, globalization is charged with multi-dimensional crimes (economic, political, cultural) of marginalizing women in unpaid or informal labor, impoverishing them through loss of traditional sources of income, excluding women from domestic political processes and denying them identity and autonomy within hegemonic global cultures.[10] A critical analysis of the situation has provoked scholars (amongst whom are Carol Gilligan,[11] Allison Jaggar,[12] Margaret Walker,[13] Lynne Roper[14] and Fainos Mangena[15]) into a consideration of ethical issues in gender, seeking to address evident imbalances emanating therefrom in societies.

Inherent in Africa's embrace of new technologies are numerous opportunities, yet the emergence of New Media poses more burden than ease for Africa, seeing how much struggle has been put into catching up with the technological developments of conventional media. Feminist research has shown how the Internet and ICTs are now part of the gender-based violence environment.[16] Statistics show that there are 4.2 million web pages that offer pornography—12 percent of the total number of websites in the world; 100,000 of them offer child pornography. The online pornography industry makes 97.06 billion dollars per year, a much higher profit than Microsoft, Google, Yahoo, Amazon, Netflix and Apple combined.[17] Although feminist ethics, a moral discourse within Gender Studies, has attracted considerable attention, an argument that Africa's religious, linguistic, political and cultural heterogeneity makes it difficult to arrive at feminist ethical positions, which will enjoy continental acceptance and usage, hampers the plausibility and possibility of exploring universals in the face of African particulars. The influence of New Media on societies which have not reflected on their media literacy skills presents moral problems; hence the importance of beaming a searchlight on how women are portrayed, interpreted and understood, especially in the New Media.

In all, the chapter calls for a deconstruction of gendered prejudices as portrayed and operationalized in New Media and suggests communicating feminist ethics and its entrenchment in the usage of New Media as essential ingredients to prevent Africa from being submerged by oppressive and unethical media usage.

The age of New Media in Africa

Among other pertinent issues to be discussed in this section, we must first embark on a brief assessment of conventional media in Africa: did they fail to meet up to expectations? Have they died or gone into extinction? Must Africa embrace New Media, and why? Is Africa in her age of New Media or is it living in other peoples' worlds, a fool's paradise?

Several qualities have been ascribed to conventional media and roles conferred on them for the benefit of society. For Omotoso and Razak,

> communication as being shared in media is the exchange of ideas, ideals, views, experiences and the sharing of meanings between persons, societies

and nations; it involves the oral, written and the analytical descriptions of imagery to trigger emotions for the sole purpose of passing information and to unearth hidden expressions.[18]

Ranging from provision of information for improved decision making and education of the masses on a wide range of issues to provision of platforms for citizens to air their views,[19] the media in Africa has undergone constant criticisms rather than applause. Such criticisms include those of miscommunication by the media, where parties fail to communicate clearly, consequently risking being misinterpreted; disinformation which involves giving false information and ultimately leading the other party to make wrong decisions; and silence, in which case, no information is made available.[20] A scrutiny of these three situations under a gendered lens shows that the media in Africa often miscommunicate and disinform on women's issues, while maintaining a disposition of silence regarding mainstreaming gender, as a result of which inefficiencies of both government and privately owned media gain prevalence. The prevalence is perpetrated through sensationalism, partisanship, polarity,[21] repression and censorships.[22] Contributory to these are the technological, political and economic setbacks facing the media in Africa. Among such setbacks are: limited internet access, nonchalant attitude toward production of Afrocentric media content, obnoxious and repressive regulatory principles, sustainability and standardization problems.[23] Onabajo reflects on how education, information and entertainment have remained main functions of media in espousing values and ideas on equality, rights, democracy, economy, development and cultural integration. However, he worries about how "success has not been significant because of government restriction on what is being transmitted."[24] He then asserts that media problems are not problems of the media alone, but are related to the problems of the community and economy.

In view of these setbacks and criticisms, do we then regard conventional media in Africa as a failure? The answer is no! The conventional media are still very much germane to Africa: television is still gaining viewership; radio keeps experiencing transitions from being a monologic to a dialogic medium; newspaper readership is also improving as literacy levels are improving; other print media (billboards, posters and so on) are flooding the streets of African states as if to justify the thriving nature of conventional media in Africa. These are unlike the Internet, which according to Madzingira "is a medium with its own audience and a source of information for the other media."[25]

Recognizably, New Media are gradually becoming inevitable aspects of daily activities in Africa. The number of internet, phone and social media users, among other technologies, have been increasing exponentially in the past few years. Kabana[26] reports that there are "over 5 million Facebook users, over 50 million tweets, over 450 million mobile internet users and about 68 million bloggers, society has changed and there is a paradigm shift in the way things are done worldwide." Interestingly, there is no age limit to people who use New Media. Internet world statistics 2016 reports that as at November 30, 2015, the population of internet users in Africa has increased to approximately 331 million, with over 125 million Facebook users.[27]

Perhaps one should pause and ask: why must Africa embrace New Media? Is Africa in its own age of New Media? The dynamic nature of information and communication technology around the world necessitates Africa's need to embrace the New Media. On this, Umeh observes that:

> There were three great scientific developments in the world that had touched man very significantly. One was nuclear energy, which at Hiroshima and Nagasaki shocked the world; the second was the discovery of man's capacity to travel in space, which thrilled the world, and the third was the discovery and invention of the computer, which was the most important of the three.[28]

For Nkwocha, a major reason to embrace the New Media is "the radical elimination of old information systems and processes characterized by slow analog technology and substituting them with the new fast and highly efficient digital technology."[29] Consequently, Bello argues that "there is a symbiotic relationship between the traditional media and the emerging communication technologies [which] is expanding the scope of media practice beyond expectations."[30] Seeing that the age of New Media is a global concept, ideology and process sweeping through continents like a tsunami willing and ready to carry with it anything that stands on its way, the question then will not be whether Africa is in its own age of New Media, rather, what is the New Media age offering Africa? The implication is that the age of New Media ensures that technology drives most, if not all, human activities and thus, cannot be ignored by anyone. Although, global technological movements cannot be ignored, this chapter is of the view that Africa is not living in its own world, considering dispositions of media users on the continent, who largely consume foreign content and produce meager knowledge from their local content for the world to consume. This practice, carried over from conventional media into New Media has spill-over effects on the portrayal and interpretations of women. New Media is a strong tool used for featuring women in particular contexts; helping society to perpetuate women's fear through promoting the idea that women are defenseless without a male companion;[31] creating images which limit and trap women through myths and stereotypes, thereby distorting women's self perception and reflecting cultural values about them, rather than realistic appraisals of their worth. As Anzaldua points out, "dominant paradigms, predefined concepts that exist as unquestionable, unchallengeable, are transmitted to us through … culture made by those in power—men,"[32] such cultures are communicated, transmitted and inculcated through the media (old and new). Noting that it is often women who have embraced the more expensive and slick aspects of mobile phones, adventurously harnessing them as "vehicles for identity and identification"[33] the suggestion is that men, motivated by pragmatism, tend to turn rationally to ICTs for their functional use, while women, who are assumed to be intensively socialized into "looking good for others,"[34] are more likely to embrace their possibilities for status and image making.

It is sad to note that just as patriarchy pervaded conventional media, New Media has also been infected, thus having larger and widespread impacts on women's portrayal in the media. Most unfortunately, too, women are not working hard enough to take their place in New Media production, dissemination and inculcation. Women oppression produced by technologies, particularly New Media, is hereby discussed in relation to gender and morality by highlighting inherent ethical issues and how they are communicated in Africa.

Feminist ethics in Africa

Feminist ethics is a field of philosophical inquiry which seeks to examine ethical issues relating to women's experiences and their everyday association with men in society. While Mama resorts to the general aim of feminism in her definition of feminist ethics as a field with "focus on the realization of equality and justice for women in all spheres of life, ending patriarchy and all its practices, transforming institutions,"[35] Scaltsas[36] succinctly describes the project of feminist ethics as that of criticizing, analyzing and, when necessary, replacing the traditional categories of moral philosophy in order to eradicate the misrepresentation, distortion and oppression resulting from the historically male perspective. Feminist ethics deals with moral questions of resolving conflict in feminist ways, the place of women's moral traits such as sympathy, nurturance, care and compassion in ethics, as well as how feminist principles can be applied in daily life. It focuses on the creation of a gendered ethics that aims to eliminate or at least ameliorate the oppression of any group of people, but most particularly women.[37] Feminist ethics therefore calls attention to the hitherto neglected gynocentric perspectives on ethics, so as to present and establish women's interpretation of, and interventions on, moral issues. But what do feminist ethics in Africa entail? Western feminist scholars have elucidated the moral framework of care as against the masculinist ethic of justice.[38] Ethics of care is a critique of the notion that women are not as morally well-developed as men, having observed a lack of neutrality in traditional ethics; as it fails to recognize that women's morality differs from that of men.[39] The primary goal of care ethics is to show that women possess equal capacity to act ethically, and it does this by bringing feminine traits inherent in motherhood, such as empathy, compassion, nurturance and kindness to the fore in ethical considerations. However, it has been argued that this ethical perspective was seen as entrenching women's traditional care-giving, as undervalued, and not fully conceptualized.[40] Following this critique, Mangena succeeded only partially in debunking the care outlook, but not in presenting a new outlook to feminist ethics in Africa. A closer look at the African situation shows that we cannot limit feminist ethics to an ethic of care.[41] The care ethic when critically considered in an African context places more moral burden on women. By womanist standards, moral rules imposed on women restrict them to the sphere of care-giving. In fact, care ethics in an African interpretation may also be held guilty of promoting objectifying and sexploiting perceptions of women, whereby an argument that it is part of woman's caring duties to present her body for all manner of obscenity would be sustained. Such an argument, alongside the necessity for a woman to 'give her all' to her husband, relatives and the community at large degenerates to the point where the so called 'care-giver' is left with no one to care for her after fulfilling her cultural and, by extension, moral obligations. Preoccupied with persistent resistance of oppressed people, and on the whole women of color over time, Welch explores an 'ethic of risk' which involves taking steps toward a desired goal, focusing on possibilities rather than outcomes, then choosing "to care and to act although there are no guarantees of success."[42] Welch's ethic of risk is characterized by three elements, each of which is essential to maintain resistance in the face of overwhelming odds: a redefinition of responsible action, grounding in community and strategic risk-taking. Although the ethic of risk is founded on principles held important by virtue of Africa's communalistic nature, Welch's strategic risk taking, which maintains that we engage issues with informed risk taking despite no assurance of success, seems pessimistic. Since it is human to desire victory in any battle, one may regard Welch's idea of focusing on responsibilities, rather than outcomes, as debasing to women. A feminist ethic primarily based on risk taking, will only encourage women to pursue possibilities and not the desired goals, hence it remains a mere negotiating process and not an ethic in its real sense.

We must begin to consider an alternative; an 'ethic of vigor,' which takes risk, care, control and justice into equal consideration in purely feminist perspectives; a platform for African woman to go all the way, multi-tasking, exemplifying her strength and resilience in struggles toward entrenching justice in care-processes. Seeing that "as pervasive as formal education is, it has become a confine such that there are still lots of unequal social relationships in modern times ..."[43] entrenching and promoting an ethic of vigor begins with widening educational horizons and expounding the untapped dynamism of the African woman through enlightened dispositions toward severing vicious customs and traditions. It calls for resonating women contextualities and optimisms in repelling oppression. Although this chapter may not be an appropriate platform to fully pursue this argument and justify an ethic of vigor as an African feminist stance, a fundamental reason to uphold such on the subject matter of this chapter is to address the various faces of oppression, marginalization, exploitation, cultural imperialism, powerlessness and systematic violence meted on women through New Media in Africa.[44] In analyzing the interplay of traditional values and modern/contemporary outlooks which have shaped or are currently shaping dispositions to New Media, one must not ignore the complexities involved in propounding an ethic of vigor. For instance, women's sexual chastity, decency, modesty, sense of responsibility, commitment, dignity and self worth are values in Africa, yet not seen as oppressive by women. However, knowledge producers using New Media in contemporary times either distort these values, replacing them with more cosmopolitan standards of womanhood, or do not even present these traditionally valued dispositions. As against an ethic of vigor which portrays African women in their contemporary struggles as virtuous, morally responsive and responsible members of community, New Media reinforces idleness, insolence, self-conscious rather than value-conscious women. Such representations have spurred feminist vilification,[45] rather than appreciation by New Media. The following section will critically expound the challenge of New Media for feminist ethics in Africa.

New Media and feminist ethics in Africa

Ethics and social responsibility are key fundamentals to the effective performance of New Media,[46] insofar as their technologies constrict global spatiotemporal gaps. Ethics places demands for liberty, value and responsibility upon New Media. It stresses that certain 'netiquettes' are required as people navigate the Internet, interact on social media, produce and disseminate information to a wide and heterogeneous array of media users. Recognizing the liberatory potentials of New Media technologies and its potential to disguise identities, ethics questions the rightness or wrongness of actions such as publishing of explicit and disturbing images, content not meant for children (particularly on children-related sites), sexual images and videos, hate speech, violence and discrimination against women, minorities and physically challenged people. This section will apply a dual approach of analyzing moral issues in New Media as well as roles women play in aiding and abetting the identified issues. The Internet provides a channel for diverse people, groups and organizations to become producers of specialized content that frames images, ideas and stories for their particular needs and desires.[47] African communities maintain a widely accepted and abiding understanding of gender roles which are sustained through communication. Notably, the media play vital roles in entrenching and sustaining such an understanding. This has been recognized as far back as the mid-1970s and 1980s, when The World Plan of Action for the International Women's Year and Decade (1975–1985) emphasized that:

> The mass communication media have great potential as a vehicle for social change and could exercise a great significant influence in helping to remove the prejudices and stereotypes, accelerating the acceptance of women's new and expanding roles and promoting their greater integration into the development process as equal partners.[48]

Despite shifting gender roles and remarkable media transitions over the years, the media has not been nurtured to be the ally of women; the oppression and subjugation of women reinforced by the New Media persists.[49] Green notes that gender is an identity that is socially constructed by New Media, enacted and reproduced to mold society.[50] Unfortunately, New Media, which at its inception was hoped by African gender scholars[51] to be a revitalized public sphere to adequately represent women, has turned out, just like conventional media, to emphasize standard stereotypical gender norms. Among issues raised by contemporary feminists are issues of sexuality, sexual harassment and rape, abortion, artistic and political representation, mass media and pornographic portrayals of women, self-presentation, self-objectification as well as the role of language in reinforcing and reflecting women's subordination.[52] This informed Chakravarty's assertion that:

> Women have no agency in the way they are represented in mass media. They become images that are locked in the ideological constructs of femininity and masculinity and are dominated by the prevalent discourse of capitalism and consumerism. Distorted images result in colonization of the body and of consciousness, and allow reiteration of dominant expectations about gender performance.[53]

The above assertion clearly indicates that New Media technologies are bound to gendered forms of representation as women are evaluated on the basis of their aesthetic values. Consequently, women are more misrepresented than underrepresented in the New Media. It is on this note that Gill asserts that "women who do not conform to the media's requirements that they be 'eye candy' are subjected to vilification."[54] New Media tops the chart when subjected to scrutiny under the five faces of oppression (exploitation, marginalization, powerlessness, cultural imperialism and systematic violence). Women are highly objectified, particularly via the new trend of meme pictures, unimaginable increase in sexploitation with the rate at which sexting, pornography, online dating, matchmaking (incited by advertisements calling for ladies to flaunt their good looks at interested suitors) and so on, are gaining ground. New Media marginalizes, demobilizes and violates women, by restricting their visibility to mere appearance devoid of reality for positive impacts. We may then bring to the fore a few stances observed as unethical in New Media and gender relations.

News: Women do not appear often in the news, but when they do, they are more often than not portrayed as trouble makers or abused and repressed persons, rather than as strong, courageous members of the society, willing to contribute their own quota to the development of that society. As such they may be described as visibly invisible. Anyanwu notes that

> a content analysis of mainstream media in Nigeria reveals one dominant orientation. Women are largely seen and not heard. Their faces adorn newspapers. However, on important national and international issues, they fade out. Even when the news is about them, the story only gains real prominence if there is a male authority figure or newsmaker on the scene.[55]

The advent of New Media has not improved the situation described above. Moreover, female New Media facilitators (journalists, bloggers and so on) are also culprits with the way they capitalize on women-centered issues like cookery skills and beauty tips in their news and event coverage while neglecting social, economic and political issues which should be brought to the table for men and fellow women to discuss so that the society is enlightened to achieve improved gender relations. Connecting this with political, economic and developmental issues, Nurka was prompted to aver that "such practices problematically delimit female participation in public because their images are too readily conscripted into aestheticizing masculinist discourses that silence them."[56]

Advertisements: As far back as the 1980s, Joseph and Lewis observed that the most salient aspect of advertisements in Black Women's Magazines was "the selling of a value-biased image of women."[57] They further maintain that the summation of that image is women as: "sexy"; subordinate to men; seductresses; isolated from other women; competitors with other women for men; alluring beauties; dependent. More than other tools, New Media use advertisements to assault women. This is done in line with existing and prevalent patterns of stereotyping and objectifying women, as seen in conventional media, which ensures that any woman who does not recognize herself within media and in fact, New Media stereotypes, is described as not aligned with current trends. Bartky argues that normative femininity is centered on the woman's body; its sexuality and its appearance.[58] However, this is tainted by series of advertisements laden with blatant and extraneous sexual appeals where varying degrees of nudity are presented as ideals of beauty.

Photography: This is a highly controversial aspect of the media (both conventional and new). McEachern[59] describes photography historically, as one of the most exploited and exploiting mediums, which has played a large role in the subjugation of the "other." Photographs are humans' physical and psychological projections helping to build identities. They depict how a person or group wishes to be portrayed in public light, but then, they could also be contextually coded otherwise. Asserting how menacing photographs could be, Lauer asserts that; "photography was not only used as a form of evidence itself, but to enhance other forms of evidence, such as handwriting and fingerprints, both of which could be magnified by photography to assist expert analysis"[60]; in addition, "the potential of photographic evidence—real or doctored—was soon realized as a tool of blackmail and guerilla activism." Prominent among gender, ethics and New Media issues are: the introduction of social media meant for sharing of pictures (Facebook, Instagram and so on) and, the introduction of softwares for fabricating pictures and creating images. Women's bodies have been created and re-created using this medium, thereby raising fundamental questions of truth and objectivity in the portrayal of images in the New Media.

Anti-feminist websites and blogspots: Women are sexually exploited through pornography sites, mail order brides, online dating sites and even sites like TheDirty.com or IsAnyoneUp.com. On such sites, men are glorified for their sexual conquests, and women are largely blamed by society, for being promiscuous. New Media, particularly sites like these, have evolved into their own public sphere and are an extension of society. In that sense, gender roles are carried over and regurgitated, and the double standards that are seen rampantly within Western society spill over into the online realm. In media like Facebook.com and online dating sites, women are put up like a line of cows for the picking.

Some believe that social networking sites were created to rate women because men's consumption of New Media was greater at that time.[61]

Fashion (modeling and musicals): Fashion is indeed a captivating expression; a form of expression in which according to Gretal,[62] women have more freedom than men. This freedom notwithstanding, stereotyping persists in fashion, particularly in modeling and musicals. Greta observes that

> it's a subtle but definite form of sexism to take one of the few forms of expression where women have more freedom, and treat it as a form of expression that's inherently superficial and trivial.... fashion and style are primarily a women's art form ... it gets treated as trivial because women get treated as trivial.

We must ask fundamental questions about whose standards determine women's fashion statements, and in whose language and at whose expense are such statements made. New Media, rather than correcting or redefining it; reinforces the sexist assumption that women's fashion statements, modeling role and tasks in musicals are basically designed to attract male attention and approval. Conversely, Greta aptly asserts that "Female fashion is often as much about women's communication with one another as it is about our communication with men."

In all, we may draw out a double-edged argument used by New Media based on the communalistic nature of African societies. On one hand is the question on the place of the 'self' as portrayed by New Media, following an argument that, if I own my body, why should anyone question my nude pictures in New Media? On the other hand, why should New Media use a few women to stereotype and generalize about African women outside communal yardsticks or criteria? It is pertinent to note that in the case of Africa, cultural imperialism has played many roles in moral issues of New Media and problems of communicating feminist ethics. This is due largely to African feminism's shortfall in audience cultivation, for unswerving de-orientation and re-orientation. While grappling with this challenge, the introduction of the Internet and subsequent New Media to a market that has not thoroughly reflected on its media literacy skills also contributed to the escalation of moral issues. Noting that the power to influence is embedded in the power to communicate,[63] scholars have questioned why some women 'buy' the distorted media image of themselves when those images are of little health or economic benefit to them,[64] help in promoting news which projects them as morally deficient, and support projects that portray them as sex objects and as vulnerable. The next section discusses challenges and prospects of communicating feminist ethics in Africa.

Communicating feminist ethics in Africa: challenges and prospects

The communication field is wide, eclectic in nature and with permeable borders. Its wideness gives room for communication issues to emerge from all disciplines, be they science, social sciences or humanities; its eclecticism makes room for an introduction of several theories which allow for its study, either as a first order discipline or second order as the case may be. It encourages diverse approaches in creation and re-creation of models and theories from multiple disciplines to address communication issues. The permeability of its borders allows for scholars and researchers to freely enter, once armed with basic tools, to exhume communication based issues and apply ideas, concepts and theories from several fields. While it is possible to study each of the concepts (communication, feminism, ethics and Africa) as separate entities, this chapter connects the concepts to bring out robust discussions on emerging issues. The major task of communication is to provide information about prioritizing development, increasing productivity and promoting healthy relations among people, which have, over time, been facilitated by the media. Recognizing that the media construct reality, Omotoso and Razak assert that

> reality construction ... could take the forms of "exact presentation" or "distorted presentation." When exact presentation is embraced, the media is held to be committed to her tenets of objectivity, truth and fairness. However, recent trends have shown that constructed reality is largely synonymous with distorted reality.[65]

Corroborating this are concerns from various African states—Egypt,[66] Nigeria,[67] Zimbabwe,[68] Ethiopia[69] and South Africa[70] among others—about the flow of undesirable communications such as pornography and violence which contaminate the values and morals of their societies. Consequently, communicating feminist ethics is vital, for juxtaposition of perspectives, the preservation of moral social relations in African states and a defense of the sanctity of womanhood in Africa.

The Habermasian[71] description of New Media as unrestricted communication presents it, without doubt, as a revitalized public sphere which is more open to public participation than conventional media and has influenced the socio-economic terrain and political participation.[72] Ironically, the emergence of New Media also poses burdens on Africa, seeing how much struggle has been put into catching up with technological developments of conventional media. On this, Madzingira stresses that:

> While Africa and other developing regions now enjoy access to worldwide information, they have opened themselves to the danger of the destruction of their own culture, traditional norms, values and lifestyles, due to the imbalance that exists in the flow of information, ideas and images from developed countries.[73]

Therefore, Madzingira posits that "the greatest challenge of Africa's internet connectivity is not access, but content, because there is a dearth of information for Africa from Africa." The fact that some women involve themselves in 'feminine degrading acts' such as prostitution and pornographic modeling for survival or fun creates a moral dilemma: accordingly, it is problematic to allocate a universal moral status to all women, without a consideration for choice or free-will—obvious examples include women who pose nude for money, refusing to challenge stereotypical roles; conforming with the norms that promote marginalization, exploitation and all forms of oppression and above all, refusing to speak or work against such ventures in New Media. Perhaps, this argument is validated because some African women have not sufficiently acquired and sharpened their media and moral literacy skills which would enable them decipher New Media essences as well as define their dispositions toward them from ethical perspectives.

Communicating feminist ethics in Africa begins with decolonizing feminist ethics. This has been attempted by a few scholars as earlier discussed in this chapter. On this, I have also argued against a total embrace of care ethics as a framework for African feminist ethics, rather, an ethic of vigor was proposed. Decolonizing feminist ethics involves a re-examination of feminist ethical principles from a 'glocal' perspective, whereby the local is factored into the consideration of global trends as presented by New Media, and the global is a conscious worldwide consideration alongside cultural and traditional values in the assessment of feminist ethical dispositions to New Media.

In communicating feminist ethics in Africa's digital age, attention must be paid to the epistemic question of identity. This throws up the question 'how does an African woman in the digital age conceive of herself, as a universal or a particular?' It presents options of either mystifying or demystifying the body; concretizing or trivializing the body. Since the identity question is symmetrically connected with the question of morality, it then leads to the question of how African womandom can be portrayed in New Media, delineating between 'is' and 'ought.' Without ignoring the wide gap between the focus of Western feminist ethicists and African feminist ethicists, including disparities as to what constitutes the obscene, modest, overtly sexist and so on, there is a need for African feminists to clarify concepts such as morality, obscenity, sexism and classism among others, in the light of cultural ethos. This, by extension, requires a clear assertion of their position on such matters in New Media. This task of decolonizing feminist ethics is an expansion of the works of post colonial feminists who object to portrayals of women from non-Western societies as passive and voiceless victims and the portrayal of Western women as modern, educated and empowered.[74] Although these works do not disregard the fact that there are points of convergence between these groups, what is important is a clear distinction between both, so as to facilitate ease of re-presenting, demystifying or exterminating New Media portrayals that contravene African feminist philosophy as need arises.

It must also be noted that, communicating feminist ethics cannot be effectively done without conscious efforts to decolonize the New Media, mainly by contextualizing its contents and presuppositions. By this, I mean a perspectival approach which questions epistemic dispositions of Africans and how they use the New Media, bearing in mind the culture of piety and vigor under-lying womanhood in Africa. Without ignoring the 'reality construction' attribute of the media, decolonizing the New Media also involves careful inter-pretation, deconstruction and reconstruction of images and identities of women via the instrumentation of African feminist epistemology. This framework will enable a commitment to sanitizing the African public sphere which has been greatly influenced by the global public sphere, so that the vision of a re-oriented New Media for Africa is vigorously pursued by all, particularly women.

Conclusion

Having espoused salient issues connected with communicating feminist ethics in Africa, this work concludes that the New Media can only contribute to peace, security, democratic development and, most especially, the development of gender sensitive societies in Africa, if African feminist scholars and activists would arise to the task of decolonizing feminist ethics and New Media, thus guiding its users toward positive goals. Without ignoring initiatives such as the African Women's Media Centre, Women's Media Watch, The Ugandan Media Women's Association, ECOWAS Gender Policy, Media Institutes of Southern Africa, Association for Progressive Africa and Gender Links, amongst others, set up to challenge gendered representations in conventional and New Media, there is still more to do.

Effective communication of feminist ethics will depend on several factors including improved access to the New Media, primarily the Internet, and con-ventional media taking proactive roles to educate the masses on the pros and cons of New Media. Also of great importance is an improved and active pres-ence of African feminists in the New Media via a revitalization of African fem-inist websites, blogspots and other social media units. These can be achieved via research and training-oriented programs which will ultimately promote media literacy and positive usage of New Media in and for Africa. Above all, seeing that New Media users consume information made available to them, African feminists must embark on knowledge production to ensure that the values and virtues of African women are widely communicated in New Media. A com-munity that consumes what it does not produce will remain perpetually sub-servient to the producers.

Notes

1 Øyvind Aadland and Mark Fackler, *Ethiopian Press, Media, TV, Radio, Newspapers*, 1999. Retrieved August 12, 2015 from www.pressreference.com/Co-Fa/Ethiopia/html.
2 Colin Oliver and R. S. Chapman, *Data Processing and Information Technology* (London: D. P. Publications, 1990).
3 Martin Lister, Jon Dovey, Seth Giddins, Ian Grant and Kieran Kelly, *New Media: A Critical Introduction*, 2nd ed. (New York: Routledge, 2009).

4 Adedapo Bello, "ICTs as a Strategic Journalistic Tool for Development (in Nigeria),"
   in *Media, Governance and Development in Africa*, edited by Lai Oso, Toyin Ajibola
   and Dele Odunlami (Proceedings of Idowu Sobowale Conference. Ago-Iwoye: School
   of Communication and Information Sciences 2009), 265.

5 Ibid. Bello provides a general description of functions of new technologies.

6 Linda Friedman and Friedman Hershey, "The New Research Technologies: Overview
   & Research Frameworks," *SSRN Electronic Journal* (2008): 1–30.

7 Andrea Kaplan and Michael Haenlein, "Users of the World, Unite! The Challenges
   and Opportunities of Social Media," *Business Horizons* 53 (2010): 59–68.

8 Carolyn Marvin, *When Old Technologies Were New* (Oxford: Oxford University
   Press, 1988).

9 Deepita Chakravarty, *Gender New Media Course*, Lecture, Tempe, Arizona, April
   26, 2012.

10 See Savitri Bisnath, "Globalization, Poverty and Women Empowerment" in *United
   Nations Division for the Advancement of Women*, Expert Group Meeting on "Empow-
   erment of Women throughout the Life Cycle as a Transformative Strategy for Poverty
   Eradication," November 26–29, 2001; Sumita Sarkar, "Globalization and Women at
   Work: A Feminist Discourse." Paper delivered at the International Feminist Summit,
   July 17–20, 2007, Townsville, Australia; and Manisha Desai, "The Messy Relation-
   ship between Feminisms and Globalization," *Gender & Society* 27 (2007): 797–803,
   on how globalization shapes women identities in societies.

11 Carol Gilligan, *In A Different Voice: Psychological Theory and Women's Development* (Cambridge, MA: Harvard University Press, 1982).

12 Allison Jaggar, "Feminist Ethics," in *Encyclopedia of Ethics*, L. Becker and C. Becker
   (New York: Garland Press, 1992), 363–364.

13 Margaret Walker, *Moral Understandings: A Feminist Study in Ethics* (New York:
   Routledge, 1998).

14 Lynne Roper, "Feminism is NOT Pacifism: A Personal View of the Politics of War,"
   Feminist Media Studies 2(1) (2002): 149–150.

15 Fainos Mangena, "The Search for an African Feminist Ethic: A Zimbabwean Perspective," *Journal of International Women's Studies* 11(2) (2009): 18–30.

16 Aimée Montiel, "Violence against Women and Media: Advancements and Challenges
   of a Research and Political Agenda," in *Media and Gender: A Scholarly Agenda for
   the Global Alliance on Media and Gender*, edited by Aimée Montiel, 15–19. (France:
   United Nations Educational, Scientific and Cultural Organization, 2014). Available at
   http://unesdoc.unesco.org/images/0022/002283/228399e.pdf. Accessed March 13, 2017.

17 Feminist Peace Network, 2006. Pornography Revenue Statistics. Available at www.
   feministpeacenetwork.org/2010/10/20/pornography-the-obscene-statistics.   Accessed
   10 September 10, 2015.

18 S. A. Omotoso and R. Olamiposi, "Exploring an Idealistic-Pragmatic Approach in
   Evolving Strategies for Ethical Conflict Reporting in Nigeria," in *Journalism Practice
   and Terrorism in Nigeria*, edited by O. Isola and M. Popoola (Ibadan: John Archers
   Publishers Limited, 2015), 136.

19 F. Windeck, *Political Communication in Sub-Saharan Africa and the Role of New
   Media* (Berlin: International Report, 2010), 18.

20 S. Omotoso, "Political Communication in Africa: Towards a Peace Policy," in *Communication, Peace and Conflict*, edited by Isaac Albert, Olusola Isola and Olusola
   Oyewo (Ibadan: Institute of African Studies, 2015), 325–346.

21 B. Shimelis, "The State of the Private Press in Ethiopia," in *Ethiopia: The Challenge
   of Democracy from Below,* 2nd ed., edited by Z., Bahiru and S. Pausewang (Addis
   Ababa: United Printers, 2006), 186–201.

22 Aadland and Fackler op. cit.

23 See P. Ansah, "The Right to Communicate: Implications for Development," *Media
   Development* 6(1) (1992): 49–52; and H. Wasserman, "The Possibilities of ICTs for

Social Activism in Africa: An Exploration." Paper presented at CODESRIA's 30th anniversary conference: *Intellectuals, Nationalism and Pan-African Ideal*. Dakar, Senegal, 2003.

24 O. Onabajo, *Deploying the Potentials of Broadcasting for Mass Education: Challenges and Prospects.* Inaugural Lecture, Lead City University, Ibadan, 2012.

25 N. Madzingira, "*Culture, Communication and Development in Africa.*" Paper prepared for the African Itinerant College for Culture and Development, African Institute for Economic Development and Planning, Senegal, October 2001, 11.

26 Kabana, cited in B. Adeyeye, I. Audu, B. Onojo, C. Ogwo, E. Ojih, "Social Media and Tools for Disseminating Agricultural Information to Farmers in Plateau State," *Journal of Communication and Media Research* 5(1) (2013): 17–28.

27 See www.internetworldstats.com.

28 A. O. Umeh, *Computer Networking, Communication and Management of Information in Banks* (Enugu: Thought Communications, 1990), 38.

29 J. Nkwocha, *Digital Public Relations, New Techniques in Reputation Management* Vol. 1 (Lagos: Zoom Lens Publisher, 2004), 145.

30 Bello, op. cit., 265.

31 H. D. Lennon, "Why Women Studies" in *Women: Images and Realities*, edited by A. Kesselman, L. D. McNair and N. Schniedewind (California: Mayfield Publishing Company, 2011), 25.

32 G. Anzaldua, "Cultural Tyranny" in *Women: Images and Realities*, edited by A. Kesselman, L. D. McNair and N. Schniedewind (California: Mayfield Publishing Company, 1995), 43.

33 M. de Bruijn, "Mobile Phones in Africa: The New Talking Drums" in *Everyday Life*, edited by F. B. Nyamnjoh and I. Brinkman, 11–22 (Bamenda/Leiden: Langaa/ASC, 2009).

34 D. Lewis, T. S. Hussen and M. van Vuuren, "Exploring New Media Technologies Among Young South African Women," *Feminist Africa* 18 (2013): 47.

35 A. Mama, "The Challenges of Feminism: Gender Ethics and Responsible Academic Freedom in African Universities," *JHEA/RESA* 9(1&2) (2011): 9.

36 P. W. Scaltsas, "Do Feminist Ethics Counter Feminist Aims?" in *Explorations in Feminist Ethics: Theory and Practice*, edited by E. B. Cole and S. C. McQuin, 15–26 (Indianapolis: Indiana University Press, 1992).

37 See Jaggar, op. cit.; Cole and Coultrap-McQuin, "Toward a Feminist Conception of Moral Life," in *Explorations in Feminist Ethics*, edited by E. B. Cole and S. Coultrap-Mcquin (Indianapolis, IN: Indiana University Press, 1992), 1–11; and Mangena, op. cit.

38 See Gilligan, op. cit. and Noddings, *Caring: A Feminine Approach to Ethics and Moral Education* (Berkeley, CA: University of California Press, 2004).

39 V. Held, "Feminism and Moral Theory," in *Women and Moral Theory*, edited by E. Kittay and D. Meyers, 111–128 (Savage, MD: Rowman and Littlefield, 1987).

40 Mangena, op. cit.

41 Margaret Walker also subscribes to this position that feminist ethics in Africa should transcend ethics of care.

42 S. Welch, *A Feminist Ethic of Risk* (Minneapolis: Fortress Press, 1990), 168.

43 S. A. Omotoso, "Education and Emancipation, an African Philosophical Perspective," *Journal of Pan African Studies*. 3(9) (2010): 228.

44 On the "Five Faces of Oppression," see Iris Marion Young, 1990.

45 This resonates in the 'feminist sex wars' which created a divide between sex-positive feminists and anti-pornography feminists. See Ann Ferguson, "Sex War: The Debate between Radical and Libertarian Feminists," *Signs: Journal of Women in Culture and Society* 10(1) (1984): 106–112.

46 M. Eid and S. J. A. Ward, "Editorial: Ethics, New Media, and Social Networks," *Global Media Journal*, Canadian Edition, 2(1) (2009): 1–4.

47 See Andrew Chadwick, "Web 2.0: New Challenges for the Study of E-Democracy in an Era of Informational Exuberance," *Journal of Law and Policy for the Information Society* 4(3) (2008): 9–42; and Gbenga Afolayan, "Mobile Technologies and Intimate Conflicts: The Case of Young Female Adults in Nigeria," in *Interdisciplinary Mobile Media and Communications: Social, Economic and Political Implications*, edited by X. Xu, 108–123 (Pennsylvania, PA: IGI Global Inc, 2014).

48 The World Plan of Action for the Implementation of the Objectives of International Women's Year, 1984, 12.

49 I. Buskens and A. Webb, *African Women and ICTs: Investigating Gender, Techno-logy and Empowerment* (London: Zed, 2009).

50 L. Green, *The Internet: An Introduction to New Media* (Oxford: Berg Publishers, 2010), 65.

51 L. Tseayo, "Culture, Mass Media and the Image of Women in Nigeria," in *Women and the Media in Nigeria*, edited by A. Odejide (Ibadan: Women Research and Docu-mentation Centre, 1996), 46–61, and Lewis, Huseen and van Vuuren, op. cit. In the two works, the scholars lament how New Media has been variously used in distorting women images.

52 See Jaggar, op. cit.; R. Gill, *Gender and the Media* (Cambridge: Polity Press, 2007); and D. Chakravarty, *Gender New Media Course*, 2012.

53 Chakravarty, ibid.

54 Gill, op. cit., 117.

55 C. Anyanwu, "Nigerian Women Demand More Representation in Governance," *Punch Newspaper* 15 (July 2001), 6.

56 C. Nurka, "Public Bodies," *Feminist Media Studies* 14(3) (2014): 486.

57 G. Joseph and J. Lewis, *Common Differences: Conflicts in Black and White Feminist Perspectives* (New York: South End Press, 1981), 157.

58 S. Bartky, "Foucault, Femininity, and the Modernization of Patriarchal Power," in *Femininity and Domination*, edited by Sandra Bartky, 25–45 (New York: Routledge, 1990).

59 S. McEachern, "Feminism, Family and Photography," *Canadian Women Studies* 11(1) (1990): 15.

60 J. Lauer, "Surveillance History and the History of New Media: An Evidential Para-digm," *New Media and Society* 14(4) (2011): 573, 571.

61 Chakravarty, op. cit.

62 C. Greta, *Fashion is a Feminist Issue*, http://theorbit.net/greta/2011/09/02/fashion-is-a-feminist-issue/.

63 Omotoso, "Political Communication in Africa," 327.

64 The works of Joseph and Lewis, *Common Differences*, and Omotoso, *An Idealistic-Pragmatic Model as an Ethical Paradigm in Advertising* extensively discussed ethical and gender issues in advertising.

65 Omotoso and Olamiposi, op. cit., 131.

66 H. Bahgat, "Egypt's Virtual Protection of Morality," *Middle East Report* 230 (2004): 22–25.

67 B. Umeogwu and I. Ojiakor, "Internet Communication and the Moral Degradation of the Nigerian Youth," *International Journal of Computer and Information Technology* 3(2) (2014): 450–463.

68 Madzingira, op. cit.

69 T. Kiros, "Zera Yacob and Traditional Ethiopian Philosophy," in *A Companion to African Philosophy*, edited by W. Kwasi, W. Abraham, A. Irele and I. Menkiti, 183–190 (Malden, MA: Blackwell, 2004).

70 De Wet, "Crime in South African Education as Reflected in the Print Media," *South African Journal of Education* 23(2) (2003): 113–121.

71 J. Habermas, *Between Facts and Norms: Contributions to a Discourse Theory of Law and Democracy* (Cambridge, MA: MIT Press, 1998).

72 P. Ifukor, "'Elections' or 'Selections'? Blogging and Twittering the Nigerian 2007 General Elections," *Bulletin of Science Technology & Society* 30(6) (2010): 398–414.
73 Madzingira, op. cit., 12.
74 S. Mills, "Postcolonial Feminist Theory," in *Contemporary Feminist Theories*, edited by Jackie Jones (Edinburgh: Edinburgh University Press, 1998), 98–112.

Bibliography

Aadland, O. and M. Fackler. *Ethiopian Press, Media, TV, Radio, Newspapers.* 1999. Retrieved August 12, 2015 from www.pressreference.com/Co-Fa/Ethiopia/html.

Adeyeye, B., I. Audu, B. Onojo, C. Ogwo and E. Ojih. "Social Media and Tools for Disseminating Agricultural Information to Farmers in Plateau State," *Journal of Communication and Media Research* 5(1) (2013): 17–28.

Afolayan, G. "Mobile Technologies and Intimate Conflicts: The Case of Young Female Adults in Nigeria," in *Interdisciplinary Mobile Media and Communications: Social, Economic and Political Implications*, edited by X. Xu, 108–123. Pennsylvania, PA: IGI Global Inc, 2014.

Ansah, P. "The Right to Communicate: Implications for Development," *Media Development* 6(1) (1992): 49–52.

Anyanwu, C. "Nigerian Women Demand More Representation in Governance," *Punch Newspaper* 15 (July 2001): 6–8.

Anzaldua, G. "Cultural Tyranny," in *Women: Images and Realities*, edited by A. Kesselman, L. D. McNair and N. Schniedewind, 43–45. California: Mayfield Publishing Company, 1995.

Bahgat, H. "Egypt's Virtual Protection of Morality," *Middle East Report* 230 (2004): 22–25.

Bartky, S. "Foucault, Femininity, and the Modernization of Patriarchal Power," in *Femininity and Domination*, edited by Sandra Bartky, 25–45. New York: Routledge, 1990.

Bello, A. "ICTs as a Strategic Journalistic Tool for Development (in Nigeria)," in *Media, Governance and Development in Africa*, edited by L. Oso, T. Ajibola and D. Odunlami, 263–273. Proceedings of Idowu Sobowale Conference. Ago-Iwoye: School of Communication and Information Sciences, 2009.

Bisnath S. "Globalization, Poverty and Women Empowerment," in *United Nations Division for the Advancement of Women*. Expert Group Meeting on "Empowerment of Women throughout the Life Cycle as a Transformative Strategy for Poverty Eradication" November 26–29, 2001, New Delhi, India.

Buskens, I. and A. Webb, eds. *African Women and ICTs: Investigating Gender, Technology and Empowerment*. London: Zed, 2009.

Chadwick, A. "Web 2.0: New Challenges for the Study of E-Democracy in an Era of Informational Exuberance," *Journal of Law and Policy for the Information Society* 4(3) (2008): 9–42.

Chakravarty, D. *Gender New Media Course*. Tempe, Arizona, April 26, 2012.

Cole, E. B. and S. Coultrap-Mcquin. "Toward a Feminist Conception of Moral Life," in *Explorations in Feminist Ethics*, edited by E. B. Cole and S. Coultrap-Mcquin, 1–11. Indianapolis, IN: Indiana University Press, 1992.

De Bruijn, M. "Mobile Phones in Africa: The New Talking Drums," in *Everyday Life*, edited by F. B. Nyamnjoh and I. Brinkman, 11–22. Bamenda/Leiden: Langaa/ASC, 2009.

De Wet, N. C. "Crime in South African Education as Reflected in the Print Media," *South African Journal of Education* 23(2) (2003): 113–121.

Desai, M. "The Messy Relationship between Feminisms and Globalization," *Gender & Society* 27 (2007): 797–803.

Eid, M. and S. J. A. Ward. "Editorial: Ethics, New Media, and Social Networks," *Global Media Journal*, Canadian Edition 2(1) (2009): 1–4.

Ferguson, A. "Sex War: The Debate between Radical and Libertarian Feminists," *Signs: Journal of Women in Culture and Society* 10(1) (1984): 106–112.

Friedman, L. and H. Friedman. "The New Research Technologies: Overview & Research Frameworks," *SSRN Electronic Journal* (2008): 1–30.

Gill, R. *Gender and the Media.* Cambridge: Polity Press, 2007.

Gilligan, C. *In A Different Voice: Psychological Theory and Women's Development.* Cambridge, MA: Harvard University Press, 1982.

Green, L. *The Internet: An Introduction to New Media.* Oxford: Berg Publishers, 2010.

Greta, C. *Fashion is a Feminist Issue* http://theorbit.net/greta/2011/09/02/fashion-is-a-feminist-issue/, 2011.

Habermas, J. *Between Facts and Norms: Contributions to a Discourse Theory of Law and Democracy.* Cambridge, MA: MIT Press, 1998.

Held, V. "Feminism and Moral Theory," in *Women and Moral Theory*, edited by E. Kittay and D. Meyers, 111–128. Savage, MD: Rowman and Littlefield, 1987.

Ifukor, P. "'Elections' or 'Selections'? Blogging and Twittering the Nigerian 2007 General Elections," *Bulletin of Science Technology & Society* 30(6) (2010): 398–414.

Jaggar, A. "Feminist Ethics," in *Encyclopedia of Ethics*, edited by L. Becker and C. Becker. New York: Garland Press, 1992.

Jaggar, A. "Feminist Ethics," in *The Blackwell Guide to Ethical Theory.* Goteborg University: EBSCO Publishing, 2000.

Joseph, G., and J. Lewis. *Common Differences: Conflicts in Black and White Feminist Perspectives.* New York: South End Press, 1981.

Kaplan, A., and M. Haenlein. "Users of the World, Unite! The Challenges and Opportunities of Social Media," *Business Horizons* 53 (2010): 59–68.

Kiros, T. "Zera Yacob and Traditional Ethiopian Philosophy," in *A Companion to African Philosophy*, edited by W. Kwasi, W. Abraham, A. Irele and I. Menkiti, 183–190. Malden, MA: Blackwell, 2004.

Lauer, J. "Surveillance History and the History of New Media: An Evidential Paradigm," *New Media and Society* 14(4) (2011): 566–582.

Lennon, H. D. "Why Women Studies," in *Women: Images and Realities*, edited by A. Kesselman, L. D. McNair and N. Schniedewind, 25–35. California: Mayfield Publishing Company, 2011.

Lewis, D., T. S. Hussen and M. van Vuuren. "Exploring New Media Technologies Among Young South African Women," *Feminist Africa* 18 (2013): 43–64.

Lister, M., J. Dovey, S. Giddins, I. Grant, and K. Kelly. *New Media: A Critical Introduction*, 2nd ed. New York: Routledge, 2009.

Madzingira, N. "Culture, Communication and Development in Africa." A paper prepared for the African Itinerant College for Culture and Development, African Institute for Economic Development and Planning, Senegal, October 2001.

Mama, A. "The Challenges of Feminism: Gender Ethics and Responsible Academic Freedom in African Universities," *JHEA/RESA* 9 (1&2) (2011): 1–23.

Mangena, F. "The Search for an African Feminist Ethic: A Zimbabwean Perspective," *Journal of International Women's Studies* 11(2) (2009): 18–30.

Manovich, L. "What is New Media?" in *The New Media Theory Reader*, edited by R. Hassan and J. Thomas, 5–10. Berkshire, UK: Open University Press, 2006.

Marvin, C. *When Old Technologies Were New.* Oxford: Oxford University Press, 1988.

McEachern, S. "Feminism, Family and Photography," *Canadian Women Studies* 11(1) (1990): 14–17.

Mills, S. "Postcolonial Feminist Theory," in *Contemporary Feminist Theories*, edited by J. Jones and S. Jackson, 98–112. Edinburgh: Edinburgh University Press, 1998.

Montiel, A. "Violence against Women and Media: Advancements and Challenges of a Research and Political Agenda," in *Media and Gender: A Scholarly Agenda for the Global Alliance on Media and Gender*, edited by A. Montiel, 15–19. France: United Nations Educational, Scientific and Cultural Organization, 2014.

Nkwocha, J. *Digital Public Relations: New Techniques in Reputation Management.* Vol. 1. Lagos: Zoom Lens Publisher, 2004.

Noddings, N. *Caring: A Feminine Approach to Ethics and Moral Education.* Berkeley, CA: University of California Press, 1984.

Nurka, C. "Public Bodies," *Feminist Media Studies* 14(3) (2014): 485–499.

Oliver, C. and R. S. Chapman. *Data Processing and Information Technology.* London: D. P. Publications, 1990.

Omotoso, S. A. "Education and Emancipation: An African Philosophical Perspective," *Journal of Pan African Studies.* 3(9) (2010): 222–231.

Omotoso, S. A. *An Idealistic-Pragmatic Model as an Ethical Paradigm in Advertising.* Unpublished PhD Thesis at Olabisi Onabanjo University, Ago-Iwoye, Nigeria, 2013.

Omotoso, S. A. "Political Communication in Africa: Towards a Peace Policy," in *Communication, Peace and Conflict*, edited by I. O. Albert, O. Isola and O. Oyewo. 325–346. Ibadan: Institute of African Studies, 2015.

Omotoso, S. A. and R. Olamiposi. "Exploring an Idealistic-Pragmatic Approach in Evolving Strategies for Ethical Conflict Reporting in Nigeria," in *Journalism Practice and Terrorism in Nigeria*, edited by O. Isola and M. Popoola, 131–151. Ibadan: John Archers Publishers Limited, 2015.

Onabajo, O. "Deploying the Potentials of Broadcasting for Mass Education: Challenges and Prospects." Inaugural Lecture, Lead City University, Ibadan, 2012.

Roper, L. "Feminism is NOT Pacifism: A Personal View of the Politics of War," *Feminist Media Studies* 2(1) (2002): 149–150.

Sarkar, S. "Globalization and Women at Work: A Feminist Discourse." Paper delivered at the International Feminist Summit, July 17–20, 2007. Townsville, Australia.

Scaltsas, P. W. "Do Feminist Ethics Counter Feminist Aims?" in *Explorations in Feminist Ethics: Theory and Practice*, edited by E. B. Cole and S. C. McQuin, 15–26. Indianapolis, IN: Indiana University Press, 1992.

Shimelis, B. "The State of the Private Press in Ethiopia," in *Ethiopia: The Challenge of Democracy from Below*, 2nd ed., edited by Z., Bahiru and S. Pausewang, 186–201. Addis Ababa: United Printers, 2006.

Tseayo, L. "Culture, Mass Media and the Image of Women in Nigeria," in *Women and the Media in Nigeria*, edited by A. Odejide, 46–61. Ibadan: Women Research and Documentation Centre, 1996.

Umeh, A. O. *Computer Networking, Communication and Management of Information in Banks.* Enugu: Thought Communications, 1990.

Umeogwu, B. and I. Ojiakor. "Internet Communication and the Moral Degradation of the Nigerian Youth," *International Journal of Computer and Information Technology* 3(2) (2014): 450–463.

Walker, M. *Moral Understandings: A Feminist Study in Ethics.* New York: Routledge, 1998.

Wasserman, H. "The Possibilities of ICTs for Social Activism in Africa: An Exploration." Paper presented at CODESRIA's 30th anniversary conference: *Intellectuals, Nationalism and Pan-African Ideal*. Dakar, Senegal, 2003.

Welch, S. *A Feminist Ethic of Risk*. Minneapolis, MN: Fortress Press, 1990.

Windeck, F. *Political Communication in Sub-Saharan Africa and the Role of New Media*. Berlin: International Report, 2010.

The World Plan of Action for the Implementation of the Objectives of International Women's Year, 1984.

Young, I. M. "Five Faces of Oppression," in *Theorizing Feminisms*, edited by E. Hackett and S. Haslanger, 3–16. Oxford: Oxford University Press, 1990.

Part II
Gender, migration and identity

4 Transnational feminist solidarity, Black German women and the politics of belonging

Tiffany N. Florvil

Introduction

> I define solidarity in terms of mutuality, accountability, and the recognition of common interests as the basis for relationships among diverse communities. Rather than assuming an enforced commonality of oppression, the practice of solidarity foregrounds communities of people who have chosen to *work* and *fight* together. *Diversity* and *difference* are central values here—to be acknowledged and respected, not erased in the building of alliances.
>
> (Chandra Talpade Mohanty, *Feminism without Borders*[1])

On August 2, 1991, over 130 women of color from six continents arrived at the Fifth Cross-Cultural Black Women's Studies Summer Institute in reunified Germany.[2] The Institute represented "an assembly of women activists, theorists, writers, peasants, and workers who [were] concerned about each other's realities and struggles," and was a "vehicle for international understanding," connecting these women.[3] While scholar Chandra Mohanty did not attend, her quotation exemplifies the Institute's ideals, especially the importance of diversity as a unifying tool for cohesion and community building.[4] Later, one Afro-German observed that the making of affective connections "to older Black women from all over the world was ... an important personal experience."[5] In an interview, Afro-German feminist Marion Kraft, the Institute Program Director, similarly conveyed that the purpose of the summer seminar is

> to build an international network of black women. To be able to find support at different levels, to gain access to resources, to form centers of information, and looking beyond the [next] three weeks to give us the chance to create an institution that does not yet exist for us."[6]

For Kraft, the Institute served important functions for Black Germans and "Black" participants from across the globe.[7] It created spaces where women of color could initiate anti-racist projects, share survival strategies and document their challenges in societies that ignored their plight.

This chapter argues that Afro-German women used the 1991 Institute to cultivate connections to Black women with varied backgrounds that became critical to their diasporic and feminist activism. Afro-Germans constructed a transnational network that promoted solidarity, extended encouragement and confronted instances of racism and sexism.[8] The Institute also represented an affective experience and a cultural moment for them, solidifying trust, encouraging further activism and affirming perceived commonalities and differences.[9] Black German women's engagement with the Institute, I contend, marked a pronounced international phase within the Afro-German movement, one that coincided with reunified Germany's attempts to reclaim its place in the global arena. Nationally, the country was also rife with xenophobic violence targeted toward actual and alleged non-white foreigners. Therefore, the Institute helped these women criticize increased racism in the years after the fall of the Berlin Wall, while also obtaining recognition for themselves as Black Germans in a nation that still considered itself to be homogeneously white. Afro-German women's participation in the Institute enabled them to engage in Black women's internationalism and redefine their positions in Germany and the African Diaspora, illustrating that the former was home to the latter.

Publicizing their feminist and African diasporic politics, Afro-German and Black participants also used the power of writing to sustain their political work, reasserting their intention to transform societies. Delegates produced and unanimously passed the "1991 Resolutions," which addressed contemporary issues concerning ethnicity, class and gender.[10] The resolutions served as a rallying call for international justice and the implementation of new legislative measures, although on these fronts little change occurred. By foregrounding the experiences of Black German women at the 1991 Institute, I consider their forms of activism, claim-making and internationalism to illustrate an example of African diasporic agency and belonging.

The chapter's first section discusses scholarship on the African Diaspora and explains the experiences of Afro-Germans to better understand how they contribute to this field. The second section addresses the sources of Black feminist and Black women's internationalism to show how they dialoged with other feminist initiatives and institutes such as at the United Nations, eventually leading to the creation of the Cross-Cultural Institute. Section three examines the 1991 Institute in Germany and how Afro-Germans used it to forge feminist solidarity and to push for more attention on the issues of racism, gender and diasporic politics. The last section demonstrates how Afro-Germans and other participants collaborated to initiate international change with their "1991 Resolutions."

The African Diaspora and Afro-Germans in reunified Germany

In the last twenty years, scholars have recentered women's histories in narratives on the African Diaspora.[11] Charting experiences from Montreal to Stockholm, some scholars have focused on the gendered dynamics that impact Black women's agency, mobility and subjectivities. They have examined the roles of Black women from different social backgrounds across the Atlantic, the Pacific and the Indian Oceans. Much of this scholarship privileges the African-American experience, while eliding the differences and parallels of these with those of other diasporic communities.[12] Building on path-breaking works on Black Europeans, this chapter expands our understanding of the African Diaspora, blackness and coalition building by analyzing the actions and practices of Black German women.[13] In doing so, I shift our focus toward women of color feminisms and diasporic activism in Germany instead of in Britain or the United States.[14] The chapter also details how these women created connections with others across the Diaspora, allowing them to establish networks and strengthen their political consciousness.

As Shelby Lewis has noted, the activism of the Institute represented "Africana feminism"—a form of diasporic activism—especially for Black German women. This is particularly significant in Germany, which has been overlooked in scholarship as an African diasporic and/or Black space—with some notable exceptions.[15] As a result, this chapter centers Afro-Germans in narratives about the Diaspora and Black European history more generally. Black Germans, according to Carmen Faymonville, have been "forced even more than their British neighbors to seek transnational identification across Europe and the globe, most often to English-speaking countries."[16] Black Germans were often isolated and scattered across post-World War II Germany instead of concentrated in a few ethnic neighborhoods, and comprise approximately half a million individuals with different backgrounds. They include African and Asian migrants and refugees, and the children of former colonial subjects, of French colonial soldiers from World War I and of African-American GIs and African students from World War II and after. Of these groups, biracial offspring constitute the largest proportion of Afro-Germans, many of who grew up having limited or no contact with their Black fathers or relatives.[17] Therefore, diasporic activism enabled Afro-German women to draw ideas and cultural tools from Third World and Black feminisms in Britain, the United States, and elsewhere and to apply those ideas to their local and national conditions.[18] It did not entail privileging communities of color over each other or the creation of a hierarchy of beliefs and customs, although this has sometimes happened within other diasporic movements. Afro-German women saw their engagement with non-German activist communities as a way of enhancing their identities and political work.

Afro-Germans' efforts at diasporic and feminist activism were inspired by Caribbean-American poet Audre Lorde, who encouraged these women to cultivate solidarities throughout the Diaspora. Lorde continued to motivate Afro-Germans during her travels to Germany from 1984 until her death in 1992. Given the heterogeneous composition of the Afro-German community, Lorde's idea that "difference [must be used] to generate energy for social change at the same time as we preserve our individuality" resonated with them.[19] She urged women to connect across their differences and advance common objectives through multiracial coalitions and international projects.[20] At a 1984 Berlin reading, she remarked that, "I am interested in making coalitions with anyone who shares a common goal." Continuing, Lorde stated, "We share common destinies, we share common goals. We have great differences and we need to be able to articulate those differences and work across them."[21] Lorde also wrote that, "Women of Color in struggle all over the world, our separateness, our connectedness, so many more options for survival. Whatever I call them, I know them for sister, mother, daughter, voice and teacher, inheritor of fire."[22] The emphasis on multicultural networks, she believed, enabled women to blend theories on "connected differences" with direct action. Lorde herself was involved in multiple attempts to build global multiracial solidarity, including co-founding the feminist organization Sisters in Support of Sisters in South Africa (SISA).[23] Lorde and her partner, Gloria Joseph, were also involved in early Cross-Cultural Institutes.

Moreover, pronounced discriminatory practices in the 1980s and 1990s drove Black German women to forge a global feminist network of Black women committed to anti-racism. Their efforts proved crucial at this time in which West, East and then reunified Germany experienced a re-emergence of nationalist rhetoric that politicians and citizens used to demarcate difference along alleged cultural lines.[24] Many white Germans espoused anti-Semitic, xenophobic and racist views that reworked traditional biological notions of difference. In 1982, Chancellor Helmut Kohl's Christian Democratic Union (CDU) Party ushered in a new conservatism (not unlike that of Margaret Thatcher or Ronald Reagan) that addressed issues of German patriotism and foreign policy (*Ausländerpolitik*) that limited asylum rights and legislation; he also referred to West Germany as "a non-immigration country."[25] Far right groups also gained more visibility through their violent attacks on refugees, asylum seekers and non-white native Germans. In November 1990, for example, German skinheads assaulted Amadeu Antonio Kiowa, an Angolan contract worker in Eberswalde (in the former East). Kiowa was beaten unconscious and later died.[26] Through the Institute, Afro-German women also elucidated that Germany was an immigration country—to invert a phrase from the Chancellor—and that racism did persist after the Second World War.[27] At the same time, politicians from across the spectrum in Europe implemented policies and citizens adopted rhetoric and practices that produced a "Fortress Europe." This Europe denied basic civil and political rights to migrants, refugees, asylum seekers and native non-white European citizens—a recurring theme at the 1991 Institute.

Situating Black feminist activism: the origins of the Institute

The Institutes offered Black women the opportunity that many had been seeking to build alliances across borders. After the United Nations World Conferences on Women in Mexico City (1975), East Berlin (1975), Copenhagen (1980) and Nairobi (1985), women throughout the globe expressed interest in sustaining a human rights dialog on racism, heterosexism, sexism, classism and eurocentrism.[28] Contemporaneously, a new series of Black and Black women's studies programs developed in the United States, and African-American feminist scholars founded organizations to explore global feminism and participate in Black women's internationalism. As scholars have shown, these practices have long been a part of Afro-diasporic women's tools of political engagement and coalition building across the globe.[29] Indeed, the Cross-Cultural Black Women's Studies Summer Institute, which was headquartered in New York City and London, served as an example of this.[30] The Institutes mirrored themes from the UN conferences while addressing the collective and intersecting experiences of women of color. Dr Andrée Nicola McLaughlin, a professor from Medgar Evers College in New York, was the founding International Coordinator. The Institutes sponsored international conferences in various countries with local host organizations. As the organizers of the 1989 Institute explained, their goal was to "foster international cooperation to promote peace, human rights, and development by presenting an opportunity for women of diverse cultures to exchange information, share experiences, identify resources and build links."[31] The organization also served as a clearinghouse for theoretical and practical information concerning Black women's experiences and helped to support research and mobilize activists.[32]

Speaking at the 1989 Institute, McLaughlin stated that the event "represent[ed] the combined efforts of women from economically-developing nations and communities worldwide," and operated as a collaborative and energizing enterprise.[33] During the opening session, McLaughlin told the participants, "we are women of diverse nationalities, cultures, religions, ages, experiences, and even ideologies," who are "bonded by a common commitment to empower women in our various struggles for self-determination and autonomy— that is, freedom of the group and the individual."[34] She, in other words, encouraged differences by privileging inclusive feminist and diasporic identities, identities that were shaped by common struggles against oppression. Within this context, "Black" was a transnational political designation as much as a cultural one that was not strictly tied to African descent or even skin color more generally.[35] As McLaughlin explained, it was "a term to express our cross-cultural identities as Black people whether based on culture, political ideas and/or social class, and thus referring to a broad range of national, ethnic, racial, and religious groups."[36] Therefore, Black served as an instrument of resistance and a malleable signifier that allowed diverse communities from Latin America, South Asia and Europe to cohere.[37]

Occurring in London, New York City, Harare, Bulawayo, Zvishavane and Auckland, the early Cross-Cultural Institutes embodied the interplay among the local, national and global. Each Institute focused on a theme that stressed the indigenous undercurrents that affected women in these locales, while also emphasizing worldwide dynamics. At the inaugural 1987 London Institute, entitled "Women's Conditions," held from July 13–August 7, McLaughlin confirmed that women:

> felt it crucial to continue to address the legacies of colonialism and feudalism which impact upon our everyday lives in real ways … issues of economic

class, national and racial oppression, gender oppression, differences of ethnicity and religion, and the contradictions of caste, region, skin color, and social class.

She clarified that due to the

power of this London exchange and the sisters' strong feeling that we could not get an accurate assessment of our condition without looking into the mirror of the world's women that we conceived of a regularly scheduled forum for the cross-cultural study of economically developing women.[38]

This intercultural emphasis remained with the 1988 New York Institute that took place from July 11–30. Bringing together women from over thirty nationalities and focusing on the topic of "Women and Communications," the three-week Institute sponsored several presentations on the media's representation and appropriation of Asian and Afro-Columbia women and on the development of national movements in Palestine, El Salvador, West Germany and New Zealand. Members from feminist organizations in Angola, Lesotho, Zimbabwe and the Netherlands attended.[39] Presentations and working groups afforded women an occasion to raise their voices and express emotions from motivation and enthusiasm to disappointment. African-American lesbian feminist Barbara Smith, along with authors Lorde and Sonia Sanchez, presented on heterosexual women and the persistence of homophobia.[40] Anjuli Gupta, an Indian-German, who identified as a "Black feminist" (*Schwarze Feministin*), attended this workshop, professing that, "the exchange gave me energy and inspired many new ideas and encouraged me to continue the fight."[41] Gupta travelled to the Institute with two Black Germans, Katharina Oguntoye and May Opitz (later Ayim), who gave a presentation on the origins of the Afro-German movement.[42] Although the Institute fostered multicultural dialog, some exchanges fell short for non-English speakers.[43]

These moments of community building were not without problems. A few conflicts re-emerged at the Third Zimbabwean Institute, entitled "Women and the Politics of Food," held on August 7–26, 1989.[44] Mrs Sekai Holland, the Program Director, sought "to facilitate [a] forum for women to discuss and define their realities," but as Marion Kraft mentioned in a 1989 letter to Lorde, emotional tensions were rife due to participants' inability to respect cultural practices and to listen to one another.[45] She posed a series of questions:

What about our sisters in Azania? What about those women from Uganda, Ethiopia, Panama—who had come a long way? What was the meaning of "Cross-Cultural"? The fact that some American sisters did not attend the closing meeting saying they felt "disrespected"? And even if they were wrong, can we discard their emotions by saying "they are very young"? How do we deal with differences among ourselves?[46]

Kraft noticed how some participants were unable to acknowledge one another's "connected differences." Yet she added that, "the 'Institute' [is] very important. We need – as African women, women of the Black diaspora—[a] forum of our own, and I am grateful to the sisters who initiated this." "Zimbabwe," Kraft stated, "was an exciting experience, worth all the hardships and frustrations."[47]

The Fourth Institute, held from March 16–23, 1990, organized around the theme of "Human Rights and Indigenous Peoples in the 'Information Age' " in New Zealand. Participants met with Maori women for a fact-finding mission and produced a documentary on indigenous and human rights.[48] Subsequent Institutes occurred in Caracas, Venezuela (1993), Honolulu, Hawaii (1995) and Johannesburg, South Africa (1998).[49] Starting in 1999, sponsored symposia and study tours took place in Trinidad, Costa Rica, Russia, Japan and Panama with the final one in 2006.[50] If not without conflicts, the Institutes continued to encourage feminist solidarity and Black internationalism. With these practices, participants showed the significance of forging forms of kinship globally and locally.

The fifth cross-cultural Black women's studies summer institute

The Fifth Institute was significant for Afro-German women because, as evidence suggests, it was the first time that an entire international conference had been hosted in Germany dedicated to the topic of Blacks in Europe.[51] The Institute shared a commitment to the theme of "Black People and the European Community" (*Schwarze Menschen und die Europäische Gemeinschaft*).[52] It occurred in Frankfurt, Bielefeld and Berlin with Kraft as the Program Director and Afro-German activists Helga Emde and Katharina Oguntoye as Regional Coordinators.[53] Members of two Black German organizations, ISD (Initiative of Black Germans or *Initiative Schwarze Deutsche*) and ADEFRA (Afro-German Women or *Afro-deutsche Frauen*) attended, presented, arranged and supported activities.[54]

The 1991 Institute tapped into existing Black German networks. In addition to spurring Afro-German women to get involved, Lorde established one sponsoring organization, the Cross-Cultural Initiative of Black Women for Minority Rights and Studies in Germany (*Interkulturelle Initiative Schwarzer Frauen für Minoritätenrechte und -Studien in Deutschland*, IISF).[55] Kraft mentioned in a 2014 article that, "this event [the Institute] was another proof of Audre Lorde's ability to turn the seemingly impossible into reality, to move the Black woman from margin to center—even in Germany."[56] Along with the IISF, Nozizwe: Project for Multicultural Feminist Education, an association that assisted migrant women in Berlin, hosted the Institute. The Institute also obtained support from a variety of organizations and institutions including the Department of Multicultural Affairs in Frankfurt, SOS Racism (*SOS Rassismus*, France and Germany), the Association of Bi-National Families (*Interessengemeinschaft der mit Ausländern verheirateten Frauen*, IAF) and other organizations.[57]

The three-week Institute came at a pivotal moment in German history, in which the re-emergence of nationalist rhetoric and violence became prevalent. As McLaughlin opined in a 1992 letter:

> Even though German society is in the throes of profound structural change and experiencing an upsurge in racist violence, our German sisters—members of a relatively young Black national community—courageously undertook initiatives to conduct the 1991 Institute and to mount a tremendous fund-raising effort. Their endeavors made possible increased national and cultural diversity of delegates in attendance and simultaneous translation at Institute events.[58]

Helga Emde was proud to host "the important conference" in "racist Germany" to show these developments to others.[59] In this context, Afro-German women constructed sites for support and transnational exchange. As some "African and American sisters" noted, Black Germans were "well-off and educated, but also more isolated and lonelier than minorities in other states."[60] Indeed, several, but by no means all, of the Afro-German participants could be considered a part of the German middle class. Yet, as these observers remarked, Afro-Germans endured isolation in majority white German environments. They, moreover, did not possess common diasporic traditions or narratives of home or community that provided other Black diasporic groups with resources that they could use as a foundation.[61] Hence, the Institute encouraged a sense of belonging among Afro-German women.

With events beginning at the University of Frankfurt on August 3, Kraft, Emde and Oguntoye wanted to address the economic and political development of the European Community and its impact on non-European immigrants.[62] A flyer expressed the aims:

> The [Institute] includes an intercultural examination of the history, present and socio-economic situation of Black people in Europe and engages with issues of cultural identity and the campaign that blacks and other minorities wage against xenophobia, eurocentrism, neo-fascism, and racism.[63]

Of particular interest to Afro-Germans were "Black Europeans' forms of political and cultural resistance ..."[64] In a local interview, Kraft explained the Institute's goals and reminded readers (and participants) that Black Europeans were complicit in the "global paradigm of oppression":

> Our theme is "Black people and the European Community," but a lot of women from the so-called Third World also are participating. These women have completely different problems than we do in western European countries. We live in countries that are directly involved in the exploitation of Third World countries. Therefore to establish a network and then to formulate the common, concrete demands for the UN and individual countries, that is the critical thing that we can do with an event like this.[65]

Attendees, German and non-German, explored these themes through a shared feminist engagement.

The Institute fostered connections, but it was not without unpleasant experiences of racism, conflict and organizational glitches. In Frankfurt, where events took place from August 3–10, participants encountered overt forms of racism. At the University of Frankfurt's bookstore, a South African attendee was told that, "she should remove her dirty fingers" from the merchandise. Moreover, child caretakers returned from a playground complaining that Germans greeted their charges with "Get lost, you Nigger[s]."[66] A 1992 IISF report mentioned a few tensions at some of the Institute sessions. Some participants, especially Black Germans, believed that having white German women in attendance created the risk that Black women's discussions about racism would be misinterpreted and questioned.[67] Some complained that the Institute left little time for more personal interactions, and some Afro-Germans wanted more involvement from ISD members. Yet the report remarked that, "regardless of these differences, after three weeks of intense work we arrived at a successful conclusion, which was positive."[68]

Institute events conveyed the organizers' ambitions. Philomena Essed and Melba Wilson were just a few of the prominent figures presenting in Frankfurt.[69] Kraft, Emde, Oguntoye and others organized events that represented the Institute's and Germany's diversity. Barbara Walker from Cologne, for example, presented an exhibition at the Dietrich-Bonhoeffer House, and African-American Broadway actress, Vinnie Burrows gave a presentation on African myths and histories at the Frankfurt Youth Center.[70] Eva Johnson, an Australian of the Mulak Mulak Nation, staged a one-woman show.[71] When events began in Bielefeld on August 11, Burrows performed the production "Sister Sister," which included texts and scenes on the international women's movement.[72] Bianca Tangande, a Dutch artist, opened an exhibition entitled "Images of Oneself," and New Zealand writer Cathie Dunsford read poetry.[73] The variety of excursions, workshops and activities allowed women to approach their differences creatively and showed how artistic expressions encouraged community. In Frankfurt and Bielefeld the focus was on the political, civil and social situation of female ethnic minorities and migration policies in the European Community. Berlin's events, which began on August 17, centered on the relationship between the European Community and the "Third World."[74] Emde also noted that contact with Black women minorities "offered an example of the political power of women for the future."[75] During the final session, McLaughlin claimed that, "We black women have to meet together the great challenge, the re-creation of the universe."[76]

The 1991 Institute facilitated Black German ties with feminists in Brazil, France, the United States and beyond. Kinship, emotions and feminist politics were intertwined as they had been in the past Institutes. Afro-German women continued to practice a postwar-World War II German tradition that involved establishing transatlantic solidarity and communal bonds with New Zealanders, Ghanaians, Americans and others.[77] Radical West German student activists from the 1960s, for example, created links and networks with American Students for a Democratic Society members, Black Power activists and Civil Rights leaders.[78] Likewise, West German activists had forged ties with and been influenced by foreign students at universities across the country.[79] Afro-German women witnessed the Institute advancing interpersonal connections, intersectional politics and linkages between the global and the local. Relationships with Black women activists and scholars from abroad, including Britain and the United States, served as a critical reference point for Afro-Germans as they dealt with similar struggles.

Unmediated interventions: the 1991 Resolutions

United through personal interactions and eager to make a difference nationally and globally, the delegates produced the "1991 Resolutions" to manifest their collective agency and their feminist and diasporic politics. The Resolutions emphasized "That the fundamental human, national, civil, and democratic rights of Black women and their communities have been and continue to be violated."[80] The Resolutions, moreover, exposed Black women's conditions and demonstrated that, while the women were from diverse regions, they faced analogous struggles. The Resolutions stressed "That the legacies of colonialism, feudalism and imperialism, as well as institutionalized racism, sexism and xenophobia, continue to reproduce social, economic and political inequality." For the delegates:

> the violation of our human, national, civil and democratic rights is characterized by the discrimination that we as black women experience in having limited or no access to work, education, housing, or health care because of our gender, race, color, social class, ethnicity, nationality, religion, language, political orientation and/or sexual orientation.

These Resolutions described how,

> the violence of colonialism, which resulted in the near extermination of First Nation peoples, as well as the enslavement and dislocation of Black people globally, continues to be perpetuated in the ongoing oppression and exploitation of Black women and children today.

This global history represented a cycle of subjugation that informed how some attendees and their children lived. Along these lines, participants at the Institute were ensnared in structural webs of inequality. Attendees hoped that their resolutions, nine in total, would "be implemented to eradicate the exploitation, oppression, and violence directed toward Black women and Black people in Africa, the Americas, Asia, Europe, the Middle East, and the Pacific."[81] Although these resolutions did not make a strong impact in their respective countries, they did encourage alliances, especially within Europe, among these women of color activists. The Resolutions signified how these women were agents whose unmediated interventions challenged their marginalization and served as public statements against the legacy of European colonialism and Fortress Europe. The Resolutions confirmed the participants' trust of each other despite their differences, as they used their common outrage and dissatisfaction.

Delegates pushed several related causes, including the "recognition of the links among oppressions based on gender, race, class, and sexual orientation, and other indexes of difference."[82] Moreover, the resolutions signified the interplay between the local/national and the international and Black women's internationalism in practice. Resolution #1, put forth by the IISF and entitled *by the host organization of the 1991 Cross-Cultural Black Women's Studies Summer Institute*, addressed the human rights struggles of migrants and ethnic minorities in Germany and the government's failure to prevent racial discrimination.[83] Refusing to decouple national and international issues, the IISF also highlighted parallels with other ethnic minorities. Resolution #2, entitled *on The Unification of Europe 1992*, stated that:

> the various existing European laws tend to restrict the freedom of movement of foreigners outside the (EEC) and Europeans born outside of Europe but living within the borders of the EEC are in violation of the UN Charter, the Geneva Convention on Refugees, and International Law.

For delegates, EEC countries had a "moral obligation to respect their commitments" to the rights of all human beings.[84] With Resolution #3, *on Migrants*, delegates insisted that basic human rights were "not subject to negotiation or tampering" and demanded

> that [the] countries of the European Community guarantee the inalienable rights of migrants as well as refugees to legal and political freedom, including the right to be politically and economically active, without fear of arrest, and the right to vote.

These women challenged Fortress Europe's restrictive and discriminatory policies. Additionally, the delegates observed that opportunities for asylum in Europe did not spare refugees from "common oppressions based on racism and social and economic injustice."[85]

With Resolutions 4 through 6, delegates articulated their solidarity with "Third World," Maori and South African women and attended to the issues of debt, indigenous sovereignty and Apartheid. Demanding indemnities from the First World "for all these centuries of exploitation our people [in the Third World] have been forced to bear," Resolution #4 *on External Debt*, tackled the question of "Who owes whom?" Delegates wanted wealthy northern "nations to use their resources responsibly and positively to encourage peace and human rights for global development."[86] With Resolution #5, *on Maori Sovereignty*, delegates urged the New Zealand government to honor the Treaty of Waitangi from 1840, which guaranteed the Maori Nation full and exclusive rights to lands, forests and fisheries.[87] Promoting feminist sisterhood, Resolution #6, *on Winnie Mandela and South Africa*, "opposed all attempts by the South African government and its police, courts, and media to discredit and destroy her and her work." This Resolution also discussed the abusive legacy of Apartheid and defended the "democratic principle of 'one person, one vote'" for South Africa.[88]

Honoring Black elders at the Institute, the women created an international council of women and a transatlantic friendship society that would continue to encourage generational attachments as a means of survival and resistance. With Resolution #7, *on* [the] *International Council of Elders*, delegates were again cognizant of their diversity, mentioning "First Nation, Third World, refugee, immigrant, and ethnic and national minority women." Elders from these groups would be "accorded every opportunity to attend all Institutes without incurring costs for fees and housing."[89] Resolution #8, *on Afro-German/Afro-American Friendship*, worked to establish a society between Afro-Germans and African-Americans, and thereby further expand opportunities for feminist dialogs and diasporic mobilization.

With their final Resolution #9, *on the Centre for Race and Ethnic Studies (CRES) University of Amsterdam*, delegates wrote "a formal letter to the Board of the University of Amsterdam about its decision to close the Centre for Race and Ethnic Studies (CRES)." They considered the disbanding of CRES—in existence since 1984—as unjust, especially as CRES was one of the first institutions in the Netherlands devoted to intersectional approaches to race, class, gender and sexuality.[90] Given the European climate, institutions such as CRES were invaluable spaces that supported scholarship on "issues in race and ethnic studies."[91]

While all of the resolutions dealt with aspects of feminism, community and politics, the first and eighth resolutions are significant for demonstrating that Afro-German women bore witness to and stressed the value of personal ties and feminist solidarity. Resolutions #1 and #8 affirmed Afro-German women's commitment to draw attention to their marginal positions in society and to foster empowering relationships with diverse Black feminists. In Resolution #1, the IISF drafters bemoaned that Germany:

> has been and remains a country that considers itself monocultural despite a large and growing number of various ethnic minorities, including Black Germans, and despite millions of immigrant workers, many of whom have been living in Germany for two or three generations and who are still denied basic human, civil and political rights, including the right to vote.[92]

As Resolution #1 made clear, Germany was an immigration country, where immigrants', their children's and Black Germans' political voices were ignored and silenced. The Resolution added that "nationalist and even fascist tendencies still exist and have increased since reunification, both in East and West Germany," where "open violence against visible ethnic minorities, people of

African descent in particular, have occurred."[93] Afro-German women also confronted Chancellor Kohl's conservative CDU Party and politicians from the liberal Social Democratic Party (SDP), demanding that they "put into practice existing UN resolutions against racial discrimination, grant immigrants in this country the right to vote, and actively support regional and national initiatives."[94]

With this difficult and violent situation, Afro-German women created an emotional economy in which they could establish trust and camaraderie with other Black women. As Sara Ahmed and Victoria Hesford have claimed, emotions do social and political work and in this way become political and revolutionary tools.[95] Forming emotional ties with Black participants enabled Afro-German women to advance political objectives about their marginal citizenship and to construct a new international network of women of color feminists and to publicize Afro-German experiences internationally. "Over the past three weeks," Afro-German women noted within the first resolution:

> we have had the opportunity to exchange our situations, our ideas and political views with women from all over the world, Black women and women of color from all continents, and we do hope that this will be the start of an international network against racism, sexism, and all forms of discrimination.[96]

Personal interactions gave Afro-German women renewed confidence to continue with their feminist and diasporic work. Their first resolution operated as a political, affective and performative act that situated Afro-German women within multiple activist communities of color. Similarly, with Resolution #8, Afro-German women solidified "the creation of an Afro-German/Afro-American Friendship Society."[97] By doing so, they wanted "to foster historical and cultural linkages between [the] ethnic minority of Black Germans and the Black population of the United States."[98] For Afro-German women one of "the most important results" of the Institute was the Friendship Society and the exchanges it would lead to.

The Institute and Resolutions gave Afro-Germans the courage to redefine and renegotiate their positions in society. Afro-German women emphasized this in the first resolution:

> As Black German women and Black women of other nationalities living in Germany, we have decided to make ourselves visible and to make our voices heard. This year's Institute and the ensuing documentation and publication of its contributions and results are important steps forward in this struggle for human rights and dignity.[99]

Black Germans hoped that this new visibility would guarantee that Black women's experiences would be observed, read and heard in a society that inaccurately imagined itself as white. Perhaps naively, these Afro-German women thought that their international and national visibility provided them with a political advantage and opened up possibilities for their budding Afro-German movement. Although the Institute gained coverage in several German newspapers, better introducing society to this African diasporic community, the publicity did not ensure that Afro-Germans could retain this recognition or that anti-Black racism would abate in Germany.

Conclusion

Through the 1991 Cross-Cultural Black Women's Studies Summer Institute, Afro-German women organized events and activities that enabled them to address local and global issues and engage in new forms of diasporic activism. Afro-Germans and others demanded social recognition from and participated in anti-racist and feminist projects that acknowledged the diversity of experiences of people of color in Germany and across the globe. Afro-German women, along with others, developed empowering Black spaces that helped them constitute bonds, accentuating and positioning their activism within their movements and communities. Black Germans cultivated transnational solidarity with individuals throughout Germany, the African Diaspora and the world. Moreover, the 1991 Institute also helped to mark Germany as an African diasporic space. Through this space, Black German women become visible agents who showcased the diversity of Germany and the African Diaspora. These Afro-German women and the other attendees of the Institute explicitly focused on women and gender in the African Diaspora, narratives of which have often centered on male experiences.

Afro-Germans made diasporic and feminist activism culturally relevant within their community and created opportunities to develop their voices and practice Black women's internationalism. The 1991 Institute helped Afro-Germans confront exclusion and discrimination as they continued to focus on critical issues in the everyday. The rise of conservatism across Fortress Europe, South African Apartheid and indigenous rights in New Zealand motivated Afro-Germans. These transnational developments also informed their work on local issues such as the persistence of racism in reunified Germany. Afro-German women's involvement in the Institute afforded them an opportunity to share their emotions and experiences, promote diasporic knowledge about their struggles and develop resistance strategies. Confronting multiple forms of discrimination, these Black Germans sought feminist connections to broadcast local and international dynamics and Black women's achievements. Even though Afro-German women and their movement were not always successful, these historical moments helped them carve out public diasporic spaces devoted to diversity and inclusivity. These moments also have critical relevance for today as women across the Diaspora continue to struggle for equality and justice, negotiating their places in societies that often render them insignificant.

Notes

1 Chandra Talpade Mohanty, *Feminism without Borders: Decolonizing Theory, Practicing Solidarity* (Durham, NC: Duke University Press, 2003), 7. The italics are my emphasis.

2 Ulrike Helwerth, "Black Coming out," *Die Tageszeitung*, August 25, 1991, no page number, The Private Collection of Ria Cheatom (hereafter cited as Cheatom Collection); Dora Hartmann, "Neues Europa—neuer Feminismus?: Schwarze Frauen über Rassismus und Sexismus," *Bielefelder Stadtblatt*, August 15, 1991, no page number; and "Strategien gegen den Rassismus: Frauen-Seminar über Schwarze in Europäischer Gemeinschaft," *Frankfurter Allgemeine Zeitung*, August 5, 1991, no page number, Cheatom Collection.

3 Dr Phyllis E. Jackson, "The Cross-Cultural Black Women's Studies Summer Institute: A History, 1987–1990," June 1, 1990, Box 14, p. 3, May Ayim Archive, Free University of Berlin (hereafter cited as Ayim Archive) and "'Schwarze Frauen stehen in Europa ganz am Rande': Interkulturelles Sommer-Seminar für Frauenstudien," *Frankfurter Rundschau*, August 5, 1991, no. 179, Cheatom Collection.

4 Mohanty was actually included in an earlier draft of the 1991 Institute program.

5 Interkulturelle Initiative Schwarzer Frauen für Minoritätenrechte und Studien in Deutschland, "Black World: Eine Boschüre von Schwarzen Frauen vol. 1. Ausgabe (Juli 1992), Ordentliche Jahres-Vereinsversammlung vom 31.1. bis 2.2. 1992 in Köln," p. 2, Cheatom Collection. The German text: "Für die deutschen Schwarzen Frauen war insbesondere der Kontakt zu älteren Schwarzen Frauen aller Welt auch eine wichtige persönliche Erfahrung." The terms "Afro-German" and "Black German" will be used interchangeably.

6 Hartmann, "Neues Europa—neuer Feminismus?" 7. The German text:

> Eine wesentliche Funktion des Sommerseminars ist die, ein internationales Netzwerk schwarzer Frauen aufzubauen. Auf ganz verschiedenen Ebenen sich informieren und unterstützen zu können, Zugang zu Ressourcen zu finden, Informationszentralen zu bilden, und uns über die drei Wochen hinaus die Möglichkeit zu geben, eine Institution zu schaffen die für uns noch nicht existiert.

7 Institute participants used the term "Black" regularly, often as an inclusive designation for all people of color.

8 For more on transnational feminist connections, see Judy Tzu-Chun Wu, *Radicals on the Road: Internationalism, Orientalism, and Feminism during the Vietnam Era* (Ithaca, NY: Cornell University Press, 2013); Cheryl Higashida, *Black Internationalist Feminism: Women Writers of the Black Left, 1945–1995* (Chicago, IL: University of Illinois Press, 2011); and Belinda Davis, "A Whole World Opening Up: Transcultural Contact, Difference, and the Politicization of 'New Left' Activists," in *Changing the World, Changing Oneself: Political Protest and Collective Identities in West Germany and the U.S. in the 1960s and 1970s*, eds. Belinda Davis *et al.* (New York: Berghahn Books, 2010), 255–273.

9 For information on emotional experiences, see Jakob Tanner, "Motions and Emotions," in *1968 in Europe: A History of Protest and Activism, 1956–1977*, ed. Martin Klimke *et al.* (New York: Palgrave Macmillan, 2008), 72 and 74.

10 Some Institute attendees contributed revised papers to Marion Kraft and Rukhsana Shamim Ashraf-Khan, eds. *Schwarze Frauen der Welt: Europa und Migration* (Berlin: Orlanda Frauenverlag, 1993).

11 Dawne Y. Curry, Eric D. Duke and Marshanda A. Smith, eds. *Extending the Diaspora: New Histories of Black People* (Chicago, IL: University of Illinois Press, 2009); Tina M. Campt and Deborah Thomas, eds. "Gendering Diaspora," special issue, *Feminist Review* 90(1) (2008); and Sandra Gunning, Tera Hunter and Michele Mitchell, eds. *Dialogues of Dispersal: Gender, Sexuality, and African Diasporas* (Malden, MA: Blackwell Publishing, 2004).

12 Mischa Honeck, Martin Klimke and Anne Kuhlmann, eds. *Germany and the Black Diaspora: Points of Contact, 1250–1914* (New York: Berghahn, 2013); Darlene Clark Hine, Tricia Danielle Keaton and Stephen Small, eds. *Black Europe and the African Diaspora* (Chicago, IL: University of Illinois Press, 2009).

13 Michelle M. Wright, "Middle Passage Blackness and Its Diasporic Discontents: The Case for a Postwar Epistemology," in *Africa in Europe: Studies in Transnational Practice in the Long Twentieth Century*, eds. Eve Rosenhaft and Robbie Aitken (Liverpool: Liverpool University Press, 2013), 217–233; Fatima El-Tayeb, *European Others: Queering Ethnicity in Postnational Europe* (Minneapolis, MN: University of Minnesota Press, 2011); and Tina M. Campt, *Image Matters: Archive, Photography and the African Diaspora* (Durham, NC: Duke University Press, 2012).

14 Tracy Fisher, "Transnational Black Diaspora Feminisms," in *What's Left of Blackness: Feminisms, Transracial Solidarities, and the Politics of Belonging in Britain* (New York: Palgrave Macmillan, 2012), 65–92; Kimberly Springer, *Living for the Revolution: Black Feminist Organizations, 1968–1980* (Durham, NC: Duke University Press, 2005).

15 Shelby F. Lewis, "Africana Feminism: An Alternative Paradigm for Black Women in the Academy," in *Black Women in the Academy: Promises and Perils*, ed. Lois Benjamin (Gainesville, FL: University of Florida Press, 1997), 48. Lewis argues that Africana feminism enables "a variety of global ideas and strategies [to] be subsumed."

16 Carmen Faymonville, "Black Germans and Transnational Identification," in "Reading the Black German Experience," eds. Tina M. Campt and Michelle M. Wright, special issue, *Callaloo: A Journal of African Diaspora Arts and Letters* 26(2) (2003): 367.

17 Marion Kraft, ed. *Kinder der Befreiung: Transatlantische Erfahrungen und Perspektiven Schwarzer Deutscher der Nachkriegsgeneration* (Münster: Unrast, 2015); May Opitz, Katharina Oguntoye and Dagmar Schultz, eds., trans. Anne V. Adams, *Showing Our Colors: Afro-German Women Speak Out* (Amherst, MA: University of Massachusetts Press, 1992); and Katharina Oguntoye, May Opitz/Ayim and Dagmar Schultz, eds. *Farbe bekennen: Afro-deutsche Frauen auf den Spuren ihrer Geschichte* (Berlin: Orlanda Frauenverlag, 1986).

18 See bell hooks, *Feminist Theory: From Margin to Center* (Cambridge, MA: South End Press, 2000); Cherrie Moraga and Gloria Anzaldua, eds. *This Bridge Called My Back: Writing by Radical Women of Color* (Watertown, MA: Persephone Press, 1981); and Shabnam Grewal, Jackie Kay, Liliane Landor, Gail Lewis and Pratibha Parmar, eds. *Charting the Journey: Writing by Black and Third World Women* (London: Sheba Feminist Books, 1988).

19 Rudolph P. Byrd, "Introduction: Create Your Own Fire: Audre Lorde and the Tradition of Black Radical Thought," in *I am Your Sister: Collected and Unpublished Writings of Audre Lorde*, eds. Rudolph P. Byrd, Johnnetta B. Cole and Beverly Guy-Sheftall (New York: Oxford University Press, 2009), 20; Peggy Piesche, ed. *Euer Schwiegen Schützt Euch Nicht: Audre Lorde und die Schwarze Frauenbewegung in Deutschland* (Berlin: Orlanda Frauenverlag, 2012).

20 Lorde coined "connected differences" to illustrate this point. See "Revolutionary Hope: A Conversation Between James Baldwin and Audre Lorde," *Essence* 15(8) (December 1984), 73–74, 129–130, and 133; Alexis De Veaux, *Warrior Poet: A Biography of Audre Lorde* (New York: W. W. Norton & Company, 2004), 330–332.

21 "Reading at BAZ (Berliner Aktions Zentrum of People of Color)," July 1984, vol. 10, p. 11, Audre Lorde Archive, Free University of Berlin (hereafter cited as Lorde Archive). White West German feminist Dagmar Schultz invited Lorde to teach at the Free University in 1984. See also Tiffany N. Florvil, "Emotional Connections: Audre Lorde and Black German Women," in *Audre Lorde's Transnational Legacies*, eds. Stella Bolaki and Sabine Broeck (Amherst, MA: University of Massachusetts Press, 2015), 135–147.

22 Audre Lorde, "A Burst of Light: Living with Cancer," in *I am Your Sister: Collected and Unpublished Writings of Audre Lorde*, ed. Rudolph P. Byrd *et al.* (New York: Oxford University Press, 2009), 129.

23 The organization has been spelled both as SISA and SISSA. I follow the spelling of Alexis de Veaux, Lorde's biographer. De Veaux, *Warrior Poet*, 279–280; Johnnetta Betsch Cole, "Audre Lorde: My Shero, My Teacher, My Friend," *I am Your* Sister, 232; "Reading at the Schoko Fabrik," November 20, 1987, vol. 12, pp. 3–4, Lorde Archive; and Cheryl Higashida, "Audre Lorde Revisited: Nationalism and Second-Wave Black Feminism," in *Black Internationalist Feminism: Women Writers of the Black Left, 1945–1995* (Chicago, IL: University of Illinois Press, 2011), 139.

24 See also Neil MacMaster, *Racism in Europe, 1870–2000* (New York: Palgrave, 2001), 190–224; May Ayim, "The Year 1990: Homeland and Unity from an Afro-German Perspective," in *Fringe Voices: An Anthology of Minority Writing in the Federal Republic of Germany*, eds. Antje Harnisch *et al.* (Oxford and New York: Berg, 1998), 105–119.

25 Rita Chin, *The Guest Worker Question in Postwar Germany* (Cambridge, UK: Cambridge University Press, 2007), 141–142.

26 Eleonore Wiedenroth-Coulibaly and Sascha Zinflou, "20 Jahre Schwarze Organisierung in Deutschland—Ein Abriss," in *The Black Book: Deutschlands Häutungen*, eds. AntiDiskrimierungs Büro (ADB) Köln and cyberNomads (Frankfurt am Main and London: IKO-Verlag für Interkulturelle Komminkation, 2004), 142.

27 Hermann Kurthen, Werner Bergmann and Rainer Erb, eds. *Antisemitism and Xenophobia in Germany After Unification* (New York and Oxford: Oxford University Press, 1997).

28 See Jutta M. Joachim, *Agenda Setting, the UN, and NGOs: Gender Violence and Reproductive Rights* (Washington, DC: Georgetown University Press, 2007), 74; Lois A. West, "The United States Women's Conferences and Feminist Politics," in *Gender Politics in Global Governance*, eds. Mary K. Meyer and Elisabeth Prügl (New York: Lanham, Rowman & Littlefield, 1999), 177–194; and Andrée Nicola McLaughlin, "Third Annual Cross-Cultural Black Women's Studies Summer Institute: Harare, Zimbabwe," *Sage: A Scholarly Journal on Black Women* 6(1) (1989): 80.

29 Erik S. McDuffie, " 'For Full Freedom of … Colored Women in Africa, Asia, and in These United States …': Black Women Radicals and the Practice of a Black Women's International," *Palimpsest: A Journal of Women, Gender, and the Black International* 1(1) (2012): 1–30; Keisha N. Blain, " '[F]or the Rights of Dark People in Every Part of the World': Pearl Sherrod, Black Internationalist Feminism, and Afro-Asian Politics during the 1930s," *Souls* 17(1–2) (January–June 2015): 90–112; and Keisha N. Blain and Tiffany Gill, eds. *To Turn this Whole World Over: Black Women's Internationalism during the Twentieth Century* (University of Illinois Press, forthcoming).

30 Stanlie M. James, Frances Smith Foster and Beverly Guy-Sheftall, eds. *Still Brave: The Evolution of Black Women's Studies* (New York: Feminist Press at CUNY, 2009), 18; Lewis, "Africana Feminism," 48.

31 Cross-Cultural Black Women's Studies Summer Institute, "Applicant Information," 1989, Box 14, no page number, Ayim Archive.

32 Lewis, "Africana Feminism," 48.

33 McLaughlin, "Third Annual Cross-Cultural Black Women's Studies Summer Institute," 80.

34 Ibid., 80.

35 Interkulturelle Initiative Schwarzer Frauen für die Entwicklung von Minoritätenrechte und -Studien in Deutschland, "5. Interkulturelles Sommer Seminar für Schwarze Frauen-Studien," 1990, Box 14, no page number, Ayim Archive.

36 Andrée Nicola McLaughlin, "International, Cross-Cultural Black Women's Studies Summer Institute: Letter and 1991 Resolutions," January 16, 1992, Box 52, p. 3, Audre Lorde Papers, Spelman College Archives (hereafter cited as Lorde Papers). Delegates were from 27 countries.

37 See also Michelle M. Wright, *Becoming Black: Creating Identity in the African Diaspora* (Durham, NC: Duke University Press, 2004); Heidi Safia Mirza, ed. *Black British Feminism: A Reader* (New York: Routledge, 1997), 255–268; and Lena Sawyer, "Engendering 'Race' in Calls for Diasporic Community in Sweden," in eds. Campt and Thomas, "Gendering Diaspora," special issue, *Feminist Review* 90(1) (2008): 87–105.

38 Interkulturelle Initiative Schwarzer Frauen für Minoritätenrechte und Studien in Deutschland, e.V. and Nozizwe: Projekt für multikulturelle feministisches Bildungsarbeit (Berlin), *Fünftes Interkulturelles Sommer-Seminar Für Schwarze Frauen-Studien Information-Programm-Ausschreibung*, August 1991, p. 4, Cheatom Collection; Cross-Cultural Black Women's Studies Summer Institute, "21st Anniversary Celebration," 6; and McLaughlin, 80.

39 Anjuli Gupta, "Überlegungen zum 'Cross-Cultural Black Womans's [*sic*] Summer Institute," *Afrekete: Zeitung von afro-deutschen und schwarzen Frauen (schwarzer Feminismus)* 2(3) (1988): 11, The Central Library of Women's and Gender Studies, Hamburg (hereafter cited as Library of Gender Studies).

40 Gupta, "Überlegungen zum 'Cross-Cultural Black Womans's [*sic*] Summer Institute," 11–12, Library of Gender Studies.

41 Ibid., 12. The German text: "der Austausch hat mir viel Energie gegeben, mich mit vielen neuen Ideen angeregt und zum 'weiterkämpfen' ermutigt."

42 Ibid., 11 and 12. As Opitz began to publish poetry, she changed her name to May Ayim, although not legally.

43 Ibid., 11. There were some Spanish and Portuguese translators available.

44 Interkulturelle Initiative Schwarzer Frauen für Minoritätenrechte und Studien in Deutschland and Nozizwe, *Fünftes Interkulturelles Sommer-Seminar Für Schwarze Frauen-Studien*, 4 and Cross-Cultural Black Women's Studies Summer Institute, "21st Anniversary Celebration," 6.

45 Cross-Cultural Black Women's Studies Summer Institute, "Applicant Information," 1989, no page number.

46 Marion Kraft letter to Audre Lorde, September 21, 1989, Box 3, p. 2, Lorde Papers.

47 Kraft letter to Lorde, September 21, 1989, 2.

48 Appendix A: Preliminary Report on the Aotearoa Institute, 1991, Box 14, p. 15, Ayim Archive.

49 The Pacific Women's Network, formed in 1994, sponsored the 1995 Institute in Hawaii. This conference predated the United Nations Women's International Conference held in Beijing in September 1995. See Robert H. Mast and Anne B. Mast, *Autobiography of Protest in Hawai'i* (University of Hawai'i Press, 1996), 232.

50 Kraft attended the 2006 Institute in Panama and reunited with McLaughlin, Lily Golden and Khosi Mbatha, individuals from the 1991 Institute.

51 Women of color activists in Germany organized several conferences that tackled racism and anti-Semitism, including *Wege zu Bündnissen* on June 8–10, 1990 in Bremen; the second national congress for immigrant, Jewish and Black German women on October 3–6, 1991 in Berlin; and *Feminism between Racism, Ignorance, and Marginalization* on October 5–8, 1990 in Frankfurt.

52 "Sommerseminar für Schwarze-Frauen-Studien," *Frankfurter Rundschau*, no page number July 27, 1991.

53 McLaughlin, "Cross-Cultural Institute Letter and 1991 Resolutions," January 16, 1992, 1.

54 Interkulturelle Initiative Schwarzer Frauen für Minoritätenrechte und Studien in Deutschland and Nozizwe, *Fünftes Interkulturelles Sommer-Seminar Für Schwarze Frauen-Studien*, 2–3 and Helwerth, "Black Coming Out," *Die Tageszeitung*, August 25, 1991. Some members included Ria Cheatom, Jasmin Eding, Judy Gummich, Ika Hügel-Marshall, Bärbel Kampmann, Shelia Mysorekar, May Opitz, Ina Röder, Modupe Laja and Eleonore Wiedenroth.

55 Marion Kraft (IISF) letter, January 2, 1991, Box 20, no page number, Ayim Archive.
56 Marion Kraft, "Cross-Cultural Sisterhood: Audre Lorde's Living Legacy in Germany," *The Feminist Wire*, February 20, 2014 http://thefeministwire.com/2014/02/cross-cultural-sisterhood-audre-lordes-living-legacy-in-germany-2/#_edn6 [accessed February 20, 2014].
57 McLaughlin, "Cross-Cultural Institute Letter and 1991 Resolutions," 2.
58 Ibid., 1.
59 Ulrike Baureitbel, "Das Universum neu schaffen."
60 "Strategien gegen den Rassismus," *Frankfurter Allgemeine Zeitung*. The German text: "Die 'deutschen Schwarze' sind nach Einschätzung ihrer afrikanischen und amerikanischen 'Schwestern' zwar wohlhabender und gebildeter, aber auch isolierter und einsamer als Minderheiten in anderen Staaten."
61 Tina M. Campt, "The Crowded Space of Diaspora: Intercultural Address and the Tensions of Diasporic Relation," in "Citizenship, National Identity, Race, and Diaspora in Contemporary Europe," ed. Ian Christopher Fletcher, special issue, *Radical History Review* 83 (2002): 102.
62 Heide Platen, "Schwarze Frauen analysieren Europa," *Die Tageszeitung*, August 5, 1991, no page number.
63 Interkulturelle Initiative Schwarzer Frauen für die Entwicklung von Minoritätenrechte und -Studien in Deutschland, "5. Interkulturelles Sommer Seminar für Schwarze Frauen-Studien."
64 Fifth Annual Cross-Cultural Black Women's Studies Summer Institute, "Focus: Black People and the European Community," Box 14, no page number, Ayim Archive.
65 Hartmann, 7. The German text:

   Das andere ist: Unser Thema heißt zwar "Schwarze Menschen und europäische Gemeinschaft". Aber es nehmen ja sehr viele Frauen auch aus Ländern der sogenannten Dritten Welt teil. Diese Frauen haben ganz andere Probleme als wir in den westeuropäischen Ländern. Wir leben in Ländern, die an der Ausbeutung der Drittweltländer unmittelbar beteiligt sind. Da ein Netzwerk zu schaffen bis dahin, gemeinsame konkrete Forderungen an die UN und die einzelnen Länder zu formulieren, das ist das Entscheidende, was wir mit solchen Veranstaltungen machen können.

66 Helwerth, "Black Coming Out." The German text: "Sie solle ihre schmutzigen Finger da wegnehmen, bekam eine Südafrikanerin am Buchstand in der Uni zu hören. Kinderbetreuerinnen kamen heulend zurück vom Spielplatz, weil ihre Schützlinge dort mit 'Hau ab, du Nigger' von AltergenossInnen begrüßt worden waren."
67 Interkulturelle Initiative Schwarzer Frauen für Minoritätenrechte und Studien in Deutschland, "Black World," 2. The German text: "Am problematischsten erwies sich jedoch an vielen Punkten die Teilnahme weißer Frauen."
68 Ibid., 2. The German text: "Das es trotz dieser Differenzen nach drei Wochen intensiver Arbeit zu einem erfolgreichen Abschluß kam, wurde als positiv eingeschätzt."
69 "Über die Identität der Schwarzen: Sommer-Seminar für Frauen mit internationalen Gästen," *Frankfurter Allgemeine Zeitung*, July 30, 1991, no page number, Cheatom Collection.
70 "Über die Identität der Schwarzen," *Frankfurter Allgemeine Zeitung*.
71 Ibid.
72 "'Schwarze-Frauen-Studien' Sommerseminar am OS-Kolleg," *Neue Westfälische*, July 26, 1991, no page number, Cheatom Collection.
73 Ibid. and "Schwarze Frauen-Studien," *Bielefelder Stadtblatt*, August 1, 1991, no page number, Cheatom Collection.
74 Baureitbel, "Das Universum neu schaffen."
75 "'Schwarze Frauen stehen in Europa ganz am Rande'" *Frankfurter Rundschau*. The German text:

> Bis zum 23. August warden sich die rund 80 Teilnehmerinnen in Frankfurt, Bielefeld und Berlin vor allem mit dem Umgang mit schwarzen Minderheiten auf dem europäischen Kontinent beschäftigen, um "durch die politische Kraft der Frauen für die Zukunft ein Zeichen zu setzen" betonte Helga Emde.

76 Helwerth, "Black Coming out." The German text: "Wir schwarze Frauen müssen uns gemeinsam der großen Herausforderung stellen, der Neuschaffung des Universums."

77 This is not to suggest that transatlantic developments did not occur in the eighteenth, nineteenth, or early twentieth centuries. See also Honeck, Klimke and Kuhlmann, eds. *Germany and the Black Diaspora*; Peter Martin and Christine Alonzo, eds. *Zwischen Charleston und Stechschritt: Schwarze im Nationalsozialismus* (Cologne: Dölling und Galitz Verlag, 2004); and Larry A. Greene and Anke Ortlepp, eds. *Germans and African Americans: Two Centuries of Exchange* (Oxford, MS: University Press of Mississippi, 2011).

78 See also Martin Klimke, *The Other Alliance: Student Protest in West Germany and the United States in the Global Sixties* (Princeton, NJ: Princeton University Press, 2010); Katharina Gerund, "Visions of (Global) Sisterhood and Black Solidarity: Audre Lorde," in *Transatlantic Cultural Exchange: African American Women's Art and Activism in West Germany*, 157–210 (Bielefeld: Transcript Verlag, 2013).

79 Klimke, *The Other Alliance*, 56–57 and 66; Davis, "A Whole World Opening Up," 255–273; and Quinn Slobodian, *Foreign Front: Third World Politics in Sixties Germany* (Durham, NC: Duke University Press, 2012), 13, 51, 61, 63–76, 95.

80 International, Cross-Cultural Black Women's Studies Summer Institute, "1991 Resolutions," 3, Lorde Papers.

81 International, Cross-Cultural Institute, "1991 Resolutions," 3.

82 Ibid., 3.

83 Ibid., 4.

84 Ibid., 5.

85 Ibid., 6.

86 Ibid., 7.

87 Ibid., 8.

88 Ibid., 9.

89 Ibid., 10.

90 Ibid., 12. See also Kwame Nimako, "About Them, But Without Them: Race and Ethnic Relations Studies in Dutch Universities," *Human Architecture: Journal of the Sociology of Self-Knowledge* 10(1) (2012), 46.

91 Nimako, "About Them, But Without Them," 47.

92 International, Cross-Cultural Institute, 4.

93 Ibid., 4. This ongoing aggression resulted in "racist murder[s]." See also Wiedenroth-Coulibaly and Zinflou, "20 Jahre Schwarze Organisierung in Deutschland," 142.

94 International, Cross-Cultural Institute, 4.

95 See Sara Ahmed, *The Cultural Practice of Emotions* (New York: Routledge, 2004) and Victoria Hesford, *Feeling Women's Liberation* (Durham, NC: Duke University Press, 2013).

96 International, Cross-Cultural Institute, 4.

97 Interkulturelle Initiative Schwarzer Frauen für Minoritätenrechte und Studien in Deutschland, 2. The German text: "Zu den wichtigsten Ergebnissen zählt die Gründung einer Afro-deutschen-Afro-amerikanischen Freundschaftsgesellschaft (Kontaktpersonen sind Dimitria Clayton und Andree Nicola McLaughlin)."

98 International, Cross-Cultural Institute, 11.

99 Ibid., 4.

Bibliography

Published sources

Ahmed, Sara. *The Cultural Practice of Emotions*. New York: Routledge, 2004.

Ayim, May. "The Year 1990: Homeland and Unity from an Afro-German Perspective," in *Fringe Voices: An Anthology of Minority Writing in the Federal Republic of Germany*, edited by Antje Harnisch, Anne-Marie Stokes and Friedemann Weidauer, 105–119. Oxford and New York: Berg, 1998.

Blain, Keisha N. "'[F]or the Rights of Dark People in Every Part of the World': Pearl Sherrod, Black Internationalist Feminism, and Afro-Asian Politics during the 1930s," *Souls* 17(1–2) (January–June 2015): 90–112.

Blain, Keisha N., and Tiffany Gill, eds. *To Turn this Whole World Over: Black Women's Internationalism during the Twentieth Century* (University of Illinois Press, forthcoming).

Broeck, Sabine, and Stella Bolaki, eds. *Audre Lorde's Transnational Legacies*. Amherst, MA: University of Massachusetts Press, 2015.

Byrd, Rudolph P. "Introduction: Create Your Own Fire: Audre Lorde and the Tradition of Black Radical Thought," in *I am Your Sister: Collected and Unpublished Writings of Audre Lorde*, edited by Rudolph P. Byrd, Johnnetta B. Cole and Beverly Guy-Sheftall, 3–36. New York: Oxford University Press, 2009.

Campt, Tina M. "The Crowded Space of Diaspora: Intercultural Address and the Tensions of Diasporic Relation," in "Citizenship, National Identity, Race, and Diaspora in Contemporary Europe," edited by Ian Christopher Fletcher. Special Issue, *Radical History Review* 83 (2002): 94–113.

Campt, Tina M. *Image Matters: Archive, Photography and the African Diaspora*. Durham, NC: Duke University Press, 2012.

Campt, Tina M. and Deborah Thomas, eds. "Gendering Diaspora." Special Issue, *Feminist Review* 90(1) (2008): 1–8.

Chin, Rita. *The Guest Worker Question in Postwar Germany*. Cambridge, UK: Cambridge University Press, 2007.

Cole, Johnnetta Betsch. "Audre Lorde: My Shero, My Teacher, My Friend" in *I am Your Sister: Collected and Unpublished Writings of Audre Lorde*, edited by Rudolph P. Byrd, Johnnetta Betsch Cole and Bevery Guy-Sheftall, 231–237. New York: Oxford University Press, 2009.

Curry, Dawne Y., Eric D. Duke and Marshanda A. Smith, eds. *Extending the Diaspora: New Histories of Black People*. Chicago, IL: University of Illinois Press, 2009.

Davis, Belinda. "A Whole World Opening Up: Transcultural Contact, Difference, and the Politicization of 'New Left' Activists," in *Changing the World, Changing Oneself: Political Protest and Collective Identities in West Germany and the U.S. in the 1960s and 1970s*, edited by Belinda Davis, Wilfred Mausbach, Martin Klimke and Carla MacDougall, 255–273. New York: Berghahn Books, 2010.

De Veaux, Alexis. *Warrior Poet: A Biography of Audre Lorde*. New York: W. W. Norton & Company, 2004.

El-Tayeb, Fatima. *European Others: Queering Ethnicity in Postnational Europe*. Minneapolis, MN: University of Minnesota Press, 2011.

Faymonville, Carmen. "Black Germans and Transnational Identification," in "Reading the Black German Experience," edited by Tina M. Campt and Michelle M. Wright. Special Issue, *Callaloo: A Journal of African Diaspora Arts and Letters* 26(2) (2003): 364–382.

Fisher, Tracy. "Transnational Black Diaspora Feminisms" in Tracy Fisher, *What's Left of Blackness: Feminisms, Transracial Solidarities, and the Politics of Belonging in Britain*, 65–92. New York: Palgrave Macmillan, 2012.

Florvil, Tiffany N. "Emotional Connections: Audre Lorde and Black German Women," in *Audre Lorde's Transnational Legacies*, edited by Stella Bolaki and Sabine Broeck, 135–147. Amherst, MA: University of Massachusetts Press, 2015.

Gerund, Katharina. "Visions of (Global) Sisterhood and Black Solidarity: Audre Lorde," in Katharine Gerund, *Transatlantic Cultural Exchange: African American Women's Art and Activism in West Germany*, 157–210. Bielefeld: Transcript Verlag, 2013.

Greene, Larry A. and Anke Ortlepp, eds. *Germans and African Americans: Two Centuries of Exchange*. Oxford, MS: University Press of Mississippi, 2011.

Grewal, Shabnam, Jackie Kay, Liliane Landor, Gail Lewis and Pratibha Parmar, eds. *Charting the Journey: Writing by Black and Third World Women*. London: Sheba Feminist Books, 1988.

Gunning, Sandra, Tera Hunter and Michele Mitchell, eds. *Dialogues of Dispersal: Gender, Sexuality, and African Diasporas*. Malden, MA: Blackwell Publishing, 2004.

Hesford, Victoria. *Feeling Women's Liberation*. Durham, NC: Duke University Press, 2013.

Higashida, Cheryl. "Audre Lorde Revisted: Nationalism and Second-Wave Black Feminism," in Cheryl Higashida, *Black Internationalist Feminism: Women Writers of the Black Left, 1945–1995*, 134–157. Chicago, IL: University of Illinois Press, 2011.

Hine, Darlene Clark, Trica Danielle Keaton and Stephen Small, eds. *Black Europe and the African Diaspora*. Chicago, IL: University of Illinois Press, 2009.

Honeck, Mischa, Martin Klimke and Anne Kuhlmann, eds. *Germany and the Black Diaspora: Points of Contact, 1250–1914*. New York: Berghahn Books, 2013.

hooks, bell. *Feminist Theory: From Margin to Center*. Cambridge, MA: South End Press, 2000.

James, Stanlie M., Frances Smith Foster and Beverly Guy-Sheftall, eds. *Still Brave: The Evolution of Black Women's Studies*. New York: Feminist Press at CUNY, 2009.

Joachim, Jutta M. *Agenda Setting, the UN, and NGOs: Gender Violence and Reproductive Rights*. Washington, DC: Georgetown University Press, 2007.

Klimke, Martin. *The Other Alliance: Student Protest in West Germany and the United States in the Global Sixties*. Princeton, NJ: Princeton University Press, 2010.

Kraft, Marion. "Cross-Cultural Sisterhood: Audre Lorde's Living Legacy in Germany," *The Feminist Wire*, February 20, 2014. http://thefeministwire.com/2014/02/cross-cultural-sisterhood-audre-lordes-living-legacy-in-germany-2/#_edn6 [accessed February 20, 2014].

Kraft, Marion, ed. *Kinder der Befreiung: Transatlantische Erfahrungen und Perspektiven Schwarzer Deutscher der Nachkriegsgeneration*. Münster: Unrast, 2015.

Kraft, Marion and Rukhsana Shamim Ashraf-Khan, eds. *Schwarze Frauen der Welt: Europa und Migration*. Berlin: Orlanda Frauenverlag, 1993.

Kurthen, Hermann, Werner Bergmann and Rainer Erb, eds. *Antisemitism and Xenophobia in Germany After Unification*. New York and Oxford: Oxford University Press, 1997.

Lewis, Shelby F. "Africana Feminism: An Alternative Paradigm for Black Women in the Academy," in *Black Women in the Academy: Promises and Perils*, edited by Lois Benjamin, 41–52. Gainesville, FL: University of Florida Press, 1997.

Lorde, Audre. "A Burst of Light: Living with Cancer," in *I am Your Sister: Collected and Unpublished Writings of Audre Lorde*, edited by Rudolph P. Byrd, Johneta Betsch Cole and Beverly Guy-Sheftall, 81–149. New York: Oxford University Press, 2009.

MacMaster, Neil. *Racism in Europe, 1870–2000*. New York: Palgrave, 2001.

Martin, Peter, and Christine Alonzo, eds. *Zwischen Charleston und Stechschritt: Schwarze im Nationalsozialismus*. Cologne: Dölling und Galitz Verlag, 2004.

Mast, Robert H., and Anne B. Mast, *Autobiography of Protest in Hawai'i*. Honolulu, HI: University of Hawai'i Press, 1996.

McDuffie, Erik S. " 'For Full Freedom of … Colored Women in Africa, Asia, and in These United States …": Black Women Radicals and the Practice of a Black Women's International," *Palimpsest: A Journal of Women, Gender, and the Black International* 1(1) (2012): 1–30.

McLaughlin, Andrée Nicola. "Third Annual Cross-Cultural Black Women's Studies Summer Institute: Harare, Zimbabwe," *Sage: A Scholarly Journal on Black Women* 6(1) (1989): 80.

Mirza, Heidi Safia, ed. *Black British Feminism: A Reader*. New York: Routledge, 1997.

Mohanty, Chandra Talpade. *Feminism without Borders: Decolonizing Theory, Practicing Solidarity*. Durham, NC: Duke University Press, 2003.

Moraga, Cherrie and Gloria Anzaldua, eds. *This Bridge Called My Back: Writing by Radical Women of Color*. Watertown, MA: Persephone Press, 1981.

Nimako, Kwame. "About Them, But Without Them: Race and Ethnic Relations Studies in Dutch Universities," *Human Architecture: Journal of the Sociology of Self-Knowledge* 10(1) (2012): 42–56.

Oguntoye, Katharina, May Opitz/Ayim and Dagmar Schultz, eds. *Farbe bekennen: Afro-deutsche Frauen auf den Spuren ihrer Geschichte*. Berlin: Orlanda Frauen-verlag, 2006.

Opitz, May, Katharina Oguntoye and Dagmar Schultz, eds., trans. Anne V. Adams, *Showing Our Colors: Afro-German Women Speak Out*. Amhers, MA: University of Massachusetts Press, 1992.

Piesche, Peggy, ed. *Euer Schwiegen Schützt Euch Nicht: Audre Lorde und die Schwarze Frauenbewegung in Deutschland*. Berlin: Orlanda Frauenverlag, 2012.

"Revolutionary Hope: A Conversation Between James Baldwin and Audre Lorde," *Essence* 15(8) (December 1984).

Sawyer, Lena. "Engendering 'Race' in Calls for Diasporic Community in Sweden," in Tina Campt and Deborah A. Thomas, eds. "Gendering Diaspora." Special Issue, *Feminist Review* 90(1) (2008): 87–105.

Slobodian, Quinn. *Foreign Front: Third World Politics in Sixties Germany*. Durham, NC: Duke University Press, 2012.

Springer, Kimberly. *Living for the Revolution: Black Feminist Organizations, 1968–1980*. Durham, NC: Duke University Press, 2005.

Tanner, Jakob. "Motions and Emotions," in *1968 in Europe: A History of Protest and Activism, 1956–1977*, edited by Martin Klimke and Joachim Scharloth, 71–80. New York: Palgrave Macmillan, 2008.

West, Lois A. "The United States Women's Conferences and Feminist Politics," in *Gender Politics in Global Governance*, edited by Mary K. Meyer and Elisabeth Prügl, 177–194. New York: Lanham, Rowman & Littlefield, 1999.

Wiedenroth-Coulibaly, Eleonore, and Sascha Zinflou. "20 Jahre Schwarze Organisierung in Deutschland—Ein Abriss," in *The Black Book: Deutschlands Häutungen*, eds. Anti-Diskrimierungs Büro (ADB) Köln and cyberNomads, 133–144. Frankfurt am Main and London: IKO-Verlag für Interkulturelle Kommkation, 2004.

Wright, Michelle M. *Becoming Black: Creating Identity in the African Diaspora*. Durham, NC: Duke University Press, 2004.

Wright, Michelle M. "Middle Passage Blackness and Its Diasporic Discontents: The Case for a Postwar Epistemology," in *Africa in Europe: Studies in Transnational Practice in the Long Twentieth Century*, edited by Eve Rosenhaft and Robbie Aitken, 217–233. Liverpool: Liverpool University Press, 2013.

Wu, Judy Tzu-Chun. *Radicals on the Road: Internationalism, Orientalism, and Feminism during the Vietnam Era*. Ithaca, NY: Cornell University Press, 2013.

Newspapers

Afrekete: Zeitung von afro-deutschen und schwarzen Frauen
Bielefelder Stadtblatt
Die Tageszeitung (taz)
Essence
Feminist Wire
Frankfurter Allgemeine Zeitung
Frankfurter Rundschau
Neue Westfälische

Film

Audre Lorde: The Berlin Years, 1984–1992, directed by Dagmar Schultz (New York: Third World Newsreel, 2012), DVD.

5   Beyond disability

The Trans-Atlantic Slave Trade and female heroism in Manu Herbstein's *Ama*

Senayon Olaoluwa

Introduction

Manu Herbstein's first novel, *Ama: A Story of the Atlantic Slave Trade*, was one of the novels from Africa to launch the twenty-first century.[1] It problematizes the history of slavery by transcending the critique of race and racism. Part of the novel's virtue consists in representing the discourse of the Trans-Atlantic Slave Trade as transcendental of space and the dialectic of freedom and bondage. While, generally, victimhood is constructed in terms of the travails of black slaves, *Ama* provides a more critical perspective on this privileged assumption in the very sense in which it shows the multiple ways in which black female slaves suffered dehumanization within the context of slavery from space to space. In spite of the physical and metaphoric tropes of disability by which female slaves are defined in the novel, the various efforts of subversion and survival against patriarchal structures are extraordinary. The efforts reinforce the assertion that the history of resistance to slavery cannot be fully accounted for without mainstreaming the role of women.

There is an understanding that African historical subjugation by Western imperial and capitalist machination substantially accounts for the metaphor of disability by which the continent is defined today. This is particularly so with respect to issues of African development in comparison with the rest of the world. An appreciable number of African scholars in the social sciences and humanities have interrogated the contemporary African predicament from this angle of slavery. However, the tendency, more often than not, is to give centrality to African masculinity in the narrative and celebrate the resilience and resistance of the African man as an allegorical resistance of Africa herself. Instances of this abound from the various slave narratives of Africans in the Americas to the space-based critical and creative reflections of other Africans. The marginalization of the African woman in this reinvention of history is, perhaps, due to the fact that many subscribe to the notion that oppression and imperialism have often been "semanticized" along sexual lines by constructing power in masculinity.[2] It may also be because there is a tendency to cast the female body in a mould that is analogous to disability—the reason whereby it is excluded "from participation in public and economic life" and at worst, "defined in opposition to a norm that is assumed to possess natural physical superiority."[3]

Generally, disability studies in the literary context adopt multiple paradigms in the unpacking of this complex discourse. One approach may be to centralize physical disability, which is understood to require remediation for narrative and curative resolution of both physical and social contradictions. In this sense, disability is aligned with loss and failure and a resilient affirmation of both against a dominant social order so as to forge an alternative to otherwise hegemonic ways of living.[4] At another level, disability in literature describes impairment and inadequacy at the level of cognition.[5] Such assumption finds further reinforcement in the sense we make of language and linguistic performance generally, such as when Berger draws a distinction between "dysarticulate" and "disarticulate" to explain the point about language disruption.[6] According to Lennard Davis,

> That distinction made is between dysarticulate as an interruption in language (ambiguously defined as either or both the inarticulate character in a literary work and the problematics of language itself in the postmodern world) and disarticulate as the interruption in a system of meaning and control.[7]

It is particularly instructive to pay attention to the extended illustration of "disarticulate" as designating the "postmodernist complications of Enlightenment thought or critiques of neoliberalism and globalism (disarticulate)."[8] In this instance, it is important to note the resonance such interpretation has for an African and global experience like the Trans-Atlantic Slave Trade, which evolved and lasted as a consequence of the Enlightenment, which produced a global order that has since continued to set the tone for the discrimination between the able and the disabled racial and spatial categories. Besides the cognitive and the metaphoric, engagement with physical disability may resonate with empowerment as a form of remediation. Such, for instance, may involve that anticipation of a future in which the disabled are empowered by technology, as captured in McCaffrey's *The Ship Who Sang*.[9] We also take seriously in this chapter Davis' contention that in the evolution of the novel "plot functions in the novel … by temporarily deforming or disabling the fantasy of nation, social class, and gender behaviors that are constructed as norms."[10] The question may then be asked, what resonances do all these imports of disability have to an understanding of its representation in *Ama*, with regard to the Trans-Atlantic Slave Trade, gender and disability?

Recent creative enterprise in African literature, especially in the twenty-first century, has continually challenged the biased notion against the place of women in the resistance to the Trans-Atlantic Slave Trade. Authors do so by centralizing the invaluable heroism of femaleness in the anti-slavery struggle.[11] *Ama* comes in a long list of twenty-first-century novels on the Trans-Atlantic Slave Trade. It distinguishes itself in the very fact that it centralizes female heroism, as embodied by Ama, the eponymous character. Two other works that immediately come to mind in reinforcing the heroism of women in the centuries of the obnoxious trade and which have received global critical acclaim similar to *Ama*'s are Yvette

Christiansë's *Unconfessed* (2007)[12] and Andrea Levy's *The Long Song* (2010).[13] While the former engages the history of slavery in the Southern African region through the repeated suffering and resistance of Sila in the hands of white slave masters, the latter critiques post-emancipation rhetoric by ascribing agency to slaves rather than the white Abolitionist. Central to the narrative of *The Long Song* is the singular subjectivity of Miss July, "a slave born on the ironically named Amity Sugar Plantation."[14] This accounts for why this chapter explores *Ama: A Story of the Atlantic Slave Trade*, a Commonwealth Prize winner, from the angle of the unparalleled heroism of Ama, the central female slave-character of the novel.

A journey toward disability

Literature on the Trans-Atlantic Slave Trade has done much to engage with the obnoxious trade and its negative impact on Africa and African peoples, both on the continent and in the Diaspora.[15] Herbstein's *Ama* is worth examining because of the centrality it accords women's resistance in the context of the Trans-Atlantic Slave Trade. Beginning with the central character, Ama, the odds that are up against her are hugely intimidating. The oppressive order of slavery into which she is led as a teenager has actually been foreshadowed in the cultural imposition of a suitor on her by patriarchal tradition. Therefore, for Nandzi, as she is called in the early unfurling of the narrative, the task of liberation from a male-dominated essence of living is the battle of her life. Whether while still a free-born in her father's house in Bekpokpam, Ghana, or from the time she is captured by Bedagbam raiders, the oppressive order of patriarchy remains a force to consistently contend with. In a sense, it is arguable that by weaving a story that is not only about resistance to slavery, but also one which seeks an interrogation of African male chauvinism which denies young women's right to marry men of their choice, Herbstein's novel harks back to the memory of Walters' late nineteenth century West African novel *Guanya Pau: A Story of an African Princess* (1891).[16] Nandzi's resistance to this sexist order is thus analogous to Guanya's response of escape in the pioneer African novel.

But the question then is how does she intend to stand out in this kind of battle of resistance? The question is pertinent in view of Baudrillard's contention that there is a constant threat of the phallic order to women's lives. Besides, within the context of women's struggles for liberation, "the danger … for the female is that she will be enclosed within a structure that condemns her to either discrimination when the structure is strong, or a derisory triumph within a weakened structure."[17] From the foregoing, the challenge before Ama is how to rise above the assumption that it is natural for women to exist in the shadows of men. Or that where it has become absolutely necessary to be heard, it has to be through the smoke screen of or with relation to men. Related to the above is the implication of male desire in the context of the female body: whether for marriage against her wish or for slavery which is also against her wish. Needless to say, in view of the spatial transition that characterizes the text for obvious reasons,

Ama's challenge is how to resist the patriarchal order that seeks to place her under slavery of a metaphoric kind where her body is desired across spaces by men across racial borders. She is also faced with the challenge of a capitalist order by which her right to self-determination is withdrawn as a result of her sale into chattel slavery. This brings the discussion into the ambience of body theory with respect to the female. According to Davis,[18] while it is important to note that "the female body is the object of processes of domination and control ... [it is also] the site of women's subversive practices and struggles for self-determination and empowerment." In other words, the phallocentric structure, both literal and metaphorical, of slavery already places some kind of social and economic disability upon her. Yet her heroism, as well as that of other female characters as will be seen shortly, lies in the ability to rise above the impediments.

Ama's earliest expression of the desire to be empowered and free is found in her efforts to confront the prescription of tradition with respect to the restriction it places on women, right from their formative years. Her resistance to all forms of enslavement manifests early in the novel when she questions the tradition that prevents girls from eating meat until they are married. Besides, she questions the rationale behind not being allowed to marry the love choice of her life, Itsho, a young man of her age who, though not having the promise of enormous wealth like Satila, an heir to a fabulous farm wealth, remains the true symbol of her love. She is the more vehemently opposed to the imposition of Satila because he is a man "approaching forty,"[19] and on whose side it appears tradition has registered its imperious endorsement. This explains why, reasoning that she will be given away against her wish in a year's time—all things being equal—she counsels herself to make the best of the passionate trysts with Itsho: "I will have to go to Satila next year: there is no avoiding it. I must just make the most of the short time I have left with Itsho."[20]

If tradition's denial of her right of love choice is already bad enough, her lot is soon to be worsened by her capture into slavery which comes in the wake of a violent rape from the leader of the raid gang, Abdulai:

> He forced Nandzi down. With his left arm he pinned her shoulders to the ground. With his right hand he took his penis and guided it into her vagina, sighing as he penetrated into the depths of her body. Nandzi continued to scream abuse at him and struggle. But now he had two hands free to pin her wrists to the ground. Nandzi twisted her head and snapped her teeth over his fat index finger She felt the bone and the warm spurt of blood in her mouth before she heard his cry.[21]

But even in her state of bondage and sexual abuse, Nandzi, as she is still called at this stage of the narrative, does not fail to take advantage of every situation to interrogate the oppressive order of slavery and masculinity, which only goes to question the injustice of a gender-biased ontology of capitalism and patriarchy. In this sense, her rape can also be said to intersect with the objectification that is prevalent in patriarchal societies and which manifests in other areas of social relations between men and women. Arguably, then, this speaks to the notion of "seeing rape as making good on the threat of sexual objectification" which is implicit in patriarchal societies.[22] While there is an indictment of African society evoked in this act of violence, it is also important to state that this also applies to Western society, as will be seen later in this discussion.

Even in co-slavery with men, the patriarchal order is to be observed, as in the fact that she is expected to do the cooking for everybody since she is the only female captive from the raid so far. After all, the men

> found it hard enough to come to terms with the psychic effects of capture and enslavement; that they should be further humiliated by being forced to do women's work was inconceivable. Fortunately for them their captors' views on what was proper work for men and women were little different from their own.[23]

Therefore, if slavery compromised African humanity in general, women, especially slave women, suffered double compromise of their humanity on account of patriarchal structures which were sustained in spite of the firm boundary between freedom and slavery. Put differently, if there is a general principle of "systemic violence" by which slavery operates in its imposition of untold suffering on slaves,[24] the extremity of women's suffering is doubly implicated in this violence. The fate of Nandzi speaks to this assertion. Nevertheless, the rights activist in Nandzi is evident each time the need arises. In the journey from Yendi to Kafaba, against her wish, she is forced to copulate with Akwasi Anoma, the old inebriated ornithologist charged with preparing a caravanserai for their camping in Kafaba. His insatiable desire for sex is as promiscuous as it is appalling. However, Nandzi finds totally unacceptable the attempt by Akwasi to summon Jaji, a "girl no more than a child" for rape.[25] Knowing that they are all leveled by the condition of enslavement, to allow Jaji to be taken for Akwasi's paedophilic desire would have been tantamount to triple slavery for the poor girl. Nandzi's courageous intervention saves Jaji from the marauding desires of Akwasi in a way that shocks the latter: "The shock of Nandzi's challenge had sobered him. His attention had been diverted and he hardly noticed that the girl had made her escape."[26]

Anchored on a strong moral ground and buoyed by the success of her intervention in the case of Jaji, Nandzi's reputation as an activist and liberation fighter even in a position of enslavement gains ascent. In the palace of Kumase where she temporarily becomes a domestic slave, she does not disguise her take on issues bordering on her rights and the rights of women in general. But above all, it is this determination to stand up to all forms of oppression that makes her a rallying point for resistance, especially during the Middle Passage and the years on the plantation. All these make her not a gendered sectarian leader, but a leader and symbol of liberation and self-determination for both sexes. Indeed, her actions and interventions through the text speak to the assumptions that women can excel in the making of history.[27] In the march toward Kumase, Nandzi raises a dirge, which, given the creative improvisation that she weaves into it, shows the artist-intellectual in her. But the fact that at inception the men refuse to join becomes another challenge from patriarchy even when the dirge speaks to their common situation of captivity. Yet one after the other the reality of their predicament is driven home in the wordings of the dirge, and ultimately they all join to lament the passage of their freedom. The impossibility of holding out forever against her prompt, and the mustering of emotions to upturn the erstwhile held notion that "the singing of dirges is women's work,"[28] reveals how Nandzi subverts the restrictive philharmonic order. Through her creative ingenuity she acquires for herself an empowerment which places her at the center stage within this captive scheme of things. It then stands to reason that Nandzi's leadership role within this context and the support that fellow women drum up for it, using the dirge analogy, validate the assertion that even in the distant past, across spaces,

> women's agency ... exceeds the strictures of patriarchal culture, for the historicity of their participation cannot be completely written out by a stilted historiography. [The] absence or silences of historiographical practice in regard to women does not change the intrinsic historical importance of their immersion in society.[29]

In the palace, Nandzi's name is changed to Ama, and she would have perhaps been the first wife of Nana Osei Kwame, the newly installed adolescent king. However, the cultural forces of masculinity combine with those of royal power to deny her this opportunity. There is no doubt that the young king prefers her to 1,000 other free women that may be brought his way for the purpose of marriage. This is why after the first love-making encounter between them, an affair in which Ama does not feel abused, but one in which, for the first time after the death of Itsho in his bid with other villagers of Bekpokpam to save her from her captors, she responds to a true desire that finds mutuality in the adolescent king's. Without doubt, Kwame has found comfort in the act, for according to him, he never wanted to be king; the restrictions that the status puts on his young life must have been responsible for this expression of reservations. However, companionship with Ama, though secretive in the palace, constitutes a source of solace and assurance for the young monarch. Barring tradition, she would have donned the toga of royal matrimony. Therefore, in the event of the final revelation of their tryst, Ama, as well as her co-slave friend Esi, gets sold to the white men "who will no doubt have [her] sold across the great water."[30] The arrogance of patriarchy and masculine monarchy and the expectations they recommend as social constructs have robbed Ama of another opportunity of experiencing true love. Needless to say, that for Kwame, it is nothing but a rocking of his love boat. Left to the custodians of the palace tradition, Ama would have been summarily executed; for it would be unheard of that a king has had an affair with a slave. Here the line between nobility and plebeianism is constructed in absolutism, thereby robbing Ama of the opportunity of bonding in matrimony with Kwame. The last statement by the Asante regent, Koranten Pete, after the trial of Ama says it all:

> What we are doing, Konadu and I, and others too, is to prepare him, to train and educate him. We all agree that we could not allow you to supplant us as the major influence on him at this time. Some of the councilors would have had you summarily executed. Both the Queen Mother and I argue that that would make it extremely difficult for us to exercise any influence over the boy.[31]

On the one hand, the above is a confirmation of the bias expressed against women as embodiments of distraction to the male body. After all, a man's cultural achievements are reinforced by his "singular anatomy.... Man is sexually compartmentalized. Genitally, he is condemned to a perpetual pattern of linearity, focus, aim, directness. He must learn to aim. Without aim, urination and ejaculation end in infantile soiling of self or surrounding."[32] In other words, the monarchical aims of Kwame stand potentially refracted and derailed because of his mix with the personage of a female slave like Ama.

In spite of the odds against her, Ama rises, as usual, to the occasion when she is sold to the white slavers and counted among the spatially unstable and doomed. Shortly before she makes it to the coast for the voyage, the binocular search of De Bruyn, the Director General of a Dutch Slave company, falls on her. Thereafter, for a period of two years, she is to live as a wife of sorts with the Dutch slaver, whose generosity of will grants manumission to Ama, whom he calls Pamela. The manumission is to be effected after his death. However, there is a dishonour of the will by De Bruyn's subordinate, Jensen, the morally dissolute lieutenant who takes over at his death. Betraying the most animalistic of instincts and by way of announcing his victory in the rivalry that had existed between him and De Bruyn before the death of the latter, he does not only burn the document permitting the manumission, he also violates her by way of a public and violent anal rape. Indeed, the incident of the rape comes in the wake of Ama's boldness to comment on Jensen's moral deficit, which accounts for his flouting of a legal document like the will of manumission. And since going down without a fight, especially in the face of oppression, is the last thing Ama would do, she reaches out to Jensen in the most unambiguous of expletives, which are just the right description for the morally unguarded Jensen: "You shit. You shit-arse. You rapist. You bastard. You pig. You filthy pig."[33]

Meanwhile, Ama's two-year stay with De Bruyn has not been without intellectual productivity. Apart from learning to speak English, she has also learnt to read and write, acquiring a prodigious proficiency that almost reaches the facility of a native speaker. This is besides her integration into the elite sports culture of the chess game. These forms of knowledge will later further distinguish her as she becomes, during the voyage and after, the intellectual among her fellow slaves, whose knowledge helps to subvert the domination of the slave masters in all areas.

The transition of space, especially into the maritime, which marks the beginning of the journey into an entirely strange world, provides some of the hardest challenges in Ama's resistance, both as an individual and member of a captive community. It will also return the discussion to the discourse of disability, especially with respect to loss and its multiple implications. Boarding the ship *The Love of Liberty* constitutes the first challenge. Being unbearably cramped with humans, it takes crawling for Ama to find a space for herself. Yet, the consciousness of her condition as well as that of others in the ship produces a response affirming their humanity. Looking at how Ama makes a space for herself, one of the women remarks, "Human beings were not created to walk on their knees like that."[34] The courage to express reservations about their dehumanization by the slave merchant Captain Williams and his crew, goes to show further how the slaves, especially the females, demonstrate their reaction to the oppressive order by which they have been turned into the subaltern *other*. And as Edward Said remarks, the reaction of the subaltern is usually informed by the understanding that the coercive formation of this group is "aware of one's self as belonging to a subject people."[35] According to Paulo Freire, the awareness causes "the deepening of the consciousness," which presupposes "learning to perceive social, political and economic contradictions, and to take action against the oppressive elements of reality."[36]

No doubt, it is this awareness of their condition that precipitates the facilitation of a revolt under the leadership of Ama with Tomba, the Futa Jalon anti-slavery fighter who is captured and sold into slavery through the complicity of both European merchants and their African capitalist collaborators. Ordinarily Ama should not have been involved in this revolt which fails abysmally. For, should she have agreed to continually cohabit with Captain Williams in exchange for the promised offer of teaching in the Caribbean where the ship is initially billed to land, she would have maintained a privileged status on the boat. But she turns down the offer, preferring to team up with fellow slaves, and exploiting her knowledge of English for the support of others. Needless to say, her integrity would have been compromised if she had succumbed to Williams's suggestion, given that in the end, the ship berths in Bahia, Brazil, contrary to schedule. As said earlier on, the revolt fails and the price she pays for it turns out to be greater than even that of Tomba. In fact, the punishment that follows leaves her body with a permanent and traumatic memento of optical disability:

> After the burial at sea, the time between the lashes became shorter. Ama tried to keep count. She was telling herself, *fifty, fifty, fifty* when Knaggs' turn came round again. He twirled the cat around and swung high, aiming at her head. One knot tore at her left ear. A bunch struck the back of her head. The knot on the longest strand took out her right eye.[37]

The site of the voyage as "transparent space" may have been truly constructed, from the perspective of Captain Williams, in the oppressive logic of what Trinh Minh-ha designates as "power, knowledge, and control,"[38] but the dignity of heroism lies in the fact that Ama bands together with fellow slaves to reject the absolutism of such imposition. For where there is such imposition, its guarantee is never absolute; indeed, "there is always a space of some kind for resistance."[39] The failure of the revolt then may not be as consequential as the fact that there is a demonstration of resistance by virtue of the space that is created.

On recovering from her brutalization and her consequent disability as a result of the punishment meted out to her on the order of Williams, Ama's critical analysis of the capitalist tendencies that inform the complicity between the Western merchants of slavery and their African collaborators is readily communicated to the reader via her pursuit of resistance to the injustice of the obnoxious trade. Clearly, Ama's predicament provides a telling commentary on the evolution of capitalism and its causal association with disability. As has been argued, in contemporary times certain categories of non-congenital impairments are constructed as workplace-related and "derive directly from the relations of production within capitalism."[40] The experience of slavery and the disability of slaves, as in the case of Ama, illustrate the intersection of such contemporary processes of impairment with the violence of slavery. This time, the opportunity to explicate this relationship presents itself when some white crew members are playing the chess game. She explains to the young boy Kwaku who is aboard together with her poor mother:

> The white men call it chess.... Now the first thing to learn is the names of the pieces. There are two armies, do you see, one is black, one white.... The king was *ohene* and the queen *ohemmaa;* the bishop was *Okomfo* and the horse *oponko;* the castle was *aban* and a pawn *akoa.*[41]

Coping with disability for remediation

On the Brazilian plantation of the Senhor (the Portuguese word for Master) in Bahia, where Ama's disability earns her the unfortunate re-christening of "One-Eye" by Vicente Texeira, the mulatto accountant,[42] she does not fail to rise to the occasion of resistance when the need arises. For instance, when on the plantation her cordial interaction with Senhora Miranda, her master's daughter, occasions playing chess, Ama boldly proposes new rules for the game not so much because of the fear of losing to Miranda as much as that of allowing for a level playing ground for both of them. Here is a metaphoric criticism of racial inequity and capitalist domination of white humanity over black humanity and of the West over Africa. Again, the intervention by way of the new rules says more about the preconceptions of white Western female personalities, which "in order to represent Woman," "require an inferior 'Other'– the woman of colour or women from non-Western countries."[43] But rather than be complicit in confirming an otherness, Ama states with categorical clarity what the relationship should be in the game– equality and fair play, her status as slave notwithstanding:

> Let's make it more interesting. I challenge you to a game. Only this time the rules will be different. I will play with the white pieces, but only eight of them: the king and the queen, knights, the bishops and the rooks; no pawns.

You'll play black and you will also have eight pieces, only they will all be pawns. What's more, when it is my turn to move, you must warn me in advance just what move you plan to make next. Oh yes, and since I'm playing white, I'll make the first move.[44]

Ama's agency in redefining the rule of the game is instructive, particularly for the present. This is because it speaks to the inequality in both racial and spatial relations in contemporary times. Beyond the empathy that disability literature provokes,[45] it is instructive to note how Ama's resistance and resilience from this stage on are geared toward remediation. As Minich has argued "Rather than merely claiming literature as a space where losers' stories are told," we should instead reflect its contemporary possibility "as a means of considering the broader capacity of politically engaged literature and literary criticism to remediate (to rectify, to correct inequities) the circumstances that produce loss."[46] For that matter, Ama's agency is significant in the way it represents her condition of disability and loss while reflecting on Africa's disability and loss. The condition is one that cries out for remediation instead of being an occasion for lamentation. Her agency in redefining the rule of the game is one sure way by which disability literature seeks empowerment for the disabled. It additionally probes the dialectic of domination and subservience as a deterministic category where race and space are concerned. The necessity of fairness then informs her agency and this is of great significance especially with respect to current global relations of power. Pragmatically, it requires that, among others, those previously constructed as powerless take up the challenge of rising to the occasion of providing agency in the review of the norms of relations, as Africa appears to be doing at the moment in response to the economic interest of the emerging powers.[47] Ama's agency is thus significant in the way it foreshadows the activation of African agency in contemporary times.

As well as all these, Ama utilizes her knowledge of literacy to read the Bible and turn the received interpretation from her master on its head. For instance, Tomba's killing of Jesus Vasconcellos, the plantation manager, for raping Ama, who has become Tomba's wife, is read to be as a valiant act that harks back to the intervention of Moses on behalf of his Israelite brother in Egypt. Such understanding in the context of slavery and resistance gives validation to what Hutton designates as "rhetorical appropriation and subversion of hostile theologies."[48] By the end of the novel, it is Ama who contemplates—and, for that matter, possesses—the power to narrate to her son, all that is past and the hope she invests in the future. This in itself is a clincher to the effect that she has been at the center of the struggle for resistance, no matter how dispossessing and deforming that has been. And indeed who else deserves such a prerogative other than the woman whose conviction about resistance to capitalist and racial oppression resonates with all the echoes of moral reinforcement?

It is pertinent to remark that Herbstein's narrative intervention in *Ama* is important for two reasons. For one, it marks a radical departure from the previous narratives on the Trans-Atlantic Slave Trade, in which the dialectic of oppression and resistance is articulated in essentially masculine terms. In such works the honour of heroism is often presented as an exclusive preserve of the African male; and this is often so whether prior to capture or during encounters with the harrowing experiences of slavery. And noting that there is a crucial way the slave trade foreshadowed the experience of occupational and settler colonization in Africa, it is not surprising then that the representation of women within the context of resistance has tended to confine them to the background of liberation struggles. This brings us back to the question of body theory and the inveterate condescending assumptions that patriarchy makes about the extent and capacity of the female body for resistance to oppression. The tendency to align the exception of disability with the female body is reinforced by the commonality of social constructs which cast "both the female and the disabled body ... as deviant and inferior; [which is why] both are defined in opposition to a norm of superiority."[49] It goes to explain why for too long and across spaces and racial lines, there seems to be an aura of ambiguity which weaves the image of women as disabled personalities in both cultural and literary texts. Usually, such permutation provides a convenient template for presenting the disabled woman figure as symbolizing otherness.[50] If thus socially constructed, then there is an automatic denial and negation of the potential for actualizing heroism of any known grandeur.

Herbstein transcends the insularity and arbitrariness which are at the base of this patriarchal bias by giving centrality not only to the personality of Ama as a woman in the narrative of resistance, but also to her disability, as well as that of other female characters like Esperanca, the deaf, and the Kongolese Jacinta who lost both hands as a result of feeding the cane mill.[51] Therefore, he deconstructs female disability from two angles and by so doing provides new insights into the assessment of the concept and the legitimization of heroism through received patriarchal practices whose unsympathetic texture to the capacity of women in matters of social and cultural heroism must be deplored. With specific reference to the memory of the slave trade, Herbstein's intervention can thus be appropriately limned as a redress of the history of the resistance to the trade. Needless to say, the intervention addresses at the same time the imbalance that has hitherto accorded undue and biased credit to men folk almost exclusively. On this score, the fact of disability which occasions "a reckoning with the messiness of bodily variety, with literal individuation run amok,"[52] pales beside the doggedness, intellection, tenderness and articulateness with which Ama, as well as the gendered groups she represents, has spoken truth to power across spaces in the context of slavery and capitalism.

On a second level, the significance of Herbstein's intervention lies in the assurance that gestures about new directions in the reinvention of the African past for the framing of both the present and the future signal heartening developments for the area of study. For too often, narratives of nationalist liberation struggles in Africa, which were essentially a reaction to the mutation of chattel slavery into colonial slavery, have also been inscribed excessively in patriarchal metaphors. This is to the extent that the good intentions of writers such as Ngugi and Achebe, to echo Elleke Boehmer, end up being eclipsed by invention of narratives that do more to reinforce rather than "disrupt existing national gender paradigms."[53] Yet, beyond liberation narratives of the nation in the African postcolony, contemporary events and the overwhelming influence of globalization on the continent remains a major challenge to everyone.

To consider but one illustration, it is a fact that since the 1980s, the "Third World governments have fallen deeper into international debt."[54] It is also a fact that the approach of Western financial institutions to the process of sinking the Third World, especially Africa, in this ocean of indebtedness harks back to the memory of the Trans-Atlantic slave trade which had encouraged the development of pawning, that is, "a system in which individuals are held in debt bondage as collateral for loans."[55] Today, slavery in its capitalist mutation has become more subtle and deadly sophisticated in the manner in which it holds nations of Africa to ransom through indebtedness to Western financial institutions like the World Bank and International Monetary Fund (IMF). One of the victories recorded on the part of Africa from Nigeria with regard to clearing such huge debts (of about $40 billion in recent times) was facilitated and executed by Ngozi Okonjo-Iweala, the then finance minister of the nation during the civilian tenure of President Olusegun Obasanjo.[56] The accumulation of such huge debt that ran into billions of US dollars was fabulous; the declaration of interest to pay back was not only considered incredible but also impossible. Yet the ingenuity of the amazon brought about the realization of the dream of the emancipation of a nation from the shackles of contemporary enslavement. Considered this way, the story of Ama finds resonance in our contemporary state in Africa and instructs to the effect that for every Mandela that is celebrated, there is always also a Winnie Mandela; and for every Joe Slovo there is always a Ruth First; indeed; for every Naguib Mahfouz, there is always a Nawal Sa'dawi; and for a Kofi Annan whose peace efforts earned him the Nobel prize, there is always also a Wangari Maathai whose sustainable development project for environmental peace and democracy also brought about the same honour.

The logic of the invocation of these personalities is that the liberation of Africa from all forms of slavery, which is a continual project, requires the intervention of both men and women. This is why the record of such intervention should be sensitive to gender balance appropriate to the achievements of these personalities. For there is much wisdom in the averment that African women are very much empowered and that their inclusion in mustering the continent's resources for development is as crucial as harnessing those of men.[57] But it is also important to cultivate the habit of acknowledgment commensurate to women's contributions. Put differently, just as in *Ama*, where Tomba has been valiant, prepared to die for killing Jesus, the rapist, in order to strike the chord of justice, there is always an Ama whose capacity for enterprise and resistance must be acknowledged for the re-invention of Africa's past of resistance to the Trans-Atlantic Slave Trade.

Conclusion

On a last note, it is apt to state that this approach to the invention of history with respect to slavery and other forms of struggle in which Africa has engaged both in the distant and recent past is not aimed at turning history on its head. But rather, it is meant to create a narrative avenue in which all categories of social stake holders, across gender lines especially, are given their due credit while aspiring toward attaining a blend of this with some measure of credible universality. To put it in Boehmer's words, particularly for writers:

> The point of still-virtual resolution may lie in a negotiated mediation between three options: neither a rewriting of masculine myths of authority alone, nor the fabrication of female icons and spaces, nor even gestures of universal solidarity made on the basis of shared oppression, but something of all three.[58]

Therefore, in literature's bid to re-invent the past the search is for nothing but historical and social justice. The inventive way in which Herbstein achieves this mandate in *Ama* remains fascinating, going by how it musters the moral strength of narrative justice by centralizing female heroism with respect to the Trans-Atlantic Slave Trade, and yet does not fail to take the male angle on board. This is why the work, while pointing back at the past, lights the path to the future, in which the balance of tales along gender lines is paramount. Overall, the work underscores disability literature's capacity to resolve social contradictions through the agency of remediation.

Notes

1 Manu Herbstein, *Ama: A Story of the Atlantic Slave Trade* (Johannesburg: Picador Africa, 2001 (2005)).
2 Jean Franco, "Beyond Ethnocentricism: Gender, Power, and the Third-World Intelligentsia," in *Marxism and the Interpretation of Culture*, edited by Cary Nelson and Lawrence Grossberg (London: Macmillan, 1988), 503–516.
3 Rosemarie Thomson, "Theorizing Disability," in *Relocating Postcolonialism*, edited by David Goldberg and Ato Quayson (Oxford: Blackwell Publishing, 2002), 231.
4 Julie Avril Minich, "Disability, Losers, and Narrative Remediation," *Comparative Literature* 66(1) (2014), 35.
5 Rachel Carroll, "'Making the Blood Flow Backwards': Disability, Heterosexuality and the Politics of Representation in Julian Barnes's *The Sense of an Ending*," *Textual Practice* 29(1) (2015), 155.
6 James Berger, *The Disarticulate: Language, Disability, and the Narratives of Modernity* (New York: New York University Press, 2014).
7 Lennard J. Davis, "A Review of *The Disarticulate: Language, Disability, and the Narratives of Modernity*," *The CI Review* (2016), 419.
8 Ibid.
9 Ria Cheyne "'She Was Born a Thing': Disability, the Cyborg and the Posthuman in Anne McCaffrey's The Ship Who Song," *Journal of Modern Literature* 36(3) (2013): 138–139.
10 Lennard Davis quoted in Minich, "Disability," 37.

11 While it is important to make the above assertion, it is also necessary to acknowledge the intervention of the likes of Toni Morrison and other African female writers in the Diaspora who have consistently centralized female heroism in their works while invoking the memory of the slave trade.

12 Yvette Christiansë, *Unconfessed* (Cape Town: Kwela, 2007).

13 Andrea Levy, *The Long Song* (New York: Farrar, Straus and Giroux, 2010).

14 Carol Haggas, "A Review of *The Long Song,*" *Booklist*, American Library Association, www.buffalolib.org/vufind/Record/1793607/Reviews (April 2010), 37.

15 Samuel Oloruntoba, "Pan-Africanism, Knowledge Production and the Third Liberation of Africa," *International Journal of African Renaissance Studies* 10(1) (2015), 7.

16 Joseph Jeffrey Walters, *Guanya Pau: A Story of an African Princess* (University of Michigan: Lauer & Mattill, 1891).

17 Baudrillard quoted in Joseph Bristow, *Sexuality* (London and New York, 1997), 141.

18 Kathy Davis, "Embody-ing Theory: Beyond Modernist and Postmodernist Readings of the Body," in *Embodied Practices: Feminist Perspectives on the Body*, edited by Kathy Davis (London: SAGE, 1997), 7.

19 Herbstein, *Ama*, 4.

20 Ibid.

21 Ibid., 8.

22 Lindsay Kelland, "Conceptually Situating the Harm of Rape: An Analysis of Objectification," *South African Journal of Philosophy* 30(2) (2011), 168.

23 Herbstein, *Ama*, 27.

24 Kirsten Dawson, " 'Did Not He Who Made Me in the Belly Make Him, and the Same One Fashion Us in the Womb?' " *Biblical Interpretation* 21(4–5) (2013), 435.

25 Herbstein, *Ama*, 52.

26 Ibid., 53.

27 Jessica Millward, "The Relics of Slavery," in *Interracial Sex and Manumission in the American South Frontiers* 31(3) (2010), 22.

28 Herbstein, *Ama*, 58.

29 Dan Ojwang, *Reading Migration and Culture: The World of East African Indian Literature* (Basingstoke: Palgrave, 2013), 106.

30 Herbstein, *Ama*, 110.

31 Ibid.

32 Paglia cited in Bristow, *Sexuality*, 45.

33 Herbstein, *Ama*, 200.

34 Ibid., 226.

35 Said in Anders Breidlid, *Resistance and Consciousness in Kenya and South Africa* (Frankfurt am Main: Peter Lang, 2002), 13.

36 Freire in Breidlid, *Resistance and Consciousness*, ibid.

37 Herbstein, *Ama*, 273.

38 Minh-ha cited in Alison Blunt and Gillian Rose, "Introduction: Women's Colonial and Postcolonial Geographies," in *Writing Women and Space: Colonial and Postcolonial Geographies*, edited by Alison Blunt and Gillian Rose (New York and London: The Guilford Press, 1994), 15.

39 Ibid.

40 Ato Quayson, *Aesthetic Nervousness: Disability and the Crisis of Representation* (New York: Columbia University Press, 2007), 3.

41 Herbstein, *Ama*, 278.

42 Ibid., 304.

43 Davis, "Embody-ing Theory," 7.

44 Herbstein, *Ama*, 352.

45 Laura Yeager, "Disability Literature can Inspire Empathy," *Reading Today* (December 2010/January 2011), 44.

46 Minich, "Disability," 35.

47 Brendan Vickers, "Africa and the Rising Powers: Bargaining for the 'Marginalized Many'," *International Affairs* 89(3) (2013), 673.

48 Jeremy Hutton, "Isaiah 51:9–11 and the Rhetorical Appropriation and Subversion of Hostile Theologies," *Journal of Biblical Literature* 126(2) (2007), 271.

49 Thomson, "Theorizing Disability," 231.

50 Ibid., 239.

51 Herbstein, *Ama*, 303.

52 Thomson, "Theorizing Disability," 231.

53 Jana Maria Giles, "Re-gendering the Postcolonial Nation," *Women: A Cultural Review* 17(3) (2006/7), 385.

54 Neil Thomas, "Global Capitalism, the Anti-Globalization Movement and the Third World," *Capital and Class* 92 (2007), 48.

55 Toyin Falola and Paul Lovejoy, "Pawnship in Historical Perspective," in *Pawnship, Slavery, and Colonialism in Africa*, edited by Toyin Falola and Paul Lovejoy (Trenton NJ: Africa World Press, 2003), 1.

56 Much as the loan pay-back that Dr Okonjo-Iweala facilitated was commendable, we should also at this stage admit that the manner of the pay-back smacked of a sophisticated strategy of imperialism which left Nigeria poorer for it, especially because there was no concrete developmental evidence of utility of the loan in the first place; neither has the payback translated into any infrastructural development as Nigerians were made to believe then.

57 Molara Ogundipe, *Indigenous and Contemporary Gender Concepts and Issues in Africa: Implications for Nigeria's Development*, (Lagos: Malthouse Press, 2007), 6–7.

58 Elleke Boehmer quoted in Giles, "Re-gendering the Postcolonial Nation," 368.

Bibliography

Berger, J. *The Disarticulate: Language, Disability, and the Narratives of Modernity*. New York: New York University Press, 2014.

Blunt, A. and G. Rose. "Introduction: Women's Colonial and Postcolonial Geographies," in *Writing Women and Space: Colonial and Postcolonial Geographies*, edited by Alison Blunt and Gillian Rose, 1–28. New York and London: The Guilford Press, 1994.

Breidlid, A. *Resistance and Consciousness in Kenya and South Africa*. Frankfurt and New York: Peter Lang, 2002.

Bristow, J. *Sexuality*. London and New York: Taylor and Francis, 1997.

Carroll, R. " 'Making the Blood Flow Backwards': Disability, Heterosexuality and the Politics of Representation in *Julian Barnes's The Sense of an Ending*," *Textual Practice* 29(1) (2015):155–172.

Cheyne, R. " 'She Was Born a Thing': Disability, the Cyborg and the Posthuman in Anne McCaffrey's The Ship Who Song," *Journal of Modern Literature* 36(3) (2013): 138–156.

Christiansë, Y. *Unconfessed*. Cape Town: Kwela, 2007.

Davis, L. J. A. "Review of *The Disarticulate: Language, Disability, and the Narratives of Modernity*," *The CI Review* (2016): 419–420.

Davis, K. "Embody-ing Theory: Beyond Modernist and Postmodernist Readings of the Body," in *Embodied Practices: Feminist Perspectives on the Body*, edited by Kathy Davis, 1–26. London: SAGE, 1997.

Dawson, K. "Did Not He Who Made Me in the Belly Make Him, and the Same One Fashion Us in the Womb?" *Biblical Interpretation* 21(4/5) (2013): 435–468.

Falola, T. and Lovejoy, P. "Pawnship in Historical Perspective," in *Pawnship, Slavery, and Colonialism in Africa,* edited by Toyin Falola and Paul Lovejoy, 1–26. Trenton NJ: Africa World Press, 2003.

Franco, J. "Beyond Ethnocentricism: Gender, Power, and the Third-World Intelligentsia," in *Marxism and the Interpretation of Culture,* edited by Cary Nelson and Lawrence Grossberg. 503–516. London: Macmillan, 1988.

Giles, Jana Maria. "Re-Gendering the Postcolonial Nation," *Women: A Cultural Review* 17(3) (2007): 385–387.

Haggas, C. "A Review of *The Long Song,*" *Booklist,* American Library Association, www.buffalolib.org/vufind/Record/1793607/Reviews (April 2010).

Herbstein, M. *Ama: A Story of the Atlantic Slave Trade.* Johannesburg: Picador Africa, 2001 (2005).

Hutton, J. Isaiah "51: 9–11 and the Rhetorical Appropriation and Subversion of Hostile Theologies," *Journal of Biblical Literature* 126(2) (2007): 271–303.

Kelland, L. "Conceptually Situating the Harm of Rape: An Analysis of Objectification," *South African Journal of Philosophy* 30(2) (2011): 168–183.

Levy, A. *The Long Song.* New York: Farrar, Straus and Giroux, 2010.

Millward, J. "The Relics of Slavery," *Frontiers* 31(3) (2010): 22–30.

Minich, J. A. "Disability, Losers, and Narrative Remediation," *Comparative Literature* 66(1) (2014): 35–42.

Ogundipe, M. *Indigenous and Contemporary Gender Concepts and Issues in Africa: Implications for Nigeria's Development.* Lagos: Malthouse Press, 2007.

Ojwang, D. *Reading Migration and Culture: The World of East African Indian Literature.* Basingstoke: Palgrave, 2013.

Oloruntoba, S. "Pan-Africanism, Knowledge Production and the Third Liberation of Africa," *International Journal of African Renaissance Studies* 10(1) (2015): 7–24.

Quayson, A. *Aesthetic Nervousness: Disability and the Crisis of Representation.* New York: Columbia University Press, 2007.

Thomas, G. "Man and Woman, Slave and Empire: 'Reconstructing (Gender) in Plantation America'," *Jenda: A Journal of Culture and African Women Studies* 7 (2005): 1–27.

Thomas, N. "Global Capitalism, the Anti-Globalization Movement and the Third World," *Capital and Class* 92 (2007): 45–97.

Thomson, R. "Theorizing Disability," in *Relocating Postcolonialism,* edited by David Goldberg and Ato Quayson, 231–269. UK: Blackwell Publishing, 2002.

Vickers, B. 2013. "Africa and the Rising Powers: Bargaining for the 'Marginalized Many'," *International Affairs* 89(3) (2013): 673–693.

Walters, J. J. *Guanya Pau: A Story of an African Princess.* University of Michigan, MI: Lauer & Mattill, 1891.

Yeager, L. "Disability Literature can Inspire Empathy," *Reading Today* (December 2010/ January 2011): 44.

6 Reverse migration of Africans in the Diaspora

Foregrounding a woman's quest for her roots in Tess Akaeke Onwueme's *Legacies*

Methuselah Jeremiah

Introduction

Reverse migration is understood to mean a remigration back to a person's original 'homeland'; a situation where a person retraces his/her steps back to their 'ancestral land.' This chapter attempts the explication of gender and identity in Africa and among Africans in the Diaspora, and how this crisis of identity, occasioned by a multiplicity of issues affecting the immigrant, pushes them to leave the Diaspora back to their home countries in Africa. King and Christou see the issue of the 'homeland' as a problematic, given that a number of returnees who re-migrate to their home countries were 'second generation' returnees who never lived there before but were born abroad. King and Christou therefore aver that this remigration is more of an "ontological return to the land of their *ancestors*" (emphasis supplied).[1] This chapter specifically discusses the phenomenon of reverse migration as captured in a play entitled *Legacies* by Tess Akaeke Onwueme, a Nigerian playwright. The play, itself, is a trenchant and convoluted narrative that dramatizes the effects of nineteenth century slavery, love and betrayal, which results in Mimi, a woman living in America, embarking on the quest to trace her Nigerian homeland. She travels from America with her son, Uli, to the fictional Idu village in the Eastern part of Nigeria, to reconnect with what she considers her ancestral roots. However, in a twist of circumstances, she also finds out that Elozie, the father of her child Uli, who walked out on her in America, is also her brother. The question that this chapter seeks to answer is why a woman should abandon the comfort of her home in a highly developed economy to travel thousands of kilometers to a remote village with no basic amenities and be subjected to the most debilitating living conditions imaginable; a village where basic amenities like pipe borne water, electricity and standard health facilities are lacking. A literary analysis of Onwueme's *Legacies* reveals some factors that propel Africans to re-migrate back to their countries of origin because the play dramatizes the threnodies of these immigrants, many of whom never really feel at home in these countries of abode in spite of the successes they record in their businesses and other pursuits.

Migration of Africans to the West

Historically, the migration of Africans to Europe and America took place in at least two 'waves'—the first, according to Toyin Falola, was the transatlantic slave trade begun in 1444 when Portuguese traders started raiding for slaves in the Senegal river.[2] While Patrick Manning agrees with this assertion, he maintains that the "important" years of this trade were between 1650 and 1850.[3] Within this period, between eight and twelve million Africans were shipped off to Metropolitan Europe and North America to work in plantations. The second wave of migration of Africans to Europe and North America, which began in the 1980s, involves millions who fled their countries for reasons such as political oppression, as in the case of exiles who fled from General Sani Abacha's regime in Nigeria to escape his brutal rule.[4] Others fled the continent because of the devastation of famine, as in the case of some African countries like Ethiopia which suffered a brutal famine in the early 1980s. Yet others who left went searching for greener pastures in the West. For example, many Nigerians emigrated to Europe and North America where opportunities abounded for "low level unskilled jobs" for immigrants.[5] John A. Arthur, an expert on migration, maintains that

> migration abroad is therefore a strategy utilized by family members to optimize their economic status while making it possible for other family members to migrate in the future.... Many in Africa see this as the most viable approach for achieving economic mobility and improving their lives.[6]

These, and a number of others, have come to be regarded as the push and pull factors in migration studies, which manifest through social, economic and political factors which push many of these people to venture into foreign lands where they feel they can get something better to do. The push factors are the conditions that propel the people to leave, while the pull factors are the 'attractions' that lure them to these areas, according to Peter Hahn and Georg Klute.[7] In another essay by John A. Arthur, he suggests that "the desire for self-improvement, to enhance human and social capital potential and to make enough money to assist in providing for extended family relatives has been behind the drive and ambition of African émigrés all over the world."[8]

Why the reverse migration?

A number of reasons have been put forward as possible explanations for the remigration of many Africans back to their ancestral homes. One of the motivations for this remigration can probably be attributed to the improvement of economies in hitherto depressed African economies. The World Bank reports that Africa is making progress at reducing poverty. Investment is improving and so economic and social conditions are improving with many countries in Africa moving into the "middle income status."[9]

The second point identified for this reverse migration hinges on the improvement of the security situation across Africa. *The Economist* reports that:

> Many have stopped fighting. War and civil strife have declined dramatically.... In the past decade Africa's wars have become a lot less deadly. Perennial hotspots such as Angola, Chad, Eritrea, Liberia and Sierra Leone are quiet, leaving millions better off, and even Congo, Somalia and Sudan are much less violent than they used to be.... The number of coups, which averaged 20 per decade in 1960–90, has fallen to an average of ten.[10]

The Economist further states that there is a gradual move from military dictatorships to democratic systems of governance which is more tolerant of criticism and invariably will also make the conditions right for the return of many people who had fled their countries fearing for their lives. Many feared 'big man leaders'—autocratic, unilateral and vicious dictators who had before now held the continent in a vice grip of high handedness, brooking no criticism of their obvious repressive policies. Coups have become old fashioned and so soldiers are more or less restricted to their barracks and focused on their primary duties of protecting the territorial borders of their countries.[11]

Yet another point that engenders reverse migration of Africans back to their countries is their inability to secure high caliber jobs that are commensurate to their qualifications in the Western industrialized countries. According to April Gordon, many of them are forced to take on menial jobs, the kind that they will not even do in their home countries. It is therefore not uncommon to see many of these immigrants engaging in these low profile jobs including being "cab drivers, parking attendants, airport workers, or waiters."[12]

On the other hand, the trauma of racism and discrimination engenders loneliness and alienation on the part of immigrants, especially in the highly developed economies of the world, even though this attitude is present in almost all countries the world over where immigrants work.[13] Hugo Kamya corroborates this statement by maintaining that many of these immigrants experience varying levels of "physical, psychological, sociological, emotional, and spiritual/religious rootlessness."[14] Joseph Takougang reports that in so many situations these immigrants are "often perceived as lazy, criminals, drug dealers and welfare cheats. This perception often results in police harassment, intimidation, unlawful arrests and even murder."[15] For some who undergo such rejection, they surmise that the best thing for them is to return to their home countries where their dignity and respect are intact, and where they think they will tap from the communal fraternity. Wilfred Ngwa and Lydia Ngwa also argue that many Africans are looked upon as second-class citizens in foreign countries and at other times "taken for granted or scorned."[16] Generally speaking, there is a paucity of data on returning immigrants but *Homecomingrevolution.com* claims in its website that up to 359,000 have returned to Africa as at 2015.[17]

But perhaps the biggest factor to be considered in the issue of reverse migration to Africa is the quest by many Diasporas to connect with their ancestral roots. What is it about roots in Africa? In yet another book, John A. Arthur avers that many Africans return to their home countries not necessarily because of the conducive conditions but because they "do not want to sever ties to their ancestral homelands."[18] In Africa, ancestry is fundamental to the identity of a person—his/her roots and bloodline are keys to his/her individuality. There is the saying that 'there is no place like home, north or south'. And so, in spite of the evidently highly developed infrastructure in Western countries where many of these Diasporas have settled in, the craving has always been there to reconnect to their roots, to reclaim their 'true identity.' Of course this feeling of nostalgia may probably be activated by factors like racism and xenophobia that we have discussed above. Even more so many of these immigrants are living in squalid conditions that are no different from the ones they thought they had escaped from in their home countries. Some who are illegal aliens do not have access to some basic amenities like health care. According to a study done by Wallace *et al.*, many immigrants are unable to access medical facilities or insurance in America.[19] However, Zauditu-Selasie affirms that it is the connection to nature that helped many slaves to combat the "traumatic terrain of American racial landscape." This in turn has had the effect of giving them a kind of comfort as if they are actually at home.[20]

Mimi's reverse migration in *Legacies*

Claude Andrew Clegg in his book *The Price of Liberty: African Americans and the Making of Liberia* discusses the migration of blacks from America back to Liberia. His incisive documentation of this mass movement undergirds the compelling need in people to identify with the roots of their origins; to establish an identity that grants them respectability and a sense of belonging. They were willing to dare into the unknown just so that they could hold their heads high in the community, not to continue to slouch around with drooping shoulders and nameless identities at the constant mercy of their white masters. According to Clegg many of them realized their dreams of freedom in varying degrees. He asserts that:

> For some, freedom came to mean dropping the hoe in favor of trade, attending churches of one's choosing, and attaining the rudiments of literacy in makeshift schools. For others, it meant having one's womenfolk beyond the predatory grasp of the slave master and raising families not subject to separation through sale or probate proceedings. Freedom was land, a farm, and independent, if drudging subsistence. It was also living on the doorstep of the roaring Atlantic and watching one's children play care free along sandy shores named liberty itself. Particularly for ex-slaves, freedom meant *legalized personhood, civil rights and documented existence.* In essence, it was the *unfettered ability to create one's own familial, communal, and civic relations* in a land beyond the control of white people (emphasis supplied).[21]

This extended quote from Clegg clearly demonstrates the kind of pitiable situation that slaves in America were faced with. The brutalities inflicted on them created a feeling of nostalgia in them even as they longed for the comfort of their roots because of the alienation they suffered in America.

Legacies by Tess Akaeke Onwueme is a dramatization of a similar phenomenon to the one above. The play foregrounds a woman's journey of rediscovery to her ancient village somewhere in Eastern Nigeria. It is a quest to catch up with her husband, Elozie, who had abandoned her and ran off to Africa after he had completed his studies in America. Mimi left the comfort of the West to travel to Idu, a remote village, to look for him because that is where she believed she will find real comfort. She was willing to forgo all the conveniences that are available in a highly developed economy to travel to an unknown less developed environment. A reading through the play indicates that many of the factors identified as having influenced many Diaspora returnees are clearly identified in this discourse, too. However, two of these factors clearly explicate the phenomenon of Mimi's return to her native land.

In the first instance, the feeling of alienation and exclusion is a huge propelling factor that succeeded in galvanizing Mimi to literally drag her unwilling son back to Idu, a village in the middle of 'nowhere.' She never felt at home in America. She always felt like a stranger, an outsider because the American society where she lived never really accepted her. She experienced loneliness and rejection and so she longed for the comfort of her native home where she will be accepted and treated as an equal.

MIMI: … the world is strange …
And we the bigger strangers.
Son,
Over there
We don't have a goddam hold
Where hope hangs on the winds
Over there,
White is the dominant colour (*sic*) of air.

(*Legacies*, 5)

She tries to make Uli understand the illusion of 'belonging' in America because it does not exist. She attempts to make him understand that American life is a mere mirage, an attempt at futility. Therefore, in spite of the sophisticated nature of life there, in spite of the fact that they may be more comfortable because they possess material things that life in Idu village can hardly offer them, they do not belong in America. As an immigrant, she encounters all manner of hostilities on the streets. She is harassed which affects her psychologically and reinforces the fear of slavery which, even though abolished, still remains in the psyche of the society. Deirdre Davis argues that even though street harassment is encountered by all women, it is even more compelling in the case of the black African American woman because of the "particular historical context to which the particular woman belongs."[22]

Mimi, therefore, affirms firmly that they belong in Africa:

MIMI: Here we are
   On earth
   This is Africa
   Son,
   Our Africa
   Where we belong
   Black this soil is
   Son
   Here's where the trees
   Are for shade
   Son

                                                                    (5)

The last three lines are an obvious reference to the brutality of slavery; where even nature seem complicit in the harrowing experiences of the immigrant. Therefore, while they are tied to the trees in America and whipped as slaves, the mere sight of a tree in Africa gives refreshment because, for once, they can sit down under its shade to rest. They do not have to look behind them in trepidation, knowing that the consequences of that will only attract the whiplash.

In this play, the pitiful state of the immigrant is brought to the fore. He/she is a nobody and even though he/she works themselves to cinder, engaged in some of the most back breaking jobs with little by way of wages paid them, they hardly get any kind of acknowledgment. If anything, they are exploited the more and suffer the ruthlessness of the system which views them as parasites and interlopers as attested to by Horowitz,[23] Marvasti and Mackinney,[24] and Obotama.[25] Harzig *et al.* further describe how these immigrants are treated more as "body parts, commodified as instruments of work: as 'hands' or 'braceros' (arms) rather than as hearts and heads."[26] This is possibly because in many of the host countries where they emigrate to, they are "said to possess mental capacities inferior to those of the receiving society and assumed to be torn from their roots by forces beyond their control, migrants were considered to be *adrift or in limbo*" (emphasis supplied).[27] No wonder Mimi calls Idu home because, probably for the first time, she felt a sense of belonging; a pride in the fact that she is looked upon not as a parasite but as a person with worth.

At the beginning of the play this is what we experience as we meet Mimi with her son Uli by the grotto in Idu. However, Uli suffers a culture shock. He fails to fit into the situation because of the obvious lack of understanding of the dynamics of African life. For him what he sees is primitivism and desolation.

ULI: Stop this mother!
   Its all in your head
   Its all in your mind, mum ...
   Look around you?

What do you see?
Trees, antiques some old skins, rags, rusty implements and skulls of
—i-don't-know-what …
No, mum! If this is the Africa,
Then it's all a huge joke!

(3)

Uli was alienated from the land. He could not fit into the scheme of things. For him, Africa is 'their' Africa. But for Mimi, his mother who understands what it is to have a place that one identifies with, Africa is 'our own' Africa. In a tremulous and trembling tone full of passion she tells him that "the roots are here … deep down here. Son, this is Africa … Africa … our OWN Africa, son …" (emphasis in the original, 3).

The seemingly raggedy stuff that Uli refers to, which to him is inconsequential, are the tools for the initiation ceremony which his own father was soon to undergo. In traditional communities among many tribal nationalities, a child cannot attain the status of an adult until he/she has undergone some special rites of passage after which he/she is allowed to, according to Ayisi, "participate in adult life."[28] The ceremonies may differ from society to society, but one thing is for sure adulthood is usually preceded by some form of initiation rites among many of these people groups, even though many of these cultural practices are in the wane and so exist only in a residual form. That Elozie, Uli's father was subjected to these rites of passage at such a late hour in his life is an indication of how important this ceremony is. Not undergoing such will mean that one is still considered a child.

This is part of the roots that Mimi tries to make her son understand; the feeling of belonging engendered by the spirit of kinship rooted in the cosmology of the people. It is a big web enveloping their way of life, something that goes beyond the bounds of the material world but more or less deeply rooted in their psyche. Mimi captures the essence of this thus:

MIMI: The world is a vast forest
   But every branch
   Has room for growth
   Every branch grows and grows
   According to its inclination
   Here's where we are
   Lets hold on to this
   Our branch, our tree
   From this we grow

(5)

This is the way Mimi perceives Africa; a place of hope and promise in spite of its 'backwardness' and stagnation. All the neon lights, and the fast trains, and the highly developed infrastructure of America, which in her words is a world of fantasy, cannot take the place of this simple but idyllic setting which is life itself. She describes how alienating the American life is with all its indignities to immigrants like them.

> MIMI: … the system out there
>   Thrives on breaking
>   Bones that bind us black
>   Fragmenting families.
>   Robbing our men
>   Of the potency of their being
>   That they may continue
>   To wander in search of life
>   Swelled by the urge
>   To regain their manhood lost …

(7–8)

This is how the system has broken the immigrants so much that they have completely lost their sense of self-esteem because many are unable to provide for their families. Their wives have assumed the roles of breadwinners in the home. This kills their ego and emasculates them into positions of subservience as their roles get reversed, as we saw with the case of Elozie. However, the communal nature of life in Africa will have helped many of these men given that the community, in most cases, will rally round to rescue them from this shameful situation. The collective nature of life in Africa ensures that everyone looks out for the other. The communal spirit in Africa is very strong. Even the advent of modernization has not taken away that attitude of looking out for one's neighbor. A strong reason for this is rooted in the belief system. Africans believe that an individual's problem is a communal affair. A person's fortune or misfortune affects the larger society. This feeling of security and warmth in her homeland propels Mimi to conclude thus:

> MIMI: … Here for once
>   In a lifetime
>   I feel warmth
>   Caressed and cradled from
>   The bosom of a mother land …

(67)

This is the key to understanding Mimi's reverse migration. She never felt at home in America but now that she finds herself in Africa, she basks in the euphoria of freedom and plenitude. Whereas Uli sees backwardness, she sees warmth and acceptability because she was on a journey for self-discovery; a journey of affirmation that, indeed, she was human with roots and an attachment to a system within the nexus of a dynamic, progressive society; a society whose value system far surpasses the one she just came from, where materialism and the quest for achievement far outweighs the values placed on communality and self-identity—a fundamental philosophical standpoint in Africa. In Africa, she was not just another face; a face to be jeered at; a face to be sneered at—one who was barely tolerated. She is a living being; one who is cherished and appreciated. The words of affirmation are captured by Anene, Mimi's mother-in-law who showers encomiums on her. Her pleasure at having Mimi is quite obvious. She is extravagant with her welcome.

> ANENE: ... welcome!
>   Welcome!
>   Welcome Egbe!
>   Woman ... Egbe
>   Woman bird
>   Who does not know a land
>   But journeys there all the same ...
>   My fellow woman and daughter ...
>   Welcome to our land ...

(65)

The point must still be made that within African ontology, the genealogical bonding is very strong. The fraternal spirit of kinship engendered by the communal nature of life makes for a very strong pull toward one's roots. Adejumo summarizes this essence thus:

> There are so many reasons for going back home, that is, for those of us who really want to go back home. One, and the most important, is that it is our country. Get American citizenship or UK citizenship, you are still Nigerian. Nothing can change that. Perhaps your children are not, but you are. Not with that thick Igbo or Yoruba accent of yours.[29]

Adejumo further argues that returning home will also avail the children the opportunity to reconnect with their roots given that they are "fast losing our identities." The reason for the nonchalance by the younger Diasporas toward their identity probably stems from the fact that they are born away from their native lands. They have grown up within these environments and therefore virtual strangers to the unique identity of their homelands. Unless they are socialized from childhood to crave for that identity, like Mimi was by her father who gave her a half of the *Ikenga*, a legacy of his roots which perpetually kept the spirit of her homeland kindled in her and encouraged her to adventure there and re-connect with her relations, they grow up even disdaining and distancing themselves from these identities.

For the immigrant who has experienced the warmth of the kinship system back home, he/she can only but crave for that, especially as he/she meets with the challenges of marginalization, discrimination and racism in the West. Wheedon maintains that:

The desire to be from somewhere, to have a sense of roots and a feeling of belonging are key features of the quest for positive identity in post-modern, post-colonial societies.... *For diasporic peoples, this concern with roots often leads to a quest for the place for which their forebears came and sometimes even for an original, authentic identity.*

(Emphasis supplied)[30]

This was the propelling desire that pushed Mimi to embark on a long tortuous journey to discover her roots. Her father had instilled in her that insatiable craving to relocate to her authentic identity—her African homeland.

Conclusion: confronting the realities of 'home'

This chapter has delved into the phenomenon of reverse migration. This was explicated using the experience of Mimi, a woman who travelled to her village from America in the quest to discover her roots. This dramatized experience is an example of the trend that has been on the ascendancy recently by many African immigrants who have been pouring back to their countries from Metropolitan Europe. It was discovered that this African remigration is engendered by factors ranging from improvement in the economies of the hitherto depressed economies of many of these African countries, to improvement in civil rights in these countries, too. However, some of these people who reverse their migration to their home countries are propelled by the quest to rediscover their roots; to have a feeling of belonging as they link up with their ancestral lands and consequently help to define their identity. A case in point to cite is that of Pete O'Neal, who has been living in Tanzania since 1972 when he left Kansas in America and relocated to the village of Imabaseni where he has acculturized and has become one of the respected elders of the community. O'Neal's ability to settle down in this backward community is hinged on the fact that he did not expect to have a rosy apartment as he had in Kansas. He accepted the harsh conditions of life and to some extent he serves as a genuine case of a person on the quest for a genuine 'home' in Africa because he came to Africa to be Africanized by immersing himself both "culturally and emotionally."[31]

This is not the case for the quest for 'home' elsewhere. Claude Andrew Clegg gives us vivid pictures of the African American slaves who remigrated back to Liberia in the late nineteenth century. He paints a very gloomy picture of what these new comers endured, some of which were worse than what they went through in America. Apart from the weather which dealt terribly with them, many of them died of malaria. They also suffered the hostilities of the indigenous Liberians who saw them as parasites who had taken over their lands. Furthermore, this their settler community was "marred by the same exclusionary, oppressive characteristic common to modern colonial regimes."[32] In other words, their romanticized idea of Africa was not what it turned out to be, it was a shattered dream.

For returning migrants to be able to settle in Africa, Okumu proposes that:

> They must learn the African cultures and languages. They cannot assume that their skin color alone will endear them to their African brothers and sisters. Second, they should not expect to find another America in Africa without discrimination and oppression. Although they will find an Africa without racial prejudice it will be one with its own unique problems which they must be willing to help solve. And, third, they should go to Africa with the intention of being Africanized. They cannot live an American lifestyle in Africa. They cannot demand special treatment for being Americans. They should be prepared to suffer alongside their African brothers and sisters. They should mingle, wiggle, and dissolve into Africa. This can easily be done by adopting one of the 1,700 vibrant cultures and becoming bona fide members of the respective ethnic groups.[33]

Another perspective to 'home' return is chronicled by Keith B. Richburg in his book, *Out of America: A Black Man Confronts Africa* where he details the woes of returning 'home.' As an African American Journalist, the author enthusiastically travels to Africa only to be met with the most despicable of horrors he had ever encountered in his lifetime. The brutality of regimes, disease and squalor, corruption and all other negativities that he encounters in his quest for identity forces him to repudiate anything African. He blurts out bluntly that

> I have been here, I have lived here and seen Africa in all its horror. I know now that I am a stranger here. I am an American, a black American and I feel no connection to this strange and violent place.[34]

Many others who manage to stay have had to daily go through the debilitating effects of corruption, poor and undeveloped infrastructure and violence occasioned by ethnic or religious sentiments among many other challenges plaguing 'home.' This is why the case of Mimi in *Legacies* remains fluid given that the play, itself, did not address the long effects of her stay at 'home'. The suggestion is that it was only a matter of time before she will start retreating back to America when the realities of the situation dawns on her unless she is able to properly acculturate with the new community like Pete O'Neal.

Notes

1 Russel King and Anastasia Christou, "Diaspora, Migration and Transnationalism: Insights from Studies of Second-Generation 'Returnees," in *Diaspora and Transnationalism: Concepts, Theories and Methods*, edited by Rainer Baubock and Thomas Faist (Amsterdam: Amsterdam University Press, 2010), 168.
2 Toyin Falola, *The African Diaspora: Slavery, Modernity and Globalization* (New York: University of Rochester Press, 2013), 5.
3 Patrick Manning, *Slavery and African Life: Occidental and Oriental and African Slave Trades* (Cambridge: Cambridge University Press, 1990), 12.

4 Toyin Falola, *The African Diaspora*, 12.

5 Toyin Falola, "Nigeria in the Global Context of Refugees: Historical and Comparative Perspectives," in *Displacement and the Politics of Violence in Nigeria*, edited by Paul Ellsworth Lovejoy and Pat Ama Tokunbo Williams (Leiden: Brill 1997), 10.

6 John A. Arthur, *African Diaspora Identities: Negotiating Culture in Transnational Migration* (Plymouth: Lexington Books, 2010), 60.

7 Peter Hahn and Georg Klute, eds., *Cultures of Migration: African Perspectives* (Munster: LIT Verlag, 2007), 9.

8 John A. Arthur, "Modeling the Determinants of Voluntary Reverse Migration Flows and Repatriation of African Immigrants," in *Africans in Global Migration: Searching for Promised Lands*, edited by John A. Arthur, J. Takougang, T. Owusu, A. Awokoya, N. Blyden, B. Tidjani, M. Kibona Clark *et al.* (Lanham, MD: Lexington, 2012), 287.

9 The World Bank, "Africa," Overview, accessed July 7, 2015, www.worldbank.org/en/region/afr/overview.

10 *The Economist*, May 16, 2012, accessed July 7, 2015, www.economist.com/news/special-report/21572377.

11 Ibid.

12 April Gordon, "Africans and African Americans from West Africa, 1940 to the Present," in *Immigrants in American History: Arrival Adaptation, and Integration*, edited by Elliot Robert Barkan (Santa Barbara, CA: ABC-CLIO, 2013), 705.

13 "Press Kit: Issues—Migration and Discrimination—World Conference Against Racism," UN News Center, accessed July 7, 2015, www.un.org/WCAR/e-kit/migration.htm.

14 Hugo Kamya, "Healing from Refugee Trauma: The Significance of Spiritual Beliefs, Faith Community, and Faith Based Services," in *Spiritual Resources in Family Therapy*, edited by Froma Walsh (Guilford Press, 2008), 289.

15 Joseph Takougang, "Contemporary African Immigrants to the United States," www.africamigration.com/archive_02/j_takougang.htm, accessed May 3, 2015.

16 Wilfred Ngwa and Lydia Ngwa, eds., *From Dust to Snow: Bush-Faller*, 201. Lulu.com, 2006, accessed July 7, 2015.

17 "Homecoming Revolution Nigeria," http://homecomingrevolution.com/nigeria/, accessed July 7, 2015,

18 John A. Arthur, *The African Diaspora in the United State and Europe: The Ghanaian Experience* (Farnham: Ashgate Publishing, 2012), 285.

19 Steven P. Wallace *et al.*, "Undocumented and Uninsured: Barriers to Affordable Care for Immigrant Populations," August 2013, www.commonwealthfund.org/, accessed July 7, 2014.

20 Kokhavah Zauditu-Selassie, "Women Who Know Things: African Epistemologies, Eco-criticism, and Female Spiritual Authority in the Novels of Toni Morrison," *The Journal of Pan African Studies* 1(7) (2007): 39–57.

21 Claude Andrew Clegg *The Price of Liberty: African Americans and the Making of Liberia* (Durham, NC: University of North Carolina, 2004), 247.

22 Deirdre S. Davis, "The Harm That Has Been Done," in *Gender Struggles: Practical Approaches to Contemporary Feminism*, edited by Constance L. Mui and Julien S. Murphy (Oxford: Rowman and Littlefield, 2002).

23 Donald L. Horowitz "Immigration and Group Relations in France and America," in *Immigrants in Two Democracies: French and American Experience*, edited by Donald L. Horowitz and Gerard Noiriel (New York: NYU Press, 1992), 8.

24 Amir B Marvasti and Katryn D. McKinney, *Middle Eastern Lives in America* (Lanham, Rowman and Littlefield, 2004), 9.

25 Raphael Obotama "Immigrants' Pilgrimage and Imagination: The Cinematic Portrayal of African Immigrants in Movies," in *Trans-Atlantic Migration: The Paradoxes of Exile*, edited by Toyin Falola and Niyi Afolabi (New York: Routledge, 2007), 109.

26 Christiane Harzig, Dick Hoerder and Donna R. Gabaccia, *What is Migration History?* (Cambridge: Polity, 2009), 4.
27 Ibid., 5.
28 Eric Ayisi, *An Introduction to the Study of African Culture* (Nairobi: East African Publishers, 1992), 47.
29 Akintokunbo Adejumo, "Reverse Migration: Time to Go Home," *Gamji*, www.gamji.com/article6000/NEWS7143.htm, accessed February 13, 2014.
30 Chris Wheedon, *Identity and Culture: Narratives of Difference and Belonging* (Mcgraw-Hill International, 2004), 85–86.
31 F. Wafula Okumu, "The Challenges Facing Diaspora Africans Who Return To Africa," www.theperspective.org/diaspora.html, n.d., accessed April 20, 2016.
32 Clegg (2004), 5–6.
33 Okumu n.d.
34 Keith B. Richburg, *Out of America: A Black Man Confronts Africa* (New York: Basic Books, 2009), 227.

Bibliography

Acholonu, Catherine Obianuju. *Motherism: The Afrocentric Alternative to Feminism.* Owerri: Afa, 1995.

Adejumo, Akintokunbo. n.d. "Reverse Migration: Time to go Home," www.gamji.com/article6000/NEWS7143.htm, accessed February 13, 2014.

Arthur, John A. *African Diaspora Identities: Negotiating Culture in Transnational Migration.* Maryland: Lexington, 2010.

Arthur, John A. "Modelling the Determinants of Voluntary Reverse Migration Flows and Repatriation of African Migrants," in *Africans in Global Migration: Searching for Promised Lands*, edited by John A. Arthur, Joseph Takougang and Thomas Owusu, 273–306. Maryland: Lexington, 2012.

Arthur, John A. *The African Diaspora in the United States and Europe: The Ghanian Experience.* Farnham: Ashgate Publishing, 2012.

Ayisi, Eric. *An Introduction to the Study of African Culture.* Nairobi: East African Publishers, 1992.

Barkan, Elliot Robert. *Immigrants in American History: Arrival Adaptation and Integration.* Santa Barbara, CA: ABC-CLIO, 2013.

Clegg, Claude Andrew. *The Price of Liberty: African Americans and the Making of Liberia.* Durham, NC: University of North Carolina, 2004.

Copeland, Larry. "Blacks return to Southern Roots," *USA TODAY.* July 1, 2011, http://usatoday.com, accessed February 24, 2014.

Davis, Deirdre S. "The Harm That Has Been Done," in *Gender Struggles: Practical Approaches to Contemporary Feminism*, edited by Constance L. Mui and Julien S. Murphy, 214–225. Oxford: Rowman and Littlefield, 2002.

Drisdelle, Rosemary. *Parasites: Tales of Humanities Most Unwanted Guests.* Berkeley, CA: University of California Press, 2010.

The Economist. "Africa: A Hopeful Continent," March 2, 2013, www.economist.com/news/special-report/21572377, accessed February 13, 2014.

Falola, Toyin. "Nigeria in the Global Context of Refugees: Historical and Comparative Perspectives," in *Displacement and the Politics of Violence in Nigeria*, edited by Paul Ellsworth Lovejoy and Pat Ama Tokunbo Williams, 5–21. Leiden: Brill 1997.

Falola, Toyin. *The African Diaspora: Slavery, Modernity and Globalization.* Rochester, NY: University of Rochester Press, 2013.

Gordon, April. "Africans and African Americans from West Africa, 1940 to Present," in *Immigrants in American History: Arrival, Adaptation and Integration*, edited by Robert Barkan, 701–712. Santa Barbara, CA: ABC-CLIO, 2013.

Hahn, Peter, and George Klute. *Cultures of Migration: African Perspective.* Munster: LIT Verlag, 2007.

Haidara, Aissata. "No Place like Home: Africa's Skilled Lagour Returns," August, 2013, www.un.org/africarenewal/magazine/august-2013/no-place-like-home, accessed February 13, 2014.

Harzig, Christiane, Dick Hoerder and Donna R Gabaccia. *What is Migration History?* Cambridge, UK: Polity, 2009.

Horowitz, Donald L. "Immigration and Group Relations in France and America," in *Immigrants in Two Democracies: French and American Experience*, edited by Donald Horowitz and Gerard Noiriel, 3–38. New York: University Press, 1992.

Kamya, Hugo. "Healing from Refugee Trauma: The Significance of Spiritual Beliefs, Faith Community, and Faith Based Services," in *Spiritual Resources in Family Therapy*, edited by Froma Walsh, 286–300. New York: Guildford Press, 2008.

King, Russel, and Anastasia Christou. "Diaspora, Migration and Transnationalism: Insights from Studies of Second-Generation Returnees," in *Diaspora and Transnationalism: Concepts, Theories and Methods*, edited by Rainer Baubock and Thomas Faist, 167–184. Amsterdam: Amsterdam University Press, 2010.

Manning, Patrick. *Slavery and African Life: Occidental and Oriental and African Slave Trades.* Cambridge, UK: Cambridge University Press, 1990.

Marvasti, Amir B., and Katryn D. McKinney, *Middle Eastern Lives in America.* Lanham, MD: Rowman and Littlefield, 2004.

Ngwa, Wilfred, and Lydia Ngwa, eds. *From Dust to Snow: Bush-Faller*, 2006, Lulu.com, accessed July 7, 2015.

Obotama, Raphael. "Immigrants' Pilgrimage and Imagination: The Cinematic Portrayal of African Immigrants in Movies," in *Trans-Atlantic Migration: The Paradoxes of Exile*, edited by Toyin Falola and Niyi Afolabi, 97–118. New York: Routledge, 2007.

Okumu, F. Wafula. n.d. "The Challenges Facing Diaspora Africans Who Return To Africa," www.theperspective.org/diaspora.html, accessed April 20, 2016.

Onwueme, Tess Akaeke. *Legacies.* Ibadan: Heinemann Educational Books, 1989.

Richburg, Keith B. *Out of America: A Black Man Confronts Africa.* New York: Basic Books, 2009.

Schapendonk, Joris. "Sub-Saharan Migrants Heading North: A Mobility Perspective," in *Long Journeys. African Migrants on the Road*, edited by Allesandro Triulzi and Robert Mackenzie, 9–24. Leiden: Brill, 2013.

Takougang, Joseph. n.d. "Contemporary African Immigrants to the United States," www.africamigration.com/archive_02/j_takougang.htm, accessed May 3, 2015.

Wallace, Steven P., Jacqueline M. Torres, Tabashir Nobari and Pourat Nadira. "Undocumented and Uninsured: Barriers to Affordable Care for Immigrant Populations," August 2013, www.commonwealthfund.org/, accessed July 7, 2014.

Wheedon, Chris. *Identity and Culture: Narratives of Difference and Belonging.* Berkshire: Mcgraw-Hill International, 2004.

World Bank. *World Bank "Africa Overview"* 2014, www.worldbank.org, accessed February 13, 2014.

Zauditu-Selassie, Kokhavah. "Women Who Know Things: African Epistomologies, Ecocriticism, and Female Spiritual Authority in the Novels of Toni Morrison" *The Journal of Pan African Studies* 2007: 39–57.

Part III

Gender, subjection
and power

7 Queens in flight

Fela Kuti's Afrobeat Queens and the performance of "Black" feminist Diasporas

Dotun Ayobade

Introduction

On the evening of July 1, 2015, Seun Anikulapo-Kuti and the Egypt 80 Band performed to a packed house at the Miller Outdoor Theatre in Houston, Texas. Seun Kuti's Houston performance was a brief stop in a five-month intercontinental tour that spanned Africa, North America and Europe. On the night, Seun performed Afrobeat classics that his late father, Fela Anikulapo-Kuti, had composed mostly in the 1970s and 1980s.[1] Certainly, many attendees at the concert had come to witness Seun perform as Fela's surrogate, carrying on the Afrobeat legacy. Besides the headliner, another important attraction was the spectacle of the two scantily-dressed dancing women who doubled as backup singers for the fourteen-person band.

An interesting series of events occurred during Seun's performance. Throughout the concert, a number of African American women clustered around the orchestra pit and executed erotic routines similar to those being performed onstage by Seun's dancers. These women in the audience shuffled their positions in the auditorium, occupying its extreme aisles as though they were seeking an opportunity to insert themselves into the spectacle onstage. Although they were never invited to mount the stage, these unnamed Black women, who spent most of the night performing their own variations of the onstage dance routines, constituted a conspicuous part of the experience. Significantly, these women attended concert wearing the "Queen" makeup, a similar facial makeup to the two dancers onstage. While Seun Kuti represented the Anikulapo-Kuti patrilineage, the two dancing women embodied a separate genealogy of women Afrobeat artists known as "Queens." This genealogy of women artists were connected neither by blood nor kinship, but rather, I argue, by the affective power of performance.

The Afrobeat Queen emerged in the Nigerian cultural scene about four decades ago. In 1969, Fela Kuti traveled to the United States in search of greater musical opportunities. Upon returning from the United States in 1970 the musician had been radicalized by the Black Power Movement (BPM). The years immediately following his return to Nigeria saw an increase in women artists in his performances. Fela also adopted the dancing Queens as a permanent feature of his routines. During Fela's performances in the early 1970s, some of the Queens were lodged in suspended cages. In these cages, they enacted sensual dances reminiscent of go-go dancers of the "discotheques" and urban bars in 1960s United States.[2] Thus, Fela recruited the Queens to tickle the fantasies of his predominantly male audience. After performances, the women freely interacted with male audience members if they so desired.[3] Both the visual spectacle of the dancing Queens and the prospect of meeting the women after performances sustained an influx of male clientele at Fela's nightclub. The Queens fuelled Fela's inspiration for several years. On February 20, 1978, Fela Anikulapo-Kuti married all twenty-seven female members of his Africa 70 Band. As one might expect, the mass marriage stirred much excitement and controversy in the Nigerian media. With the marriage, Fela bestowed upon the young women the designation, "Queens."[4] Part of the musician's intention was to rid the women of the disrepute by which the public held them as 'prostitutes.' The marriage also represented the musician's ultimate gesture of appreciation of the women's struggles with him in the face of incessant state-sponsored violence.[5] The women participated in running Fela's large communal household. They also collaborated as backup singers and dancers in Fela's music. As stage assistants, wives and advertisers, the women supported Fela's work off the stage.[6] Through their overlapping domestic and artistic labors, the women outlined what the Nigerian public would identify as the *life* of the Afrobeat Queen. More than anything, however, the Queens were most famous for their exotic facial makeups as well as their eroticized routines, which entailed controlled gyrations of the buttocks and thighs to Afrobeat's fast-paced rhythms.

During Fela's performances, the Queens typically adorned two-piece *ankara* dresses. One piece covered their breasts, while a skimpy skirt of the same material covered their pelvic region, but it revealed their legs all the way to their upper thighs. Their tight-fitting costumes usually revealed their midriffs and thighs. The Queens' stage appearances had a titillating effect on Fela's audiences and the Nigerian public. Vivien Goldman describes this effect as invoking the "primeval pussy power."[7] Their erotic performances consolidated the public's view of the Queens as sexually deviant women. Yet, on a certain level, the women's performances were deliberately subverting the politics of respectability that characterized postcolonial Nigeria in the 1970s. Shayne Lee suggests in *Erotic Revolutionaries: Black Women, Sexuality, and Popular Culture* that this kind of sexual politics, which undergirds many Black feminist interventions, fails to "produce a discourse on sex and sexuality that celebrates the erotic theatricality of the sexual female body."[8] It is, however, feasible that when the Queens were performing erotic routines and experimenting with bold makeups in the 1970s, they were unaware that they were in fact defining a cultural movement that would outlive them. Although they understood the immediate political implications of their everyday artistic and aesthetic practices, they were likely incognizant of the long-term implications of these practices on women beyond Nigeria.

This chapter examines how the figure of the Afrobeat Queen has inspired Black women artists to perform by imitation, as well as how specific performances by Black women forge an alternative, emergent Black Diaspora. I will suggest that the aesthetic and affective connection between the figure of the Queen, as in the case of Seun Kuti's dancing women, and women in the Black Diaspora provides a basis for imagining a "Black" feminist Diaspora. Proceeding from the premise that the Queen represents a paradoxical symbol of power and subjection, I consider the works of three artists—Aya Yem, a Japanese singer and dancer; Wunmi Olaiya, a British-born, Nigerian-raised singer, choreographer and fashion designer; and an online photo album featuring a group of Black women by a US-based photographer, Alim Muhammad—who, operating in different performance contexts, reinterprets the nature and complexities of the Queen in complex and interesting ways. These artists forcefully gender Afrobeat history even as they stage a resurgence of the Queen in contexts far removed from Fela's patriarchal domain.

By examining these artists' works and/or life histories, this chapter demonstrates that the Queen's erotic power as well as her susceptibility to patriarchal violence imbues her with an affective power to *take flight* between women's bodies across time and space. The flight that I contend that the Queen takes argues for an appreciation of the ways that time, space and ideology collapse into one another in performance. Also, this flight raises pertinent questions upon which I elaborate in the following pages: how does the Queen mobilize performance to sanction momentary manifestations of Black feminist diasporic subjectivity? What notions of race, gender and sexuality does the Queen invoke in this conceptualization of Diaspora? How do racialized, gendered and sexualized aesthetics map Diaspora? From Fela's women at the Afrika Shrine[9] to other women artists in the Black Diaspora, the Queen resurges as a symbol of strength and beauty that is connected to but not reducible to her erotic power. In so doing, the figure complicates the discourses that constrict the terms on which her erotic subjectivity is understood at home. Although Fela's Afrika Shrine—his nightclub that was also a hub for marijuana-smoking, sexual rebellion and leftist philosophies—constituted home for the Queen, she necessarily transcends this space through the bodies and creativity of Black women in the Diaspora.

The performance scenarios I analyze differ both in context and in their subject's relationship to the Black Diaspora. But for their mobilizing the Queen through the use of movement and facial makeup, these women differ by race, nation and personal history. I employ their performances to demonstrate instances when the Afrobeat Queen has resurged, aesthetically and politically, through Black women's bodies. These iterations of resurgence, I conclude, chart a tentative (even tenuous) notion of Black feminist Diaspora. Quite unlike migration, or even movement that suggests motion between points in space, the notion of *taking flight* implies a more spectral, phantasmal motion. This flight ruptures space, defies linear time and challenges the logics of roots and relocation that dominate thinking about the Black Diaspora. The Queen's flight derives its potency from Black women's bodies. Yet, it defies domestication to coherent and spatially-bound notions of body.

Queens and the Black Diaspora

In the same way that Afrobeat music can be imagined as diasporic in its fusion of styles and sounds—pop, jazz, funk, highlife, African rhythmic patterns and soul—the Black Diaspora can be understood, Jasmine Johnson argues, as mediated performance.[10] Within this conception of the Black Diaspora, the Afrobeat Queen emerges as a diasporic figure that embodies postcolonial Nigerian regimes of gender and sexuality. In this way, the Queen can be said to animate a politics of the body that is simultaneously feminist and diasporic. Yet, it is critical to problematize the Queen's movement and emergence between Nigeria and the Black Diaspora.

Black Studies scholars have advocated a more nuanced understanding of the construction of blackness in the New World. Their thinking has challenged ideas that privilege Africa as home and the Diaspora as exile or dispersal. Moving past such dualisms as home and Diaspora, motherland and exile, these scholars are increasingly interrogating the complex ways through which realities like slavery, capitalism, colonialism and globalization continue to condition blackness. In "Unfinished Migrations," Tiffany Patterson and Robin Kelley critique such conception of Diaspora with a view of moving beyond dualisms. These authors propose a notion of the Black Diaspora that neither fixes itself on tracing cultural continuities to make claims of belonging to Africa (essentialism), nor contends that culture is too much in flux and that claims to cultural continuity are dubious (antiessentialism). For Patterson and Kelley, Diaspora is "process and condition":

> As a process it is constantly being remade through movement, migration, and travel, as well as imagined through thought, cultural production, and political struggle. Yet, as a condition, it is directly tied to the process by which it is being made and remade. In other words, the African diaspora itself exists within the context of global race and gender hierarchies which are formulated and reconstituted across national boundaries and along several lines.[11]

These authors point to the historical processes through which Blacks were inaugurated into global modernity through slavery, colonialism and imperialism. Yet, they argue that it is pertinent to account for the ways that Black Diasporas overlap with, and are being re-forged through, unfolding socio-political conditions. These conditions shape how Blacks experience and continually express Diaspora.

To echo Patterson and Kelly, as process and condition, Diaspora is contingent upon emergent power structures. Lily Cho argues in "The Turn of Diaspora" that Diaspora should be apprehended not as a unit of analysis but rather as "a condition of subjectivity" framed by long histories of dispossession and displacement. Even though Diaspora bears correlation to colonialism, slavery and globalization, it should not be reduced to tangibles like demographics and geographies. Rather, Diaspora emerges from deeply subjective processes of racial memory, of grieving for losses which cannot always be articulated and longings which hang at the edge of possibility. It is constituted in the spectrality of sorrow and the pleasures of "obscure miracles of connection."[12]

For Lily Cho, Diaspora is not just *there*, evidenced in the physical-ness of communities bound by race, religion or history. Rather, Diaspora emerges in its subject's relation to power. Lily Cho's articulation of the relationship between Diaspora as subjectivity and as constituted in "the spectrality of sorrow" resonates with Grace Cho's work in *Haunting the Korean Diaspora*, where she examines the possibilities that trauma holds for constituting affective Diasporas.

There is also a way in which Diaspora manifests as fragmented and sporadic. In this idea of Diaspora, cultural figures become crucial agents that underline the instances when Diaspora emerges in fragmented form. Cultural figures become a way of interrogating Diaspora both as process and condition of subjectivity, but also as constituted through affect. It is in this sense that Grace Cho's *Haunting the Korean Diaspora* makes an important contribution. Cho analyzes the ways that the figure of the *yanggongju* constitutes a source of haunting for the South Korean Diaspora in the United States. The *yanggongju*, or the Yankee whore, emerged in South Korea as a comfort worker for US soldiers during the Korean War. Even though the war lasted roughly three years (June 1950–July 1953), the phenomenon of *yanggongju* endures to the present. Also referred to as the "Western Princess" or "GI Bride," the *yanggongju* worked as a prostitute to soldiers in the United States military when faced with the alternative of starvation and death that the war guaranteed. According to Grace Cho, the figure of the *yanggongju* embodies the contradiction of shame and envy, both as a result of her betrayal of South Korean pride through her sexual unrestraint on the one hand and, on the other hand, her relative proximity to realizing the American Dream through marriage to a US soldier. However, the experience of forced sexual labor that the Korean War inaugurated for the *yanggongju* came to constitute a source of trauma for these Korean women.

Efforts at *silencing* the *yanggongju* in the family and at the level of US–Korean relations—for the sake of national diplomacy—transforms her trauma into a phantom. In what Cho calls "transgenerational haunting," the act of keeping the *yanggongju* a family and national secret causes her to re-emerge in the unconscious of her progeny. In the process, she ruptures official narratives around her trauma and diffuses her haunting among "Korean" bodies in the United States. Additionally, Grace Cho explores the "affective potential of haunting."[13] In so doing, she offers, "the accumulated grief and rage (*han* in Korean) transmitted by the yanggongju creates spaces of possibility within the ruptures she has made but also in a realm beyond narrative."[14] Thus, the *yanggongju* acquires spectral agency through this capacity to inhabit multiple bodies through haunting. The figure assumes a ghostlike agency that transcends the body of the primary subject of the trauma, and haunts other bodies even generations after the original cause of the trauma. Indeed, the *yanggongju*'s power derives from her capacity to act upon bodies, while being essentially independent of the materiality of bodies. The women's trauma and the unjust silencing of that trauma spurs the *yanggongju*'s haunting. Even when uninvited, she *flies* into and through bodies, invades the privacy of homes, and makes her trauma powerfully felt in the present moment. Trauma gives her flight.

The *yanggongju*'s agency is evidenced in her ability to traverse the temporal and spatial limits of power. To frame it differently, the power of the *yanggongju* is contiguous with the power of affect. Therefore, insofar as affect can be apprehended as always in a body's capacity to forge connections with other bodies through and within the interstices of encounters, then it remains potentially subversive, even under strict, highly-regulated power regimes. Affect, as Melissa Gregg and Gregory Seigworth put it,

> can be understood then as a gradient of bodily capacity—a supple incrementalism of ever-modulating force-relations—that rises and falls not only along various rhythms and modalities of encounter but also through the troughs and sieves of sensation and sensibility, an incrementalism that coincides with belonging to comportments of matter of virtually any and every sort.[15]

The "in-between-ness" or "beside-ness" of affect which Gregg and Seigworth describes lends force to the *yanggongju*'s capacity to haunt through the "sieves of sensation and sensibility" of bodily encounters, whether these encounters are imagined as bodily, sexual encounters between soldier and *yanggongju* or between the *yanggongju* and her diasporic progeny. Affect equally reveals its sheer power in the subtleties of its trail and travel between bodies, times and spaces. If in the US–Korean example, the United States can be imagined as the patriarch who holds the power to arbitrate the conditions of his bride (South Korea)'s power, then the ghost of the *yanggongju* becomes a potential albatross of that patriarchal regime. In other words, the force of affect imbues the *yanggongju* with the power to confound the patriarchy of the United States, if only in her ability to sporadically inhabit bodies within the United States.

Like the *yanggongju*, the Afrobeat Queen possesses spectral agency. Clearly, the constitution of the Korean Diaspora differs radically from that of the Black Diaspora. Also, there is no direct equivalent of the *yanggongju* in the Black Diaspora; neither does the *yanggongju* explain the emergence of the Afrobeat Queen. Still, the affective power of the *yanggongju* offers a way of understanding the sporadic ways emergence of the Queen in the bodies of women in the Black Diaspora. The *yanggongju* and the Queen offer a way of understanding how Black women, who are routinely written out of Black diasporic discourse, reimagine and re-perform the Black Diaspora. Through performance, the Queen is able to randomly appear in the bodies of women artists. However, unlike the *yanggongju* who creates affect through trauma and shame, the Afrobeat Queen creates affect through erotic energy. The affective capacity of the figure of the Queen has continued to spread along with the global reach of Afrobeat. As more Afrobeat bands spring across the world, has the Queen emerged as a vital component of the genre's politics? How then might the figure of the Queen be excavated as one of Black feminist possibilities considering the overlapping discourses that constrict her at "home?" With her emergence, the Queen opens up possibilities for reimagining transnational feminist poetics that emerge through the affective power of performance.

Large swaths of the Black Diaspora are constituted by historical, transgenerational trauma, that are passed down both genetically and affectively. Yet, there is a way in which the Black Diaspora is constituted by gender and sexuality as much as by race and nation. Edmund T. Gordon argues for reading patriarchy into the formation and articulation of Diaspora. According to Gordon, modernity and the anti-Black violence upon which it rests is not only gendered; it is sanctioned and supported by patriarchy. Patriarchy also produced and is a product of the Black Diaspora not simply because of the predominance of Black males as agents in the processes of chattel slavery, anti-Black genocide and colonialism; but also the prevalence of male figures in resistance to these processes.[16] The dominant theorists of Diaspora—Paul Gilroy, Stuart Hall, James Clifford to name a few—have made much of the diaspora as "sowing" and "scattering" of seed, as root and routes. However, Jonathan Sell argues, "the sowing and scattering of seed may imply the taking of root, but does not necessarily entail it."[17] We, thus, require a conception of Diaspora that delinks from patriarchy, while also destabilizing the common symbols and metaphors—such as home, dispersal, nostalgia, loss, exile and so on—that undergird it. In this vein, Samantha Pinto suggests that the sporadic eruption of aesthetic form allows for a disruptive reading of Diaspora that is Black and feminist. Pinto argues that a Black feminist Diaspora can be understood not simply as a set of physical movements but also "a set of aesthetic and interpretive strategies" practiced by Black women writers.[18] Aesthetic form, thus, allows us to appreciate seemingly incongruous points in/between time and space as potential for Black feminist diasporas. In other words, a Black feminist Diaspora charts alternative modes of identification and being that Black woman practice in the New World.

Understanding the Queen as a figure implies that the Queen can be known as a cultural, political and aesthetic figure distinct from, but connected to, the actual lives of Fela Kuti's women. As a figure, the Queen potentially disrupts bodies, time and space since she appears in performance. Therefore, when the Queen emerges diasporically, she assumes an aesthetic form characterized by the signature makeup and an erotic presence. These elements make it possible to trace her movement across space, and beyond Afrobeat. In the following section, I examine three different performance scenarios in which women artists have embraced elements of the Queen's persona to assert themselves as "Black" diasporic subjects.

Aya Yem: a Japanese dancer

Aya Yem is a Japanese dancer, singer and choreographer who finds expression for her *Blackness* through Afrobeat music. The progeny of a biracial grandfather, who was half-Black, half-Japanese, Aya claims her Blackness through cultural expressions such as hip-hop and R&B. Although she incorporates these diverse styles into her work, she often approaches them from the distinct standpoint of the Afrobeat Queen. In the last few years, Aya has been crucial to the successful hosting of Felabrations in Japan.[19] Aya, who also leads a team of women artistes, performs in spaces like art clubs, nightclubs, wrestling rings and city halls. More prominent is her performance as a singer and dancer in Oremi, a Japanese Afrobeat dance group. In some of her appearances, Aya replicates the baring of the legs and midriff while enacting free-flowing movements. Her performances range from group choreographies executed with other women dancers to solo dance renditions to some of Fela Kuti's classics. In other performances—and this is close to Fela's model—Aya's team perform as part of an ensemble of live instrumentalists who play either Fela's songs or Afrobeat originals that the band has composed. When the women perform with a live band, they might be con-stricted in the use of space and by how much time they perform. Like Fela's ori-ginal Queens, Aya's dances rely heavily on the hips and the torso, which are characteristically flexed and released in coordination with the arms. Also, Aya retains the dotted white chalk around the eyes, a makeup choice that she occa-sionally complements with other symbolic elements such as cowries and palm fronds, as well as body painting.

Although Aya does not name herself "Queen," she inserts herself within Jap-anese Afrobeat culture as an embodiment of the Nigerian Afrobeat Queen. For Aya, Afrobeat does not simply represent "African power," it constitutes a powerful medium for expressing sexuality.[20] Further, the Queen represents a spe-cific vehicle through which she can mobilize both the power of Afrobeat and her own sexual and political identity.[21] Through social media and travel, Aya stays connected to the Nigerian Afrobeat community, especially with the women dancers within the community.

Aya's work with Oremi represents a strategy for reimagining Afrobeat's pol-itics in her Japanese performance context. Specifically, Aya's work is one of reinterpretation; not only of Afrobeat's aesthetics, but also of its gender and sexual politics. For instance, Aya leads a team of dancers in an interpretation of Fela Kuti's "You No Go Die Unless You Wan Die" (1976). The title roughly translates, as "You will not die unless you want to." Mostly rendered in Yoruba, Fela composed this funky tune to share his opinion on the basic principles of survival in the increasingly precarious Nigeria of the 1970s. Fela's basic advice to the listener is couched in condemnation: if you die in Lagos then you deserve to. The musician suggests that flight is a basic strategy for survival in cosmopol-itan Lagos. In other words, if you see a snake, run for your life; if you spot a recklessly-driven car approaching you, flee.

Aya approaches "You No Go Die" with a broad range of interpretive move-ments that wilfully circumvent Fela's pointed injunctions. Along with seven other dancers (a total of six women and a man), Aya downplays the dangers of which Fela warns. Embracing the more cynical aspects of Fela's work, Aya favors a celebratory aesthetic. The only man present in the scene appears to be an appendage to the more central presence of the women. The women are adorned in one-piece *ankara* print materials that cover the frontal section of their upper bodies, while revealing the backs but for the strings holding the piece together around their necks and backs. The dress does not extend beyond their upper thighs, as a result baring most of their legs and accentuating the movements across the stage. Revealing the thighs in this manner, as well as the measured exposure of the women's bodies, lends their performance the erotic edginess for which the Afrobeat Queen is notorious. Moyo Okediji suggests that Aya's ingenuity can be found in her ability to expand the Afrobeat Queen's vocabulary of movement without sacrificing the Queen's erotic energy:[22]

> [Aya] adds inventive movements to the music of Fela Anikulapo Kuti. Aya Yem reinterprets [You No Go Die] with lean lines that are both poetic and painterly, using frozen and fluid phrases, imbued with a fine range of restrained yet colorful palettes, utterly surprising and erotic in their linear and cyclic fullness of volumes.[23]

Okediji underlines the tact with which Aya uses her body to reinterpret Fela's art in her Japanese context. It is important to add that Aya's resourcefulness transcends the aesthetic appeal of her works or her ability to conjure the Queen's eroticism (these are salient considerations). Aya's resourcefulness extends to her ability to inflect Afrobeat's gender and sexual politics with a kind of feminist praxis. In the example of "You No Go Die," Fela is disembodied; he only "supplies" the music from the speakers. The act of absenting Fela, or any central male figure for that matter, extols the figure of the Queen as a complete political subject in and of herself. Additionally, as the women claim the stage flailing their arms, flexing their torsos and wriggling their hips, they activate a discourse of female sexuality not being dictated by a central male figure. If anything, Fela's voice is only relevant in the performance because it *serves* the women's primary desire to dance.

Aya's solo and the ensuing freestyle dancing by the other women invite a most visible reading of this kind of erotic autonomy. Flanked by two lines of women on either side of the stage, Aya takes center stage to execute a range of freestyle movements. Beginning with her back to the audience, she jiggles her waist to the audience. Her vibrating waist and torso elicits wails of delight from the audience. Amidst the appreciation, Aya proceeds to execute a fast-paced routine that involves flexing her torso and punctuating the rhythm with her extremities in angular formations. She then segues into circular movements of the torso and arms as she rotates on a spot. This culminates into leg movements that involve opening and closing both legs in flaps. Her body's lines and the pulsing of her thighs invite attention to her pelvic region. As Aya completes her routine, the other dancers reoccupy the center stage area in turns. Their freestyle movement features a flexing of their torsos in semi-squatting positions. This sequence then culminates into an orgasmic moment in which the women continue jerking their waist to the pointed cry of the trumpet. The queer energy of

Figure 7.1 Aya Yem and Oremi.
Photo credit: Aya Yem.

this moment is hard to miss. Not only are the women reveling in an erotic bliss of their performance together; they symbolically subvert heterosexual masculinity by decentering the only man in the frame. The sole man in the routine enjoys neither visual emphasis nor emotional attention.

This moment in the performance presents the most perceptible moment of the Queen's resurgence in the bodies of these Japanese women. In brief moments of charm, these women inhabit the Queen, lend her energy and spectral agency, and identify, however tenuously, with the figure as one domesticated by colonial and postcolonial patriarchies. In performance, diasporic collectivities are forged through the force of affect.

Wunmi Olaiya: Wunmigirl's "More Expensive Shit"

Wunmi Olaiya was born in Britain and raised in Nigeria, but splits her time as a performing artist between Europe, Africa and the Americas. As a singer, dancer, choreographer and fashion designer, Wunmi grounds her work in the Afrobeat aesthetic. Following in the shoes of Victor Olaiya, her uncle and famed Nigerian highlife musician, himself Fela's contemporary, Wunmi continues to produce music that combines Afrobeat, folk, jazz and, to a certain extent, rock. This fusion of styles that Wunmi espouses in her art evidences the diasporic reach of

Figure 7.2 Wunmi in performance at Hornings Hideout, North Plains, Oregon, July 2012.

Photo credit: Brandan Jaffer-Thom.

her own life. A writer manages to capture some of the complexities of Wunmi's style in a 2009 article: "In the world of dance music, Wunmi is a one-off, an artist that effortlessly joins the dots between Nigeria's Afrobeat music, New York's house pedigree and London's jazz, broken beat and classic street soul sounds."[24] Her repertoire ranges from personal originals to remakes of Fela classics. Despite not being a mainstream artist, Wunmi manages to produce some of her music in video. Otherwise, most of her performances take place in clubs or concert halls in major cities across the world.

The Afrobeat subculture and Fela's radicalism have been formative to Wunmi's artistic identity. Although Wunmi holds deep admiration for Fela, she recognizes that Fela's genius derives in part from the Queens' power. According to Wunmi, the Queens remained the essential force behind the groove. They enchanted the audience and kept them craving more music, more rebellion. For Wunmi, the Queens' influence was not limited to the audience, but to Fela Kuti himself:

> I love the fact that the women control. They controlled it! They controlled it! You can talk about Fela all day long, but when you went to the show, you went to check the women out. So as a female artist stepping into myself and doing what I do with music and dance, it made it very easy for me because I didn't have to explain myself to anybody.[25]

By speaking of an artistic self that she "steps into," Wunmi upholds the Queen as an artistic forebear. Like Aya, she understands the Queen as a figure that invokes potentially subversive notions of gender and female sexuality. In some ways, the Queen's inhabitability made it so that Wunmi "didn't have to explain [her]self to anybody." In a similar light, when Wunmi speaks of Fela's Queens, she reveals a deep respect for the women. The act of "checking out" the women during performances could entail appreciating the strength and control of their bodies. Also, this idea of "checking out" could entail taking in the eroticism of their gyrating bodies, while simultaneously (re-)reading the sexual scripts for which the women's bodies were choreographed. In a separate interview with Vivien Goldman, Wunmi explains that "when you see how the woman can control [the hip and buttocks], so smooth— ooooh!"[26] As Goldman describes it, this moment in the interview culminates as something of a sensual union with the Queen: "[Wunmi] shudders deliciously."[27] Fela would have taken no delight in realizing that *his* women could elicit this kind of same-sex admiration. Nonetheless, the affective power and reach of the women's bodies trumps his desire to regulate their sexuality.

Wunmi adapts aspects of the Queen's aesthetic to her own work. Yet, Wunmi's relationship with the Queens is far from seamless. Unlike Aya, who might perform as a backup singer or as a dancer in Oremi, Wunmi is the lead singer in her own performances. She leads her own band of mostly male musicians, who collaborate as instrumentalists and vocal backups. Occasionally, she deploys female backup singers and male instrumentalists. Although Wunmi does not self-identify as a "Queen," her fans and friends insist that she is "The Queen of Afrobeat," a reincarnation of Afrobeat's feminine principle.[28] While her aesthetics invokes the Afrobeat Queen, Wunmi's work clearly transcends the politics of the Queen. Some folks think of her as a "modern living truth of Afro-Futurism,"[29] an indication of her mobilizing the Queen's aesthetic to extant and imagined political realities. In framing Wunmi as a Queen, it is important to remain cognizant of the different musical and aesthetic genres that her work straddles. Yet, the Queen continues to shape Wunmi's artistic work in poignant ways. Wunmi explains the nearly-spiritual manner in which the Queen acts upon her composition process: "[O]ften I hear Fela's Queens' voices in my head when working out my hooks ... the power of all their voices singing in unison."[30] In this artistic relationship, the Queen assumes a spectral agency. She is able to act upon Wunmi's artistic creative subconscious even as she helps expand the political limits of what can be said through Wunmi's music. In this way, Wunmi animates the Queen in the same way that the Queen acts upon Wunmi.

It is easy to misread Wunmi's work as an imitation of Fela's more acclaimed work. For instance, Wunmi has a penchant for singing Fela classics or employing scat singing, a vocal mannerism for which Fela was famed. However, Wunmi's performances reveals subtle and deliberate acts of feminist subversion. In a London tribute performance to Fela, to cite an example, Wunmi riffs on the late musician's 1975 "Expensive Shit." Her edition is titled "More Expensive Shit." The original song recounts Fela's harrowing experience with the Nigerian police after being arrested for marijuana possession. In this tribute performance, however, Wunmi fuses "Expensive Shit" with Fela's 1974 "Upside Down" in which Fela collaborated with Sandra Izsadore, his friend and lover who is credited with radicalizing him.[31] By inhabiting the role of Sandra, who is revered in Afrobeat circles as the Mother of Afrobeat, Wunmi actively inserts herself into a genealogy of Afrobeat women artists. In Wunmi's interpretation of "Expensive Shit," Sandra doubles both as herself and as the Afrobeat Queen. Crucially, the figure of the Queen transforms from a "docile" artistic appendage into a vibrant, "fierce" lead vocalist. Wunmi's "More Expensive Shit" allows her to simultaneously appropriate the energies of the Queen and that of Fela into something novel. At moments during the performance, Wunmi turns and wiggles her buttocks to the audience, most of which is comprised of women. Midway through her performance Wunmi makes her way to a Black woman in the audience. For a few seconds, she sings to this woman who smiles back. The performance is electric. The erotic charge of Wunmi's performance and the intense singing and dancing animates the audience.

Therefore, when Wumi shuffles between Lagos, London and the numerous cities in the United States, she circulates with the ever-present potential of invoking the Queen or of being read as embodying the Queen. Her movement across these spaces and national contexts troubles stable categories such as roots, home, exile, dispersal and so on. Rather, Wunmi maps the Black Diaspora as moments of performance, which the figure of the Afrobeat Queen sanctions.

A photographic collective: Alim Muhammad's "The Art of Fela's Queens"

I now turn my attention to another mode of performance: a group photography session by Alim Muhammad, a Dallas-based photographer. Muhammad describes himself simply as a "travelling photographer" on his 500px.com page.[32] Through this online photo-sharing platform, Muhammad shares his work, which ranges from landscape to portrait and travel photography. 500px.com allows its users to not only create and upload their portfolio of photos online; it also gives them the platform to sell these photos to interested buyers. Muhammad offers an intriguing interpretation of the Queens in a series titled "The Art of Fela's Queens." Comprising sixty-nine photographs, Muhammad's interpretation of the Queens is arguably one of his most striking works.[33]

Importantly, Alim Muhammad's "The Art of Fela's Queens" invokes an idea of joy and, quite radically I will say, a demeanor of peace in the "private" world of the Queens. Colorfully made up with the Queen's signature multicolored makeup, the palette of colors invokes a carnival-esque ambience. Some of the photos can be understood as sneak-peeks into the process of *becoming*. They highlight the ways that the Queen is a performed identity. That is, an identity that comes into being through the process of reiterated enactments. In other words, such identities are contingent upon the very act of their performance.[34] Some of these photos feature Queens making up one another, covering their faces in layers of colors that transform them into Queens. Muhammad documents this act of becoming as one occurring within an environment of joy and mutual care among Black women.

The posed portraits in the series capture the Queens already transformed through makeup. These portraits show the women either staring squarely into the camera or peeking just out of focus of the camera's gaze. This category of photos capture the Queen as a figure of strength. By this sequence in the series, *Queen* as a denotative category begins to refer to both the women who historically collaborated with Fela Kuti, as well as the women who perform the Queen in Alim Muhammad's photo-shoot. Since Diaspora is "mobilized choreographically," as Jasmine Johnson argues,[35] it becomes counterintuitive to claim that the women in the photoshoot are inauthentic Queens. To say that they *are not* Queens, or that they do not do justice to the Queens,[36] is to misunderstand the very constitution of the Queen as a diasporic subject herself. The broad swath of colors across the face was often overlaid with dotted rings or lines of white paint around the eyebrow and the cheeks. In part, the Queens' elaborate makeup represented an attempt to invoke a similar practice from ancient Egyptian makeup traditions.[37] Additionally, the dotted *efun* or white chalk around the eyes invoked the idea of purity predominant in Yoruba spiritual practice. Laced in dotted arcs around the eyes, this white became symbolic of an extraterrestrial vision that some Yoruba women were believed to possess. The combination of these elements—cage, chalk, beads, dress, song and dances— combine as core elements in making the Queen a social and artistic entity that culls performance practices and philosophies from disparate cultures. What such a claim about cultural authenticity misses is the idea that the figure of the *Queen* is herself a contested and unstable identity that is shaped and reshaped constantly by the women who have inhabited her and who continue to inhabit her, either to make a political statement or for purely aesthetic events such as Muhammad's photo-shoot.

The posed group photos in the series highlight the connection between the Queens. This category of photographs captures the Queens in variations of collectivity; in small groups of three or in larger groups as many as fourteen. These photographs highlight the subtle ways that the women are affectively and erotically connected by their bodies. In several of the photos, the Queens maintain poses in which their bodies touch, in which they support one another's weights or in which their bodies form a human chain, a visual metaphor both for slavery and for connectivity. Whether they are arranged as a chain of bodies, as a human pile with outstretched arms, or simply as a group of women engaged in casual chitchat, these Queens underscore the interconnectivity of their worlds. The force of bodily contact emits homoerotic current, even as it evokes the subtleties of the women's relationship to one another. In other words, the collage of photographic moments prioritize the women's relationships within the collective.

The women's relationship to objects or symbols of the Afrobeat aesthetic further illustrate this notion of relationality. In one photograph, the women are engaged in what seems like a casual chat around an erect silver saxophone. While the saxophone is centrally positioned in the photo, it cedes focus to the women who all look like they are immersed in lively conversation. Half smiling, half-chatting, each of the women looks at first sight to be jesting with another specific woman within the group. However, a closer look at their lines of sight tells a slightly different story. Most of the women render both a broad and specific visual focus to another woman, so that the perceived out-of-focus spaces become a commentary on their intersubjective existence. The overlapping [or crisscrossed] fields of visions seem to form an invisible kaleidoscope of connections among the women, which simultaneously captures the idea of looking *at* one another as well as looking *out for* one another. The secondary object of focus in this combination, a saxophone (which might be read as Muhammad's metaphor for Fela) underscores the women's commitment to the collectivity despite the presence of objects. Although the objects receive visual emphasis in certain photographs in the collection, the majority of photographs emphasis the connection between the women.

Although the collection is organized, curated and mediated by a man, the visual power of the collection is to be found in the individual and collective performances of its subjects, the Black women. This is not to underplay Muhammad's mediatory authority, but, rather, to highlight (a) the power of the Afrobeat Queen to inspire collectivities of Black women, and (b) power of the subject of a photograph to affect interpretations of that photograph. On this second point, Wendy Garden argues, "The poses adopted by the [photographic subject], their gaze and gesture, together with the vestments and accoutrements worn on the body all contribute to the meanings produced in photographic space."[38]

The women do not simply re-enact the Queen. In Muhammad's photo session, they reinterpret themselves as Black diasporic subjects. Their embodying the Queen in turn extends the potential for the Queen to be reperformed by other women in the Black Diaspora.

Emergent Queens: performing affect and charting Diaspora

The Afrobeat Queens' subjugation under Fela's patriarchal authority leaves them unattractive for Nigerian feminisms that have heretofore ignored them as subjects of political possibilities.[39] In fusing this performance of sexuality with "Black Power" concerns, the Queen reconciles the seeming contradictory categories of racial consciousness and erotic subjectivity. On another level, the Queen's body traces the archeology of colonial power on the female body, a power that rigs erotic desire and the erotic imagination in favor of the African man upon whom the tripartite forces of colonial polity, religion and trade have invested often-arbitrary powers.[40] One might argue that the unattractiveness of the Queen as a subject of political possibilities in the Nigerian context is rooted in her curious relationship with patriarchy and violence. The Queens were susceptible to state-sponsored violence enacted by the army and police. The targeted assault on the Queens' sexual body parts during the invasion powerfully illustrates one mode of the Nigerian State's disciplining of its sexually deviant women.[41] In particular, sexualized violence also suggests that the state imagined the women as being sexually violable. Thus, her relationship with violence leaves the Queen unworthy of celebration in a feminist sense. She is thus "silenced" because she is too entangled with two key sources of gendered violence: domestic patriarchy and State patriarchy. Yet, it is in the nexus of eroticism and violence that the Queens' performances appear to derive potency. In the varied diasporic contexts in which the Queen is performed, violation becomes strength while eroticism becomes a feminist position.

The works of Aya Yem, Wunmi and Alim Muhammad reveal the multiple ways that the figure of the Queen moves between time, space and bodies. They also illustrate how the Queen manifests spectral agency in her ability to act with and through the bodies of Black women. The nature of Diaspora in which the Queen operates is not necessarily one of displacement, loss or longing but one of affect. The women's Diaspora is constituted through identification with Afrobeat's racial politics or with the erotic subjectivity of Fela's original Queens. In this sense, the potency of the Afrobeat Queen becomes, quite like the *yanggonju*, encoded in the spectrality of her agency.

In the flight and resurgence of the Queen, the performing body becomes crucial to forging new notions of Black feminist Diasporas. For Aya, diasporic subjectivity emerges in her *performing* Diaspora through dance and music rather than in the volume of "Black" blood that runs in her veins. Through her artistic and political work, Aya argues for a recalibration of the Black Diaspora to include Japan and the larger Asian continent—these spaces typically get excluded from Black diasporic discourses. In Wunmi's case, playing around the

Queen (by simultaneously embodying Fela and the women) represents one way she navigates the New World. More than race, citizenship or shared histories of displacement or dispersal, the ephemerality of performance, the contagion of Queen's affect, is what connects Aya to Wunmi.

The women in Alim Muhammad's "The Art of Fela's Queens" reveal an even more nuanced idea of Diaspora. Even though the fourteen anonymous women share space, time and performance of *queenliness*, it will be disingenuous to place them into the category of Diaspora. More than likely, they share radically different personal histories as well as different relationships to political and racial citizenship. Yet, their inhabitation of the Queen in the time and space of the photography session marks them as performing, momentarily, a notion of Diaspora steeped in Afrobeat history. Without the benefit of knowing their personal histories, their embodying the Queen opens up space for imagining them part of a diasporic collective. Filtered through the lens of Afrobeat music, this collective is simultaneously Black and feminist. The collective is Black not simply because it is peopled by Black bodies, but because it visually activates the Pan-Africanist ethos of Afrobeat music. The three foregoing scenarios are feminist because they actively displace Fela Kuti or a patriarchal figure in favor of named or unnamed Black women. In this way, the women stage an identification with Afrobeat's politics while enacting a critique of its patriarchal ethos.

While Aya, Wunmigirl and the women in "The Art of Fela's Queens" do not share an articulated Black feminist agenda, their engagement with the Queen, even their choice to perform the Queen, opens them up to a Black feminist reading. In these scenarios, the potential of *becoming* Queens through performance unites the women in the category of a Black feminist Diaspora. If some of the women subtly identify with Afrobeat's pro-Black, pan-Africanist and anti-colonial ethos, then performing the Queen allows them to embrace this politics without naming it. Afrobeat dance, Jasmine Johnson points out, "shows the ways that the body indexes Diaspora without verbal utterance."[42]

By suggesting that the Queen charts a Diaspora through performance, I point to the way that performance rearticulates diaspora. Rather than being an objective condition, Diaspora becomes performed and re-performed. And, as in performance, Diaspora is always in the making. Diaspora is unresolved. For the Afrobeat Queen, Diaspora is made in the moments and the fragments of space beyond subjection by Fela's patriarchy. It is also made in the way the figure sporadically inhabits the bodies of women artists globally.

Conclusion

In this chapter, I have argued that the Afrobeat Queen, a figure imagined as victim in Nigeria, has been imagined as a symbol of strength and beauty in a Black diasporic context. I examined the works of three artists to discuss how they interpret the Queen as a figure of the Black Diaspora. In their different ways, these artists contend with the contradiction of the Queen as a figure imbued with erotic power but susceptible to violence. As such, they each stage performances that interpret the Queen without her subjection to postcolonial patriarchy. In examining how Black women inhabit the Queen in diasporic contexts, I have demonstrated that they offer a way of imagining a Black feminist Diaspora that neither takes "Black" for granted as an objective locus for gauging Diaspora, nor assumes shared feminist poetics based on race.

This Black feminist Diaspora is contested and takes its substance from being performed and performable. In other words, it derives its impetus from the contagion of affect. The difficulty, if not impossibility, of disciplining affect into rigid categories like race, nation and class makes it a productive way to rethink how the Black Diaspora is being re-enacted. My treatment of the Afrobeat Queen extends conversations not only about how a gendered, sexualized and racialized figure might transform across time, place and bodies, but also how this figure might generate fresh political possibilities as well as emerging, experimental collectivities. The Queen forges ephemeral collectivities of Black women from Nigeria to the Black Diaspora. In short, the Queen is mapping her own Black Diaspora.

Notes

1 Afrobeat is a style of music that fuses elements of soul, jazz, funk, Nigerian Hi-Life, African rhythmic patterns; all these complemented by scathing political commentary. Fela Kuti developed Afrobeat as a highly political art in the early 1970s.
2 G. Gonos, "Go-Go Dancing: A Comparative Frame Analysis," *Urban Life* 5(2) (1976): 189–220, doi:10.1177/089124167600500203.
3 Interview with Elutunde Eludoyin, close associate of Fela Kuti.
4 Carlos Moore, *Fela: This Bitch of a Life* (London: Allison and Busby, 1982), 162.
5 Ibid.
6 Ibid., 166.
7 Vivien Goldman, "Thinking Africa: Afrobeat Aesthetic and the Dancing Queens," in *Fela: From West Africa to West Broadway*, edited by Trevor Schoonmaker (New York: Palgrave Macmillan, 2003), 105.
8 Shayne Lee, *Erotic Revolutionaries: Black Women, Sexuality, and Popular Culture* (Lanham, MD: Hamilton Books, 2010), xi.
9 The Afrika Shrine was Fela Kuti's notorious nightclub. From the Shrine, Fela performed his Afrobeat music and delivered political diatribes to an anxious audience.
10 Jasmine E. Johnson, "Queens' Diaspora," *African and Black Diaspora: An International Journal* 9(1) (2016), 12.
11 Tiffany Ruby Patterson and Robin D. G. Kelley, "Unfinished Migrations: Reflections on the African Diaspora and the Making of the Modern World," *African Studies Review* 43(1) (2000): 20, doi:10.2307/524719.
12 Lily Cho, "The Turn of Diaspora," *TOPIA: Canadian Journal of Cultural Studies* 17:15.
13 Grace M. Cho, *Haunting the Korean Diaspora: Shame, Secrecy, and the Forgotten War* (Minneapolis, MN: University of Minnesota Press, 2008), 25.
14 Ibid.
15 Melissa Gregg and Gregory J. Seigworth, *The Affect Theory Reader* (Durham, NC: Duke University Press, 2010), 2.
16 Edmund T. Gordon, "Patriarchy and the Diaspora," 2014 Distinguished Africa Lecture, The University of Texas at Austin. Austin, TX, September 23, 2014.
17 Jonathan Sell, *Metaphor and Diaspora in Contemporary Writing* (New York: Palgrave Macmillan, 2012), 6.

18 Samantha Pinto, *Difficult Diasporas: The Transnational Feminist Aesthetic of the Black Atlantic* (New York: New York University Press, 2013), 3–4.

19 Felabration is an annual celebration of Fela Kuti's art and politics. According to the Felabration website (www.felabration.net), the occasion

> originated from his eldest child Yeni who conceived it in 1998. With the exception of 1999, Felabration has taken place annually. Currently Felabration [...] has grown into a mega week-long musical event in Nigeria which attracts thousands of visitors annually to the New Africa Shrine from all over the world and is an official tourist destination of The Lagos State Government which is a major sponsor of the event.

20 Aya Yem, E-mail to Author, September 18, 2014.

21 Ibid.

22 Moyo Okediji coordinates an online forum on Facebook (University of African Art) for discussing and reviewing African art and performance. Okediji's work through the UAA allows for critical commentary on lesser-known artists like Aya Yem, whose art might require circulation within African art circles to expand understanding on art in the African Diaspora.

23 Moyo Okediji, Facebook, July 17, 2013.

24 "Ghana or Bust: Wunmi Olaiya AKA WunmiGirl," Afrobeatradio.com, December 12, 2009, http://afrobeatradio.net/2009/12/12/our-guest-this-week-wunmi-olaiya-aka-wunmigirl/, accessed December 2, 2013.

25 Wunmi Olaiya, "Wunmi—Thoughts On Fela," YouTube, www.youtube.com/watch?v=VtyM_ovlGgY, accessed January 23, 2014.

26 Vivien Goldman, "Thinking Africa: Afrobeat Aesthetic and the Dancing Queens," in *Fela: From West Africa to West Broadway*, edited by Trevor Schoonmaker (New York: Palgrave MacMillan, 2003), 106.

27 Ibid.

28 Wunmi Olaiya, Email to the Author, September 18, 2014.

29 Ibid.

30 Ibid.

31 Sandra Izsadore's contribution to Fela's radicalization can be found in Carlos Moore's *Fela: This Bitch of a Life*, 91–107.

32 500px is a photography-sharing website. Alim Muhammad's page can be found at http://500px.com/Markmillionz.

33 The entire collection of photographs in Alim Muhammad's "The Art of Fela's Queens" is available online at 500px.com. However, the link to the specific photograph that I analyze in this section can be found in the following link: https://500px.com/photo/22856409/fela-kuti-queens-554-by-m-alim-muhammad?ctx_page=1&from=gallery&galleryPath=19044865&user_id=654229.

34 For a detailed treatment of the concept of performativity, see Judith Butler, "Performative Acts and Gender Constitution: An Essay in Phenomenology and Feminist Theory," *Theatre Journal* 40(4) (1988), doi:10.2307/3207893.

35 Johnson, "Queens' Diaspora," 2.

36 One commentator at the 2014 Africa conference, where I first presented this research, launched into an "inauthenticity" critique of Bill T. Jones's interpretation of Fela in the Broadway show, *Fela!* According to the commentator, Jones does not represent Fela "authentically" because the lead actor "mispronounced" some Nigerian words given his American accent. Such a critique of inauthenticity, which is faulted in many ways, can easily be extended to the Queens.

37 One of the Queens, Alake Kuti, explains this in Vivien Goldman, "Thinking Africa: Afrobeat Aesthetic and the Dancing Queens," in *Fela: From West Africa to West Broadway*, edited by Trevor Schoonmaker (New York: Palgrave Macmillan, 2003), 108.

38 Wendy Garden, "Photographic Space and the Indian Portrait Studio," *Double Dia-logues*, 2 (Winter 2007), www.doubledialogues.com/article/photographic-space-and-the-indian-portrait-studio/, accessed March 2, 2015.
39 LaRay Denzer, a prominent figure in Nigerian feminist discourse, is a huge exception to this practice. In an essay titled "Fela, Women, Wives," Denzer attempts to recover the Queen as a figure in the development of Fela's art.
40 One of the most prominent work on the intersection between coloniality and gender in Nigeria can be found in Oyèrónké Oyěwùmí, *The Invention of Women: Making an African Sense of Western Gender Discourses* (Minneapolis, MN: University of Minnesota Press, 1997). The book's preface offers a concise exposition of this connection.
41 Carlos Moore, *Fela: This Bitch of a Life* (London: Allison & Busby, 1982), 177–232.
42 Johnson, "Queens' Diaspora," 12.

Bibliography

Babayale, Olaide. Personal Interview. August 16, 2014.
Butler, Judith. "Performative Acts and Gender Constitution: An Essay in Phenomenology and Feminist Theory," *Theatre Journal* 40(4) (December 1988): 519–531.
Cho, Grace M. *Haunting the Korean Diaspora: Shame, Secrecy and the Forgotten War.* Minneapolis, MN: University of Minnesota Press, 2008.
Cho, Lily. "The Turn of Diaspora," *TOPIA: Canadian Journal of Cultural Studies* 17: 11–30.
Collins, John. *Fela: Kalakuta Notes.* Amsterdam: KIT Publishers, 2009.
Denzer, LaRay. "Fela, Women, Wives," in *Fela: From West Africa to West Broadway*, edited by Trevor Schoonmaker, 111–134. New York: Palgrave Macmillan, 2003.
Eludoyin, Elutunde. Phone Interview with Author. August 8, 2014.
Garden, Wendy. "Photographic Space and the Indian Portrait Studio," *Double Dialogues* 2 (Winter 2007), www.doubledialogues.com/article/photographic-space-and-the-indian-portrait-studio/, accessed March 2, 2015.
"Ghana or Bust: Wunmi Olaiya AKA WunmiGirl," *Afrobeatradio.com*, December 12, 2009. Web. December 2, 2013. http://afrobeatradio.net/2009/12/12/our-guest-this-week-wunmi-olaiya-aka-wunmigirl/.
Goldman, Vivien. "Thinking Africa: Afrobeat Aesthetic and the Dancing Queens" in *Fela: From West Africa to West Broadway*, edited by Trevor Schoonmaker, 103–110. New York: Palgrave Macmillan, 2003.
Gonos, George. "Go-Go Dancing: A Comparative Frame Analysis," *Urban Life* 5(2) (July 1976): 189–220.
Gordon, Edmund T. "Patriarchy and the Diaspora." 2014 Distinguished Africa Lecture, The University of Texas at Austin. Austin, TX, September 23, 2014.
Gregg, Melissa and Gregory J. Seigworth, eds. "Introduction" in *The Affect Theory Reader*, 1–25. Durham, NC: Duke University Press, 2010.
Higginbotham, Evelyn Brooks. "African-American Women's History and the Meta Language of Race," *Signs* 17 (1992): 251–274.
Johnson, E. Jasmine. "Queens' Diaspora," *African and Black Diaspora: An International Journal* 9(1) (2016): 1–13.
Johnson-Odim, Cheryl and Nina Emma Mba. *For Women and the Nation: Funmilayo Ransome-Kuti of Nigeria.* Urbana and Chicago, IL: University of Illinois Press, 1997.
Lee, Shayne. *Erotic Revolutionaries: Black Women, Sexuality, and Popular Culture.* Maryland: Hamilton Books, 2010.

Moore, Carlos. *Fela: This Bitch of a Life*. Chicago, IL: Lawrence Hill Books, 2009.

Muhammad, Alim. "The Art of Fela's Queens," *500px.com*. Web. December 2, 2013. http://500px.com/Markmillionz/sets/the_art_of_fela_s_queens.

Okediji, Moyo. July 17, 2013. n.p., Online Posting to *Facebook*. Web. December 1, 2013. www.facebook.com/aya.yem?fref=ts.

Oyěwùmí, Oyèrónkẹ́. *The Invention of Women: Making an African Sense of Western Gender Discourses*. Minnesota: University of Minnesota, 1997.

Patterson, Tiffany Ruby and Robin D. G. Kelley. "Unfinished Migrations: Reflections on the African Diaspora and the Making of the Modern World," *African Studies Review* 43(1) *Special Issue on the Diaspora* (Apr. 2000): 11–45.

Pinto, Samantha. *Difficult Diasporas: The Transnational Feminist Aesthetic of the Black Atlantic*. New York: New York University Press, 2013.

Sell, Jonathan. *Metaphor and Diaspora in Contemporary Writing*. New York: Palgrave Macmillan, 2012.

"Wunmi—Live at Momo, London (More Expensive Shit)," *YouTube*. Enchanted Tunes, June 9, 2012. Web. December 2, 2013. www.youtube.com/watch?v=eFUfsuPmSJQ/.

"Wunmi—Thoughts on Fela" *YouTube*. Fela Kuti, October 17, 2013. Web. January 23, 2014. www.youtube.com/watch?v=VtyM_ovlGgY.

"yemAya Afrobeat Class 'Oremi'" *YouTube*. Afrofunksystem, July 13, 2013. Web. December 1, 2013. www.youtube.com/watch?v=EjcWQItLsLo/.

Yem, Aya. Email to the author. September 18, 2014.

8 Women and *tfu* in Wimbum Community, Cameroon

Elias K. Bongmba

Introduction

This chapter presents and discusses *tfu* (witchcraft) discourses in the Wimbum society that involved women in their communities. The Wimbum people live on the Nkambe plateau in the Northeast of the Western Grassfields of Cameroon in the Northwest Region of Cameroon. The Administrative unit they belong to is called Donga Mantung Division and the Wimbum people live in two subdivisions; the Nkambe Sub Division and the Ndu Sub Division. The chief towns of the Wimbum community include Nkambe/Binju, the Divisional Headquarters, Ndu Town which is the seat of the Ndu Sub Division. Other large villages include Ntumbaw, Binka and Tabeken Villages.

The research for this chapter was conducted in Cameroon and in dialog with Cameroonians in the Diaspora between 1998–2001. In Cameroon, I visited Ndu and Ntumbaw Villages in Ndu Sub Division, and interviewed members of the families whose relatives were accused of practicing witchcraft. The account from Talla Village was gathered from informants during one-on-one informal interviews at Ndu Market. My goal was not to discuss this account, but to get information about the accusations that were made against Mrs Njingti, whom I had interviewed at her new home near Ndu Town in 1999 after she was evicted from her marriage home at Mbah on suspicion that she had killed her husband. That interview was conducted with Miss Eunice Ringda Ngala, who served as a research assistant for me during that research visit. Nearly eighteen years later, the issues are still compelling because issues raised in witchcraft discourses at the time are still relevant today. I also interviewed relatives of the family members who were exiled from Ndu. During the intervening years, witchcraft accusations have been made in the Wimbum community. More than five years ago (2011) it was widely reported in the villages of Ntumbaw and Njirong that the land dispute between the two villages defied solution because witches were preventing the two villages from reaching an amicable solution. In 2014, *New Watch Cameroon* reported that witchcraft practice in the region was alarming.[1] The report alleged that witchcraft accusations were made in five villages; Bih, Saah, Kungi, Binka and Konchep. It was alleged that ten children were given human flesh to eat on February 10, 2014 at Bih Village. They were to repay this meat with the flesh of their relatives whom they were going to kill using witch-craft. These allegations were taken seriously by His Royal Majesty the King of Binka who reportedly performed traditional rites to protect his people and also warned that anyone who was practicing witchcraft would be punished. The vil-lages affected, the people who were reportedly tied by witches and waiting for the day when they would be killed and their flesh eaten by witches, were freed from their captivity. Many people still take complaints about witchcraft to the divisional administration, the court system in Nkambe, the Divisional Headquarters.

I returned to this chapter because when these allegations were made, it was also reported that in the Village of Kungi a certain Pa Ngwang was accused along with Mami Siberia of Nambong. The fact that these two accused people were summoned by the youths (vigilantes) of the village to give an account reminded me of the research I conducted in Wimbum land for this chapter. I was struck by the fact that the reporters pointed out that it was Mami Siberia who had given the children human flesh to eat, thus recruiting the children to practice witchcraft. But more than that, she then asked the children to pay for the meat by killing their own relatives.

In this chapter, I will use the term witchcraft to refer to the widely held belief that some people have innate powers that they can use to cause harm to other people. This is a narrow view of witchcraft which the Wimbum people call *tfu*. *Tfu* belongs to a family of words and ideas which include activities which some people consider benign. These include to pull off actions which some people may consider wonders or miracles; these actions can range from preventing dis-aster to appearing as the double of oneself or similar things. In some cases it is believed that these powers include the ability to detect the evil plans of other members of the community. Therefore, when the Wimbum people talk of *tfu*, they refer to the type that can be used to see things which others cannot see with their eyes, the ability to destroy some one's property and the ability to go to some distant land in spirit and to bring wealth to one's community. The under-standing of *tfu* which many people fear and which is the subject of many rituals and so-called witch hunts and witch eradication, is the belief that some people have the power to cause harm to other people and can use those powers to kill another person and eat their flesh.

Studies of this kind of witchcraft (*tfu*) have long demonstrated that the belief in the existence and sometimes efficacy of witchcraft remains strong in many African communities and the Wimbum community is no exception.[2] This belief system in many ways offers a structure for understanding the world for some people, while some dismiss belief in witchcraft as nonsense. As a researcher, time has elapsed since I collected some of the initial data and followed the con-versations with other Cameroonians on chat forums, but I return to the account to examine the impact of *tfu* accusations on individuals, especially women, in the Wimbum community. My goal is not to provide a broad and systematic ana-lysis of gender and *tfu* in Wimbum society, but to call attention to the gender dynamics of *tfu* beliefs and make a case for alternative ways of dealing with witchcraft accusations. Elsewhere in Africa, recent studies demonstrate that witchcraft is still considered a formidable force, as recent accounts of witches' villages have surfaced in Northern Ghana.[3]

I know some of the people involved in these narratives. I am aware of the problems and ethical issues one faces in doing research on issues with which one has some connections. One's connections, as in this case, have to be stated clearly, and one's interest in such a project should not go beyond the issues and objectives of the research and the presentation of an objective analysis of the issues. My interest in *tfu* studies lies in raising broad moral questions about the discourse and practice, and I will in this chapter give an account and state the simple fact that the majority of the people accused of being witches are women who thus bear the burden of witchcraft beliefs and accusations. The material has been gathered from interviews with members of the community, written accounts and online discussions between Cameroonians in the Diaspora who read some of these narratives posted online in the late 1990s. I have not revealed the real names of the individuals who were accused or made the accusations, except in the cases that were published in newspapers, nor the names of those who exchanged positions on witchcraft in online discussions.

Since 1998, the Wimbum community has been plagued by *tfu* crises that has surprised and shocked people. The Late Archbishop Paul Verdzekov of the Bamenda Archdiocese told me in Bamenda that he was shocked and dismayed at these accusations and would continue to pray for the people in the region to find better ways of resolving conflicts.[4] The Archbishop pointed out that witchcraft crises continue to plague the country, but he did not expect several cases to come from the region in such a short time. Wimbum *bkfu* (chiefs)[5] met to reflect on the crises. People were accused of practicing *tfu* in several Wimbum villages. These accusations involved men as well as women and, in all cases, stiff penalties were exacted from those who were accused. I focus on the accusations leveled against women. In highlighting these *tfu* accusations, I revisit the gender dimension of witchcraft because the number of women accused of being witches is still high. The accusations against women are serious and happen frequently, especially when a woman's husband dies. As part of this discussion, I highlight two perspectives on witchcraft that have changed witchcraft discourses in Wimbum land; namely modernity and the growth of religion. Finally, these stories and drama are important because there were no longer confined to the families that were involved. The broader Wimbum community and, to a certain extent, the Cameroon community are increasingly being drawn to these discourses and made to feel as though they are part of the drama through the mass media and the internet. These communication tools also make it possible for us to gauge a wide range of opinion on the allegations and I will discuss some of the newspaper accounts and internet discussions.

Witchcraft accusations in the Tang community

The first case comes from one of the villages in the Tang clan of the Wimbum society. The discourse on *tfu* was provoked by the death of Adam Kanjoh who died at the age of forty-four.[6] Kanjoh worked as an accountant in Douala, the economic capital of Cameroon. In August 1998, Kanjoh attended his father's funeral in the village and after the funeral, he set out to return to his place of residence in Douala but he fell ill. His relatives took him to a Catholic hospital where he was admitted but his health deteriorated. His family decided to seek treatment from a traditional healer. However, that treatment did not help Kanjoh and he eventually died on December 5, 1998. My informants commented that his death shocked the community to the extent that *Nkwi Tala*,[7] the head of the Tang clan went to see the dead body of Kanjoh, despite the fact that Wimbum culture forbids a *nkfu* (chief) from seeing a corpse. *Nkwi Tala* decided to find out what led to the death of this man at the prime of life. He sent three teams to consult different diviners and they all reported that their consultations revealed that some members of Kanjoh's family were responsible for his death.

On the orders of *Nkwi Tala*, the elders of the village went to the deceased's compound to declare the result of the divination and make the accusations against the suspects. These elders gave the villagers the impression that this was such a dangerous mission because the witches responsible for the death of Kanjoh were preventing them from entering the compound and they had to use stronger power to defuse the power of the witches. They even claimed that some of the witches had incarnated into a snake, and the elders had to kill one of the snakes to have access into the compound. When they got to the compound, the leader of the group accused nine people for using *tfu*, to cause the death of Kanjoh. Mr Bungong, the stepfather of Kanjoh, was accused of being the leader of the group of *tfu* people who caused Kanjoh's death. The group included Kanjoh's wife and Kanjoh's stepmother. The women were accused of playing a leading role because it was Mrs Kanjoh and his stepmother who made the decision to offer up Kanjoh to be killed by the witches. In the Wimbum community, it was assumed that they were the ones who killed Kanjoh and the other members of the witch society were merely accomplices because they shared in consuming the flesh of Kanjoh in the witch society. The elders who carried out the divination and reported their findings claimed that Kanjoh's wife and his stepmother gave up Kanjoh as a payback for consuming the meat of another victim of witchcraft. By eating the flesh of a victim of witchcraft, she had also agreed that someday she would give her own relative so the group would eat that person's flesh, and it was Kanjoh this time.

In addition, the elders of the village also accused Bungong and his group of using *tfu*, to kill several unnamed people in the compound. Bungong denied these claims. The delegation of elders also accused him and his group of planning to kill three more people. This last revelation was considered a good omen and successful divination because the Wimbum people believe that if they are able to detect the plans of witches, the villagers can take action to prevent the witches from carrying out their plans. The elders of the village can authorize certain rituals, which would forestall the killing if the accused persons confess and abandon their plans. The people accused of killing Kanjoh were stripped of their membership in the village and expelled with immediate effect. The *nwarong*, a regulatory society in the village that maintains law and order, gave them a bamboo to signify that they were *persona non grata*. Since they were considered dangerous witches, other members of the village were ordered to cut off connections with the exiled witches.

My informants reported that even though others were involved in this accusation, the elders of the village who were asked to investigate this accusation, reported that Mrs Kanjoh and Kanjoh's stepmother were considered the ringleaders, an indication that gender is still at work in cases of witchcraft. In a context where women are often accused of killing their close relatives in a disproportionate manner, there are gendered issues that should be highlighted in the interpretation of witchcraft in Wimbum villages and in Cameroon. The leaders who carried out the investigation made the accusation and pronounced the punishment because they were convinced that their findings were correct. The elders who made the accusation warned the villages not to seek redress of this action from the state of Cameroon by appealing to the local divisional administration. They claimed that the divisional administration was going to support the decision taken by the elders of the village. In order to ensure that others in the village were not involved in the death of Kanjoh, the team of leaders prepared medicines, soaked the clothes of the late Kanjoh in the mixture of medicines, and asked the villagers to drink the mixture to establish their innocence. I asked my informants what the villagers thought of this modern day oracle used to get people to proclaim their innocence through drinking what could be dangerous; they told me that members of the village accepted the findings and thought that these measures were appropriate because if they did not do so, *witfu* (*tfu* practitioners) would continue to kill people. They actually said that the villagers present indicated their support for the proceedings, applauding the representatives of *Nkwi Tala* for acting so swiftly to remove the alleged evildoers.

The second case of *tfu*, in Wimbum land was reported in the Cameroon press and was carried by the online publication, the *Herald*, as well as a Cameroonian online discussion forum, *Camnet*, on July 21, 1998.[8] Here are the details of this *tfu* accusation as reported by Isaha'a Boh, in *Herald*. Four members of one of the quarters of Ndu village were suspected of killing people with *tfu* powers. The death that brought this accusation was that of Pius Njingti, a head teacher of a primary school in the area.[9] The details about the circumstances of Njingti's death were terse. Some of his friends who had seen him in June claimed that he was in good health, but were very surprised that a day after their meeting he became ill. Njingti was taken by car to the Baptist Health Center at Ndu. His condition deteriorated and the staff at the health center decided to transfer him to Baptist hospital at Banso, but he died on the way to the hospital. His body was returned to his home for burial. Before the funeral rituals, some of the youths of the community suspected that something was wrong and consulted diviners. The diviners accused four people including Mrs Merina Njingti, the wife of Njingti, and Selina Malah, whose husband died two years earlier. The diviners also claimed that the suspects were planning to kill a pastor who was working at Ndu.[10] This prompted the leaders of the village to take immediate action, and the *nwarong* society was dispatched to the community to discipline the suspects. Two of the women who were accused, Mrs Njingti and Selina Malah, were told to leave the quarter. They were exiled from their place of residence. It is also alleged that these two women were also beaten by *nwarong*, before they were banished from the community.

On the day they were accused and exiled, members of the local Baptist Church had come to the compound to condole with Merina Njingti, since she was the choir director of the church. My sources have confirmed this story.[11] In an interview I conducted with Mrs Njingti, she confirmed this account and told me she was shocked that the elders of the community decided to punish her for a crime she had not committed, and send her away from her home on the same day the church came to visit her. In addition to the torture from the *nwarong* society, the public jeered and booed her and the others whom the elders exiled that day. One of the accused women cried and called on one of the pastors who was present to help them, but the pastor reportedly refused to give them assistance and instead told them to carry their *tfu* out of the community. When I expressed surprise to the many people I talked with when I was in Wimbum land, they simply said that the death of Njingti frightened members of the community because it was the fifteenth death in that area within a short period of two weeks. However, neither Talla Tantor, my other source, nor the people I interviewed knew if the leaders of the community accused anyone of being responsible for the death of the other fourteen people. It is important to consider this as one raises questions about these recent trials. I will return to this later.

The third case of *tfu* in Wimbum land happened also in 1998. I am aware of this case because I visited the village where the events happened and talked to relatives of many of the people involved in the allegations. I also interviewed some of the elder members of the extended family where these accusations were made against an elderly woman in their family, Mami Regina, affectionately called Mami Ngwankfu because one of her daughters was called Ngwankfu. She was a member of a successful extended family, by the standards of the village. Regina's husband died in the early 1980s. Regina depended on her extended family, but she also cultivated corn, beans and other subsistence foods.

Regina's problems began when some of her relatives accused her of planning to use *tfu* to kill two important elites of the family. This was the third time she was being accused of practicing *tfu*. Ezekiel, one of my informants, says that when she was first accused he appealed to one of the elites who was said to be a victim of Mami Regina's *tfu* to resolve the problem by persuading the members of the family this was not true. The elite declined to get involved because he did not believe in those accusations. When she was accused again, Ezekiel claims that he persuaded the same elite to do something about these false accusations, but the elite said there was nothing he could do to change the beliefs of people who think only about *tfu*. Ezekiel claimed that he then persuaded the senior elite to take Regina to live with her to demonstrate that he was not afraid of these allegations, but the elite thought nothing was going to happen to Regina.

When they accused Regina for the third time, they also charged that she had tied the two elites on a tree (in the *tfu* way) and she was waiting to sacrifice them at Christmas time. One of the elders who reportedly possessed *tfu yebu* (this *tfu* enables those who have it to have prior knowledge of things that will happen and persons who do not have *tfu* cannot have this prior knowledge) made this third and serious accusation.[12] The members of the community met and agreed that Regina would be given three weeks to free the people she held captive. They adjourned the discussion, but later that day, the population started to agitate and ask the elders what if, in waiting for three weeks for Mami Regina to free the captives, something went wrong, implying that they could die before their day of freedom.

There are two accounts about what followed. In the first account, some people in the village claim that Regina genuinely feared for her life and left the compound, but when she tried to return to the compound to take additional clothing, she was beaten by the *nwarong* society and she died three days later. Others claim that the *nwarong* society ordered her to leave the village and not return, but she resisted. It was at that point that vigilantes beat her up and she died three days later from injuries she sustained because of the beating. However, when I asked if they think that Regina had been beaten to death, none of my informants were willing to say categorically that Regina died from the beating. I sensed a great remorse in some of the people in the village as they talked about this incident. Others speculated that given her age, it is possible to suspect that she died from the beating, but my informants refused to admit that Regina died from injuries from the beating.

Although Regina, who was suspected of practicing *tfu*, was taken out of the extended family, things were not going well. The community continued to struggle with quarrels, illness and deaths. They decided to consult with the *fai*, (sub chief)[13] who is the custodian of the land on behalf of the village. This *fai* was also concerned about these problems and encouraged the family to consult a diviner. He volunteered to go with them to consult the diviner to demonstrate the extent to which he believed that the practice of *tfu* threatened the wellbeing of the family and their entire village. The elders of this family, now accompanied by a senior *fai* from the village, consulted a diviner but to their surprise, the diviner pointed out that the *tfu*, practiced by Mami Regina was not dangerous or life threatening. The diviner also named members of the family who were engaged in *tfu*, but said they were engaged in it just to get attention, even though such *tfu* also brought discord, jealousy and bad feelings in the community. As if to demonstrate that he knew what he was talking about, the diviner reportedly told one of the members of the team that had come to consult him that *tfu* people were trying to make him go blind. He gave him protective medicines and assured him this was going to take care of everything.

When the delegation brought up the case of Regina, the diviner agreed that she had *tfu*, but added that Regina did not do any harm. He told them that she had *tfu bsaa*, a form of *tfu* which is generally used to bring bounty and abundance to the family.[14] They told the diviner that she had been exiled because she was accused of negative *tfu*. The diviner reportedly told them that it was unfortunate that they did this to Regina. He asked them to go and beg her to return to the village otherwise they would see their fortunes go away. Surprised and embarrassed,[15] the members of the team said the she died three days after *nwarong* punished her. The diviner told them that they were going to suffer for this act. He then told them to go back and see the *fai*, who is the custodian of the land and ask him to offer sacrifices and purify the land because they had spilled the blood of Regina who was a good woman. If they did not do that, the entire family and the village would suffer. The *fai* who had accompanied them told the diviner that he was the one who did the rituals to cleanse the land. The diviner told them to collect twenty-five CFA francs from all members of his extended family and buy a goat for sacrifices and *kfu bfaa*, a ritual that atones for an evil act. Wimbum people use this expression only in serious infractions such as incest and adultery, especially when one commits adultery with the wife or husband of a relative. They were to ask for forgiveness for the "evil" they had committed against Regina and polluted the land. He also told them that three members of the family who accused Regina were gossipers. They were to warn those people at a public ceremony. When the team returned to the village they did exactly as the diviner told them. At the public ceremony, the elders who consulted the diviner named some whom they believed were the gossipers in the family and warned them to desist from gossiping. They offered sacrifices and performed *kfu bfaa*, to atone for the exile and eventual death of Regina.

The *tfu* accusations I have discussed led to the infamous declaration by the Wimbum *bkfu*, (chiefs) calling on all in the Wimbum community to take a hard line on *tfu*. In a news dispatch about the Nkambe area of Donga Mantung Division, on March 28, 1999, Isaha'a Boh reported that the Wimbum *fons*[16] who met at the village of Sehn in Ndu Sub-Division "took a resolution against the practice of witchcraft, endorsing lynching and/or banishment from the village as an acceptable sentence for those caught in the act."[17] The dispatch quoted the Cameroon Post as reporting that after that resolution, about twelve people were banished from another village, and five other people were beaten to death.[18] When one individual attempted to return, the village levied a hefty fine on him:

> According to Cameroon Post, the man was invited by the traditional council of the village to provide a male descendant to work as a messenger for the Fon and a girl descendant who would be trained to qualify as one of the Fon's wives. He was also asked to provide seven goats, seven calabashes of traditional wine and seven chickens as part of his fine giving him a right to re-settle, adds the paper.[19]

The only dissent was voiced by the sub-section president of the ruling Cameroon People's Democratic Movement, Fai Ndishirnfu, who charged that people were taking the law into their hands, "inflicting wounds on suspects, expelling entire families from their homes and even killing people on claims that they were engaged in wrong-doing."[20]

Some people I talked to were thankful that the *bkfu* wanted to resolve these *tfu* problems even though these individuals thought that the resolutions the *bkfu* adopted were extreme. Other Wimbum people were worried that the resolutions pointed to the fact that Wimbum leaders had given up finding a solution to the problems and decided that they would only use certain types of punitive measures. Some expressed concerns that in trying to eliminate what they perceived as a bad practice, many of the *bkfu* were eager to exploit the situation for their own benefit. The fines proposed by the *bkfu* indicated that they wanted to turn this tragedy to their own advantage by asking people who were suspected of practicing *tfu* to atone for their alleged crimes by giving their relatives as wives for the *bkfu*. Many of the people I talked to expressed the concern that leaders might be tempted to conclude without evidence that someone was guilty of practicing *tfu* because those leaders would collect the spoils of that behavior that now include servants and wives.

Tfu accusations: women as targets

These narratives of *tfu* accusations paint the portrait of the Wimbum community in transition to modernity, yet still rooted in some of the core traditional beliefs that have provided ways of handling misfortune in the past. These accounts offer today's reader different angles from which to analyze the beliefs of contemporary Wimbum people and other Cameroonians on *tfu* by analyzing the position that the Wimbum people have always believed in *tfu*. While the belief and response deal with normative ethical regulation of society through the idiom and logic of witchcraft, these narratives present difficult issues from the perspectives of gender studies. Esther Goody and Alma Gottlieb argue that people regard women suspected and accused of being witches negatively, while men who may possess similar power are respected in the community.[21] The accusations against women often leave something to be desired for several reasons. First, women face the risk of being accused more often than men are. In the three cases discussed here, the people who died were men who held jobs and were considered economic assets to their families and their communities. Their wives and other women were accused of being instrumental in causing their deaths. Some people I talked to during my research think that it was the place of these individuals in society that made even a *nkfu* to go see the body of a dead person. Since these people were respected in their communities, some of my informants claimed that only their wives who were close to them could have given them over to witches. When I asked some of the people, they simply said that since these individuals were helpful to other people, their wives were selfish and decided that rather than have their husbands continue to help others, they should kill them.

Second, women are not merely at risk; they are actual victims. In these narratives, women were accused and punished for allegedly doing things that would cause the death of their husbands. In many Wimbum communities, when a woman dies, it is only in rare cases that the husband is suspected or even accused of giving his own wife to *tfu* people to kill. Some therefore suggested that these accusations indicated that many people thought that women are a danger to the community. One cannot understand why in the case of Tala, the fear that about fourteen people had died in two weeks would make people believe that two women played a leading role in the death of another person. No one talked about the cause of these deaths, but everyone reportedly was afraid and people thought that *tfu* people must have caused these deaths. Fifteen deaths in two weeks may have come from some epidemic, but we have no indication that such a prospect was entertained in the community. If someone pointed out that there was some outbreak that caused these deaths, some people who already believed that the women are evil might still have suggested that it is the women and their *tfu* accomplices who caused the epidemic. This is a well-known logic employed in witchcraft accusation, reported by Edward E. Evans-Pritchard when he studied witchcraft among the Azande. In the Azande case, the people believed that termites had destroyed the poles that supported the granary and a small wind pushed it down, but the people still wanted to know why granary collapsed at the particular time it did when a certain individual was sitting under it. In this case, people could argue either that the women caused the epidemic, or their claims about *tfu* are justified on grounds that fifteen people died only in the village of Tala.

Wimbum people are beginning to ask new questions about women and *tfu*. Wimbum families value marriages, spend much money on engagement and marriage and cherish women as wives and mothers of their children, and of their families. A woman in Wimbum society is often called "*ma bo*," literally mother of the children. For example, Evelyn, a professional Wimbum woman in Bamenda told me that to assume that a woman would kill her husband is counterintuitive to this cultural logic. She added that when women in Wimbum society marry, their husbands become the breadwinners and to assume that the woman would kill him was claiming too much. Such accusations assume that women do not know what is good for them. The concerns Evelyn raised about the accusation that women kill their husbands surprised me because in the past women would not have raised these questions publicly. Let us take the example of Mrs Njingti. She is one of the women who depended on her husband as an employed person to provide for the family and one wonders if she would have done anything to cause the demise of her own husband who was employed and held in high regard in the community and the church. I can see why some women who told me they respect their culture would also raise questions about some of the claims that women would do things that endanger the life of the person whom they love, and on whom they depend, and expect to raise their children with, claims which make a big assumption about the intelligence of women.

Third, these accusations mirror arguments made about witchcraft in other parts of Africa. Recent literature from other parts of Africa suggest that the claim that women generally are guilty of practicing witchcraft could be read as a reflection of the eternal conflict between male and female over the control of life forces.[22] Karin Barber points out that witchcraft among the Yoruba is connected to femaleness and women who lack *oriki*, in spite of the fact that they hold high economic status.[23] However, Ibitokun argues that the powers of *Iya mi* (mother-hood cult) cannot be equated with evil or witchcraft, but in the *gelede* perform-ance, female power is an object of fear by the men.[24] This fear of female power is often projected to the belief that they are witches. These issues invite a critical appraisal of *tfu* to problematize accusations against women. Such a task should not involve a denial that women may be and are often also implicated in witch-craft accusations, but should be an exercise that calls attention to the dispropor-tionate nature of the accusations in contexts where the vulnerability of women ought to caution against generalized accusations. Likewise, any discussion of practices that allege the women are doing these evil things need not see such allegations as an affirmation of the power women have, or as the continuation of such an eternal struggle to maintain and control their husbands and male kin. I came away from my conversations with many of the people I talked to in the Wimbum community aware that some women are willing to ask tough questions about the stigmatization of women as witches.

There seems to be a sense that some women want to ask tough questions even at a time when the public is quick to judge and take revenge. The case of Regina is a good example. Some of my informants told me that Regina had actually been exiled and she was returning to her marriage home to take additional clothes, when *nwarong* retainers met her on the road and beat her. Normally, they would have listened to her perspective since Regina was also an elderly widow; she had earned a right not only to speak for herself but also to be heard. However, she was denied this courtesy in this case. Denying whatever mediation role her maternal home could have played in this particular case, the traditional system failed to adjudicate for the good of all involved.

Wimbum elites, gender and tfu

The escalation of *tfu* in Wimbum land has emerged as a challenging or embar-rassing issue for some Wimbum elites at home and abroad, depending on whom you talk to about these issues in the Wimbum community. I got this impression when I talked to people in Bamenda during my research trip to Cameroon. Several of the people with whom I discussed *tfu* told me that they have Wimbum friends who feared going back to live in their villages because of these *tfu* accu-sations. For example, Albert Njingti, who grew up in Ntumbaw Village told me in Bamenda that he could not live in the village of Ntumbaw because he feared witchcraft. He told me "*tata a faa bi mbi wir ndap weh a tfu*" (Our sub chief has given all members of my family to witches to kill). One Wimbum woman living at Bamenda told me on condition of anonymity that a certain elite and former government official who lived in Bamenda, could no longer go home because his relatives had told him that if he goes to the village, he will be killed by witches. Some also claimed that the relatives of some Wimbum elites constantly tell the elites not to visit home because *tfu* people could hurt them when they are back in the village. Others agreed that *tfu* was a serious problem but indicated that they thought the claims that some Wimbum elites fear to return to their homeland were exaggerated. Others just dismissed the claims of fear as baseless rumors. What was also clear to me was that there is still a rather strong perception that if a person dies young or even in midlife, someone must have done something to make that person die.

Second, in most cases when a socially prominent Wimbum person dies, people often suspect that witches have killed the person. In the death of Njingti, his wife was suspected to have used *tfu* to kill him. When Kanjoh died, his stepmother was suspected and accused of killing him. Mami Regina was accused of trying to kill two elites. I do not want to give the impression that men are not witches or do not practice *tfu* in Wimbum land. However, during my research, I heard very few people think of the idea that a husband could use witchcraft to kill his wife. It is rare that a man would be beaten for allegedly killing his wife. Men have been sent into exile for practicing *tfu*, but in these villages where these accusations took place, it would have been strange to suspect that a man had killed his own wife. I asked many people I talked with in the Wimbum area if they remembered a case where a man was killed for bewitching his wife and no one remembered such a case.

The third way we think of the challenging times in which Wimbum elites find themselves with growing fear of *tfu*, is to consider the discussion of *tfu* in popular literature. The Wimbum elites of Yaoundé published a newsletter called *KINFER*, which literally means conversations. In its inaugural edition in December 1997, the editorial focused on the theme of *tfu*, and the editors claimed: "Today, the Mbum[25] man is abandoning the old habits—hatred, petty jealousy and wizardry."[26] Yet a *tfu* story was front page, and the opening lines were very dramatic: "Fear and suspicion have gripped the Wimbum community in Yaoundé following persistent rumor that some Wimbum women have formed a society of witches with the pledge to offer their husbands as sacrificial lambs."[27] We should note that the writer calls this a "rumor" and goes on to acknowledge that the source of this "rumor" is difficult to trace. However, the editors add that they had interviewed a "renown[ed] soothsayer" who confirmed that such a society exists, but they declined to disclose the location and the identity of the women. One of them said that people might die before the end of the year—that is, in just thirty days—if the group did not do something about it. It is then that the writer pointed out:

> Some members of the Mfuh, an exclusive traditional society for men are promising the wrath of the mfuh, on any woman who is part of the witchcraft gamble … the matter is under investigation and those involved would be presented to the public to face the music as per Wimbum tradition.[28]

While this might sound like a sensational story, the idea was serious business and the accusations in Yaoundé came at the time the ones we have discussed were taking place. Thus, there was a *tfu* scare among the Wimbum people at home and abroad. In this case, women were suspected of being the *tfu* people who would give up their spouses as sacrifices.

The second issue of *KINFER* carried a short story on the *tfu* again, this time stating that the Douala branch of the dance group *mnkung*, (also called *Nei*) of Tabeken Village visited the Wimbum community in Yaoundé and warned the women, and other people to desist from their practice of *tfu*. This time they argued that Wimbum "traditional beliefs have it the *mnkung* juju is a place of people who 'see beyond', so their confirmation about the existence of witchcraft cannot be taken lightly."[29] They claim that this mask dance is composed of people who "see beyond", an expression which refers to the view that some people have the power to know what is taking place in the world of *tfu*, and report it to the rest of the society to seek remedy for the evil plans of *tfu* people. Another expression for this ability is a second pair of eyes.[30] Some people I talked to thought this was a strange accusation because they considered the *mnkung* to be only a mask dance society and thought that the claim that this society can now detect *tfu* practices was new. Regardless of what anyone thought at the time, the editors of *KINFER* emphasized that there were three *tfu* groups among Wimbum women in Yaoundé and then the editors claimed that they were withholding the names of those involved, an indication that they knew who the suspects were.

In its third volume, *KINFER* carried a story that claimed that one woman tried to demonstrate her supernatural powers with the *nwarong* masquerade, *wanmabuh*, by causing the *wanmabuh* to act confused and having difficulties ending its display because it was trapped.[31] As with *tfu* accounts in the previous editions of the paper, the writer warned, "the issue of witchcraft amongst Wimbum women in Yaoundé has of late been a matter of great concern to their husbands."[32] Referring to their previous issue, the paper pointed out those "reliable" sources that told them that there are now three groups in Yaoundé where *tfu*, is practiced. The May issue of *KINFER* carried a letter from Brother Nju-Nyu Nfor Moses of GBSS Niété, stating that only God Almighty can enable people's progress.[33] He lamented, "Despite the high level of the Mbum educational profile, despite the gospel preaching that Jesus has powers in conquering the devil and giving us authority over Satan, the Mbums are still much entrenched in the fear of witchcraft."[34] Brother Nju-Nyu pointed out that the talk and warnings against *tfu* have not changed anything because people still die. He argued that *tfu* results from jealousy and lack of love and unity among members of the family. In a rather open statement, he argued:

> Prosperous members of the family are often targeted by lazy family members. Instead of pleading for help, they resort to killing him or her. Just the mere presence of soothsayers and traditional doctors to combat witchcraft is the proof of its existence. Indeed, non-believers of Mbum origin are caught up in the web of witchcraft. Any misfortune, illness, or death is attributed to witchcraft. The consequences of witchcraft mentality are many

and disastrous. One of the most shocking is self-exile. Some hard working people have deliberately refused to progress. They prefer to remain poor so as to protect themselves from witchcraft.[35]

He ended by lamenting that other groups treat their own cases of witchcraft privately but the Wimbum talk about it so openly as if witchcraft applied only to their culture. Nju-Nyu does not deny the existence of *tfu*, but merely says that it is a devilish activity. He thinks that educational attainment and preaching of the gospel should have stopped the spread of *tfu*. However, that has not happened. He thinks it is there because people lack love and unity. He also thinks it is practiced by lazy people. He talks of self-exile, but what he actually is referring to is that some people among the Wimbum do not want to work and do well so that they will not be targets of the kind of jealousy that results in *tfu*. This is a claim that can be contested.

   This critique is welcome, but I must point out two problems imbedded in his argument. First, he assumes that the Christian gospel can do away with *tfu*. Second, he assumes that educational attainment should have done away with belief in *tfu*. Colonials and missionaries promoted the idea that a more educated populace would abandon belief in *tfu*. This view was grounded on the belief that if Africans studied science they would understand the laws of nature or recognize the chanciness of life and come to accept that things either happen according to the laws of nature or at random. Hence one could not continue to believe that some individuals have these innate powers that allows them hurt other people.

   It is important to note that the Wimbum Cultural and Development Association (WICUDA) of Yaoundé publish the paper and this discussion of *tfu* reflects a conversation that many of the members and elites of Wimbum community in urban areas might be having. The June 1998 issue of *KINFER* carried two stories on the subject of *tfu*.[36] The first reported that two people suspected of practicing *tfu* in Nkambe, the chief town of Donga Mantung Division, were killed. The two individuals, Naka Isaac and his sister Martha, were alleged to have killed their relative, Angoh Martin. Angry villagers stoned the two suspects to death. The same story about this *tfu* accusation and stoning included the following report:

> In a separate incident on May 29, at Mbiyeh-Talla, life was squeezed out of one Shey Chifu who was resisting the *nwarong* injunction to leave the village for good. He too was accused of killing his brother Chifu Matthew through witchcraft mystics.[37]

I am interested in this account because in this particular issue of the publication, there was a challenge of gender-biased perspective on *tfu*. The paper reported that at the May meeting of WICUDA, there was a heated debate about the reports carried in that paper about witchcraft in its previous issue. The President of the group reported that the paper was not selling well.

Mrs Barthson asserted that the poor sales [could] be attributed to the fact that the newsletter carried very negative reports about Wimbum women in Yaoundé. She referred to the *tfu* accusations that were carried in the previous edition of the paper as "mere rumors." She said the inclusion of such "negative news" in *KINFER* only tarnished the image of the women to the outside world.[38]

Mrs Barthson also pointed out that such powers were valued in many Wimbum families, but it was wrong for the community to tarnish the image of women with such rumors. The paper pointed out that the women applauded Mrs Barthson. This is an indication that the women rejected such bias and negative representation by the Wimbum elites of Yaoundé. Mrs Barthson's position was supported by Mrs Bridget Ngeh, who pointed out,

No one had the authority to settle cases of witchcraft out of Wimbum villages, let alone trying to do it on the pages of a newsletter. She lamented that the witchcraft rumor had led to blackmail among the women, some of who settled personal scores by tagging their enemies as witches.[39]

By accusing women, the men encouraged fighting among the women. Mrs Emelda Tala urged women to stay out of male business like the *wanmabuh* masquerade, and if any woman tampered with it in the future, she suggested that such a woman should just be killed instantly. Such a perspective reflects patriarchal perspectives.

Several things stand out from this part of the engagement among the Wimbum in Yaoundé. First, some women reject perspectives that tarnish their image. Second, they challenged the rights the Wimbum community in Yaoundé had assumed in settling these disputes. Third, I must point out that many of the people I spoke to in Cameroon were of the opinion that the elites in Yaoundé are certainly inventing the tradition. By making the case that these closed associations, the *nfuh*, and the mask dance *mnkung*, were to take action and discipline women accused of practicing *tfu*, the Wimbum elites in that city were doing something different because these are not the associations that carry out such disciplines. The approach of the Yaoundé elites is novel to the extent that they want to use institutions that do not normally handle these issues to solve these problems and by doing so demonstrate clear gender bias. Mrs Bridget Ngeh pointed this out to the members of WICUDA.

I must add that the Wimbum community in Yaoundé is not considered a village and because of that, they cannot legally operate a *nwarong* society, but they do have a *nfu* house which is also a regulatory society. In the past, the *nfu* house was the forum that discussed and planned strategies for battles, hunting expeditions and other social activities. The elites of Yaoundé warned Wimbum women that the wrath of the *nfuh* would be extended to them. According to some of my informants, this is a violation of Wimbum traditions because the *nfuh* never had such authority. In this case, the elites are clearly inventing a tradition that caters mostly to their own fears and whims. However, I do believe that Wimbum elites in places like Yaoundé, Douala, Baffuosam, Bamenda, Buea and other towns in Cameroon do have an important role to play in the on-going discussion about *tfu* among the Wimbum. They may not have authority to decide what each village can do, but they certainly have great influence over opinions in the village because they provide the members of the village with money for development projects. They can begin a conversation on witchcraft that could alter the way accusations are treated and the type of punishment given to people. It is simply cruel for elites to assume that rumors constitute a genuine claim, let alone that on such rumors Wimbum institutions should rain wrath on the accused persons. It is regrettable that Wimbum elite are not willing to take a closer look at such accusations against their wives, mothers and sisters. Some of the women who have spoken on this subject think that the men do not know what they are talking about because it is based on rumors, and their so-called "renown[ed] soothsayers" cannot even give names of suspects when the matter is so serious that they fear that people might be killed at the end of the month. Furthermore, there is no indication that any of the senior women in Yaoundé are involved in the investigation—it is the *mfuh*, which they clearly indicate is a male society. Who is to say that the male society has the interest of the women at heart?

Women and tfu in an old/new world

What was going on in Wimbum land was not strange to the rest of the country because incidents of witchcraft were reported in other places in Cameroon. In a dispatch filed August 3, 1998, in Yaoundé, Isaha'a Boh reported a native court upheld judgment against a woman. The chief of the Ekombe Bonji, Lebialem Division of the South West Province, recently upheld a sentence handed down by a lower native court on a "witch." The Paramount Chief of Ekombe Bonji Peter Ekwaro Ekwaro, ordered the woman to pay fines of "a cow, 400 bottles of beer and two bottles of whisky." Ma Ache was accused of transforming herself "into the python to devour her neighbours' domestic animals and cause havoc where necessary."[40]

The Herald News of June 28, 2000 reported that two barren women became pregnant after consulting with a traditional doctor in Yaoundé.[41] After visiting the traditional healers the women became pregnant because the healer had

> purified [them with] "Keghepshu Ngang" which was recently installed in Yaoundé by a three-man delegation from the Oku palace. The cult is headed by Shey Ndifon Samuel, one of six traditional doctors who have been initi-ated into "Keghepshu Ngang." The women had claimed that they were barren because witches prevented them from getting pregnant.

Dr Bah Tanwi, who criticized the claims, dismissed them as nonsense. Such an attack forced Sam Monono to point out:

Calling this story "nonsense" was probably not the correct reaction from our very own Cameroonian MD. At least it has given us food for thought. Many of us are fully aware of alternative healing or traditional medicine that really works. Modern day medical scientists have already acknowledged that they cannot cure all diseases, and in some cases, traditional or alternative medicine has worked for the patients. If you ask the opinion of the ladies who became pregnant after visiting the Oku traditional medicine men, they will not call their experience "nonsense" and it is their opinion that really counts.[42]

Dr Tanwi responded stating:

The use of witchcraft to "cure" infertility is nonsense. Investigations of the curative properties of witchcraft, magic, voodoo, mungang, telepathy, psychic surgery and the like, for verifiable organic disease has been consistently proven false in all controlled scientific settings for centuries. There is an organization called CSICOP (The Committee for the Scientific Investigation of Claims of the Paranormal) headquartered in New York with worldwide chapters. You may want to contact them to see if there is a branch in Cameroon. Perhaps they could meet with the Oku men (and women) in Yaoundé and have them cure organic disease with witchcraft under controlled reproducible conditions. Why are these Oku men not using witchcraft to cure AIDS, an organic process? Please read this carefully my dear brother.[43]

This was a lively debate and I will return to it again later. But it is instructive to note here that there was virtually no debate on an earlier story on the same discussion list which accused Ma Acha of stealing the python head. In the second story, the debate among Cameroonians in the Diaspora focused on the reality of witchcraft and the practices related to it. Joan Foretia raised different kinds of questions in *KINFER*, which are related to ethical concerns that I am interested in:

Without disputing any claims in the original article, please be informed that a lot of women in Cameroon are labeled barren who are not. Undeniably, in Cameroon, and most parts of Africa infertility is seen as a Woman's problem. This outlook predisposes them to bear all the burden of infertility until a traditional doctor a.k.a. "*Mungang* man" is contacted etc. Abuses from some of these "*Mungang* men" are appearing in contemporary African Women's Writings. Most of the children from the so called barren women are fathered by these *Mungang* men, a situation created by the women's powerlessness and the mysterious and magical claims that often characterize these traditional practices (e.g., claims that he has to deliver the concoction himself etc.) I am yet to meet a Cameroonian who doesn't know of a barren woman who got pregnant right after she was divorced. For the most part these women had no infertility problem, they were not barren.

The role of religion

The narratives do open several issues from a religious perspective. First, it is clear that among the Wimbum people *tfu* is an equal employer because some of the people accused were members of the church. Mrs Njingti was a member of the Baptist Church at Mbah. She was the choir director. There was no doubt in the minds of the people that members of the church practice *tfu*. One of my informants, whose father was a pastor from the area, answered emphatically that *tfu* is real and members of the church practice it. Second, the church or church leaders also believed in the existence of *tfu*. It is reported that one of the pastors from the area refused to help the women, as they were being tortured and driven away from the community.

Religion was more of an issue among certain members of the Cameroonian Diaspora. The comments came in a general discussion about witchcraft and flowed postings of the stories filed from Cameroon by Isaha'a Boh. On July 23, 1998, Dr Cabinda de-Gaulle argued that he believed in the reality of witchcraft because the ancestors of the present Bali people used it when they migrated to the present settlement. Witchcraft was considered a gift and was always handed down in the family to the favorite child. He also pointed out that a professor at the faculty of biomedical sciences in Yaoundé was conducting research on the issue. He lamented,

> Unfortunately modern society does not handle these situations appropriately nor do they think that the traditional society has a place in running the African society.... So the traditional African Society still has a role in running the "modern African society" because the root of the society will forever remain traditional no matter how democratic or technologically advanced we become. The only way modern influence can be of help to us will be when we use it to integrate in our existing structures. Not trying to fit African structures into the modern schemes or just outright ignoring the traditional system when we are supposed to use it in instances like fighting witchcraft. This is the price we pay.[44]

Dr Ndamunkong Tangeh argued that the Bali indeed used such powers in the past. Sam Akuma stated that Cameroonians today consult "witch doctors" on all matters dealing with appointments, promotions, and where to go when they are home.[45] Others on the forum such as Jude Anoma called these assertions "hearsay," and Dr J. Asongu argued that the logic of witchcraft exists only in the minds of those who believe in it. Irene Keine raised the question of source, but it was Alaine Maashe-Mengueme writing from Liberty University who presented an evangelical Christian position, arguing that witchcraft if it exists is of the devil and nothing more. He pointed out that it was part of the old religious beliefs and concluded: "I am not against traditional values but witchcraft is definitely wicked."[46] He argued consistently that witchcraft was a diabolical practice and urged others to look to Jesus for a solution.[47]

Joseph Nkemontoh on November 11, 1998, argued that witchcraft is practiced today even though the practitioners do not like to be associated with it for fear that they might be killed. He attributed the increased witchcraft practice to:

> The resurgence of paganism, religious pluralism and new age religions [which] have recently made it easier for witchcraft to return to mainstream western society. Thus, many newspapers advertise wicca /coven meetings just as churches advertise services in the religion section. In the past, it was branded as superstitious nonsense. Witchcraft has always been part of the experience of every "third world" society as evidenced by the literature of various literary periods. While there are quacks in every profession, genuine witchcraft is ultimately diabolic, involving demonic powers with which witches and wizards are able to control subjects, or those who fall victim to their craft. And the "contrary" force that demolishes all demonic powers is the LIGHT of Christ, when allowed to shine in the darkness.[48]

This prompted Dr J. Asongu to invite anyone with witchcraft to teach him how to practice it. Wawa Ngenge, a Zen Buddhist from Cameroon responded, pointing out that someone also wondered why people who claim to be a "great magician (witch, wizard, marabou, etc.) "has never won the lottery."[49]

Some of the Cameroonians in the Diaspora do not doubt it exists, but attribute it to the devil, or, as Nkemontoh indicates, it is a diabolical practice that has been strengthened by new religions. For some scholars who study African witchcraft, the reactions by Cameroonians, which I have reported here, might simply be their way of trying to deal with a cultural and ideological position which they find unacceptable, but they lack the resources and contextual positioning to discuss or debate it in their villages where their position might matter most. I also think that while these debates are informative and interesting, the emphasis on the reality of witchcraft and attempts to demonize it misses an opportunity for a rigorous discourse on a complicated world of meaning and its ethical implications. I continue to see *tfu* power as neutral power that becomes problematic if it is used against someone. I am not sure that I can answer the question about its reality now, but I know the world the discourse has constructed is real and concrete for many people.

Conclusion: *tfu* and the media

In the narratives I have presented, the popular press in Cameroon carried the cases and those in turn were broadcast to a global audience over the internet, making them available to hundreds of Cameroonians who might have ignored them if they read them in papers in Cameroon. However, when it came to them in form of email from their favorite discussion group, many of them were forced to react to the story and the question of witchcraft and *tfu*. This is not a new phenomenon, but the broadcasting of these incidents over the internet provides another opportunity for the examination of the questions involved. This has several implications. First, it will continue to encourage discussion of the issues even if the discussions spend far more time on the reality or otherwise of witchcraft, ignoring the reality that the discourse has created. My assumption is that by keeping such discussions alive, there is the possibility that more women will join the debate and raise questions that could help members of the Wimbum community to rethink the easy assumptions they make about women and witchcraft. From my own reading and understanding of witchcraft discourses, women tend to be disadvantaged because it is assumed most of the time that they have powerful witchcraft and deploy it often at the expense of their husbands. These stories demonstrate the bias women face and a broad discussion, as we have seen in the debates by Cameroonians in the Diaspora, has the potential of providing further criticism of beliefs and practices that already condemn women with little evidence.

Second, some of my informants in Cameroon insisted that the time has come when one cannot make a statement about these issues and not expect to be challenged. Recently some of the members of the Southern Cameroons Movement, which is now called the British Southern Cameroon Nation, alleged that a gendarme suspected in the killing of people in Kumbo died.[50]

> A gendarme officer, Corporal Ahidjo, who has been identified by the British Southern Cameroons Provisional Administration (BSCPA) as being one of those who opened fire on unarmed BSC citizens in the City of Kumbo is dead. Reliable sources say he died on Wednesday October 3, 2001, after being struck by lightning. Victory will be ours, not that of the aggressors and BSC shall be free. No further comments.[51]

This sparked a debate again that did not last very long. Some members wondered why a nation that calls itself British Southern Cameroon would believe that such tactics would be used to fight its war of independence. This response implied that the British would not support such kind of tactics today.

Third, this development offers a new opportunity for questions about gender bias in witchcraft discourses and practices. I pointed out earlier that Joan Foretia raised ethical questions about the practice of healers, who claim that they have used *mungang*,[52] to heal barrenness. The tacit accusation is that in the past some of them were the ones who have impregnated the women. The charge here is not merely adultery and malpractices involving sexual exploitation and abuse. What is implied here is the position that people should revisit barrenness in Cameroonian society. If the *mungang* practitioners impregnate the women, does this suggest that at some time men should be the ones treated for barrenness? This might solve a lot of problems and limit accusations leveled against some women for closing their wombs or the wombs of others.[53]

Notes

1 Marcel Abanda, "Witchcraft Attains Alarming Proportions in Nakambe," in *News Watch Cameroon,* http://newswatchcameroon.blogspot.com/2014/03/witchcraft-attains-alarming-proportions.html, accessed April 25, 2016.
2 Patrick Mbunwe, *Witchcraft, Magic and Divination: Accounts from the Wimbum Area of the Cameroon Grassfields* (Mankon, Cameroon: Langaa Press, 2012). For a comparative analysis see Khaukanani Mavhungu, *Witchcraft in Post-Colonial Africa: Beliefs, Techniques and Containment Strategies* (Mankon, Cameroon: Langaa Press, 2012).
3 Mensah Adinkrah, *Witchcraft, Witches and Violence in Ghana,* (New York: Berghan Books, 2015).
4 Personal communication at Ntarikom, Bamenda, January, 2000.
5 The Wimbum term for *fon* (chief) is *nkfu,* the chief of a Wimbum village. The plural is *bkfu.*
6 Richard Tanto Talla, personal communication at the "Cameroon Transitions and Transformations: Multidisciplinary Perspectives on a Society at the Crossroad." Conference at Rice University, Houston, Texas April 6–8, 2001.
7 The term *nkwi* is another title for the chief of a village. It is used when one refers specifically to the *nkfu* of a village therefore *Nkwi Tala* is the *nkfu* (chief) of Talla Village.
8 I have used the names of the communities where these events took place.
9 This is not his real name.
10 My informants at Ndu did not know the identity of the pastor.
11 My informant was not at Mbah at the time, and recalls the account given to her by close relatives.
12 *Tfu yebu,* is the power to know what other *tfu* people are doing. In some communities, such *tfu* power is considered a good thing. See Elias K. Bongmba, "Towards a Hermeneutic of Wimbum *tfu*," *African Studies Review* 41(3) (December, 1998): 165–191; *African Witchcraft and Otherness: A Philosophical and Theological Critique of Intersubjective Relations* (Albany, NY: SUNY Press, 2001).
13 *Fai* is the Wimbum title for a sub chief.
14 I have discussed different conceptions of *tfu,* but I was informed of this form when I was in Wimbum land. See Bongmba, *African Witchcraft and Otherness,* 2001, Chapter 2. See also, Elias K. Bongmba, 1998, 165–191.
15 My informants suggested the language about embarrassment.
16 *Fon* is a more popular title used in the literature for chief in the Northwest Province.
17 See Isaha'a Boh 1999, www.boh.org.
18 I have not been able to determine this village. The paper might be referring to "Kuyah" which is a quarter in Ndu—in that case it is not a village.
19 Isaha'a Boh, 1999.
20 Ibid.
21 See Esther Goody, "Legitimate and Illegitimate Aggression in a West African State," *Witchcraft Confessions and Accusations,* edited by Mary Douglas, 207–244 (London: Tavistock, 1970); Alma Gottlieb, "Witches, Kings, and the Sacrifice of Identity among the Beng of Ivory Coast," in *Creativity of Power: Cosmology and Art in African Societies,* edited by W. Aren and I. Karp, 245–272 (Washington DC: Smithsonian Institution Press, 1989).
22 Judith Hoch-Smith and Anita Spring, eds, *Women in Ritual and Symbolic Roles* (New York: Plenum Press, 1978).
23 Karin Barber, *I Could Speak until Tomorrow* (Edinburgh: Edinburgh University Press, 1991).
24 B. M. Ibitokum, *Dances as Ritual Drama and Entertainment in Gelede of the Ketu-Yoruba Subgroup of West Africa* (Ilé-Ifè, Nigeria: Ọbàfẹ́mi Awólọ́wọ̀ University Press, 1993).

25 Abbreviation for Wimbum.
26 *KINFER, A Monthly Newsletter of the Wimbum Cultural Development Association, Yaoundé*, Vol. 1 No. 001 December 1997: 1. In nearly all of their reports, they use the term "witchcraft" to refer to the practices I am calling *tfu*, in this chapter.
27 Ibid.
28 Ibid., 3.
29 *KINFER*, Vol. 1 No. 002 (January 1998), 2.
30 See Bongmba, "Toward a Hermeneutic of Wimbum *tfu*," *African Studies Review* 41(3) (December 1998): 173.
31 *KINFER*, Vol. 1 No. 003 (February 22, 1998), 3.
32 Ibid.
33 *KINFER*, Vol. 1 No. 006 (May 1998) p. 2.
34 Ibid.
35 Ibid.
36 *KINFER*, Vol. 1 No. 007 (June 28, 1998), 1.
37 Ibid., 3.
38 Ibid.
39 Ibid.
40 Isaha'a Boh, www.boh.org. Other stories about witchcraft did not deal directly with women. In a dispatch on March 13, 1999 Isaha'a Boh in Bulletin n° 425 reported that one Robert Carlos Orome Nambu killed his father with an axe in Kake Bokoko Village near Kumba, because it was alleged that the father wanted to kill him through witchcraft. This event took place in a drinking house. He had been informed by a diviner that he had only three days to live because his father was planning to use witchcraft and kill him and he believed the diviner because his father was suspected of causing the death of his elder brother, who was a Presbyterian pastor, the previous year. Isaha'a Boh pointed out in this dispatch the murderers who kill on claims that the diviner told them someone was going to take their lives were on the rise in the area, and forces of law and order were not doing anything about it. Meanwhile on May 20, 2000, a former student leader in Cameroon posted a message on the Social Democratic Forum discussion group forwarding a message, which alleged that the government in Cameroon was using occult powers and as a result students at newly created universities, were dying as a result of these occult practices.

> When the Biya government decided to create fake universities in 1993, we refused and let them know that Cameroon didn't have the financial means to take good care of the seven universities since they couldn't even handle the only existing one university of ngoa-ekele. We were expelled from the university and many universities were created. Since then, more than three deadly accidents have taken place in the Soa road to the university and killing many innocent students. Now fourteen other students have been killed in a car accident. In fact, in 1993, we said that this corrupt government was using some foreign sects to rule Cameroon and that Biya needed more blood to stay in power. For the past seven years, there isn't a year without an accident in this Soa road.

41 Posted on the Southern Cameroon Forum of June 28, 2000.
42 Southern Cameroon Forum July 12, 2000.
43 It solicited a response from Emil (I suspect Dr Mondoa) on the Southern Cameroon Forum, in which he intimated that witchcraft might be nonsense. Taking a scientific line, he argued:

> Witchcraft, ESP, vodou and so on might not be reproducible because even the practitioners do not understand exactly how it works, that is why there tends to be so much extraneous stuff. Occasionally the right conditions could be reproduced and then it might work on that occasion. As Dr Nkohkwo said, statistical methods,

which are what abound in many of these "proof of cure" scenarios in medicine are inherently unsatisfactory because they do not delve into the inner workings of things to see how they actually work. I have had rare personal unbidden experiences of so called paranormal phenomena, tried to reproduce them with practically no success but they would recur occasionally after some years without my apparent bidding. Imagine what would happen if I told all the world of my experience, and people started showing up on my doorstep offering me money to "do it again for them." I would quickly become a charlatan because I would not be able to reproduce a certain vivid experience at will. The present cognitive tools and methods might have limitations in some of these things. I am still concerned about the absolute certainty of your tone, which is reminiscent of a disciple of a religion. Bottom line: Non reproducible = non reproducible. Non reproducible, false usually, but not every time. By the way, I expect that you would disbelieve that I have had interesting paranormal experiences, and that would be OK by me.

44 Camnet July 24, 1998.
45 Camnet, November 7, 1998. See also studies by Peter Geschiere, Cyprian Fisiy.
46 Ibid.
47 Camnet July 24, 1998.
48 Joseph Nkemontoh, Camnet, November 11, 1998
49 Camnet discussion forum, November 12, 1998.
50 Posted on the bscnation@yahoogroups.com discussion forum on October 5, 2001.
51 Ibid.
52 Occult powers
53 See Mark Auslander, "'Open the Wombs': The Symbolic Politics of Modern Ngoni Witchfinding" in *Modernity and its Malcontents: Ritual and Power in Postcolonial Africa*, edited by Jean Comaroff and John Comaroff, 167–192 (Chicago, IL: University of Chicago Press, 1993).

Bibliography

Abanda, Marcel. "Witchcraft Attains Alarming Proportions in Nakambe," in *News Watch Cameroon,* http://newswatchcameroon.blogspot.com/2014/03/witchcraft-attains-alarming-proportions.html, accessed April 25, 2016.

Adinkrah, Mensah. *Witchraft, Witches and Violence in Ghana.* New York: Berghan Books, 2015.

Auslander, Mark. "'Open the Wombs': The Symbolic Politics of Modern Ngoni Witchfinding," in *Modernity and its Malcontents: Ritual and Power in Postcolonial Africa*, edited by Jean Comaroff and John Comaroff, 167–192. Chicago, IL: University of Chicago Press, 1993.

Barber, Karin. *I Could Speak until Tomorrow.* Edinburgh: Edinburgh University Press, 1991.

Bongmba, Elias K. "Toward a Hermeneutic of Wimbum *tfu*," *African Studies Review* 41(3) (December 1998): 165–191.

Bongmba, Elias K. *African Witchcraft and Otherness: A Philosophical and Theological Critique of Intersubjective Relations.* Albany, NY: SUNY Press, 2001.

Comaroff, Jean, and John Comaroff. "Introduction," in *Modernity and its Malcontents: Ritual and Power in Postcolonial Africa*, edited by Jean Comaroff and John Comaroff, xi–xxxvi. Chicago, IL and London: The University of Chicago Press, 1993.

Douglas, M. "Introduction," in *Witchcraft Confessions and Accusations*, edited by Mary Douglas, xiii–xxxviii. London: Tavistock Publications, 1970.

Evans-Pritchard, E. E. *Witchcraft, Oracles and Magic Among the Azande.* Oxford: Clarendon Press, 1937.

Fernando, K. *The Triumph of Christ in African Perspective: A Study of Demonology and Redemption in the African Context.* Carlisle, Cumbria UK: Paternoster Press, 1999.

Fisiy, C. F. and Peter Geschiere. "Judges and Witches, or How is the State to Deal with Witchcraft: Examples from Southeastern Cameroon," *Cahiers d'Etudes Africaines* 118(1990): 135–156.

Geschiere, P. *The Modernity of Witchcraft: Politics and the Occult in Postcolonial Africa.* Charlottesville, VA and London: University Press of Virginia, 1997.

Goody, Esther. "Legitimate and Illegitimate Aggression in a West African State," in *Witchcraft Confessions and Accusations*, edited by Mary Douglas, 207–244. London: Tavistock, 1970.

Gottlieb, Alma, "Witches, Kings, and the Sacrifice of Identity among the Beng of Ivory Coast," in *Creativity of Power: Cosmology and Art in African Societies*, edited by W. Aren and I. Karp, 245–272. Washington DC: Smithsonian Institution Press, 1989.

Hoch-Smith Judith, and Anita Spring, eds. *Women in Ritual and Symbolic Roles.* New York: Plenum Press, 1978.

Ibitokum, B. M. *Dances as Ritual Drama and Entertainment in Gelede of the Ketu-Yoruba Subgroup of West Africa.* Ilé-Ifè, Nigeria: Ọbàfẹ́mi Awólọ́wọ̀ University Press, 1993.

Irele, A. "Introduction," in *African Philosophy: Myth and Reality*, edited by Paulin J. Hountondji, translated by Henri Evans and Jonathan Rée, 7–30. Bloomington, IN: Indiana University Press, 1983.

Karp, I. and D. A. Masolo. "Introduction: African Philosophy as Cultural Inquiry," in *African Philosophy as Cultural Inquiry*, edited by I. Karp and D. A. Masolo, 1–18. Bloomington and Indianapolis, IN: Indiana University Press, 2000.

Kiernan, J. "Introduction," in *Power of the Occult in Modern Africa: Continuity and Innovation in the Renewal of African Cosmologies*, edited by James Kiernan, 1–18. Berlin: LIT Verlag, 2006.

Mavhungu, Khaukanani, *Witchcraft in Post-Colonial Africa: Beliefs, Techniques and Containment Strategies.* Mankon, Cameroon: Langaa Press, 2012.

Mbunwe, Patrick, *Witchcraft, Magic and Divination: Accounts from the Wimbum Area of the Cameroon Grassfields.* Mankon, Cameroon: Langaa Press, 2012.

Moore, H. L., and Todd, S., eds. *Magical Interpretations, Material Realities: Modernity, Witchcraft and the Occult in Postcolonial Africa.* London: Routledge, 2001.

Mulago, V. "Traditional African Religion and Christianity," in *African Traditional Religions in Contemporary Society*, edited by Jacob K. Olupona, 119–134. St. Paul, MN: Paragon House, 1990.

Parrinder, G. *Witchcraft: European and African.* London: Faber and Faber, 1958.

Schmidt, P. *The Culture and Technology of Iron-making in Africa.* Gainesville, FL: University of Florida Press, 1996.

Thomas, K. "The Relevance of Social Anthropology to the Historical Study of English Witchcraft," in *Witchcraft Confessions and Accusations*, edited by Mary Douglas, 47–79. London: Tavistock Publications, 1970.

9 Women's agency and peacebuilding in Nigeria's Jos crises

Omotola Adeyoju Ilesanmi

Introduction

This chapter analyses the decade-long (2001–2011) crises in Jos, Plateau State, in North Central Nigeria, particularly within the ambit of the peacebuilding roles played by women in the crises. Plateau State, for several years, was embroiled in widespread violence and conflict with a heavy toll on the lives and properties of its people. However, Jos, the capital of Plateau State can be regarded as the epi-center of the grave violence with widespread killings and destruction of lives and livelihoods experienced massively in the city.[1] Additionally, the chapter highlights the negative impact of the conflict on women and girls. More importantly, it brings into sharp focus the roles women played in bringing an end to the violence and armed conflicts, and in entrenching peace in their communities, demonstrating the fact that women's positions transcend being passive victims in armed conflict and war situations to being active agents of peace. The crises that engulfed the Tin city of Jos,[2] Plateau State for over a decade had transmuted the state celebrated as "The Home of Peace and Tourism" to a "Theatre of War."[3] The first major outbreak of violence occurred in 1994 but was contained by military intervention and concession to local demands.[4] The subsequent outbreak of conflict in 2001, followed in quick succession by episodes of violence in 2004, 2008, 2010 and 2011, engulfed Jos City and its environs.

However, the recent and gradual return of peace to Plateau State, with a reduced spate of violence, brings a great deal of relief and gratitude to the people of the State, and to Nigerians at large. The peace currently experienced in Jos can be attributed to the implementation of a wide range of peace programs carried out by several stakeholders in the state including civil society groups, women groups, faith based organizations and government. Pro-peace non-governmental organizations within the Plateau have embarked on strengthening the peaceful co-existence of inhabitants of the state. Non-governmental organizations such as the Centre for Humanitarian Dialogue (HD), Search for Common Ground (SFCG) and Apurimac Onlus amongst others have been working with the people at the grassroots and community levels to mediate peace and prevent a recurrence of violence. As noted in a *Daily Trust* article by Onimisi Alao on January 16, 2015,[5] the Centre for Humanitarian Dialogue in particular works mainly with communities in surrounding municipal council areas of Jos North and Jos South Local Government areas to develop local peacebuilding initiatives. Since 2013, the Centre for Humanitarian Dialogue has had series of consultations with leaders of the five major ethnic communities in Jos, namely: Anaguta, Afizere, Berom, Fulani and Hausa; as well as with government officials, women representatives, religious leaders, civil society, youths and the business community as a way of facilitating a community driven conflict prevention and peacebuilding process. Similarly, Chijioke Kingsley in an article in the *Daily Times* of Nigeria on June 6, 2016[6] also attributed the current peaceful atmosphere in Jos, and other parts of Plateau state to the efforts of the current administration of Governor Lalong in running an all-inclusive government, with every ethnic group in the state represented in his cabinet, as well as greater efficiency on the part of all the security agencies. The conflict prevention and peacebuilding mechanisms put in place by the different stakeholders in the Plateau has indeed borne great dividends, as no major crises and violence have erupted in Jos and its environs since 2011. This is, however, not denying the existence of fighting brought about by Boko Haram terrorist activities, and the Fulani herdsmen/farmer conflicts. These cannot however be compared in magnitude to the decade-long intermittent armed conflicts that overwhelmed Jos and its environs between 2001 and 2011. Although the decade-long crisis that plagued the city of Jos has been significantly contained, and peace restored to the city, it is imperative that women's contributions to ending these conflicts and building sustainable peace in Jos are highlighted. Women's roles in conflict prevention, conflict resolution and peacebuilding have received global attention, particularly in the Global South, and their activities have been documented in the literature. From the activities of the Sixth Clan in Somalia's peace processes in 1992, to the story of the Mano River Women's Peace Network, the women's organization of the Mano River Union countries of Guinea, Liberia and Sierra, and others working in Sudan and Burundi amongst others, these narratives of women's peacebuilding activities at the grassroots level and in formal peace processes have been documented. This chapter therefore advances existing literature by showcasing the critical peacebuilding roles women played in ending the protracted conflict in Jos City and its environs, and their activities in entrenching peace in their communities. While the conflict in Jos lasted, the women demonstrated their resolve not to compromise their quest for peace in their communities, and by using a series of non-violent methods contributed to the restoration of peace in their communities. The chapter therefore is primarily aimed at demonstrating how women's agency for peace was valuable for bringing an end to the Jos Crisis.

Women, armed conflict and peacebuilding

A large proportion of the entire global system remains engulfed in violence, as pervasive conflicts and wars continue to ravage the world. Unlike the twentieth century, that was dominated by a legacy of devastating global wars, colonial struggle and ideological conflicts, the twenty-first century is characterized by violent conflicts precipitated by communal, ethno-religious and resource based crises within nation states, in addition to terrorist activities that are trans-border in nature transcending several countries. Research has shown that these post-Cold War conflicts have resulted in large scale civilian casualties and the widespread internally displaced persons (IDPs) and refugee crises. Many countries and sub national areas now face cycles of repeated violence, weak governance, and instability and these conflicts often are not one-off events, but are ongoing and repeated.[7] Africa in particular has a large share of these armed conflicts that ravage the continent with negative implications for its socio-economic development.

Violent conflicts in sub-Saharan Africa are responsible for the direct and indirect deaths of millions of civilians on the continent in addition to the low level of human security in the region.[8] There is hardly any country in Africa that has not experienced armed conflict, with several African countries either embroiled in conflicts or just coming out of one.[9] Several theories exist on the causes of conflicts in Africa including Greed and Grievance, Protracted Social Conflict, Asymmetrical Warfare and Regional Security Complex theories.[10] The causes of armed conflicts are multifarious and complex and cannot be explicated by single monolithic arguments; a hybrid model that considers many variables as the causal factors of intra-state armed conflicts in Africa seems more appropriate. Consequently, those causal factors for African conflicts will include a combination of state failure, weak governance structures and inability of government to transmit dividends of natural resources endowments to the people; horizontal and vertical inequality among identity groups and feelings of marginalization; as well as stagnant economies that lead to the impoverishment and alienation of people.[11]

Although armed conflict causes suffering for everyone, women and girls are uniquely affected by its short- and long-term effects. Wars and conflict situations result in widespread atrocities and violence perpetrated against women and girls, ranging from rape, prostitution, torture, sexual slavery and trafficking to death. Since women and children are generally perceived to be less of a threat they are lesser targets for death compared to men; they, however, face a fate worse than death as they become victims of sexual violence through rape and sexual abuse while escaping the conflict zone or in the post conflict era.[12] Women and girls are affected differently for several reasons including the fact that because they are differently embodied they symbolize different things to their communities, and because they are targeted differently their injuries have different social and livelihood impacts.[13] Although women and girls experience sexual and gender based violence in peacetime, it is heightened in periods of armed conflict with increased occurrence and intensity. A 2006 UN Secretary General's Report aptly captures the experiences of women to include all forms of physical, sexual and psychological violence perpetrated by both State and non-State actors, including

> murder, unlawful killings, torture and other cruel, inhuman or degrading treatment or punishment, abductions, maiming and mutilation, forced

recruitment of women combatants, rape, sexual slavery, sexual exploitation, involuntary disappearance, arbitrary detention, forced marriage, forced prostitution, forced abortion, forced pregnancy, and forced sterilization.[14]

In addition, terrorist organizations use women and girls as strategic tools in their activities. From the Islamic State in the Middle East to Al Shabaab in East Africa and Boko Haram in North East Nigeria, women and girls have continually been targeted and used a strategic part of these groups in achieving their goals. Women and girls are abducted and used as sex slaves, prostitutes, terrorists, wives and combatants; they are forcefully impregnated and forcefully married and sold off. Additionally, they are used as fighters, recruiters, mobilisers, spies and suicide bombers. A wide array of scholarship including reports by non-governmental organization exists on the impact of conflict on women.[15] The dominant image of women with regards to conflicts and wars remains that of victims, highlighting their vulnerability to sexual violence such as rape and its attendant consequences. Despite the horrific impact of armed conflict on women as highlighted above, women worldwide have not remained passive victims, as highlighted in the literature and in the media images portrayed globally. Women are active agents of conflict resolution and peacebuilding in their communities, drawing on the resources available to them to entrench a culture of peace in their communities.

The term "peacebuilding" emerged from United Nations peacekeeping operations in Namibia. However, the concept gained popularity in the 1992 and 1995 editions of former UN Secretary-General Boutrous Boutrous Ghali's "An Agenda for Peace." In general terms, peacebuilding refers to preventive measures that can be applied in all stages of conflict including efforts at promoting peace and non-violence.[16] A fundamental objective of peacebuilding is the creation and fostering of stability and functioning of a region or state.[17]

> Ultimately, peacebuilding is a dynamic process of resolving conflict and rebuilding society: it refers to a wide variety of activities and methods of intervention aimed at bring about sustainable peace.[18]

Women's activities in peacebuilding have been recognized, beginning with the roles played by women activists in ending the carnage of World War I, when women groups transcended borders in a novel way, seeking an end to the carnage brought about by the war. This resulted in the gathering of over 1,000 women from twelve countries to convene the first ever International Congress of Women (ICW)[19] in 1915, demanding equality between women and men, and among nations, as well as the creation of a neutral international organization to mediate disputes among countries.[20] In contemporary times, women's peace activism and contribution to peacebuilding particularly at the grassroots and informal levels have attracted attention and have been acknowledged. As aptly captured by Kofi Annan, the former UN Secretary-General, "for generations, women have served as peace educators, both in their families and in their societies. They have proved instrumental in building bridges rather than walls."[21]

Similarly, women's engagement in peacebuilding is recognized by many international institutions as a crucial element of recovery and conflict prevention —a fact reflected in UN Security Council Resolution 1325. In particular, the resolution calls for the increased participation of women in conflict prevention and conflict resolution while recognizing the unique contributions women make to peace processes and the unique perspective they bring to bear in creating peaceful societies.[22] Indeed, women's peacemaking roles have been widely recognized based on the assumption that they have unique attributes which make them better suited for peace than for war. As International Alert's draft Code of Conduct states:

> We explicitly recognize the particular and distinctive peacemaking roles played by women in conflict afflicted communities. Women and women's organizations are often reservoirs of important local capacities which can be used in peace-building activities.[23]

Women's agency as peace builders is well documented in the literature, and there are several portrayals of women rising up as a critical mass, cutting across language, ethnic and religious divides to entrench peace in their communities.[24] In Africa, there are case studies of women and women groups organizing for peace at the grassroots and community levels, as well as in formal peace processes to engender the peace agreement.[25] Some examples include the Save Somali Women and Children (SSWC) who, in 1992, organized themselves into the Somali Sixth Clan and got a place as a constituency on the peace process, bringing the clan lords together.[26] In the Great Lakes region of Africa (Burundi, Rwanda, the eastern Democratic Republic of Congo), Kenya, Liberia, South Africa and in Sudan, women have organized for peace and an end to armed conflict and violence.[27] Women organizing for peace cut across borders, language, race and ethnicity, and carry out a wide range of peacebuilding activities including provision of food and shelter for individuals affected by conflict, psychological healing and provision of trauma counseling services, dialog and peace meetings with warring parties, and inspiring other women by sharing their stories.[28] These peacebuilding roles have been attributed to women's innate peaceful and compassionate qualities that stem out of their roles as mothers and caregivers. Galtung avers that women possess innate qualities that make them peace loving, and more prone to peaceful relationships.[29] Similarly, Alonso maintains that women have been portrayed by numerous groups as being more sensitive, more caring, thoughtful and committed to a more humanistic and compassionate world than men.[30] In her work *Maternal Thinking*, Sara Ruddick postulates that women's experience and natural roles as mothers, and their nurturing and protective qualities make them more suited to peacemaking.[31]

This argument has, however, been debunked by feminist scholars who argue that mothering is not instinctive but acquired through the process of socialization, and that some women have rejected the motherly role but still belong to peace movements.[32] Additionally, it is argued that this essentialist and gender stereotyping of women as naturally peaceful and suited for peacemaking roles and men as aggressive and perpetrators of violence further reinforces patriarchy and androcentric tendencies that constrain women's equal participation in decision making. In their contribution, Kaufman and Williams posit that although essentialist notions of women's behavior such as nurturing, peacefulness and caregiving are bases for women's engagement in peacebuilding reinforce gender norms, such peace activism in itself is seen as a challenge to gender norms as women transcend beyond the private sphere of family and domestic responsibilities to engage in the public sphere dominated by men. These scholars therefore predicate women's peacebuilding activities as

> a conscious choice and form of political activism sometimes driven by feminist goals (defined as promoting political, social, and economic equality of women and men, and overturning patriarchal, political, economic and social structures), and sometimes by more traditional values (specifically a wife or mother who wants peace in her community).[33]

This study aligns itself with this notion that women's engagement in peacebuilding is a form of political activism and a challenge to gender norms that restrict women to the private sphere.

A history of the Jos crisis

Jos, the capital of Plateau State in North Central Nigeria has historically been known for its peace and tranquility. Located on the high mountainous plateau from which the state derives its name, it is blessed with a temperate climate leading to a tremendous influx of both foreigners and Nigerians into the state from the colonial era onwards. Another factor that led to influx of people into Jos was the establishment of the colonial tin mining industry which led to an expansion of commerce and industry. The mining industry attracted people from all over Nigeria, such that by the mid-1940s, more than 200 mining camps had been built on the Plateau with the miner population exceeding 40,000.[34] Plateau State, including its capital Jos, is inhabited by both Christians and Muslims, and diverse ethnic groups that can be broadly divided into indigenes—namely the Afizere, Berom and Anaguta[35]—and those termed as settlers, notably the Hausa/Fulani, Yoruba, Igbo and other ethnic groups. These various groups have lived peacefully together for years and co-habited without problems and recourse to violence until recently when bloodbath and killings pervaded the land. Nigeria has had her fair share of violent conflicts since her return to democracy in 1999. Nigeria has witnessed several ethnic, political, religious and communal conflicts in which thousands of people were killed and properties involving billions of Naira were lost.[36] These conflicts not only pose a major threat to her democracy, but to the stability and corporate existence of the country. The protracted crises that pervaded Jos and its environs have attracted both national and international attention. These incessant outbreaks of violence have left a large percentage of women widowed, poorer and displaced at the death of their husbands, with many of them becoming heads of households. The crises have also led to an increased level of poverty due to the massive disruption of economic activities and business which has affected the women more.[37] This has resulted in an increase in the number of school children dropouts; creating a critical mass of youths that are ready tools for the perpetration of more violence.

Various factors have been advanced as causes of the violent clashes, ranging from politics, religion and ethnicity, to claims to ownership of land and resources. Some scholars attribute the causes of the violence to tension between ethnic groups rooted in allocation of resources, electoral competition, fear of religious domination and contested land rights that have amalgamated into an explosive mix.[38] The dominant discourses in the conflict refer to political exclusion on the basis of ethnicity and religion, on the Muslim side, and fears of religious and cultural domination among Plateau Christians.[39] Similarly, others see the transformation of the conflict from a political conflict over control of the traditional and other forms of political space (between Afizere, Anaguta and Berom indigenes on the one hand, and Hausa/Fulani immigrants on the other hand), to now a religiously polarized and increasingly polarizing conflict.[40]

A major factor that has been identified by scholars as being one of the remote causes of the protracted crisis is the contestation between the Hausa/Fulani group and the indigenous ethnic groups of Berom, Afizere and Anaguta over the ownership of Jos city, with each group relying on historical records to justify their claims.[41] Closely related to the dispute over the ownership of Jos is the so-called indigene/settler problem. While the Hausa/Fulani claim that they are indigenes of Jos alongside the Berom, Afizere and Anaguta, the claim is refuted by the indigenous groups who claim that they are the authentic indigenes, while the Hausa/Fulani are settlers. Indigene/settler problems are not unique to Plateau State but remain a challenge to Nigeria as a whole. Conflict revolves around privileges and resources that are deemed for indigenes vis-à-vis those perceived as settlers. Although the Nigerian Constitution grants every citizen the right to settle and live in any part of the country, in practice persons living in states other than their state of origin may lack access to some resources such as recruitment by the state civil service and political representation, amongst others.[42]

Another remote causal factor of the Jos crisis was the balkanisation of the Jos Local Government Area (LGA) into the Jos North LGA and the Jos South LGA in 1991. This singular act was perceived as symbolic by the indigenous groups (Berom, Afizere and Anaguta) as it altered the demography and political configuration of the Jos North LGA by making the Hausa/Fulani the majority ethnic group and the indigenous group the minority ethnic group in the area.[43] Ethnicity and religion are related factors that greatly contributed to the protracted Jos crisis. The Hausa/Fulani who are parties to the conflict are predominantly Muslims, while the other parties to the conflict—the Berom, Anaguta and Afizere—are predominantly Christians. This has resulted in the conflicts taking on religious dimensions at the slightest opportunity. Religion remains a very sensitive issue in Nigeria and is a major cause of crisis in the country. The fear of the dominance of one religion over the other remains a key source of social tension in Nigeria, and this clearly manifests in the political representation and voting in elections. Shedrack Best therefore maintains that Christian leaders in Plateau State viewed the conflict primarily as a religious one, motivated by a jihadist agenda to conquer and Islamize the state.[44]

Other factors considered as immediate triggers of the conflict include the 1994 crisis, regarded as the first crisis in Jos, which was as a result of the appointment of a Hausa Muslim man as Chairman of the Caretaker Management Committee of the Jos North Local Government area by the then Military administrator, Col. Mohammed Mana—an action that was swiftly rejected by the Berom, Anaguta and Afizere indigenous groups on the basis that he was not an indigene. Accordingly, this action was seen as a substantiation of the fear by the indigenous group that the Hausa/Fulani were bent on taking over political power in Jos. Similarly, the 2001 violence that erupted on September 7 resulted in the death of several persons and destruction of properties. The immediate cause included the appointment of a Hausa/Fulani man as the new National Poverty Eradication Coordinator, and an attempt by a Christian lady to pass through a Muslim congregation that had blocked a road,[45] resulting in bloody carnage and reprisal attacks in different parts of the city which left hundreds dead. This crisis also resulted in the segregation of Jos along ethnic and religious lines. In 2002, the election of ward officials in Eto Baba, an area in Jos, led to an eruption of violence and destruction of property. An election into the Jos North Local government area in January 2010 led to the death of young men, women and children[46] with an estimated number of 400 people killed, and 18,000 injured.[47] Other episodes of violence erupted later in the year with the March 2010 killings in Dogo Nahawa in Jos South LGA, where groups of armed men suspected to be Fulani herdsmen sacked villages, killing over 300 persons, predominantly women and children. In December of the same year, several lives were again lost in the Christmas Eve bombing and the subsequent riots.

In a bid to examine the causes, effects and actors in these crises, as well as the various dimensions to it, both the federal and state governments have set up judicial commissions of inquiry and panels since 1994, with the mandate to look into the remote and immediate causes of the crisis as well as proffer solutions as a means of engendering sustainable peace in the state. These included: the Hon. Justice Aribiton Fiberesima Judicial Commission of Inquiry into the 1994 crisis; Hon. Justice Niki Tobi Judicial Commission of Inquiry into the September 2001 crisis; Presidential Peace Initiative Committee on Plateau State, headed by Shehu Idris of Zazzau, May 2004; Plateau Peace Conference ("Plateau Resolves") August 18–September 21, 2004; The Declaration of a State of Emergency in the State by President Olusegun Obasanjo in 2004; the Hon. Justice Ajibola Commission of Inquiry into the 2008 crisis, the Emmanuel Abisoye Panel of Investigation; and the Presidential Advisory Committee on the Jos crisis, March–April 2010.[48] However, the disregard for these probe panels and commissions of enquiry as well as the non-implementation of the recommendations of their findings remains a major challenge for the quest for peace on the Plateau, and are seen by many as a reason for the recurrence of violence. In addition to the above, the Federal Government also created the Special Joint Military Task Force to maintain law and order in Jos and environs, however, there were several criticisms of the Task Force including delayed response in cases of attacks, extrajudicial killings and lack of neutrality, amongst others.[49]

Women and peacebuilding in Jos

The decade-long Jos Crisis has to a large extent negatively affected women: since its emergence, women and children have been at the receiving end; with many killed, displaced, tortured, raped or denied of their means of livelihood, and many more have become widows and heads of households at the death of their spouses.[50] Several cases of gender based violence against women have also been perpetrated as there were reports of sexual violence against women occurring on both sides during the crises.[51] Similarly, because women were mostly in the informal and small business sector in Jos, the frequent clashes with the concomitant destruction of homes and properties including shops impacted negatively on the livelihoods of women. Women became more impoverished as a result of frequent attacks and destruction of their retail businesses and shops. Additionally, there was displacement and exit of female traders from markets situated in conflict flashpoints such as Dilimi, Bukuru, Farin-gada, Gangare and Yan Doya markets in Jos.[52]

In particular, the crises has seen women in large numbers killed and brutally murdered in the privacy of their homes. According to a *Daily Champion* 2010 report, Chugwui community in Vwang district of Jos South local government area lost over 250 women since 2001, as well as able family men and youths who have died leaving behind women and children to cater for themselves. The Dogo Nahauwa massacre of March 2010 brings to mind the terrible toll the Jos crisis had on women. Dogo Nahauwa, a mining settlement in Jos Plateau State, saw over 500 people, mostly defenseless women and children massacred and killed in the night by assailants alleged to be Fulani herdsmen.[53] However, women did not belong to a monolithic category in the Jos crises as they occupied multifarious positions and assumed different roles including as peace activists, victims, supporters and combatants. Higazi reports that women on both sides to the conflict in Jos participated in the riots and killings, and actively supported their male folk to fight.[54] Women were also involved as peace activists and worked relentlessly to end the crises.

Women and women groups in Jos have not remained passive victims in the crisis as most literature usually portrays women in conflict situations; instead they have been actively involved in seeking ways to end the conflict, although this is predominantly within the informal sector. Right from the initial outbreak of violence in 2001, women have employed various strategies of ending the conflicts. One of the ways through which they have sought to achieve this has been through the staging of peaceful protests and demonstrations. On August 28, 2002, women from several women's organizations such as the Country Women

Association of Nigeria (COWAN), the National Council for Women Societies (NCWS), Federation of Muslim Women's Association in Nigeria (FOMWAN) and ZAMATA MATA (women Christian fellowships) in Jos metropolis embarked on a "peacewalk" to protest against the widespread killings in Jos.[55] This was in response to the series of violence that erupted at the Peoples Democratic Party (PDP) ward congress in Eto Baba where at least 100 persons had been killed and properties destroyed.

In the wake of the November 28, 2008 local government election violence and the killings that followed, thousands of women, in black attire, gathered at Riyom on the outskirts of Jos, marching through the streets of the city, and blocking the major Abuja–Jos highway to protest the incessant attacks on their villages by suspected Fulani herdsmen. Also, in the wake of the March 2010 Dogo NaHauwa killings, in which hundreds of Fulani herdsmen were said to have invaded three Christian villages of Dogo NaHauwa, Ratsat and Zot at midnight, with no fewer than 500 people, mostly women, children and elderly killed in the attack, an army of women decked in black with sticks in hands and fresh leaves on the head demonstrated peacefully against the massacre of women and children. Women of Plateau origin living in Abuja also carried out similar protest to the National Assembly in Abuja, the Federal Capital Territory. Similarly, women also rose in protest against the killings at Wareng in Riyom, Fan in Barkin Ladi and K/Vom in Jos South. In a surprising and unprecedented move, the women had swooped on soldiers deployed in the areas, after accusing them of complacency and complicity in the spate of attacks in the state, carrying placards and chanting war songs against the military presence in the area.[56] However, what could be described as the mother of all protests took place on Monday January 25, 2011 when women in their thousands marched through the streets of Jos demanding the removal of soldiers and their commanding officer. The women defied the heavy presence of riot policemen and marched to the Government House at Jishe. They brandished placards with different inscriptions, but with a common message to the soldiers to stop aiding the killings in Jos.

Additionally, in a bid to end the recurrent violence in Jos and its environs which had claimed the lives of their husbands and children, local women groups and nongovernmental organizations organized press briefings, calling the attention of government to the escalating bloodbath in the state. In one such press briefing, the women's group called the "Women Without Walls Initiative" (WWWI), led by Pastor Esther Ibanga, while addressing journalists threatened to adopt the strategy employed in Tunisia, Egypt and other parts of Northern Africa during the Arab uprisings as a last option to draw the attention of stakeholders to the suffering of women and children in Jos.[57] The women also carried out advocacy visits to the Government House in Jos, where they were received by the then Deputy Governor, Mrs Pauline Tallen, and to the palaces of various traditional and community leaders with a view to seeking an end to the crisis.

Women groups were also established in mixed neighborhoods of Christians and Muslims as a way of preventing the eruption of violence. The case of Dadin

Kowa, a mixed community that remained relatively peaceful during the crisis underscores the roles of women in peacebuilding. Dadin Kowa is a community in Jos North LGA that comprises of a Christian majority and Muslim minority. Krause observes that after the 2008 crisis in Jos, over 200 women across religious and ethnic divides came together after participating in training by the Damitta Peace Initiative (DPI), meeting regularly in smaller groups to dialog and deliberate on ways to keep their communities safe. By the time the 2010 crisis erupted, the women groups prevailed on their religious leaders to forbid violence and undertake conflict prevention measures in the community. This resulted in meetings and dialogs between pastors, imams and elders of the community, and a "Peace Declaration" for the community. Mixed vigilante groups were also established for the community to ward off external attacks.[58]

Women groups and non-governmental organizations also played key roles in the ending of the Jos crisis and ensuring sustainable peace. The Jos based Islamic Counselling Initiative of Nigeria (ICIN), a non-governmental organization (NGO) working on gender issues, girl child education and peacebuilding provides trauma healing seminars for women who have become traumatized as a result of the death of loved ones brought about as a result of the conflict. In addition, relief materials were provided by the NGO to women affected by the conflicts irrespective of religion, ethnicity and social class.[59] Another women group actively involved in peacebuilding activities in Jos, Plateau State is the Christian Women for Excellence and Empowerment in Nigeria (CWEENS), with Professor Oluwafunmilayo Para-Mallam as the National Coordinator. CWEENS carries out training and capacity building programs for the empowerment of women including providing trauma counseling training to victims of conflicts. The organization blew the whistle in respect of the killings of females in Bukuru, Jos South Local government area in a wave of secret killings in Jos.[60] The organization also provided training on trauma counseling after the March 2010 Dogo NaHauwa killings.[61]

The Women Without Walls Initiative founded by Pastor Esther Ibanga is made up of Christian and Muslim women who reach out to warring Muslim and Christians communities in Jos to establish dialog and peaceful co-existence. The group also embarked on advocacy campaigns to traditional rulers as well as religious leaders, and trained women in peace building initiatives/activities, dialogs and mediation between warring parties. In 2010, Pastor Esther Ibanga led 100,000 Christian women in a protest through the streets of Jos to the Government House calling for peace and an end to the wanton loss of human lives, especially those of women and children. This was followed by a peaceful protest by Muslim women, led by Hajiya Khadijat Hawaja, also demanding an end to the bloodbath that had killed their husbands and children.

It is instructive to note that the roles women played in demanding the restoration of peace and an end to the violence in Jos and its environs contributed to a very large extent to the current atmosphere of peace being experienced in Jos and other parts of Plateau. Taking their fate in their own hands, and tired of the men's inability to end the bloodbath, both Christian and Muslim women defied all odds, crossing ethnic, religious and language divides to forge together as a force to demand the restoration of peace and human dignity in the land. During these periods of armed conflict and violence, women refused to remain as passive victims as usually portrayed in the literature, instead the women on the Plateau rose up above their limitations and saw beyond the violence inflicted on them to fight non-violently for peace in their communities.

Regrettably, however, in spite of the critical roles women play in the informal and grassroots peace processes, they are usually denied positions in formal peace processes. This was the case in Jos, as women were not well represented in the various Tribunals and Commissions of Enquiry set up by government to look into the Jos crises. Out of the three tribunals set up by government, and a total of twenty-three members, only two were women.[62]

Conclusion

While women remain veritable partners in resolving conflicts and achieving sustainable peace in society, they are usually constrained in achieving this due to lack of recognition of the inherently unique abilities that they can bring to bear in conflict situations, and the patriarchal societal values that limit peace and security discourses within the masculine enclave. Women are not passive victims of conflicts as most literature on peace and security would want us to believe; on the contrary, women in conflict regions worldwide are actively involved in seeking ways of ending conflicts and entrenching peace in their communities. There have, however, been calls for increased recognition of the roles women play in resolving conflicts, as well as greater inclusion of women in the formal process of conflict resolution and peacebuilding. The campaign for the inclusion of more women in peacebuilding scored a landmark victory with the October 2000 adoption of the United Nations Security Council Resolution 1325 on Women, Peace and Security. This Resolution recognizes that civilians—particularly women and children—are the worst affected by conflict, which is a threat to peace and security. It includes calls for women's participation in conflict prevention and resolution initiatives; the integration of gender perspectives in peacebuilding and peacekeeping missions; and the protection of women in regions of armed conflict.

As highlighted in the paper, the women in Jos have been actively involved in seeking an end to the incessant killings and bloodbath that have pervaded the state. This has been largely through peaceful protest and demonstrations which are usually reactive in nature, that is, coming up after a major incident of killings, instead of being preventive and proactive. Also, most of the women activists involved were members of local community women groups and local non-governmental organizations, thus there is need for women of diverse socioeconomic status including professionals, market women and others to be more involved in the cause for peace. Although women from opposing groups are already working together to achieve peace in Jos, there is still room for greater synergy between women as a way of sustaining the current peace experienced in

Jos and other parts of Plateau State. Gender balance in the composition of the members of the judicial commissions and panels set up by government is also an imperative for seeking an effective end to the crises, as this will ensure the articulation of the interest and needs of women. Closely related to this also is the need for the inclusion of women in the Special Task Force assigned to quell the violence in conflict zones, as this will engender a more sympathetic attitude by the force toward women and children during conflicts.

Notes

1 Adams Higazi, *The Jos Crises: A Recurrent Nigerian Tragedy* (Abuja: Friedrich-Ebert Stiftung, 2011).
2 Jos City was known for its Tin mining industry that attracted thousands of people in the early 1940s during the colonial era.
3 In Nigeria, states have slogans officially adopted to identify them. The slogan for Plateau State is "Home of Peace and Tourism."
4 Oluwafunmilayo Para-Mallam, "Introduction," in *Finding Durable Peace in Plateau*, edited by Oluwafunmilayo Para-Mallam (Kuru: National Institute for Policy and Strategic Studies, 2011), 1.
5 Alao Onimisi, "Plateau Communities Charting Own Way to Lasting Peace," *Daily Trust*, January 18, 2015, www.dailytrust.com.ng/sunday/index.php/travelogue/19345-plateau-communities-charting-own-ways-to-lasting-peace.
6 Kingsley Chijioke, "Governor Lalong Ushers in Peace in Troubled Plateau," *Daily Times*, June 6, 2016, http://dailytimes.ng/gov-lalong-ushers-peace-troubled-plateau/.
7 World Bank, *World Development Report—Conflict, Security, and Development.* (Washington DC: World Bank, 2011), available at https://openknowledge.worldbank.org/handle/10986/4389 License: CC BY 3.0 IGO.
8 R. Bowd and A. Chikwanha, "Introduction," in *Understanding Africa's Contemporary Conflicts: Origins, Challenges, and Peacebuilding*, edited by R. Bowd and A. Chikwanha, x–xxii (Addis Ababa: African Human Security Initiative, 2010).
9 Victor Adetula, "African Conflicts, Development and Regional Organization in the Post-Cold War International System," *Current Issues* 61(8) (2015): 7–73.
10 D. J. Francis, *Uniting Africa: Building Regional Peace and Systems* (Hampshire: Ashgate 2006).
11 Adetula, "African Conflicts,"13–25.
12 Maria Lourdes Veneracion-Rallonza, "Women and Armed Conflict in the Phillipines: Narrative Portrait of Women on the Ground," *Philippine Political Science Journal* 36(1) (2015): 35–53, DOI: 10.1080/01154451.2015.1024676.
13 Dyan Mazurana, "The Gendered Impact of Conflict and Peacekeeping in Africa," *Conflict Trends* 2 (2013): 3–9.
14 United Nations Secretary-General Report, *In-depth Study on All Forms of Violence Against Women* (New York: UN, 2006).
15 UN Secretary General's Report on *Women, Peace and Security* (New York: UN, 2002).
16 Berghof Foundation, "Peace, Peacebuilding, Peacemaking," in *Berghof Glossary of Conflict Transformation: 20 Notions for Theory and Practice* (Berlin: Berghof Foundation, 2011), 62.
17 Mary Elizabeth King, "What Difference Does It Make? Gender as a Tool in Building Peace," in *Gender and Peace Building in Africa,* edited by Dina Rodriguez and Edith Natukunda-Togbon (Costa Rica: University for Peace, 2012).
18 Mary K. McCarthy, "Women's Participation in Peacebuilding: A Missing Piece of the Puzzle?" April 8, 2011. *CUREJ: College Undergraduate Research Electronic Journal*, University of Pennsylvania, http://repository.upenn.edu/curej/132.

19 The International Congress of Women (ICW) later became the Women's International League for Peace and Freedom (WILPF), which advocates for disarmament and human rights.

20 Elisabeth Rehn and Ellen Johnson Sirleaf, *Women, War and Peace: The Independent Expert Assessment on the Impact of Armed Conflict on Women and Women's Role in Peacebuilding* (New York: UNIFEM, 2002).

21 Swanee Hunt and Cristina Posa, "Women Waging Peace," *Foreign Policy* 124 (2001): 38–47.

22 United Nations Security Council (UNSC) 2000, Resolution 1325, S/RES/1325. (October 31).

23 International Alert, *Code of Conduct.* July 13, 1998: 6.

24 For accounts of women's active roles in entrenching peace in their societies see Simoni Sharoni, "Rethinking Women's Struggle in Israel-Palestine, and in the North of Ireland," in *Victims, Perpetrators or Actors? Gender, Armed Conflict and Political Violence*, edited by Caroline Moser and Fiona Clark, 85–98 (London: Zed Books, 2001).

25 Nadine Peuchguirbal, *"Gender and Peace Building in Africa: Analysis of Some Structural Obstacles,"* 2005, www.upeace.org (accessed 4 November 2016).

26 Mary Elisabeth King, "What Difference Does It Make?"

27 Rehn and Sirleaf, 2002; UN Secretary General Study on Women Peace and Security 2002 Pursuant to Security Council Resolution 1325(2000) (New York: UN, 2002).

28 K. A. Korb, "Peacemaking as a Woman's Issue," *Theological Education in Africa Conference.* Jos: University of Jos, held August 9, 2011.

29 Johan Galtung, *Peace by Peaceful Means: Peace, Conflict, Development and Civilization* (London: Sage, 1996).

30 H. Alonso, *Peace as a Women's Issue*: *A History of the US Movement for World Peace and Women's Right* (New York: Syracuse University Press, 1993).

31 Sara Ruddick, *Maternal Thinking: Towards a Politics of Peace* (London: Women's Press, 1990).

32 Michael Potter, *Women Civil Society and Peacebuilding: Paths to Peace through the Empowerment of Women* (Belfast: Training for Peace Network, 2004) accessed at www.twnonline.com.

33 Joyce P. Kaufman and Kristen P. William, *Women at War, Women Building Peace: Challenging Gender Norms* (Boulder, CO: Lynne Rienner Publishers, 2013).

34 Jane Krause, *A Deadly Cycle: Ethno-religious Conflict in Jos, Plateau State, Nigeria.* Working Paper (Switzerland: Geneva Declaration, 2011).

35 Other indigenous ethnic groups include the Ngas, Goemai and Tarok

36 E. O. Alemika, "Prevalence, Sources and Resolutions of Conflicts in Nigeria," in *Issues of Peace and Security: Essays in Honor of Major General Charles B. Ndiomu*, edited by D. A. Briggs and J. G. Sanda (Kuru: National Institute for Policy and Strategic Studies, 2004).

37 Women on the Plateau are known for their hard work and success in business and farming.

38 Jane Krause, *A Deadly Cycle,* 19.

39 Adams Higazi, *The Jos Crises.*

40 Shedrack Best and Kate Hoomlong, "Literature Review of Academic Publications and International Papers," in *Finding Durable Peace in Plateau*, edited by Oluwafunmilayo Para-Mallam, 58–76 (Kuru: National Institute for Policy and Strategic Studies, 2011).

41 Umar Habila Dadem Danfulani and Sati U. Fwatshak, "Briefing: the September 2001 Events in Jos Nigeria," in *African Affairs* 101(403) (2002): 243–255.

42 Jane Krause, *A Deadly Cycle,* 19.

43 Jos North Local Government Area is the epicenter of commercial activities in Plateau State, and accommodates the Jos Main market and other commercial ventures.

Additionally, the palace of the paramount ruler of Jos, the *Gbong Gwon Jos*, is located there.

44 Shedrack Best, *Conflict and Peacebuilding in Plateau State, Nigeria* (Ibadan: Spectrum Books, 2007).

45 Shedrack Best, *Conflict and Peacebuilding in Plateau State*; Phillip Ostien, *Jonah Jang and the Jasawa: Ethno-Religious Conflict in Jos, Nigeria. Muslim–Christian Relations in Africa.* August 2009, www.sharia-in-africa-.net/media/publication/etno-religious-conflicts-in-jos-nigeria/Ostien_jos.pdf.

46 Rotgak Gofwen, "A Historical Overview of Ethno-Religious Conflicts in Plateau State: Government Interventions and Strategies," in *Finding Durable Peace in Plateau,* edited by Oluwafunmilayo Para-Mallam, 11–57 (Kuru: National Institute for Policy and Strategic Studies, 2011).

47 Jane Krause, *A Deadly Cycle.*

48 International Crisis Group, *Curbing Violence in Nigeria (1): The Jos Crisis,* Africa Report 2012, 196.

49 Jane Krause, *A Deadly Cycle.*

50 Habiba Muhammedu, living in the abattoir area in Jos, said her mate (co-wife) and she with their eight children watched helplessly as their breadwinner was slaughtered and their home burnt; children have dropped out of school and there remains no hope to date. See www.gbooza.com/grond aup/nigeriapolitics/forum/topic/fury-as-jos-crisis-clocks-ixzz1joUsMEDf.

51 Adams Higazi, "Violence urbaine et politque a jos (Nigeria), de la periode colonial aux elections de 2007," ("The Politics of Urban Violence in Jos, Nigeria: From Colonial Rule to the 2007 Elections") *Politiqueafricaine* 106 (2007): 66–91.

52 Lohna Bonkat, "Survival Strategies of Market Women and Violent Conflicts in Jos, Nigeria," *Journal of Asia Pacific Studies* 3(3) (November 2014): 281–299.

53 Segun Joshua and E. Ajibade Jegede, "Ethnicization of Violent Conflicts in Jos," *Global Journal of Human Social Science* 13(7) (2013): 39–44.

54 Higazi, "The Politics of Urban Violence in Jos," 2007.

55 Victor Adetula, "Ethnicity and the Dynamics of City Politics: The Case of Jos," in *Urban Africa: Changing Contours of Survival in the City,* edited by A. M. Simone and A. Abouhone, 232–233 (New York: Zed Books, 2005).

56 During the riot at K/Vom, even the commander was said to have been held hostage by the women and it took reinforcement from the other sectors before he could be rescued.

57 *Daily Independent* February 23, 2011.

58 Jane Krause, *A Deadly Cycle.*

59 *National Express* (Nigeria), *Inclusiveness best Panacea to Violence in Plateau State.* Retrieved from www.nationalexpress.com.ng/inclusiveness-best-panacea-to-violence-in-plateau-state/ May 19, 2016.

60 Seriki Adinoyi. "Nigeria: Jos Killings—'We Found 16 Decomposed Bodies of Women'," *This Day,* June 4, 2010. http://allafrica.com/stories/201006071576.html.

61 Felix Akpan, Angela Olofu-Adeoye and Simon Odey Ering, "Women and Peace Building in Nigeria," *African Journal of Social Science* 4(11) (2014): 170–182.

62 Felix Akpan et al., "Women and Peace Building," 2014.

Bibliography

Adetula, V. "Ethnicity and the Dynamics of City Politics: The Case of Jos," in *Urban Africa: Changing Contours of Survival in the City,* edited by A. M. Simone and A. Abouhone, 232–233. New York: Zed Books, 2005.

Adetula, V. "African Conflicts, Development and Regional Organizations in the Post-Cold War International System," *Current Issues* 61 (2015): 7–73.

Adinoyi, S. "Nigeria: Jos Killings—'We Found 16 Decomposed Bodies of Women'" *This Day*, June 4, 2010. http://allafrica.com/stories/201006071576.html.

Alemika E. O. "Prevalence, Sources and Resolutions of Conflicts in Nigeria," in *Issues of Peace and Security: Essays in Honour of Major General Charles B. Ndiomu*, edited by D. A. Briggs and J. G. Sanda, 95–110. Kuru: National Institute Press.

Alison, M. *Women and Political Violence: Female Combatants in Ethno-National Conflict*. New York: Routledge, 2009.

Alonso, H. *Peace as a Women's Issue: A History of the US Movement for World Peace and Women's Rights*. New York: Syracuse University Press, 1993.

Akpan, F., A. Olofu-Adeoye and S. Odey Ering. "Women and Peace Building in Nigeria," *African Journal of Social Science* 4(11) (2014): 170–182.

Berghof Foundation, "Peace, Peacebuilding, Peacemaking," in *Berghof Glossary of Conflict Transformation: Notions for Theory and Practice*. Berlin: Berghof Foundation, 2011.

Best, Shedrack. *Conflict and Peacebuilding in Plateau State, Nigeria*. Ibadan: Spectrum Books, 2007.

Best, S., and K. Hoomlong. "Literature Review of Academic Publications and International Papers," in *Finding Durable Peace in Plateau*, edited by O. J. Para-Mallam, 58–76. Kuru: National Institute for Policy and Strategic Studies, 2011.

Bonkat, L. "Survival Strategies of Market Women and Violent Conflicts in Jos, Nigeria," *Journal of Asia Pacific Studies* 3(3) (2014): 281–299.

Bowd, R., and A. Chikwanha. "Introduction," in *Understanding Africa's Contemporary Conflicts: Origins, Challenges, and Peacebuilding*, edited by R. Bowd and A. Chikwanha, x–xxii. Addis Ababa: African Human Security Initiative, 2010.

Chijioke, K. "Governor Lalong Ushers in Peace in Troubled Plateau," *Daily Times*, June 6, 2016. http://dailytimes.ng/gov-lalong-ushers-peace-troubled-plateau/.

Danfulani, H. B. D., and S. U. Fwatshak. "Briefing: The September 2001 Events in Jos Nigeria," in *African Affairs* 101(403) (April 2002): 243–255.

Francis, D. J. *Uniting Africa: Building Regional Peace and Systems*. Hampshire: Ashgate, 2006.

Galtung, J. *Peace by Peaceful Means: Peace, Conflict, Development and Civilization*. London: Sage, 1996.

Gofwen, R. "A Historical Overview of Ethno-Religious Conflicts in Plateau State: Government Interventions and Strategies," in *Finding Durable Peace in Plateau*, edited by O. J. Para-Mallam, 11–57. Kuru: National Institute for Policy and Strategic Studies, 2011.

Higazi, A. "Violence urbaine et politique a Jos (Nigeria), de la periode colonial aux elections de 2007' (The Politics of Urban Violence in Jos, Nigeria: From Colonial Rule to the 2007 Elections) *Politiqueafricaine* 106 (2007): 66–91.

Higazi, A. *The Jos Crises: A Recurrent Nigerian Tragedy*. Abuja: Friedrich-Ebert-Stiftung (FES) Nigeria, 2011.

Hunt, S. and C. Posa. "Women Waging Peace," *Foreign Policy* 124 (2001): 38–47.

International Alert, *Code of Conduct*, July 3, 1998.

International Crisis Group. "Curbing Violence in Nigeria (1): The Jos Crisis," *Africa Report* 196, 2012.

Joshua, S., and E. Jegede. "Ethnicization of Violent Conflicts in Jos," *Global Journal of Human Social Science* 13(7) (2013): 39–44.

Kaufman, J. P. and K. P. William. *Women at War, Women Building Peace: Challenging Gender Norms*. Boulder, CO: Lynne Rienner Publishers, 2013.

King, M. E. "What Difference Does It Make? Gender as a Tool in Building Peace," in *Gender and Peace Building in Africa*, edited by D. Rodriquez and E. Natukunda-Togbon, 27–50. Costa Rica: University for Peace, 2012.

Krause, J. *A Deadly Cycle: Ethno-religious Conflict in Jos, Plateau State, Nigeria.* Working Paper. Switzerland: Geneva Declaration, 2011.

Korb, K. A. "Peacemaking as a Woman's Issue," *Theological Education in Africa Conference.* Jos: University of Jos, 2011.

Mazurana, D., and K. Carlson. *From Combat to Community: Women and Girls in Sierra Leone.* Washington, DC: Women Waging Peace, 2004.

Mazurana, D. "The Gendered Impact of Conflict and Peacekeeping in Africa," *Conflict Trends* 2: 3–9. South Africa: ACCORD, 2013.

McCarthy, M. K. "Women's Participation in Peacebuilding: A Missing Piece of the Puzzle?" *CUREJ: College Undergraduate Research Electronic Journal*, University of Pennsylvania, 2011, http://repository.upenn.edu/curej/132.

National Express. "Inclusiveness Best Panacea to Violence in Plateau State," *National Express*, May 19, 2016. www.nationalexpress.com.ng/inclusiveness-best-panacea-to-violence-in-plateau-state/.

Onimisi, A. "Plateau Communities Charting Own Ways to Lasting Peace," *Daily Trust*, Jan 18, 2015. www.dailytrust.com.ng/sunday/index.php/travelogue/19345-plateau-communities-charting-own-ways-to-lasting-peace.

Ostien, P. "Jonah Jang and the Jasawa: Ethno-Religious Conflict in Jos, Nigeria. Muslim-Christian Relations in Africa," www.sharia-in-africa-.net/media/publication/etno-religious-conflicts-in-jos-nigeria/Ostien_jos.pdf.

Para-Mallam, O. J. "Introduction," in *Finding Durable Peace in Plateau*, edited by O. J. Para-Mallam, 1–10. Kuru: National Institute of Policy and Strategic Studies, 2011.

Peuchguirbal, N. "Gender and Peace Building in Africa: Analysis of Some Structural Obstacles," 2005, www.upeace.org.

Potter, M. *Women, Civil Society and Peacebuilding: Paths to Peace through the Empowerment of Women.* Belfast: Training for Peace Network, 2004. www.twnonline.com.

Rehn, E. and E. J. Sirleaf. *Women, War and Peace: The Independent Expert Assessment on the Impact of Armed Conflict on Women and Women's Role in Peacebuilding.* New York: UNIFEM, 2002.

Rehn, E. and E. J. Sirleaf. "UN Secretary General Study on Women Peace and Security Pursuant to Security Council Resolution 1325 (2000)," 2002.

Ruddick, S. *Maternal Thinking: Towards a Politics of Peace.* London: Women's Press, 1990.

Sha, D. P. *The Politicisation of Settler-Native Identities and Ethno-Religious Conflicts in Jos, Central Nigeria.* Ibadan: Stirling-Horden Publishers Ltd, 2005.

Sharoni, S. "Rethinking Women's Struggle in Israel-Palestine and in the North of Ireland," in *Victims, Perpetrators or Actors? Gender, Armed Conflict & Political Violence*, edited by C. Moser and F. Clark, 85–98. London: Zed Books, 2001.

United Nations Security Council (UNSC). Resolution 1325. S/RES/1325. October 31, 2000.

United Nations. Secretary-General Report. *In-Depth Study on all Forms of Violence against Women.* 2006.

Veneracion-Rallonza, M. L. "Women and Armed Conflict in the Philippines: Narrative-Portraits of Women on the Ground," *Philippine Political Science Journal* 36(1) (2015): 35–53. DOI: 10.1080/01154451.2015.1024676.

World Bank. *World Development Report—Conflict, Security, and Development.* Washington, DC: World Bank. 2011. https://openknowledge.worldbank.org/handle/10986/4389.

10 Contesting the notions of "thugs and welfare queens"

Combating Black[1] derision and death

Leamon Bazil

Introduction

Shortly after the police killing of Michael Brown led to civil unrest in Ferguson, Missouri in August 2014, Mark Lamont Hill, a popular television personality and Distinguished Professor of African American Studies at Morehouse University, appeared on CNN Live. Hill was invited to the network to discuss whether President Obama should appear in the small Saint Louis suburb in order to ease racial tensions. Hill argued that the president should go to Ferguson, but only if he would be willing to "speak truths and demand justice" and not just preach calm and denounce the protestors. While engrossed in a heated debate about Black on Black crime and police brutality with the conservative Black pundit Larry Elders, Hill made a highly contentious and controversial claim. Drawing statistics from a nonacademic report developed by the Malcolm X Grassroots Movement, Hill argued that every twenty-eight hours a government official or a vigilante citizen kills an unarmed Black man, woman, or child in the United States.[2] The comment was so controversial that it gained the attention of several fact checkers who promptly denounced it as false. After being accused of making an inaccurate statement, Hill reluctantly amended his position. Instead of claiming that an unarmed Black person is killed every twenty-eight hours by a government official or a vigilante citizen, Hill unenthusiastically adduced that a Black person is killed, *armed or not*, every twenty-eight hours. Hill's amended position is not as strong as his initial claim, but if it even approximates the truth, it is cause for serious concern.

According to Rutgers University sociologist Paul Hirschfield, "multiple independent researchers, journalists, and the federal government itself have compiled a virtually exhaustive record of civilians recently killed by U.S. police"[3] and, compared to European countries, rates of police killings in the United States are disproportionately high.[4] For instance, in England and Wales, only fifty-five fatal police shootings have occurred within the past twenty-four years, whereas fifty-nine fatal police shootings occurred in the United States over the first twenty-four days of 2015.[5] Consider also Iceland, a small Scandinavian nation-state comprised of roughly 300,000 citizens. Only one person has suffered a police death in this country in the past seventy-five years, as compared to Stockton,

California, a United States county comprised of nearly the same number of citizens, but in which three fatal police shootings were registered within the first five months of 2015.[6] The racial disparity in police killings in the United States is also problematic. Although Blacks were twice as likely to be unarmed than whites that were the victims of police killings in 2015, they were overrepresented among those slain by police by a factor of 2.3.[7] In short, among all industrialized nations, the United States is unmatched in its police lethality,[8] particularly in its lethality of Blacks, *unarmed or not.*

Hirschfield offers two reasons why police killings in the United States are so pronounced. One, police violence is both a tool and product of strategies to maintain racial segregation and inequality.[9] Two, elevated rates of police killings are rooted in America's prevailing ideology (and mythology) of self-reliance and limited government.[10] This chapter explores the first component of Hirschfield's argument and explains how the imagery of Blacks as thugs and welfare queens contributes to the frequency of Blacks' death at the hands of police.[11] This issue ought to be of prime importance for the descendants of the Old African Diaspora, who have settled permanently in the United States, Europe, the Caribbean and the rest of the Americas, but also for the Blacks of the New African Diaspora, who toggle back and forth between the same geographical locations and the African mainland.

The paper aims to show that thug and welfare queen iconographies are forms of oppression, which fall under the category of cultural imperialism. As the renowned feminist philosopher Iris Young convincingly points out:

> The culturally dominated undergo a paradoxical oppression, in that they are both marked out by stereotypes and at the same time rendered invisible. As remarkable deviant beings, the culturally imperialized are stamped with an essence. The stereotypes confine them to a nature which is often attached in some way to their bodies, and which thus cannot easily be denied.[12]

In unison with Young, I argue that thug and welfare queen iconographies are depictions of Black men and women's bodies that render them invisible by concealing who they really are, while paradoxically marking them out as the Other.[13] Furthermore, thug and welfare queen iconographies are derisive conceptualizations designed to cut off empathy for Black men and women, such that their violent deaths and constant disparagement are unproblematic. The first part of the paper analyzes the genealogy of Black gender and sex roles in United States in the context of institutionalized white supremacy. The second part suggests that there is a need for the creation and maintenance of a program of Pan-African education and cultural identification for the men and women of both the Old and New African Diasporas. Such a program will help them to more adroitly resist their oppression in the United States and abroad.

Overall, the paper draws its inspiration from the project of Western liberal feminism, as characterized by the social and cultural anthropologist Saba Mahmood. Mahmood suggests that Western liberal feminism has a dual function.

On one hand, feminism serves as a critical analysis of social structures and relations that dominate and oppress women.[14] On the other hand, feminism operates as a practical emancipatory political project whereby women and their allies are called upon to change patriarchal and misogynistic social structures and relations in substantial ways. One may refer to the first horn of Mahmood's formulation of feminism as consciousness raising in that it brings to awareness the myriad ways in which women are prevented from flourishing and thriving. The second horn of Mahmood's formulation of feminism can be described as radical feminist democracy in the sense that it requires women to exercise autonomy and to actively change social structures and relations that work to women's detriment. Mahmood further argues that the overarching coherence of the project of feminism is established through the premise "that where society is structured to serve male interests, the result will be either a neglect, or a direct suppression of, women's concerns."[15]

This chapter's interpretation of the Pan-African project is similar to that of Mahmood's characterization of the Western liberal feminist project. On one hand, Pan-Africanism is the critical analysis of social structures and social relations that dominate and oppress people of African descent. On the other hand, Pan-Africanism is a practical emancipatory political project whereby Black people and their allies are obligated to change white supremacist and anti- Black social structures and relations in substantive ways. One may refer to the first horn of Pan-Africanism as consciousness raising in that it brings to awareness the countless ways in which Black people are prevented from flourishing and thriving. The second horn of Pan-Africanism can be described as Black radical democracy in the sense that it requires Black people and their allies to actively challenge social structures and relations that work to Blacks' detriment. This chapter further asserts that the overarching coherence of the project of Pan-Africanism is established through the premise that where society is structured to serve the aims of white supremacy, explicitly or implicitly, the result will be either a neglect, or a direct suppression of, Black people's concerns.

> It is my contention that black people of all stripes have an obligation to diagnose the numerous causes of anti-black racism and to develop plans to eradicate and/or diminish their effects. Just as the diagnosis of a patient with a curable or manageable disease is useless without a prognosis and a practical plan for treatment, the acknowledgement of injustices against black people is useless if black people and their allies do not make sincere efforts to eradicate them. However, black people's allies cannot dictate the terms of blacks' political engagement and analysis, lest they unwittingly undermine blacks' autonomy and political agency. As Brittney Cooper, Assistant Professor of Women's and Gender Studies and Africana Studies at Rutgers University, asserts: White people should recognize that the best way to be good allies is to go work among their own people (white people) to create more allies. Too frequently, white allies think we are asking them to come into our communities to affirm our account of racist acts and structures.

What we are really asking is for them to (1) affirm that account boldly among other white people; and (2) use their privilege to confront racial injustices when they see them happening, whether in the grocery store or the boardroom.[16]

I agree with Cooper here, any more involvement than this from white allies is an insult to Black people's inherent moral dignity and political agency.

Analysis and consciousness raising: the gendering and sexualization of death and derision for Black male and female bodies

Frequently, in the United States, Black men are characterized as thugs and Black women as welfare queens, which give sanction to their continued derision and death. To be a thug is to be gendered, sexualized and racialized as a hyper-violent Black rapist/super-predator who engages in conduct that makes him deserving of scorn, carceral confinement and/or death. To be a welfare queen is to be gendered, sexualized and racialized as a promiscuous free-riding Black woman, rendering her the appropriate object of derision, carceral confinement and/or death. These negative gender, sex and race representations cause persons to have reduced levels of empathetic concern for Black men and women.[17] For instance, one popular Fox News correspondent, Doug Giles, recently argued that Black thugs don't deserve to be the recipients of empathy because they are high school dropouts, absentee fathers, consumers of foulmouthed rap music and disrespectful to law enforcement. They are abusers of drugs and alcohol, robbers and thieves, disrespectful to white people and walk around with chips on their shoulders.[18]

Giles's depiction of young Black men as thugs falls neatly into the groove of recent media coverage surrounding the police killing of Michael Brown. Initially, the media portrayed Brown as a gentle giant. However, as further details about the shooting began to emerge, Michael Brown was increasingly characterized as a thug. No sooner than the name of the police officer that was involved in the death of Brown was disclosed (Darren Wilson), a video was released by the Ferguson Police Department that implicated the slain teenager in a nearby robbery. A smear campaign against Brown ensued and right wing media outlets all over the country began running a deluge of stories characterizing him as a thug. For instance, Mathew Vadum, from *FrontPage Magazine*, wrote an article entitled "Michael Brown: A Criminal and a Thug."[19] Dylan Scott, for *Talking Points Memo*, wrote "Far Right Says Michael Brown's Raps Show He was a Criminal and a Thug."[20] Robert Rich, for *Mr Conservative*, penned an article with a title that read "Prominent Black Pastor: Michael Brown was a Thug."[21] Mike Brown was not the only target of such disdainful labeling. Stories depicting the Ferguson protestors as hoodlums and thugs are just as ubiquitous as those deriding Brown. United Press International published "Hug a Thug Fails: National Guard coming to Ferguson."[22] USBACKLASH.ORG circulated "Mobs of Looting Thugs again Target Ferguson."[23] Dave Blount wrote "Ferguson Thug is Proud to Combat Injustice by Looting and Vandalizing,"[24] and the blog *Absolute Rights* published the article "Missouri Protesters ... Common Street Thugs or Justified Protestors?"[25]

That the right wing media would portray Michael Brown and the Ferguson protestors as thugs is not surprising, as the media in general tends to "[over-represent] whites as victims of crimes perpetrated by people of color."[26] Such negative media representation leads white Americans to "overestimate the proportion of crime committed by people of color, and associate people of color with criminality."[27] Also, it should come as no surprise that Blacks and whites have radically different reactions to Brown's shooting and its aftermath, as Blacks typically have different quantitative and qualitative experiences with the criminal justice system than do whites. A recent Pew poll shows that just 44 percent of whites questioned thought that Michael Brown's case raises important issues about race, compared with an overwhelming 80 percent of Blacks.[28] Likewise, 65 percent of Blacks questioned say that the police's response to Ferguson protesters has been too harsh, compared to just 33 percent of whites.[29] Such stark differences in opinions about Brown's shooting and the police's subsequent handling of the political protestation after the shooting suggests that Black and white Americans possess significant differences in opinion about the value of Black men's lives and the kinds of political responses that are appropriate when their lives are taken away or jeopardized.

What is troubling about Michael Brown's death is that it is not an isolated incident. He was the fifth Black man to be killed by US law enforcement officers in the month of August, 2014.[30] These five deaths are not isolated either, as it is possible to connect them to over 200 police deaths that have occurred in the US over the past fifteen years, including that of the unarmed West African immigrant Amadou Diallo, who was gunned down by four New York police officers because they mistook his wallet for a pistol. A study conducted by the psychologist B. Keith Payne suggests that negative racial stereotypes may have contributed to Diallo's and the other men's deaths. Payne argues that unconscious race bias, prompted by racial stereotyping "can lead police to claim to see a weapon where there is none."[31] Payne's study goes on to show how "[s]plit-second decisions magnify [racial] bias by limiting people's ability to control responses."[32] Amadou Diallo's shooting, then, and scores of others like it, indicates that Black thug imagery and iconography creates and promotes racial bias and is a palpable source of death for Black male bodies. This is the case for both the descendants of the Old African Diaspora, like Michael Brown and Eric Garner, and for members of the New African Diaspora, like Osmaune Zongo, Tendai Nhekario and Amadou Diallo.

Consider also negative historical representations of Black women in the media, ranging from mammies, jezebels and sapphires,[33] to fat, ugly, nappy-headed and trampish. Each is disdainful and injurious. No representation of Black women, however, is as pervasive or is as derisive as that of the Black welfare queen. Ronald Reagan and his political consultants first coined the term welfare queen in 1976. While campaigning for the presidency Reagan broke the story of a Southside Chicago woman named Linda Taylor, who had been arrested for welfare fraud and investigated for a host of other pernicious crimes, including kidnapping and homicide. During a radio press release, Reagan said of Taylor,

> [S]he has eighty names, thirty addresses, twelve Social Security cards and is collecting veteran's benefits on four non-existing deceased husbands. And she is collecting Social Security on her cards.... She's got Medicaid, getting food stamps, and she is collecting welfare under each of her names. Her tax-free cash income is over $150,000.[34]

Instead of characterizing Taylor as an exceptional kind of criminal exhibiting a unique kind of pathology, he implied that her activities were typical of most single Black mothers on welfare. The implication that most Black women were abusing public assistance in the way that Reagan claimed Linda Taylor did was misleading, as Reagan heavily exaggerated her criminal offenses and welfare abuses. The imagery, however, was profoundly effective and has left an indelible print on the average American's psyche. "As late as 1990, the majority of white Americans expressed the belief that Blacks were less intelligent, lazier, more prone to violence, and more likely to prefer living on welfare compared to whites."[35]

Contemporary images of welfare queens differ slightly from those contrived during the seventies, eighties and nineties but their scripting is eerily similar. For reasons that will be discussed in more detail below, the contemporary welfare queen takes the form of a pathologically lazy and/or morally deficient single Black mother who must be *forced to work* and *forced to care* for her children. We see the harmful effects of such scripting in the narrative of Shanesha Taylor, a homeless Arizona mother who was recently taken into custody for leaving her two children in an SUV while she went on a job interview, and in the story of Debra Harrell, who was recently arrested for leaving her nine year old daughter in a park while she worked at a nearby McDonald's. Both of these women had brushes with law enforcement due to their violation of child protection laws. However, it is important to acknowledge that current welfare policy is the cause of their violations. Their actions were poor, but their poor actions must be scrutinized in the context of harsh workfare requirements spurred and sustained by derisive welfare queen iconography.

Consider also a seemingly innocuous YouTube video, which has now gone viral, of a little Black boy named Tre entitled "Mommy's Big Secret." Tre's parents, both African-American, had been trying to hide that an addition to their family was imminent. When his mother finally decided to break the news, she captured Tre's reaction on camera. Upon hearing the news, Tre responded angrily, "What were you thinking? This is exasperating!" He continued in broken English, "Why you wanna get another baby and just replace one of your babies if there's just too much." Tre then asks, pointing his finger obstinately at his mother, "What kinda baby is that?" His mother replies, "I don't know, could be a boy, could be a girl." At this point Tre places his hands over his ears and prays that it is not a boy because, "They cry even louder than Amaya," his little sister. He then folds his arms, looks out of the window, and demands, "Buy me some earplugs too." The video was intended to be an illustration of an articulate and charming boy displaying sibling rivalry, and for many that is all it was. For many others, however, it became an insidious platform for commenters to depict Tre's mother, Shanee Hart, as irresponsible.[36] Despite the fact that both of Tre's parents are active members of the United States Armed Forces, many could not see Shanee Hart as anything more than a hypersexual and lazy Black welfare queen, because the default position in much of white America is that fertile Black women, whether they are receiving public assistance or not, are seeking to siphon money away from hard working white people.

The impetus behind labeling Black men as thugs and Black women as welfare queens has genealogical ties to slavery. Prior to being subjected to this malevolent form of servitude, Blacks were scarcely thought to be different than whites.[37] Clearly, people of African descent are phenotypically dissimilar from Europeans because of their sable skin and wooly hair, but these dissimilarities did not stop them from eating, sleeping, socializing and even running away together under the harsh and oppressive conditions of new world bondage. Neither did differences in skin color stop Black and white indentured servants and slaves from taking up arms together, which they did during Bacon's Rebellion, where they joined forces in Virginia in 1676 in order to challenge the economic hegemony of the planter class.[38]

The members of the planter class, however, were stunned by this black/white alliance and developed a potent strategy to neutralize it. Using balkanization techniques, they supplanted this multi-racial populist movement with a bribe.[39] As long as whites promised to keep their sable fellows in check, they would be granted an "honorific" status above them and would be regarded as wage earners instead of slaves. As a result, and as if with the wave of a wand, whites were placed in a higher social category than that of their dispossessed Black brethren and sistren. It was thus asserted that black skin and wooly hair were devilish marks revealing a natural taint. This pernicious racial lie, fabricated for the sake of justifying the institution of slavery and for separating the mutual economic interests of Black and white laborers, began to stand on its own legs, and persists in the form of the myth of the Black thug and the Black welfare queen.

The genealogy of Black thug iconography

In "From Slavery to Mass Incarceration: Rethinking the 'Race Question' in the US,"[40] the noted sociologist and ethnographer Loic Wacquant argues that "America's first three 'peculiar institutions,' slavery, Jim Crow, and the ghetto, had one thing in common: they were each instruments for the conjoint *extraction of labour* and *social ostracization*."[41] That is, they were each designed with the express intent of exploiting Black labor and creating an almost impenetrable form of social cleavage. Wacquant shows how each of these forms of domination and oppression have morphed into a fourth "peculiar institution," mass incarceration. Before examining the details of how Wacquant connects these institutions, I will offer a brief outline of them. Afterwards, an understanding of how they each naturally evolved out of one another and how the system of mass incarceration upholds many of the same social functions as slavery should become clear.

Slavery

Slavery in the Americas can be most simply described as an agrarian based economic institution that exploited an unfree Black labor base and that developed a rigid racial caste system. From the sixteenth to the nineteenth century, it is conjectured that approximately nine to twelve million Black men, women, and children were transported from Africa to the new world in slave ships.[42] These African diasporites provided a secure labor pool for the harsh and exacting agricultural work deemed undesirable and unsuitable for Native Americans and European immigrants.[43] Slavery was highly lucrative and those poor persons that survived the middle passage were assigned to plantations all over the Americas where their behavior and work performance could be tightly monitored and regulated. One unfortunate but secondary effect of slavery was the creation of a racial caste system that separated "civilized" whites from "primitive" Blacks. Once the biological lines were artificially drawn onto their bodies, they became calcified culturally. Racism was used as a conceptual tool to reconcile the apparently contradictory practice of slavery alongside the avowed high ideals of democracy and individual freedom.

In 1865, union abolitionists and Black freedom fighters helped to eradicate the institution of slavery, and for a brief period of time after the Civil War Blacks were granted the right to vote, to hold and seek public office and to fraternize with whites.[44] But these hard gained rights and privileges would prove to be ephemeral, for white Southerners could not bear their loss with dignity and worked fiercely to re-establish social and economic hegemony over the newly freed slaves. In answer to Reconstruction, they created Jim Crow.

Jim Crow

Jim Crow was a stern set of laws and bigoted cultural norms established for the purpose of continuing the exploitation of Black labor and for reinforcing the practice of relegating Blacks to a permanent second-class status.[45] On the social front, Blacks were strictly prohibited from sharing public transportation, restrooms, water fountains and housing accommodations with whites. Also, Blacks were prevented from shaking white hands, speaking derisively in reference to white men, and, most importantly, expressly prohibited from commenting on the appearance of white women. Any violation of these race norms would result in either mob terror or severe legal sanctions.[46] On the economic front, Jim

Crow served as a way for wealthy planters to maintain the agrarian based economy of the South, which had been placed under threat by the Civil War. Black farmers were forced into a merciless sharecropping system, which replaced slavery as a cheap source of labor. Although Blacks no longer labored under threat of the whip, they were forced to sign usurious rental agreements with unscrupulous landowners, which they were often unable to fulfill. A small number of Black sharecroppers were fortunate enough to turn a profit, which enabled them to buy land, freeing them from the yoke of the sharecropping system. However, the vast majority of Black farmers were not so lucky, and found themselves mired in an endless cycle of poverty and peonage.[47]

Ethno-racial enclosure

Tired of the ill treatment and social debasement they were suffering at the hands of hostile whites under Jim Crow, many Southern Blacks became enamored with the idea of heading North, which for them represented something akin to the biblical Promised Land. This attraction was further enhanced by the lure of economic improvement, made available by a shortage in the influx of non-skilled European laborers. This shortage in workers, caused by WWI, necessitated the recruitment of two previously undesirable groups into the Northern urban workforce: Southern Blacks and white women. Thus, if the North represented a social Promised Land for Southern Blacks, their movement, numbered in the millions, symbolized something analogous to the Hebraic exodus out of pharaonic Egypt. But instead of finding a utopia in Northern American and Mid-western cities, they found themselves wandering around in pockets of dark urban deserts. They were now ethnically enclosed in urban dystopias in which they were forced to accept the most menial work, meager wages and vile social conditions.

During this phase of Northern and Midwestern migration Blacks found themselves forced into slums and ghettoes because of comprehensive communal violence.[48] Spontaneously and anonymously, any Black could be singled out because of their skin color and be subjected to indiscriminate beatings and lynchings. Blacks, thus, had an incentive to cluster together, because of the safety that accrues through numbers.[49] But after the initial wave of wanton and impersonal violence, the violence became more specific and targeted. It was not uncommon for Blacks who were nestled in or too close to white neighborhoods to be given threatening letters, to suffer personal harassment or to undergo intense intimidation. Rock throwings, cross burnings, ransackings, shootings, gang beatings and bombings were often used to drive specific Blacks out of designated white neighborhoods.[50]

When the direct use of violence was inconvenient, organizational solutions were employed. Neighborhood associations whose explicit purpose was to preserve property value and provide security, but whose implied purpose was to restrict the entrance of Blacks into white neighborhoods, were created. Such organizations checked and limited the scope and range of residential possibilities for urban Blacks through zoning regulations and through boycotting real estate agents and businesses that would cater to them. However, the most effective and powerful tool that neighborhood associations used to ward off Blacks came in the form of restrictive covenants, contracts drawn up by neighborhood associations which expressly forbid its members to allow Blacks and other minorities to buy, lease or occupy their properties.[51]

Because violence and calculated organizational practices fostered the growth and development of the Black ghetto, it is safe to say that the Black ghetto was formed by deliberate design. Initially, the Black ghetto was a device for caste control, a mechanism for quarantining alterity while utilizing menial labor. But this mechanism of marginalization and exploitation, as effective as it was, is now becoming increasingly ineffective at managing the growing horde of urban poor persons created by America's new post Fordist/Keynesian economic and cultural vision.[52] The emerging consensus, on both the left and right end of the American political spectrum, on how to deal with the "negro" problem, seems to be through the upsizing of the penal sector of the state. Hence, we appear to be in the middle of a transitional period where the institution of ghettoization is permutating into the institution of mass incarceration and the aim is to manage Black males' bodies, and to manage Black females through paternalistic administrative bureaucracies. The way the penal state manages Black males will be outlined first, followed by an adumbration of how Black females are managed by administrative welfare bureaucracies.

Mass incarceration

The Black ghetto is metamorphosing into something significantly different than its prior self because of the state's new socio-economic imperatives. The belt-tightening of wage labor and diminishment of welfare protection—a post Keynesian/Fordist concoction—coupled with the increased use of penalization as a means of social control signals that the ghetto is increasingly becoming tied to the prison. Wacquant argues that the two are joined

> by a triple relationship of functional equivalency, structural homology, and cultural syncretism, such that they now constitute a single *carceral continuum* which entraps a redundant population of younger black men (and increasingly women) who circulate in closed circuit between its two poles in a self-perpetuating cycle of social and legal marginality with devastating personal and social consequences.[53]

What Wacquant says here is accurate, but it is important to remember that the use of the carceral state to control the Black population is nothing new, for directly after Emancipation and Reconstruction a law and order rhetoric was devised, which served the purpose of justifying the use of penal institutions to exploit newly freed Blacks' labor and to keep them in their place.[54]

Throngs of Blacks, who were once required to be subservient by law, were instantaneously imbued with the same rights as their previous owners. They could own guns, vote and engage in enterprise. This bothered the members of the Southern aristocracy, who were afraid that revenge might be taken out upon them and that their source of wealth would be completely uprooted. It also bewildered the masses of poor and illiterate whites that had grown accustomed to the racial caste system and symbolic privileges it afforded them. It must have seemed strange to both classes of white Americans that "their niggers" were no longer following the established rules of racial etiquette and were no longer comporting themselves obsequiously. From both of their perspectives, something had to be done. The solution was to criminalize Black life itself.

Southern legislators drafted new laws that targeted Blacks for the express purpose of controlling and managing their existence. Pig laws, vagrancy statutes, laws against walking too closely to railroads, laws against speaking too loudly in the presence of white women and laws against loitering, etc.... were indicative of the kinds of unjust statutes that were contrived in cities and counties all over the South for the purpose of returning Blacks to a condition as close to slavery as possible. Although slavery was outlawed upon the basis of race, it was not outlawed in cases where persons were convicted of felonies. The penal system, with its practice of convict leasing, became an institution that supplied the continued exploitation and management of Black men.[55]

The difference between the law and order rhetoric of America's past and its implementation today is that in the past it served the dual purpose of justifying exploitation and marginalization. Today, however, because of market deregulation, mechanization, welfare downsizing and the outsourcing of labor, law and order rhetoric and the imagery of Black male thuggery primarily serve the purpose of social ostracization and devaluation of Black male life. That is, the expansion of the penal state and its attendant law and order propaganda is predicated upon managing annoying and dispensable Black male bodies.

Recovering Wacquant's line of reasoning, the contemporary penal system in the US is functionally equivalent to the ghetto in that it uses controlled violence to restrict and contain a dishonored group; it is structurally homologous to the ghetto in that it comforts the same types of dominating and oppressive social relations, and it is culturally welded to the ghetto in that it upholds several of its main functions. But the chief problem with the symbiotic relationship between the ghetto and the penal state is that the ghetto is no longer able to serve its Janus-faced functions.[56]

Although the ghetto is a means of carving a dishonored group off of the social body, it is also the means by which that dishonored group can bond to protect itself. However, with the rise of mass incarceration, the ghetto is permutating into a hyperghetto (superghetto), which no longer encourages such bonding and collective protection. The reality of the Black hyperghetto can be best understood by distinguishing it from the traditional communal Black ghetto or by identifying the four main characteristics that render it exceptional.[57] One, the hyperghetto is comprised of a homogeneous population of uneducated and unemployed Black masses, whereas the ghetto of the twentieth century was integrated along class lines.[58] Two, the hyperghetto is merely the repository of unwanted Black bodies, but the ghetto of the twentieth century was a "reservoir for cheap and pliable labor."[59] Three, the hyperghetto is filled with top down bureaucratic agencies that custodialize and survey, while the communal ghetto of the twentieth century was filled with socially beneficial institutions that paralleled those of prosperous white Americans. Finally, as mentioned in the previous paragraph, the hyperghetto offers no buffering protection from a dominating and oppressive police state, whereas the communal ghetto offered some solace in the form of a sheltered space, where decent Blacks would not be harassed by "hostile white folk."

As the two worlds of prison and ghetto collide, they become increasingly indistinguishable. The ghetto begins to take on characteristics of the prison and vice versa. This *deadly symbiosis*, as Wacquant refers to it, is virtually destroying the Black community. The prison is becoming increasingly divided among racial lines and gang affiliations, whereas it once was predicated upon inmate unity so as to negotiate better prison conditions.[60] Further, the code of the streets and gang violence is beginning to permeate the reality of prison life to such an extent that inmates are finding it increasingly difficult to do their "own time," once a valued way of serving a prison sentence, as many of today's inmates are pressured by threat of violence to take sides in nihilistic contraband wars. Finally, the role of the prison as an instrument for rehabilitation has been replaced by its role as a space in which undesirables are incapacitated and resigned to a life of pain and suffering. The penitentiary is no longer perceived as a place of penance and redemption, it is merely a storage facility for abject bodies.

Although the institution of mass incarceration is modally different than slavery, Jim Crow and ethno-racial enclosure, it is functionally similar to them in key respects. They each confirm that Blacks bear an inextinguishable taint, justifying their social and political exclusion. The exploitative element of Black labor is admittedly absent in mass incarceration, but covertly present. The cardinal difference between mass incarceration and these others, then, is that the prior institutions explicitly exploited Black labor and cleaved Blacks off from the social body. The current system of mass incarceration, however, exploits Black labor creatively and circuitously through the proliferation of the prison industrial complex and the media's characterization of Black males as thugs.

The prison industrial complex exploits Black labor through the revolving door of publicly funded military style policing, draconian sentencing and the warehousing of Black bodies. Under the aegis of community protection and the "war on drugs," police departments all over the United States use SWAT teams that employ paramilitary tactics such as no knock raids and that use paramilitary equipment like flash bang grenades and battering rams to stun, capture and detain suspected criminals, drug dealers and drug addicts. Once booked, municipal, state and federal courts jail and imprison convicted felons and non-violent drug dealers and attach hefty restitutions to their sentencing statements and release arrangements. If the offender cannot pay the fines, they are often sent back to prison shortly after their release. In addition to being subjected to military style occupation by police and economic exploitation by a draconian justice system, convicted felons who serve time in prison are forced to work menial jail jobs for pennies per hour. There are long lists of both public and private corporations that make use of prison labor for profit.

Likewise, the media exploits Black labor through the proliferation of hyper sexualized thug imagery. News outlets sell advertisement space by fomenting racial xenophobia and paranoia. Racialized media coverage is perceived as titillating and sexy, and is systematically used to bump up ratings. Demagogues, like Bill O' Reilly and Rush Limbaugh, have sustained lucrative careers by race baiting and playing on white peoples' racial sensitivities and fears. Record, television and film production companies draw a fair share of their profits from presenting Black males as violent, ignorant and hypersexualized criminals. Unfortunately, the Black men who sing, rap, dance and act on records, television shows and motion pictures are often complicit in their own exploitation and debasement. As Black men portray themselves as gangsters and thugs for profit, they become the contemporary equivalent of minstrels.

The unfortunate consequence of such modern day minstrelsy is that many Black men in hyperghettos have begun to wholeheartedly identify themselves as those who deride, kill and exploit them, as essentially criminals and thugs. Through the negative evaluation of honor, many Black men are attempting, in vain, to "flip the script" on criminality through the wholesale cooptation of the criminal image. It is a logic that says, "if you're going to be perceived as a criminal, then you may as well be the best damned criminal you can be." The tragedy of such self-deprecation is sorrowfully exposed by the rapper Tupac Shakur, who painfully recites the truth about many Black ghetto youths on one of the most popular songs off of his posthumous studio album *All Eyez On Me.* "He say he wanna be/he say he gonna be/he say he wanna be/shorty wanna be a thug." The sad thing is that many Black boys have *ambitions* to become thugs and hoodlums, because, as the popular rapper 2 Chainz candidly exhorts, "The dope man my motherfucking role model/not Tiger, not Jordan, not Charles Barkley." This respect for the dope man is grounded in the outlaw's ability to carve out an opulent living, even in the midst of extremely harsh and impossibly cruel structural conditions. However, no matter how we try to spin thug imagery and lore, the tragic fact remains that no sublimation of a negative mark will result in a positive and healthy self-conception.

It is imperative, then, that new Black social critics and leaders analyze how the complex system of mass incarceration stifles positive Black self-understandings and self-images, thwarts Black self-determination and foils black self-development. The tag "thug" may be different from the tag "slave," "sharecropper" or "menial laborer" but the deleterious effects are just the same. Labeled as thugs and criminals, Black men exist in a degraded and dishonored second-class status, lacking voting rights, the ability to engage in substantive and satisfying work and are often regarded as dishonorable citizens deserving of death.

So, if it is egregious to characterize Black men as criminals and thugs, how should they be depicted? Put differently, how should others regard them, and how should they regard themselves? Since answering this question requires some insight into how Black women ought to be perceived, I will hold off answering it until I offer a deep historical overview of the origins of the characterization of Black women as welfare queens.

Welfare queens and the myth of dependency

In the early 1940s, the members of the National Resources Planning Board (NRPB)[61] were intent on developing "an ambitious program for postwar economic growth and security."[62] Their policy initiatives would culminate in the development of two bills, the Wagner–Murray–Dingell bills of 1943 and 1945, which would never see the floor of Congress. With these bills, NRPB members and other New Deal advocates were seeking to frame welfare as a broad form of public insurance designed to mitigate a vast constellation of social, structural and economic problems. However, the position of fiscal conservatives in Congress, lack of support from labor unions and an increase of middle class entitlements for WWII veterans signaled doom for any chance of these bills' passage.[63] Conservative Congressmen on both sides of the aisle formed loose coalitions that effectively blocked the growth of postwar social welfare programs, which they perceived as dangerous threats to free enterprise and negative liberty. Labor unions such as the American Federation of Labor and the Congress of Industrial Organizations pulled financial and lobbying support from comprehensive social-welfare reform as they secured bread-and-butter contracts for themselves and their members via deals with private corporations. Also, congressional and administrative focus on middle class entitlements such as the GI bill drew attention away from the needy and the poor and directed it toward the creation and expansion of a carefully selected middle class.

If comprehensive welfare reform initially signaled the effort to guarantee public insurance for all Americans, it underwent a radical change in meaning after the Wagner–Murray–Dingell bills of 1943 and 1945 died. Instead of "comprehensive" entailing the expansion of those deemed worthy of receiving welfare or public insurance, it increasingly came to be understood as the expansion of therapeutic social services provided to "problematic" women.[64] Thus, in place of characterizing poor persons as victims of inegalitarian economic arrangements, social injustice or unfortunate circumstances, the poor became feminized and stigmatized. That is, overwhelmingly the poor came to be regarded as "troubled women" in need of professional social services.

"Divorced, deserted, and unmarried mothers" were characterized as having "moral, social, and psychological impairments," for they were entering extant public assistance programs such as Aid to Dependent Children in large numbers and were causing public relations problems for prominent public policy makers. One such policy maker, Rudolph Danstedt, the executive director of the Social Planning Council in St. Louis in the early 1950s, proposed a solution. He argued for "the creation of a social rehabilitation center analogous to … physical rehabilitation centers … for A.D.C. mothers." For such women he would:

[p]rovide for services of case workers, psychiatric and medical consultation, psychological testing, educational and vocational counseling, planned vocational training, job placement, and of course, day-care or homemaker service[s].[65]

Droves of public policy experts echoed Danstedt's sentiments, making rehabilitation the main focus of public assistance programs and the preeminent goal of an extensive number of social work experts. The acceptance of Danstedt's goal was further enshrined into federal law with the passage of the 1956 Social Security Amendments, which solidified the change in orientation from a comprehensive plan for public insurance to the comprehensive plan for rehabilitation; that is, the movement away from structural explanations of poverty and dysfunction toward subjective culpability accounts that could best be remedied through personal counseling.[66]

As income grants became less of a concern for those heading the ADC, providing rehabilitative social services became the focal point. The result was the commitment to a public policy that would eventually become ever more intrusive and paternalistic; while, ironically, encouraging independence and self-sufficiency.[67] Oxymoronically, women were expected to bring home the bacon *and* fry it up in a pan. And although the rehabilitation paradigm had become settled, it was merely a veneer. Underneath it all lay the true problem: the ADC's shifting clientele. The ADC had its inception in the continuation of mother's pension programs that began in the early twentieth century.[68] Most of the recipients of aid from these programs were white widows. Over time these programs permutated into ones in which the clientele increasingly changed to unwed nonwhite mothers. When the ADC's clientele was comprised mostly of widowed white women, it scarcely, if ever, came under public fire. However, as its clientele changed, it became heavily scrutinized. The problem for public policy experts, then, was how to justify income grants to poor unwed mothers, particularly Black mothers, when most of the public harbored hostile racial prejudices.[69]

In order to handle the backlash against the ADC, public policy experts simply changed the programs' initiatives. As was mentioned earlier, instead of merely offering monetary support to poor women, they would now offer them family rehabilitation services. Still, rehabilitation was going to be a hard sell, and public policy experts knew it. Thus, they devised a strategy that they hoped would sidestep rampant racial animus toward and public repudiation of the ADC: they would misleadingly whiten the image of their clientele while vigorously promoting the ADC's ability to foster family values.[70] In so doing, they created program and policy initiatives that were ill suited to serving their true clientele. In other words, they managed to ignore the primary sources of poverty and dysfunction amongst poor Black unwed mothers in urban environments: ghettoization and deindustrialization. This point is underscored by Middlestadt, who writes:

Knowledge of racism [by welfare professionals], did not translate into action on civil rights. Though some welfare professionals recognized that racial discrimination contributed to poverty and welfare use, and existed within the ADC program itself, welfare policy makers in the late 1950's did not fight for civil rights within the welfare system. Welfare policy makers distinguished between recognizing the existence of racial discrimination and incorporating this analysis into their policy agenda.[71]

Ultimately, too many welfare professionals, in the late 40s and throughout the entire 50s, were willing to turn a blind eye toward racial injustice. Instead of attacking racial domination and oppression head on by adjoining themselves with reputable civil rights organizations and leaders, they sought to mitigate racism's effects by providing services to a supposedly "psychologically impaired" group of women. These welfare reformers may have meant well, but they merely delayed the inevitable. By ignoring racial discrimination and promoting the rehabilitation of dysfunctional families, they were partly responsible for etching into the public consciousness the image of the Black welfare queen and for bringing into existence an excessively punitive workfare system.

As if the harm from welfare professionals were not enough, the National Urban League's leaders, Lester Granger and Whitney Young, added insult to injury by following the ADC's lead in downplaying racial discrimination in the area of public assistance, while highlighting and supporting the ADC's mission to rehabilitate troubled families.[72] The impetus behind this awkward coupling lay in the Nation Urban League's leaders' avowed mission to improve Negro family life, while avoiding the stigmatization and embarrassment that attends public assistance. Instead of pushing the envelope for social, structural and distributive justice simultaneously, the Urban League opted to keep doing what was popular and successful at the time: opening up social spaces for Blacks through civil disobedience.[73] There was simply no room in their publicity campaign to fight for the cause of what they considered to be an embarrassment: the growing phenomenon of poor single Black mothers. This they would soon come to regret.

In the early 1960s, Louisiana governor Jimmie Davis and Newburgh, New York city manager, Joseph Mitchell, waged war against the ADC.[74] The former by dropping tens of thousands of poor unwed mothers from public assistance rolls for having "unsuitable" households, the latter by framing public assistance as an unfair redistributive system that burdens taxpayers by rewarding "lazy chiselers and loafers." These powerful political objections to public assistance put welfare advocates on edge, for it threatened the very core of their justification of public assistance: family rehabilitation.

Welfare reformers were reacting to negative publicity and growing disapproval of public assistance rather than being proactive in framing the issue the way they wanted. It was as if they were engaged in a game of chess, where their every move was a defensive move due to a constant series of clever offensive checks. Their timidity in squaring up with the subject of racial discrimination in public assistance made matters worse than they had to be. By continually sidestepping the race issue, the issue became more and more prominent. Eventually, welfare professionals had to deal with the issue of race, but in a way not to their liking. In order to avoid the charge of being supportive of free-loaders, welfare advocates capitulated to the demand that women receiving public assistance work for it. Again, I turn to Middelstadt.

> In the year or so after Newburgh, the public and policy discourse regarding gender, work, and welfare grew muddier. Contradictory images of mothers as stay-at-home caregivers were juxtaposed with images of them as potential workers. Criticisms of their laziness were given as much stress as criticisms of their care-giving or sexual status. Critics of welfare like Mitchell in Newburgh argued that all ADC mothers, if they were simply able bodied, were de facto employable. Welfare advocates opposed this broad claim and drew a line in the sand. But they nevertheless found themselves responding subtly to such criticism by beginning to publicly emphasize how rehabilitation promoted work for ADC mothers.[75]

It may be impossible to discover their precise reasons or motivations, but the actions of those social welfare policy makers who vehemently denied the relevancy of racial discrimination to either the acceptance or rejection of their policies only makes sense in terms of the following possibilities: (a) they were straddling the fence in regards to following racial imperatives, (b) they were attempting to secure long-term work for specialists in the social service industry or (c) they were attempting to remain diplomatic such that they could maneuver politically in hostile territory. None of these reasons or motivations is mutually exclusive with the others and it is highly likely that they avoided the subject of race, more or less, for all of these reasons. Whatever the case may be, their racial dodging had adverse consequences. In their attempt to preserve the ADC program, social welfare professionals failed to advance the interests of all poor single mothers and succeeded in reinforcing the image of the lazy Black welfare queen. Also, they contributed to the development of an overly paternalistic workfare bureaucracy that monitors and enforces top-down mandates, turns social workers into constabularies and which devalues care work, leading to the neglect of poor children.[76]

At this juncture, one may argue that I have attributed too much blame to social welfare professionals, who were merely implementing law or working within the existing framework of welfare law and policy. However, it is important to understand that early welfare professionals, Rudolph Danstedt in particular, played a direct role in drafting and promoting early ADC law and policy initiatives. My overall point here is that most transfer programs, such as Section 8, Aid to Families with Dependent Children, Temporary Assistance for Needy Families and the Children's Health Insurance Program, are administered by governmental bureaucracies that are arranged hierarchically and that utilize instrumental thinking in setting and achieving objectives. I do not seek to eliminate these "top down" bureaucracies, which would be impossible, but rather to constrain them so as to make them more "compatible with the 'horizontal' egalitarian and participative demands of the democratic ideal."[77]

While it is important to acknowledge that thug imagery and iconography lead to Black male derision and death, it is equally important to acknowledge that welfare queen imagery and iconography lead to Black female derision and death, as it prevents the extension of empathy to Black female bodies. Welfare queen imagery generates contempt for Black women and creates situations in which people like Shanesha Taylor and Debra Harrell have to choose between working or childrearing, because xenophobic whites don't want lazy Black women to steal their tax dollars. Welfare queen iconography causes people like Shanee Hart to be treated as objects of derision and contempt, even though they are among the best and brightest of hardworking Americans. Welfare queen imagery leads to the death of women like Yvette Smith, who was gunned down on her own property in Bastrop, Texas by a policeman who initially stated that she was armed, but retracted the statement after an internal investigation. Welfare queen iconography leads to the death of women like Eleanor Bumpurs, who was shot twice by a shotgun in her apartment by a Bronx policeman who claimed she attacked him with a butcher knife. Welfare queen imagery leads to the death of women like Tyisha Miller, Kathryn Johnston, Gabriella Nevarez, Rekia Boyd Pearlie Golden and many others.

So, if it is egregious to characterize Black women as welfare queens, how should they be depicted? Put differently, how should others regard them, and how should they regard themselves? The next section illustrates that the answer lies in the development of a program of Pan-African education for the men and women of both the Old and New African Diasporas. In order to prove this point it is first necessary to detail the ineffectiveness of contemporary Black leadership and the dearth of practical Black political consciousness in the United States. After doing so, the need for a program of Pan-African education should naturally emerge, along with a need for Black radical democracy.

Pan-Africanism and its connection to radical democracy

What little freedom Black people have been able to gain in the United States, and elsewhere, has been born out of an undying spiritual struggle against a terrible admixture of forms of domination and oppression. It should come as no surprise, then, that Blacks' struggle against such manifold forms of subjugation took up guises just as terrible. Individually and collectively Blacks combated slavery through deception, stealing and destroying property, directly disobeying orders, absconding and armed rebellion. During the Jim Crow era Blacks organized underground cotton markets, liberated convicted laborers through jailbreaks, developed occupational strikes and boycotts and, in some instances, got involved in small-scale gun skirmishes with racist landowners. During the civil rights era many Blacks took to high ground and resisted their mistreatment through moral suasion, litigation, non-violent civil disobedience and economic protest. There is no denying that such diverse forms of struggle were effective, and even when not, at least understandable.

From slavery to the civil rights movement, then, there have always been strong and successful Black leaders, social critics and activists ready to galvanize, organize and make sense of Blacks' struggle for freedom. Abolitionists such as Sojourner Truth, Harriet Tubman, James Forten Sr., William Whipper, David Walker and Frederick Douglass were powerful and effective Black leaders who substantively contributed to the cause of Black emancipation. In the face of the unremitting terror of Jim Crow, Benjamin "Pap" Singleton, Booker T. Washington, Lucy Laney, Ida B. Wells, Homer Plessy and W. E. B. DuBois made similar contributions to the freedom fight. Civil rights leaders and activists such as Martin Luther King, Jr., Malcolm X, Bayard Rustin, Fannie Lou Hamer, Ralph Abernathy and Medgar Evers, did no less. However, when we examine and weigh Blacks' current efforts in the struggle for freedom against the efforts of men and women of the past, it reveals that something is missing. Contemporary Black folk seem to have reached a point where they lack prophetic vision and the very soul of the political.

Cornel West emphasizes this problem in his latest book, *Black Prophetic Fire*, in which he argues that the ascendency of Barack Obama to the presidency of the United States has rendered current critiques of the American system of imperialism by Blacks as tantamount to disloyalty.[78] In *Betrayal: How Black Intellectuals Have Abandoned the Ideals of the Civil Rights Era*, Houston A. Baker argues that the popular and well-circulated musings of neo-conservatives are far from progressive, and are "in no way allied to the best practices of and ideals of race men and women of countless American generations."[79] Eddie Glaude, Jr. argues that the "Black Church is Dead," and "the idea of this venerable institution as central to Black life and as a repository for the social and moral conscience of the nation has all but disappeared."[80]

Even so, to some, the assertion that Black leadership and Black political consciousness are in crisis may seem oxymoronic, because today, so many Blacks are thriving like never before. There are Black politicians like President Barack Obama, Representative Maxine Waters, Attorney General Eric Holder and Senator Corey Booker. On the right side of the political spectrum sit Herman Cain, Clarence Thomas, Michael Steele, Condoleezza Rice, Colin Powell and Allen West. There are popular and prosperous Black entertainers and athletes such as Jay Z, Oprah Winfrey, Shaquille O' Neal, Michael Jordan and LeBron James. Also, there are extremely wealthy Black businesspersons and entrepreneurs like R. Donahue Peebles, Quinton Primo III, Janice Bryant, Herman Russell and Ulysses Bridgeman Jr. These Black persons' anomalous prosperity and limited social-political power, however, provides neither consolation nor solace for nearly one third of the Black population who live in poverty in the United States and an even larger number of Blacks who live in a constant state of social and political dysfunction and dis-ease. Well-noted Black liberals, conservatives, clergy members and intellectuals have attempted to take up the banner of the Black struggle, but their leadership efforts have failed to provide the Black community with pragmatic strategies for dealing with its most deep-seated problems.

The liberal/democratic platform promoted by Barack Obama, and the agenda currently pushed by most African-American liberals, consists in advancing middle class growth and distributive justice. Their goal is to restore accessibility to the American dream, such that anyone who "works hard" and "plays by the rules" will receive their fair share of material and/or social goods. This program, however, provides very little impetus for critical analysis of the hierarchical structure of the division of labor itself, which is what actually prevents people in poverty from having any real chance of climbing up. Something analogous can be said about the transfer programs that Black and white liberals support so zealously. Means-tested social programs like TANF, WIC, SNAP and Section 8 are usually administered by governmental bureaucracies that employ condescending officials who seldom take up the concerns and interests of their clients, and thereby rarely provide them with services that might truly ameliorate their condition.

More importantly, policy initiatives undergirded by the principles of distributive justice offer no feasible solution to problems related to white supremacy and Blacks' subjection to race based violence. Both Trayvon Martin and Jordan Davis were the sons of gainfully employed and "respectable" middle class African-Americans, but their class status did not prevent them from being gunned down in the streets by men who "felt threatened" by them. Thus, although fair distribution ought to be of great concern to African-Americans, equitable distribution should not be perceived as the *summum bonum* of justice. The demand for meaningful, self-directed and self-affirming work, the ability to manage one's own imagery and symbols, and the ability to have decision-making power over the course of one's life are issues just as significant as issues related to distribution.[81]

The shortcomings of liberalism have caused many blacks to turn toward the Republican Party and Black conservativism for guidance, but black conservatives offer prescriptions for African-Americans that are even more problematic than those offered by Black liberals. Borrowing from the playbook of the "politics of respectability," Black conservatives urge African-Americans to be resourceful, industrious and responsible: to pull themselves up by their own bootstraps. At first glance, such a position seems reasonable, even laudable. Upon reflection, this argument is, at best, simpleminded, at worst, disingenuous. The politics of respectability is misguided principally because it leads Black conservatives to downplay the significance of structural domination and oppression, to overemphasize personal responsibility and individualism and to uncritically endorse neo-liberal economic theory. Black conservatives offer no substantive program for dealing with African-Americans' most deep-seated problems; they merely encourage them to imitate the comportment and values of the white middle class so as to achieve the impossible: to become invisible and be absorbed into the white social body while being indelibly marked as Black and abject.

Finding little comfort in the musings of electoral politicians, some African-Americans would rather stick with what is safe and familiar, and it could be argued that no institution is more familiar to or safe for African-Americans than the Black church. At one time the Black church served as the back bone of the African-American community, undergirding most of its activities in both public and private life. In the same way that the salons of the eighteenth century served as the meeting place of the public sphere in Europe, the Black church served as the meeting place of the Black public sphere in the United States. But today's Black church has lost its prophetic vision because of too many scandals and its failure to provide practical political guidance.

On one hand, too many Black preachers are charlatans enjoying the spoils of money and sex pilfered from their congregations. They offer their members little if any leadership, but merely entrance them with loud music and shouting. On the other hand, the prophetic vision of too many Black preachers has become clouded by the gospels of prosperity and favor, which more closely resemble principles derived from new age spirituality, rather than the fiery sermons of traditional preachers who possessed a strong sense of social and political justice. If the Black church is to be considered relevant again, Black preachers must do more than preach variations of the gospel. They must use the pulpit as a means to address the concrete social and political needs of Black people. In the words of Otis Moss, the well noted civil rights activist and esteemed evangelist, Black preachers must

> preach the gospel on Sunday, but walk picket lines on Monday. The church needs to be the headlight not the taillight of political activism. There needs to be more than a praise gospel. The church must promote revolutionary change in the community.[82]

Until the Black church harkens this message, it will remain peripheral to the struggles of Blacks for freedom.

In spite of the failures of today's Black liberals, conservatives and Black clergy to manage the African-American community's most deep-seated problems, all is not lost. It is my contention that the crisis of Black leadership and political consciousness in America can be resolved by arming new Black social critics, potential Black leaders and the Black community with a Pan-African education that reveals their rich history of consciousness raising and radical democracy. The problem, however, is that the minds of many African Americans have become so colonized, that they see the politics of resistance and struggle as zealotry and extremism. Quite frankly, I am speaking here of the Black Lives Matter movement. In other words, many Blacks in the United States have unwittingly, through dint of habit, adopted a passive, market-based model of democracy and see those who are struggling against it as wrongdoers.

Why market democracy is insufficient for the members of all African Diasporas

Democracy is routinely construed as a form of government in which persons rule themselves through voting mechanisms, either directly or by proxy. When a society's institutions are arranged in such a way that its citizens primarily vote directly, it is said to be a direct democracy. When a society is arranged such that its citizens govern themselves indirectly it is said to be a representative democracy. It is interesting to note that most ordinary persons who are accustomed to living in Western democratic societies, particularly the United States, tend to think that having more democracy is favorable to having less. For this reason many Americans assume that direct democracy is better than representative democracy and several studies suggest that this attitude may be linked to citizens' overall distrust of elected officials and representative institutions.[83] But many well-noted political theorists and statesmen have argued against this disposition. In fact, several of the framers of the United States constitution and signatories of the Declaration of Independence have warned against the dangers associated with direct democracy, or as it is often construed, populism.

Although there is not enough space to cover such thinkers' viewpoints here, it is interesting to note that, ironically, today's Black politicians and social critics, even those who were participants in the civil rights movement, tend to characterize democracy as the anti-populists do: as consumer-like voting. Black Americans have become so preoccupied with voting and with interest group politics that they have neglected to take stock of their current political reality. Certainly, voter ID laws, voter protection proposals, the shortening of early voting periods, unfair redistricting and ominous billboards that intimidate Black voters with jail time are all unjust forms of voter suppression and should be condemned. But, voting has not, nor will it ever, stop the growth of the prison industrial complex and the paternalism of the welfare state. That is, punching a hole in a ballot box or electing Black politicians will not solve most of the problems currently facing the Black community in the United States, especially white supremacy as a source of Black male and female derision and death.

The crucial downside of this unreflective acceptance of the economic characterization of democracy for African-Americans is that it keeps Black citizens balkanized and prevents Black leaders from recognizing that the extra-constitutional measures and insurrectionist actions of the participants of the civil rights movement, abolitionist movement and transatlantic mutinies were, *in fact*, democracy. Instead of encouraging an emerging Black public to *act* democratically in order to improve its condition, Black politicians and social critics have fooled themselves and members of the Black community into thinking that voting *is* democracy and that voting *is* the principal means by which to practice self-governance. This is unfortunate. The result is that no more action and no more insurgency is expected or required from the members of the Black community, because the members of previous freedom movements are perceived as having done all of the important work for them. By imagining voting to be the principal means by which to practice self-rule, the Black public has lost the fervor—the very *soul*—of the political.

It is clear, then, that the new Black social critic is confronted with a significant problem. How can he convince a diverse multitude of Black persons that their conception of democracy is significantly flawed? How can he convey to the Black public that the civil rights movement and prior liberation movements, if they are perceived chiefly as struggle for suffrage and desegregation, were exercises in futility? The new Black social critic can begin to manage this crisis through a program of Pan-African education.

Pan-Africanism is a political ideal designed to help Blacks overcome the colonization of their cultural memory. It is the critical analysis of social structures and relations that dominate and oppress Black people. As such, it is a form of political awareness that mitigates Black miseducation and Black double consciousness. Pan-Africanism also operates as a practical emancipatory political project whereby Black people and their allies are called upon to change racist and anti-Black social structures and relations in substantive ways. It is the acknowledgement of Blacks' history of resistance and rebellion against slavery and colonialism, in a variety of forms. It is knowledge of and dedication to actively challenging social structures and relations that work to Blacks' detriment as told through brown, not blue, eyes. As the historian Toyin Falola states:

> When millions of people were enslaved and when their continent was forcefully conquered, it was a strategy both of justification and domination to deny the people a past, a memory. The maintenance of power also meant the creation of a new history to erase the previous one.[84]

From the perspective of this twisted historical narrative Africans were taught that they *benefited* from slavery. They were raised from their backwardness by being Europeanized and Christianized. Such twisting must be untwisted.

Pan Africanism helps Blacks to understand that their ability to thrive and flourish as a group will not be achieved through blind assimilation to Western culture, which tells the descendants of Africans "that they had no history and that they did not make any significant contribution to world civilization."[85] Blacks must become aware that, from the inception of slavery, there has been a sustained attempt to silence their history of resistance and rebellion. Blacks must thwart this effort my studying their insurrectionist history and ethics meticulously.[86] Such study will lead to the recognition of events and ideals that have challenged the notion of Blacks as inferior and passive. Knowledge of the various forms of historical Black resistance will help contemporary Blacks to more easily identify current forms of resistance, such as the Black Lives Matter movement, as essentially democratic and compel them to mobilize and rally around them when possible, rather than ridicule them, as justice for a few Blacks has the potential to translate into justice for a large number of Blacks.

Conclusion

Overall, I have been leading up to a point at which I can confidently make the case that democracy is an ideal that demands the mutual assignment of obligations and duties, which culminate in laws, policies and institutions that are legitimate to the extent that all citizens are substantively included in their creation and maintenance. Furthermore, democracy is constitutive of justice in human affairs when all citizens recognize the creative and normative powers of all other citizens and when every person is able to effectively order "the terms of their common life together."[87] Democracy, then, is an ideal that orders interactive processes. More accurately, democracy manifests itself as a moral intercommunicative happening or event directed toward inclusion and fairness in human affairs. It must be noted that democracy is not an institution, a particular form of government, or a procedure, although institutions, governments and procedures can be arranged to more or less reflect the democratic ideal.

I refrain from characterizing democracy as anything more than a happening or an ideal so as not to lay claim to having developed any concrete democratic form, for in my view democracy is episodic and modal. Democracy is episodic in that it is an exception and not the normal means by which we govern ourselves, as all are typically not included in assigning themselves duties and obligations. The inspiration for this assertion of democracy's episodic or fugitive character is provided by Sheldin Wolin, who states:

> Democracy in the late modern world cannot be a complete political system, and given the awesome potentialities of modern forms of power and what they exact of the social and natural world, it ought not to be hoped or striven for. Democracy needs to be reconceived as something other than a form of government: as a mode of being that is conditioned by bitter experience, doomed to succeed only temporarily, but is a recurrent possibility as long as the memory of the political survives. The experience of which democracy is the witness is the realization that the political mode of existence is such that it can be, and is, periodically lost ... Democracy is a political moment, perhaps the political moment, when the political is remembered and re-created. Democracy is a rebellious moment that may assume revolutionary, destructive proportions, or may not.[88]

That democracy is episodic should not be discouraging, but rather, it ought to be inspiring, for it signals that when injustice becomes intolerable, the most average and lowly of citizens can rise up and create new cultural patterns, meanings and news ways of thinking, being and doing.

Though democracy be episodic, it is also modal, for it manifests in no definite form. Just as the forms of human interaction and decision making are fluid and shifting, so too are forms of domination and oppression that stifle self-determination and self-development. Such modalities give rise to the need for critical theory (consciousness raising) and uncover its link to democracy (radical political action). Pan-Africanism explains the various forms and manifestations of Black domination and oppression in modern societies with the aim of diminishing them. Pan-Africanism, then, is both descriptive and prescriptive. It is descriptive in that it explains how various forms of domination and oppression emerge to diminish the prospects of Black freedom. It is prescriptive in that it offers practical proposals for the enhancement of Black freedom and development.

Prejudice and race bias are often unintentional because they are habitual practices that have been "ordered" within a pre-reflectively disclosed world. The origins of such biases are clear: the transatlantic slave trade required a racially stratified society, and Blacks were to occupy the lowest position in that society. The social practices that made the inhumane treatment of African diasporites tolerable, although contradictory to modernity's central themes, has left an indelible print on our current social practices, even though we publicly disavow them. The fact is that the pre-reflectively disclosed world that many Americans take for granted, causes great psychic and physical pain for marginalized others.

An even worse problem is that some African-Americans accept this pre-reflectively disclosed world as an ontological fact, for it is the only world they know. A world of dis-ease and dis-pleasure is one that they acknowledge as real. Utopian dreams of better tomorrows and brighter futures are eclipsed by nightmares of waking horror and nihilism. Many African-Americans live in nightmarish conditions, giving rise to crime and dysfunction. Prisons are built in rural areas to warehouse them and exploit their dysfunction for profit and are deemed more important than the construction of excellent schools designed to channel and develop their talents and capacities.

Although some cannot be roused from their nightmares, most African-Americans are aware that there is something wrong with the way the world currently is. They may lack the words to say it eloquently, the scientific rigor to represent it symbolically or the philosophical acumen to articulate it argumentatively, but they know something is amiss. The new Black social critic's job is to use Pan-Africanism as a means by which to express these intuitive sentiments in an intelligible and meaningful way. In the best way she knows how, the new Black social critic must express what the majority of Black people would say if they knew how. She must explain to Westerners that the world they seek to sustain is hurtful and harmful, and that it does not have to be this way. She must convince them, even if it makes them uncomfortable, that there is a different way of viewing the world and that there is an alternative way that they can view themselves, and that together we can successfully bring about this much needed transformation into reality.

Notes

1 I use the term Black here instead of African or African-American because it contrasts better with the social and political ideology of whiteness. It must be noted, however, that I often use the terms Black, African and African-American interchangeably in order to illustrate that Africans, African-Americans, or any other peoples who are visibly descendants of Africans, have shared social, political and economic interests. Blacks' problems are not mostly geographical, cultural or ethnographic, they are primarily color based.

2 Arlene Eisen, "Operation Ghetto Storm," *Operation Ghetto Storm*, accessed May 4, 2016, www.operationghettostorm.org/.

3 Paul J. Hirschfield, "Lethal Policing: Making Sense of American Exceptionalism," *Sociological Forum* 30(4) (December 2015): 1110.

4 Ibid.

5 Jamiles Lartey, "By the Numbers: US Police Kill More in Days than Other Countries Do in Years," *Guardian*, June 9, 2015, www.theguardian.com/us-news/2015/jun/09/the-counted-police-killings-us-vs-other-countries.

6 Ibid.

7 Hirschfield, "Lethal Policing," 1110.

8 Ibid., 1111.

9 Ibid.

10 Ibid., 1112.

11 The death I am referring to here is, of course, physical, but it is also social. Physical death is the cessation of life, whereas social death is the inability to function or attain well-being in a specific social environment. Tommy J. Curry's "The Eschatological Dilemma: The Problem of Studying the Black Male Only as the Deaths that Result from Anti-Black Racism," (Texas A&M: forthcoming) gives an excellent account of what Black death is and the kinds of conceptions that sustain and promote it.

12 Iris Marion Young, *Justice and the Politics of Difference* (Princeton, NJ: Princeton University Press, 1990), 59.

13 Ibid.

14 For the purposes of this chapter I define domination as does Iris Marion Young. She characterizes domination as a state in which persons are not able to make choices freely and oppression as a condition in which persons are not able to develop powers and capacities that are socially useful. Iris Marion Young, *Inclusion and Democracy* (Oxford: Oxford University Press, 2000), 31–33.

15 Saba Mahmood, "Feminist Theory, Embodiment, and the Docile Agent: Some Reflections on the Egyptian Islamic Revival," *Cultural Anthropology* 16(2) (2001): 202–236.

16 Kali Holloway, "11 Things White People Can Do to Be Real Anti-Racist Allies," *Salon*, accessed May 6, 2016, www.salon.com/2015/04/29/11_things_white_people_can_do_to_be_real_anti_racist_allies_partner/.

17 J. D. Unnever and F. T. Cullen, "Empathetic Identification and Punitiveness: A Middle-Range Theory of Individual Differences," *Theoretical Criminology* 13(3) (2009): 283–312.

18 Doug Giles, "Dear Black Thugs: You're Making It Hard for White Devils to Believe You're Innocent Children," *Clash Daily*, August 25, 2013. Web, September 10, 2014, http://clashdaily.com/2013/08/dear-black-thugs-youre-making-it-hard-for-white-devils-to-believe-youre-innocent-children/.

19 Matthew Vadum, "Michael Brown: A Criminal and a Thug," *FrontPage Magazine*, August 18, 2014. Web, September 10, 2014, www.frontpagemag.com/2014/matthew-vadum/michael-brown-a-criminal-and-a-thug/.

20 Dylan Scott, "Far Right Says Michael Brown's Raps Show He Was a Criminal and a Thug'," *Talking Points Memo*, August 18, 2014. Web, September 10, 2014, http://talkingpointsmemo.com/livewire/michael-brown-rap-lyrics-ferguson-shooting.

21 Robert Rich, "Prominent Black Pastor: Mike Brown Was a Thug," *Mr Conservative*, August 18, 2014. Web, September 10, 2014, http://mrconservative.com/2014/08/47883-prominent-black-pastor-michael-brown-was-a-thug/.

22 United Press International, "Hug a Thug Fails: National Guard Coming to Ferguson," *GOPUSA*, Acquire Media, August 18, 2014. Web, September 10, 2014, www.gopusa.com/news/2014/08/18/hug-a-thug-fails-national-guard-coming-to-ferguson/.

23 USBACKLASH.ORG, "Mobs of Looting Criminal Thugs Again Target Ferguson Businesses While 'Riot Friendly' Police Sat Back and Watched," *USBACKLASH.ORG*, 2014. Web, September 10, 2014, http://usbacklash.org/mobs-looting-criminal-thugs-target-ferguson-businesses-riot-friendly-police-sat-back-watched/.

24 Dave Blount, "Ferguson Thug Is Proud to Combat Injustice by Looting and Vandalizing," *Moonbattery*, 2014. Web, September 10, 2014, http://moonbattery.com/?p=49402.

25 *Absolute Rights*, "Ferguson Missouri Riots | Thugs or Justified Protestors?" *Survival Life*, August 21, 2014. Web, September 10, 2014, http://survivallife.com/2014/08/21/ferguson-missouri-riots-protestors/.

26 Nazgol Ghandnoosh and Christopher Lewis, "Race and Punishment: Racial Perceptions of Crime and Support for Punitive Policies," *The Sentencing Project: Research and Advocacy for Reform* (2014): 22.

27 Ibid., 3.

28 Pew Research Center, "Stark Racial Divisions in Reactions to Ferguson Police Shooting," August 18, 2014. Web, September 18 Sept, 2014, www.people-press.org/2014/08/18/stark-racial-divisions-in-reactions-to-ferguson-police-shooting/2/.

29 Ibid.

30 Eric Garner of Staten Island, John Crawford of Ohio, Ezell Ford of Los Angeles and Dante Parker of Victorville, California, represent the other four lives lost at the hands of police.

31 B. Keith Payne, "Weapon Bias: Split Second Decisions and Unintended Stereotyping," *Current Directions in Psychological Science* 15(6) (Dec 2006): 287.

32 Ibid.

33 Dorothy E. Roberts, *Killing the Black Body: Race, Reproduction, and the Meaning of Liberty* (New York: Vintage, 1999), 10–19.

34 Ronald Reagan, "Gilford New Hampshire Campaign Speech," reprinted in *Welfare in the United States: A History with Documents, 1935–1996*, edited by Permilla Nadasen, Jennifer Mittelstadt and Marissa Chappell (New York: Routledge, 2009), 189.

35 Ghandnoosh and Lewis, "Race and Punishment," 30.

36 John Prager, "Fox Posts Adorable Video of Black Child, Commenters Go FULL RACIST (Screenshots)," *Americans Against the Tea Party*, August 29, 2014. Web, September 19, 2014, http://aattp.org/fox-posts-adorable-video-of-black-child-commenters-go-full-racist-screenshots/.

37 For an alternative to the argument presented here see Winthrop Jordan's *White over Black: American Attitudes toward the Negro, 1550–1812* (Chapel Hill, NC: University of North Carolina Press, 2012). In this work, Jordan argues that Westerners, especially Englishmen, have always thought disparagingly about Blacks. For an alternative to Jordan, however, see Frank Snowden's *Blacks in Antiquity: Ethiopians in the Greco-Roman Experience* (Cambridge, MA: Belknap Press, 1970). In this work Snowden argues that Blacks were held in high esteem by both the ancient Greeks and Romans, the ideological progenitors of occidental culture.

38 Michelle Alexander, *The New Jim Crow: Mass Incarceration in the Age of Colorblindness* (New York: New Press, 2010); See also Amechi Okolo, *The State of the American Mind: Stupor and Pathetic Docility* (Bloomington, IN: xlibris, 2010), Chapter 7; see also Sherrow O. Pinder, *The Politics of Race and Ethnicity in United States: Americanization, De-Americanization, and Racialized Ethnic Groups* (New York: Palgrave Macmillan, 2010), 43–48. See also Michael Staudenmaier, *Truth and Revolution: A History of the Sojourner Truth Organization, 1969–1986* (Oakland, CA: AK Press, 2012), 84–85.

39 Alexander, *The New Jim Crow*, 24–25; Rocky Mirza, *Rise and Fall of the American Empire: A Re-interpretation of History, Economics, and Philosophy: 1492–2006* (Victoria: Trafford Publishing, 2007), 155–156; and Howard Zinn, *A People's History of the United States* (New York: Harper Perennial, 1995), 55–56. See also Sherrow O. Pinder's *Whiteness and Racialized Ethnic Groups in the United States: The Politics of Remembering* (Lanham, MD: Lexington Books, 2012), 19–20.

40 Loic Wacquant, "From Slavery to Mass Incarceration: Rethinking the 'Race Question' in the US," *New Left Review* 13 (2002): 41–60.

41 Ibid., 44.

42 Robert Fogel and Stanley Engerman, *Time on the Cross: The Economics of American Negro Slavery* (Boston, MA: Little, Brown, & Company, 1974), 15. See also David Mustard's *Racial Justice in America: A Reference Handbook* (Santa Barbara, CA: ABC-CLIO, 2003), 2. See also Stephen Behrendt's "Transatlantic Slave Trade," in

Africana: The Encyclopedia of the African and African American Experience edited by Kwame Anthony Appiah and Henry Louis Gates Jr (Oxford: Oxford University Press, 2005), 195–204.

43 Nancy C. Curtis, *Black Heritage Sites: The South* (New York, The New Press, 1996), 5. See also Talmadge Anderson and James Stewart's *Introduction to African American Studies: Transdisciplinary Approaches and Implications* (Baltimore, MD: Black Classic Press, 2007), 52–53. See also Peter McCandless' *Slavery, Disease, and Suffering in the Southern Lowcountry* (Cambridge, UK: Cambridge University Press, 2011), 9.

44 John Hope Franklin's classic work, *Reconstruction: After the Civil War* (Chicago, IL: University of Chicago Press, 1961) provides a detailed account of the kinds of privileges that Blacks enjoyed during the era of Radical Reconstruction. Also insightful is Eric Foner's *Forever Free: The Story of Emancipation and Reconstruction* (New York: Knopf, 2005). See also Eric Foner and Olivia Mahoney's *America's Reconstruction: People and Politics after the Civil War* (Baton Rouge, LA: Louisiana State University Press, 1995).

45 Wacquant, "From Slavery to Mass Incarceration," 44–45.

46 For a vivid and excoriating account of Jim Crow see Stetson Kennedy's *Jim Crow Guide to the U.S.A.: The Laws, Customs, and Etiquette Governing the Conduct of Nonwhites and Other Minorities as Second-Class Citizens* (Tuscaloosa, AL: The University of Alabama Press, 1990). For African-American narrative accounts of Jim Crow see William Chafe, Raymond Gavins and Robert Korstad's *Remembering Jim Crow: African Americans Tell about Life in the Segregated South* (New York: The New Press, 2001) and Anne Valk and Leslie Brown's *Living with Jim Crow: African American Women and Memories of the Segregated South* (New York: Palgrave Macmillan, 2010).

47 For a concise, but accurate, account of the oppressive conditions surrounding the southern sharecropping see Daniel Fusfeld and Timothy Bates' "The Black Sharecropping System and Its Decline," in *African Americans in the U.S. Economy*, edited by Cecilia Conrad (Lanham, MD: Rowman and Littlefield, 2005), 32–37. For a fuller account see Edward Royce's *The Origins of Southern Sharecropping* (Philadelphia, PA: Temple University Press, 1993). See also Noralee Frankel's *Break Those Chains at Last: African Americans 1860–1880* (Oxford, UK: Oxford University Press, 1996), Chapter 4.

48 Douglass S. Massey and Nancy A. Denton, *American Apartheid: Segregation and the Making of the Underclass* (Cambridge, MA: Harvard University Press, 1993), 34. See also Harriette McAdoo's *Black Families* (Thousand Oaks, CA: Sage Publications, 2007).

49 It is important to understand that enclosed Northern American urban ghettoes, where recently emancipated southern Blacks found themselves, were not the product of ecological dynamics or undesigned processes, but instead were the result of deliberate acts of communalized violence. For a descriptive account of this process, see Massey and Denton's *American Apartheid*. An ecological paradigm of residential agglomeration asserts that racial and group clustering occurs spontaneously and unintentionally. The paradigm attempts to show that persons belonging to a specific cultural or racial group have a natural affinity to others who belong to that same group and that they, therefore, tend to benignly cluster together in order to preserve their peculiar form. The ecological paradigm may help to explain residential patterns in numerous places, but it simply misses the mark in attempting to explain the racial dynamics which governed urban residential patterns at the turn and middle of twentieth century America. For an explanation of the ecological account of group clustering see the introduction of Ray Hutchison's *The Ghetto: Contemporary Global Issues and Controversies* (Boulder, CO: Westview Press, 2012).

50 Geoffrey R. Skoll, *Social Theory of Fear: Terror, Torture, and Death in a Post-Capitalist World* (New York: Palgrave Macmillan, 2010), 108–110. See also Thomas J. Sugrue's *The Origins of the Urban Crisis: Race and Inequality in Postwar Detroit*

(New Jersey: Princeton University Press, 1996), Chapters 8 and 9. See also Kevin Gotham's *Race, Real Estate, and Uneven Development: The Kansas City Experiment, 1900–2010* (Albany, NY: State University of New York Press, 2014), 45–49.

51 Beverly I. Moran, *Race and Wealth Disparities: A Multidisciplinary Discourse* (Lanham, MD: University Press of America, 2008), 26–33. See also William Wayne Griffin's *African Americans and the Color Line in Ohio, 1915–1930* (Columbus, OH: Ohio State University Press, 2005), Chapter 5. See also Frank L. Samson's "Race and the Limits of American Democracy: African Americans from the Fall of Reconstruction to the Rise of the Ghetto," in *The Oxford Handbook of African American Citizenship, 1865-Present*, edited by Henry Louis Gates Jr., Claudia Steele, Lawrence D. Bobo, Michael Dawson, Gerald Jaynes, Lisa Crooms-Robinson and Linda Darling-Hammond (Oxford: Oxford University Press, 2012), Chapter 3 (71–81).

52 Loic Wacquant refers to post-Fordism/Keynesianism as desocialized wage labor and welfare retrenchment in "Deadly Symbiosis: When Ghetto and Prison Meet and Mesh," *Punishment and Society* 3 (2000): 98.

53 Wacquant, "From Slavery to Mass Incarceration," 52–53.

54 Alexander, *The New Jim Crow*, Chapter 1.

55 Ibid.

56 Loic Wacquant, "A Janus-Faced Institution of Ethnoracial Closure: A Sociological Specification of the Ghetto," in *The Ghetto: Contemporary Global Issues and Controversies*, edited by Ray Hutchinson and Bruce Haynes (Boulder: Westview Press, 2012), Chapter 1 (1–31).

57 Wacquant, "Deadly Symbiosis," 103.

58 Ibid., 104.

59 Ibid.

60 Ibid., 109.

61 The National Resources Planning Board was a government organization created during the Great Depression in order to carry out Franklin Delano Roosevelt's New Deal policies. See Marion Clawson, *New Deal Planning: The National Resources Planning Board* (Baltimore, MD: Johns Hopkins University Press, 1981).

62 Alan Brinkley, "The New Deal and the Idea of the State," in *The Rise and Fall of the New Deal Order, 1935–1980*, edited by Steven Fraser and Gary Gerstle (Princeton, NJ: Princeton University Press, 1989), 106.

63 Jennifer Mittelstadt, *From Welfare to Workfare: The Unintended Consequences of Liberal Reform, 1945–1965* (Chapel Hill, NC: The University of North Carolina Press, 2005), 29–30.

64 Mittelstadt, *From Welfare to Workfare*, Chapter 2; and Rudolph Danstedt, "A Possibility for Social Rehabilitation," *Public Welfare* 10(2) (April 1952). See also James Leiby, *A History of Social Welfare and Social Work in the United States* (New York: Columbia University Press, 1978), 181–184, and Regina G. Kunzel, *Fallen Women, Problem Girls: Unmarried Mothers and Professionalization of Social Work, 1890–1945* (New Haven, CT: Yale University Press, 1993), Chapter 6.

65 Danstedt, "A Possibility for Social Rehabilitation," quoted in Mittelstadt, *From Welfare to Workfare*, 41.

66 Mittelstadt, *From Welfare to Workfare*, 64–68.

67 Many influential philosophers have convincingly argued that the kind of reasoning typically employed by officials in bureaucratic institutions leads to the marginalization and domination of dependent persons. Experts, who "know better" than those they are supposed to serve, create policies that old persons, the mentally ill, women and the poor are required to obey, or run the risk of being "cut off" from their benefits. See Young, *Justice and the Politics of Difference*, 53–55; Nancy Fraser, "Women, Welfare and the Politics of Need Interpretation," *Hypatia* 2(1) (1987): 103–121; Henry Richardson, *Democratic Autonomy: Public Reasoning about the Ends of Policy* (Oxford, UK: Oxford University Press, 2002).

68 Winifred Bell, *Aid to Dependent Children* (New York: Columbia University Press, 1965), Chapters 1–4; See also Mittelstadt, *From Welfare to Workfare*, 3; Michael B. Katz, *In the Shadow of the Poorhouse: A Social History of Welfare in America* (New York: Basic Books, 1996), 133; James T. Patterson, *America's Struggle against Poverty in the Twentieth Century* (Cambridge, MA: Harvard University Press, 2000), 65–70.

69 Kenneth J. Neubeck and Noel A. Cazenave, *Welfare Racism: Playing the Race Card Against America's Poor* (New York: Routledge, 2001), Chapter 3; Mittelstadt, *From Welfare to Workfare*, 3, 13, 44–45, 96; Bell, *Aid to Dependent Children*, Chapter 2.

70 Mittelstadt, *From Welfare to Workfare*, Chapter 3

71 Ibid., 78.

72 Daryl Michael Scott, *Contempt and Pity: Social Policy and the Image of the Damaged Black Psyche, 1880–1996* (Chapel Hill, NC: University of North Carolina Press, 1997), 148–149; and Mittelstadt, *From Welfare to Workfare*, 82–85.

73 Mittelstadt, *From Welfare to Workfare*, 85.

74 Neubeck and Cazenave, *Welfare Racism*, Chapter 4; Mittelstadt, *From Welfare to Workfare*, 91–106.

75 Mittelstadt, *From Welfare to Workfare*, 104.

76 Richardson, *Democratic Autonomy*, 222. Any government bureaucracy that is responsible for providing aid to needy people cannot successfully achieve that end unless its officials have some knowledge of what their clientele actually needs. The best way that this kind of knowledge can be secured is by *involving* needy people in policy development and review. To the extent that we support transfer programs, without a corresponding support for their periodic evaluation and revision through participative democratic means, we encourage a stifling form of paternalism and dependency that impedes the recipients' functioning and that fails to meet the transfer programs' true objectives.

77 Ibid.

78 Cornel West and Christa Buschendorf, *Black Prophetic Fire* (Boston, MA: Beacon Press, 2014), 11.

79 Houston A. Baker, *Betrayal: How Black Intellectuals Have Abandoned the Ideals of the Civil Rights* Era (New York: Columbia University Press, 2010).

80 Eddie Glaude Jr., "The Black Church Is Dead," *The Huffington Post*, www.huffington post.com/eddie-glaude-jr-phd/the-black-church-is-dead_b_473815.html.

81 Young, *Justice and the Politics of Difference*, 18–24.

82 Rev. Otis Moss, "Civil Rights Leadership Forum," C-SPAN. New York, NY. April 6, 2013. Television.

83 Shaun Bowler, Todd Donavan and Jeffrey Karp have written an interesting article covering this subject entitled "Popular Attitudes Towards Direct Democracy," which was prepared for the American Political Science Association Meeting in 2003.

84 Toyin Falola, *The African Diaspora: Slavery, Modernity, and Globalization* (New York: The University of Rochester Press, 2013), 56–57.

85 Ibid., 56.

86 Leonard Harris, "Insurrectionist Ethics: Advocacy, Moral Psychology, and Pragmatism," in *Ethical Issues for a New Millennium*, edited by John Howie (Carbondale: Southern Illinois University Press, 2002), 192–210. See also Lee McBride III, "Insurrectionist Ethics and Thoreau," *Transaction of the Charles S. Pierce Society* 49(1) (Winter 2013): 29–45.

87 James Bohman, *Democracy Across Borders* (Massachusetts: MIT Press, 2007), 45.

88 Sheldon Wolin, "Fugitive Democracy," reprinted in *Democracy and Difference*, edited by Seyla Behabib (New Jersey: Princeton University Press, 1996), 43.

Bibliography

Absolute Rights. "Ferguson Missouri Riots | Thugs or Justified Protestors?" *Survival Life*, August 21, 2014. Web, September 10, 2014, http://survivallife.com/2014/08/21/ferguson-missouri-riots-protestors/.

Alexander, Michelle. *The New Jim Crow: Mass Incarceration in the Age of Colorblindness*. New York: New Press, 2010.

Allen, Danielle. "Political Philosophy: The Origins," in *The Oxford Handbook of the History of Political Philosophy*, edited by George Klosko, 75–95. Oxford: Oxford University Press, 2011.

Anderson, Talmadge and James Stewart. *Introduction to African American Studies: Transdisciplinary Approaches and Implications*. Baltimore, MD: Black Classic Press, 2007.

Appiah, Anthony and Henry Louis Gates, Jr. *Africana: The Encyclopedia of the African and African American Experience*, 2nd edition (Oxford, UK: Oxford University Press, 2005.

Baker, Houston A. *Betrayal: How Black Intellectuals Have Abandoned the Ideals of the Civil Rights* Era. New York: Columbia University Press, 2010.

Bell, Winifred. *Aid to Dependent Children*. New York: Columbia University Press, 1965.

Behrendt, Stephen. "Transatlantic Slave Trade," in *Africana: The Encyclopedia of the African and African American Experience,* 2nd edition, edited by Kwame Anthony Appiah and Henry Louis Gates Jr., 195–204. Oxford, UK: Oxford University Press, 2005.

Blount, Dave. "Ferguson Thug Is Proud to Combat Injustice by Looting and Vandalizing," *Moonbattery*, 2014. Web, September 10, 2014, http://moonbattery.com/?p=49402.

Bohman, James. *Democracy Across Borders*. Massachusetts: MIT Press, 2007.

Bowler, Shaun, Todd Donavan and Jeffrey Karp. "Popular Attitudes Towards Direct Democracy," prepared for the American Political Science Association Meeting in 2003.

Brinkley, Alan. *The End of Reform: New Deal Liberalism in Recession and War*. New York: Knopf, 1995.

Brinkley, Alan. "The National Resources Planning Board and the Reconstruction of Planning," in *The American Planning Tradition: Culture and Policy*, edited by Robert Fishman, 173–192. Baltimore, MD: Johns Hopkins University Press, 2000.

Chafe, William, Raymond Gavins and Robert Korstad. *Remembering Jim Crow: African Americans Tell about Life in the Segregated South*. New York: The New Press, 2001.

Clawson, Marion. *New Deal Planning: The National Resources Planning Board*. Baltimore, MD: John Hopkins University Press, 1981.

Curry, Tommy J. "The Eschatological Dilemma: The Problem of Studying the Black Male only as the Deaths that Result from Anti-Black Racism," Texas A&M (forthcoming).

Curtis, Nancy C. *Black Heritage Sites: The South*. New York: The New Press, 1996.

Dahl, Robert. *A Preface to Democratic Theory*. Chicago, IL: University of Chicago Press, 1977.

Danstedt, Rudolph. "A Possibility for Social Rehabilitation," *Public Welfare* 10(2) (April 1952): 46–48.

Dewey, John. *The Public and Its Problems*, reprinted in *John Dewey: The Later Works, 1925–1927 Volume 2*, edited by Jo Ann Boydston. Carbondale, IL: Southern Illinois University Press, 1988.

Downs, Anthony. *An Economic Theory of Democracy*. New York: Harper, 1957.

Eisen, Arlene. "Operation Ghetto Storm," *Operation Ghetto Storm*, accessed May 4, 2016. www.operationghettostorm.org/.

Falola, Toyin. *The African Diaspora: Slavery, Modernity, and Globalization*. New York: The University of Rochester Press, 2013.

Fogel, Robert William and Stanley L. Engerman. *Time on the Cross: The Economics of American Negro Slavery*. Boston, MA: Little, Brown, & Company, 1974.

Foner, Eric. *Forever Free: The Story of Emancipation and Reconstruction*. New York: Knopf, 2005.

Foner, Eric and Olivia Mahoney. *America's Reconstruction: People and Politics after the Civil War*. Baton Rouge, LA: Louisiana State University Press, 1995.

Fraser, Nancy. "Women, Welfare and the Politics of Need Interpretation," *Hypatia* 2(1) (1987): 103–121.

Frankel, Noralee. *Break Those Chains at Last: African Americans 1860–1880*. Oxford, UK: Oxford University Press, 1996.

Franklin, John Hope. *Reconstruction: After the Civil War*. Chicago, IL: University of Chicago Press, 1961.

Fusfeld, Daniel and Timothy Bates, "The Black Sharecropping System and Its Decline," in *African Americans in the U.S. Economy*, edited by Cecilia Conrad, 32–37. Lanham, MD: Rowman and Littlefield, 2005.

Ghandnoosh, Nazgol, and Christopher Lewis. "Race and Punishment: Racial Perceptions of Crime and Support for Punitive Policies," *The Sentencing Project: Research and Advocacy for Reform* (2014).

Giles, Doug. "Dear Black Thugs: You're Making It Hard for White Devils to Believe You're Innocent Children," *Clash Daily*, August 25, 2013. Web, September 10, 2014, http://clashdaily.com/2013/08/dear-black-thugs-youre-making-it-hard-for-white-devils-to-believe-youre-innocent-children/.

Glaude Jr., Eddie. "The Black Church Is Dead," *The Huffington Post*, www.huffington post.com/eddie-glaude-jr-phd/the-black-church-is-dead_b_473815.html.

Gotham, Kevin. *Race, Real Estate, and Uneven Development: The Kansas City Experiment, 1900–2010*. Albany, NY: State University of New York Press, 2014.

Griffin, William Wayne. *African Americans and the Color Line in Ohio, 1915–1930*. Columbus, OH: Ohio State University Press, 2005.

Hamilton, Alexander. "Speech in the New York Ratifying Convention on Representation," in *Alexander Hamilton: Writings*, edited by Joanne Freeman, 487–495. New York: Library of America, 2001.

Harris, Leonard. "Insurrectionist Ethics: Advocacy, Moral Psychology, and Pragmatism," in *Ethical Issues for a New Millennium*, edited by John Howie, 192–210. Carbondale, IL: Southern Illinois University Press, 2002.

Hirschfield, Paul J. "Lethal Policing: Making Sense of American Exceptionalism," *Sociological Forum* 30(4) (December 2015): 1109–1117.

Holloway, Kali. "11 Things White People Can Do to Be Real Anti-Racist Allies," *Salon*, accessed May 6, 2016. www.salon.com/2015/04/29/11_things_white_people_can_do_to_be_real_anti_racist_allies_partner/.

Hutchison, Ray. *The Ghetto: Contemporary Global Issues and Controversies*. Boulder, CO: Westview Press, 2012.

Jones, Richard. *Natural ... The Beautiful 'N' Word: Breaking the Psychological Bondage of the American Standard of Beauty*. Lincoln: iUniverse: 2007.

Jordan, Winthrop D. *White Over Black: American Attitudes Toward the Negro, 1550–1812*. Durham, NC: University of North Carolina Press, 2012.

Katz, Michael B. *In the Shadow of the Poorhouse: A Social History of Welfare in America*. New York: Basic Books, 1996.

Kennedy, Stetson. *Jim Crow Guide to the U.S.A.: The Laws, Customs, and Etiquette Governing the Conduct of Nonwhites and Other Minorities as Second-Class Citizens*. Tuscaloosa, AL: The University of Alabama Press, 1990.

Kunzel, Regina G. *Fallen Women, Problem Girls: Unmarried Mothers and Professionalization of Social Work, 1890–1945*. New Haven, CT: Yale University Press, 1993.

Lartey, Jamiles. "By the Numbers: US Police Kill More in Days than Other Countries Do in Years," *Guardian*, June 9, 2015, www.theguardian.com/us-news/2015/jun/09/the-counted-police-killings-us-vs-other-countries.

Leiby, James. *A History of Social Welfare and Social Work in the United States*. New York: Columbia University Press, 1978.

Mahmood, Saba. "Feminist Theory, Embodiment, and the Docile Agent: Some Reflections on the Egyptian Islamic Revival," *Cultural Anthropology* 16(2) (2001): 202–236.

Madison, James. "Federalist #10," in the *Federalist Papers*, edited by Clinton Rossiter. New York: New American Library, 1961.

Massey, Douglass S., and Nancy A. Denton. *American Apartheid: Segregation and the Making of the Underclass*. Cambridge, MA: Harvard University Press, 1993.

McAdoo, Harriette. *Black Families*. Thousand Oaks, CA: Sage Publications, 2007.

McBride III, Lee. "Insurrectionist Ethics and Thoreau," *Transaction of the Charles S. Peirce Society* 49(1) (Winter 2013): 29–45.

McCandless, Peter. *Slavery, Disease, and Suffering in the Southern Lowcountry*. Cambridge, MA: Cambridge University Press, 2011.

Mittelstadt, Jennifer. *From Welfare to Workfare: The Unintended Consequences of Liberal Reform, 1945–1965*. Chapel Hill, NC: The University of North Carolina Press, 2005.

Mirza, Rocky M. *The Rise and Fall of the American Empire: A Re-Interpretation of History, Economics and Philosophy: 1492–2006*. Victoria: Trafford Publishing, 2007.

Moran, Beverly I. *Race and Wealth Disparities: A Multidisciplinary Discourse*. Lanham, MD: University Press of America, 2008.

Moss, Otis. "Civil Rights Leadership Forum," C-SPAN. New York, NY. April 6, 2013. Television.

Mustard, David B. *Racial Justice in America: A Reference Handbook*. Santa Barbara, CA: ABC-CLIO, 2003.

Neubeck, Kenneth J., and Noel A. Cazenave, *Welfare Racism: Playing the Race Card Against America's Poor*. New York: Routledge, 2001.

Okolo, Amechi. *The State of the American Mind: Stupor and Pathetic Docility Volume II: Stupor and Pathetic Docility* Bloomington, IN: xlibris, 2010.

Osborne, Robin. *Athens and Athenian Democracy*. Cambridge, UK: Cambridge University Press, 2010.

Patterson, James T. *America's Struggle against Poverty in the Twentieth Century*. Cambridge, MA: Harvard University Press, 2000.

Payne, B. Keith. "Weapon Bias: Split Second Decisions and Unintended Stereotyping," *Current Directions in Psychological Science* 15(6) (Dec 2006): 287–291.

Pew Research Center, *Stark Racial Divisions in Reactions to Ferguson Police Shooting*, August 18, 2014. Web, September 18, 2014, www.people-press.org/2014/08/18/stark-racial-divisions-in-reactions-to-ferguson-police-shooting/2/.

Pinder, Sherrow O. *The Politics of Race and Ethnicity in the United States: Americanization, De-Americanization, and Racialized Ethnic Groups*. New York: Palgrave Macmillan, 2010.

Pinder, Sherrow O. *Whiteness and Racialized Ethnic Groups in the United States: The Politics of Remembering*. Lanham, MD: Lexington Books, 2012.

Prager, John. "Fox Posts Adorable Video of Black Child, Commenters Go FULL RACIST (Screenshots)," *Americans Against the Tea Party*, August 29, 2014. Web, September 19, 2014, http://aattp.org/fox-posts-adorable-video-of-black-child-commenters-go-full-racist-screenshots/.

Reagan, Ronald. "Gilford New Hampshire Campaign Speech," reprinted in *Welfare in the United States: A History with Documents, 1935–1996*, edited by Permilla Nadasen, Jennifer Mittelstadt and Marissa Chappell: Document 31. New York: Routledge, 2009.

Rich, Robert. "Prominent Black Pastor: Mike Brown Was a Thug." *Mr Conservative*, August 18, 2014. Web, September 10, 2014, http://mrconservative.com/2014/08/47883-prominent-black-pastor-michael-brown-was-a-thug/.

Richardson, Henry. *Democratic Autonomy: Public Reasoning about the Ends of Policy*. Oxford, UK: Oxford University Press, 2002.

Roberts, Dorothy E. *Killing the Black Body: Race, Reproduction, and the Meaning of Liberty*. New York: Vintage, 1999.

Royce, Edward. *The Origins of Southern Sharecropping*. Philadelphia, PA: Temple University Press, 1993.

Samson, Frank L. "Race and the Limits of American Democracy: African Americans from the Fall of Reconstruction to the Rise of the Ghetto," in *The Oxford Handbook of African American Citizenship, 1865-Present*, edited by Henry Louis Gates Jr., Claudia Steele, Lawrence D. Bobo, Michael Dawson, Gerald Jaynes, Lisa Crooms-Robinson and Linda Darling-Hammond, 71–81. Oxford: Oxford University Press, 2012.

Schumpeter, Joseph. *Capitalism, Socialism, and Democracy*. New York: Harper, 1942 (1976).

Scott, Daryl Michael. *Contempt and Pity: Social Policy and the Image of the Damaged Black Psyche, 1880–1996*. Chapel Hill, NC: University of North Carolina Press, 1997.

Scott, Dylan. "Far Right Says Michael Brown's Raps Show He Was a Criminal and a Thug'," *Talking Points Memo*, August 18, 2014. Web, September 10, 2014, http://talkingpointsmemo.com/livewire/michael-brown-rap-lyrics-ferguson-shooting.

Skoll, Geoffrey R. *Social Theory of Fear: Terror, Torture, and Death in a Post-Capitalist World*. New York: Palgrave Macmillan, 2010.

Snowden, Frank M. *Blacks in Antiquity: Ethiopians in the Greco-Roman Experience*. Cambridge, MA: Harvard University Press, 1970.

Staudenmaier, Michael. *Truth and Revolution: A History of the Sojourner Truth Organization, 1969–1986*. Edinburgh: AK Press, 2012.

Sugrue, Thomas J. *The Origins of the Urban Crisis: Race and Inequality in Postwar Detroit*. New Jersey: Princeton University Press, 1996.

Thorley, John. *Athenian Democracy*. New York: Routledge, 1996.

United Press International. "Hug a Thug Fails: National Guard Coming to Ferguson," *GOPUSA*, Acquire Media, August 18, 2014. Web, September 10 2014, www.gopusa.com/news/2014/08/18/hug-a-thug-fails-national-guard-coming-to-ferguson/.

Unnever, J. D. and F. T. Cullen. "Empathetic Identification and Punitiveness: A Middle-Range Theory of Individual Differences," *Theoretical Criminology* 13(3) (2009): 283–312.

USBACKLASH.ORG. "Mobs of Looting Criminal Thugs Again Target Ferguson Businesses While "Riot Friendly" Police Sat Back and Watched," *USBACKLASH.ORG*, 2014. Web, September 10, 2014, http://usbacklash.org/mobs-looting-criminal-thugs-target-ferguson-businesses-riot-friendly-police-sat-back-watched/.

Vadum, Matthew. "Michael Brown: A Criminal and a Thug," *FrontPage Magazine*, August 18, 2014. Web, September 10, 2014, www.frontpagemag.com/2014/matthew-vadum/michael-brown-a-criminal-and-a-thug/.

Valk, Anne, and Leslie Brown. *Living with Jim Crow: African American Women and Memories of the Segregated South*. New York: Palgrave Macmillan, 2010.

Wacquant, Loic. "Deadly Symbiosis: When Ghetto and Prison Meet and Mesh," *Punishment and Society* 3 (2000): 95–134.

Wacquant, Loic. "From Slavery to Mass Incarceration: Rethinking the 'Race Question' in the US," *New Left Review* 13 (2002): 41–60.

Wacquant, Loic. "A Janus-Faced Institution of Ethnoracial Closure: A Sociological Specification of the Ghetto," in *The Ghetto: Contemporary Global Issues and Controversies*, edited by Ray Hutchinson and Bruce Haynes, 1–32. Boulder, CO: Westview Press, 2012.

West, Cornel, and Christa Buschendorf. *Black Prophetic Fire*. Boston, MA: Beacon Press, 2014.

Wolin, Sheldon. "Fugitive Democracy," reprinted in *Democracy and Difference*, edited by Seyla Behabib, 31–45. New Jersey: Princeton University Press, 1996.

Young, Iris Marion. *Justice and the Politics of Difference*. Princeton, NJ: Princeton University Press, 1990.

Young, Iris Marion. *Inclusion and Democracy*. Oxford, UK: Oxford University Press, 2000.

Zinn, Howard. *A People's History of the United States*. New York: Harper Perennial, 1995.

11 Culture of silence and gender development in Nigeria

Gift U. Ntiwunka and Rachael Oluseye Iyanda

Introduction[1]

Gender inequality and violence against the female gender is not a new phenomenon in Africa.[2] These have persisted due to traditional practices, beliefs and discriminatory legislations which forbid women to have a voice in matters concerning them and to also advance in the society. These practices range from domestic violence, child marriages, widowhood rites, female genital mutilation, to inheritance rights that discriminate against women and girls, and polygamy. Women are deprived of their fundamental rights such as the right to human dignity, right to education, right to employment, freedom of expression, right to property and inheritance, right to fair hearing, reproductive rights, other social and political rights and freedom from violence and all forms of discrimination amongst others.

The patriarchal nature of many African societies, by which men dominate every sphere of life, has worsened the situation as the fate of women is determined by men. Women are seen as subordinate to the men and are denied certain roles in the society. Obasola opines that "these inhibitions imposed on women by culture and in most cases religion has negatively affected their positions in the society," as well as their contribution to national development.[3] For example, over 70 percent of the women population in Nigeria, (which makes up about 50 percent of the whole) are living below the international poverty line of one dollar per day.[4] This implies that majority of them cannot make meaningful contributions to the development of their homes, communities and country.

Governments at the international level have concluded treaties, conventions and declarations which states are expected to key into and domesticate at the state level in order to protect the rights of women. These include the African Charter on Human and Peoples' Rights (the Maputo Protocol), which asserts the right of women by guaranteeing that they have social and political equality with their male counterparts and also control their own reproductive health;[5] the Beijing Declaration of the Fourth World Conference on Women 1995; Convention on the Elimination of All Forms of Discrimination Against Women (CEDAW), ratified as of March 2014 by 187 countries out of the 194 member states of the United Nations;[6] International Covenant on Civil and Political

Rights; International Convention on Economic, Social and Cultural Rights; Convention Against Torture and Other Cruel, Inhuman or Degrading Treatment or Punishment;[7] and the Sustainable Development Goals. In addition to these, the constitution of a country is expected to spell out the fundamental rights of citizens and how these rights are to be protected. For instance, in Nigeria, the rights are contained in Chapter 4 of the 1999 constitution. The National Gender Policy was introduced in 2006 to promote equal and fair treatment of men and women, prevent and eliminate violence against women and encourage women empowerment programs.[8]

It is unfortunate that not all countries in Africa have been able to domesticate these international human rights instruments. Additionally, not all that have domesticated them have been able to enforce them. As at 2011, the African Charter on Human and Peoples' Rights signed by forty-six out of the fifty-three African countries had been ratified by only thirty countries.[9] The inability of states to curtail cultural anachronisms and legislations which prevent women from having equal rights as their male counterpart to a great extent contributes to the silence by women.

Culture of silence is a situation whereby women who have been sexually assaulted and/or whose rights have been denied in other ways due to discriminatory laws and traditional practices refuse to speak out for fear of discrimination, exploitation and stigmatization by men and the society at large. This is coupled with the fact that the services and support systems needed to protect and defend them are sometimes ineffective. It is true that the "majority of women in Nigeria and Africa at large suffer one form of violence or another but have unfortunately and helplessly accepted the maltreatment as the norm rather than the exception."[10] A culture of silence coupled with weak laws and limited support for victims of violence against women and girls are the reasons for the increase in the violation of women's fundamental human rights. India and South Africa are top on the list of countries with a high rate of Gender Based Violence.[11]

This chapter therefore addresses how a culture of silence has undermined women development in Africa and examines the interface between culture of silence and development which is defined as "a multidimensional process involving major changes in social structures, population attitudes and national institutions, as well as the acceleration of economic growth, the reduction of inequality, and the eradication of poverty."[12] Its essence is to increase the availability and widen the distribution of basic life; raise the level of living through increase in income, provision of more jobs, better education and greater attention to cultural and human values and expand the range of economic and social choices available to individuals and nations.[13]

The theory adopted for this analysis is the Gender and Development theory (GAD) which emerged in the late 1980s as a pre-Beijing perspective in response to the failure of the Women in Development (WID) approach to change the lives of women and influence the broader development agenda.[14] GAD involves the social, economic, political and cultural forces which determine how men and women participate in, benefit from and control project resources and activities differently.[15] GAD examines women's material conditions and class positions as well as the patriarchal structure and ideas that define and maintain women's subordination.[16] The theory "seeks to ensure that all decisions concerning development are reached through the local equitable participation of men and women in the development process."[17] GAD supports gender equality and promotes treaties, conventions, declarations and policies that promote human rights and advancement of women.[18]

This chapter is structured into four parts: the introduction presents the problem of study as well as the theoretical underpinnings for the analysis in the chapter; the second section reviews the literature pertaining to issues, problems and policies associated with gender equality and inequality in Africa; the third section discusses the influence of silence on development in Africa; the fourth section is a conclusion which highlights the possible remedies to the challenges posed by the issues raised in the chapter.

Gender inequality in Africa: issues, policies, problems

Although power imbalance and structural inequality exist between men and women, the role of women in development in Africa cannot be overemphasized.[19] Women have made significant contributions in the area of agriculture and industry even though they are found mainly in the informal sector with minimal access to finance. In spite of this, women on the continent are yet to achieve their full potentials due to restrictive practices, discriminatory laws and the highly segmented labor markets. Many are yet to be fully mobilized and empowered to contribute to national development.[20]

Domestic violence is an inhuman treatment that some African cultures promote. This involves physical, sexual or psychological harm or suffering to women. Such cases when reported are very often treated as domestic conflicts that should be resolved at home by the parties involved. Unfortunately the Penal Code[21] and the Sharia legal system in the Northern part of Nigeria give men the permission to violate their wives. Victims of rape are seen as culprits and blamed for the assault on their persons.[22] This promotes a culture of shame and silence and makes it difficult to ascertain the prevalence of violence against women as well as develop measures to curb them. The police and other security agencies that are supposed to defend and protect victims have themselves become perpetrators of rape and sexual exploitation. The recent report of rape and sexual exploitation by members of the security forces of women and girls displaced by Boko Haram in the internally displaced persons' (IDPs) camps in North East Nigeria is an example. According to Human Rights Watch, forty-three cases of rape and sexual exploitations were reported in these IDP camps in July 2016 alone.[23]

Widowhood rites are another "debasing and dehumanizing treatment that culture is unleashing on women after the demise of their husbands."[24] Widows are tortured, exposed to health risks and deprived of their husbands' properties. In some parts of Africa like Nigeria, Uganda and Zambia, women are forbidden from owning properties independent of their husbands. Female children do not inherit any part of their father's properties.[25] This affects their education as many of them withdraw from school due to financial constraints. Moreover, education of the girl child in many communities in Africa is seen as a waste of resources since the girl role is seen as beginning and ending in the kitchen. Even the presence of modern education and socialization has failed to discountenance this belief. In Niger, Chad, Bangladesh and Guinea, girls are given out in marriage at a very tender age.[26] The Child Rights Act of 2003 which was enacted to, among other things, prohibit the betrothal and marriage of children has been passed into law in twenty-four states in Nigeria but it is yet to be fully domesticated.[27]

Marriage for many in Africa is primarily for the purpose of procreation. The woman is voiceless as to whether she will have children or not, the number of children she will have and she does not have the right to abortion.[28] Women who do not have children are ridiculed and oppressed even by their fellow women. The issue of female genital mutilation (FGM) is another abuse of women's reproductive rights. This has resulted in death and other complications as the procedure is often carried out under crude conditions with the use of unsterilized instruments. Women also constitute barriers to one another's development as many have imbibed these practices as normal.

Political institutions and social attitudes also contribute to the subordination of women and unequal gender relations in society. Only a few women occupy key positions in the public and private sector. In Nigeria, women occupy fewer than 30 percent of all posts in the public sector. In South Africa, according to the South African Business Women's Association, women's share of CEOs in 2012 was 3.6 percent. In Kenya, "women hold 44 or 9.5 per cent of the 462 board seats of the fifty-five companies listed in the Nairobi Security Exchange."[29] This implies that women contribute minimally to decision making, leading to low investment in the health and education sectors of the economy which are crucial to human development.[30]

Despite laws, treaties and conventions agreed by governments at the global, national and state levels, these cultural practices persist. Article 2 (1) of the International Covenant on Civil and Political Rights (ICCPR), 1966 states that:

> Each State Party to the present Covenant undertakes to respect and to ensure to all individuals within its territory and subject to its jurisdiction, the rights recognized in the present Covenant, without distinction of any kind, such as race, colour, sex, language, religion, political or other opinion, national or social origin, property, birth or other status.[31]

The article postulates that each party to the Covenant is expected to ensure that all individuals within its territory and all subjects under its jurisdiction have their rights recognized without distinction of any kind, such as race, color, sex, language, religion, political or other opinion. Article 26 below also postulates that all persons are equal before the law and are entitled without any discrimination to the equal protection of the law:

All persons are equal before the law and are entitled without any discrimination to the equal protection of the law. In this respect, the law shall prohibit any discrimination and guarantee to all persons equal and effective protection against discrimination on any ground such as race, colour, sex, language, religion, political or other opinion, national or social origin, property, birth or other status.[32]

In the same vein, the Convention on the Elimination of All Forms of Discrimination against Women (1981) states that:

States Parties shall take in all fields, in particular in the political, social, economic and cultural fields, all appropriate measures, including legislation, to ensure the full development and advancement of women, for the purpose of guaranteeing them the exercise and enjoyment of human rights and fundamental freedoms on a basis of equality with men.[33]

The African Charter on Human and Peoples' Rights (2006), also known as the Banjul Charter, in its Article 2 provides that:

Every individual shall be entitled to the enjoyment of the rights and freedoms recognized and guaranteed in the present Charter without distinction of any kind such as race, ethnic group, colour, sex, language, religion, political or any other opinion, national or social origin, fortune, birth or other status.[34]

Section 42 (1) of the 1999 Constitution of the Federal Republic of Nigeria provides that:

A citizen of Nigeria of a particular community, ethnic group, place of origin, sex, religion or political opinion shall not, by reason only that he is such a person
(a) be subjected either expressly by, or in the practical application of, any law in force in Nigeria or any executive or administrative action of the government, to disabilities or restrictions to which citizens of Nigeria of other communities, ethnic groups, places of origin, sex, religion or political opinions are not made subject; or
(b) be accorded either expressly by, or in the practical application of, any law in force in Nigeria or any such executive or administrative action, any privilege or advantage that is not accorded to citizens of Nigeria of other communities, ethnic groups, places of origin, sex, religion or political opinions.[35]

Based on the provisions of these laws/articles, a woman is entitled to equal treatment as a man, which makes the longstanding argument of traditions unjustifiable on the issue of unequal treatment between men and women.

Customary practices prohibit equality of treatment between men and women. Oraife customary law in Nigeria prohibits women and children from dealing in and owning landed property. They are prevented from having direct link to matters in relation to landed property such as giving evidence in landed property cases. This practice was evident in the Nigerian case Ajajemba Uke and Anor V. Alber Iro,[36] where the defendant wanted to be a witness but was denied the chance to be one on the grounds that she was a woman and was not qualified to give evidence in relation to land by the Nnaeto Custom in Imo state.

In the case of Mojekwu v Mojekwu,[37] it was asserted that the oli-ekpe customs of Nnewi, Anambra State, Nigeria permits the son of the brother of the deceased to inherit property to the exclusion of the daughter of the deceased. Also, in Mojekwu v Ejikeme,[38] the respondent sought to rely on the Nrachi custom where the father may keep a female child in his house and prevent her from marrying as she continues to bear children in her father's house for her father. The Court in the above-mentioned cases found that these practices were repugnant to natural justice, equity and good conscience and so they ought not to stand. This stresses the need for government to eliminate cultural anachronisms that stand in the way of women development and harmonize the laws in its domain.

In its effort to ensure that women contribute to development by participating in national activities like their male counterparts, the Nigerian government adopted the National Gender Policy in 2006 and established institutions that will see to its implementation.[39] The Policy, which is in support of CEDAW and the African Protocol on the Rights of Women in Africa, the 1995 Fourth World Conference on Women in Beijing and the Sustainable Development Goals, is a document prepared by the Federal Government of Nigeria containing its plan toward achieving the equal and fair treatment of men and women, as well as its rationale and objectives.[40]

Based on these situations faced by women, the Policy set out to build a just society devoid of discrimination, harness the full potentials of all social groups regardless of sex or circumstance, promote the enjoyment of fundamental human rights and protect the health, social, economic and political wellbeing of all citizens in order to achieve equitable rapid economic growth and evolve an evidence based planning and governance system where human, social, financial and technological resources are efficiently and effectively deployed for sustainable development.[41]

Even though there are guiding principles, policy delivery strategies and institutional framework provided by Government through the Ministry of Women Affairs and Social Development, these objectives are yet to be achieved. Social, economic, traditional, cultural and religious factors are still forces militating against gender equality in Nigeria. These, for instance, still affect the enrolment of girls in school. Although the number of enrolments into primary and secondary schools has increased, as in many countries in sub-Saharan Africa, equal participation for boys and girls have not been achieved.[42] At the tertiary level, gross enrolment ratio in Nigeria is less than 20 percent. This is also the situation in Angola, Chad, Uganda, Ghana and a host of other countries in sub-Saharan

Africa.[43] According to the Gender Parity Index, sub-Saharan Africa dropped from the sixth to the eighth position on this issue.[44] On political participation, there is low representation of women due to the array of barriers that women face in their quest for full participation in various aspects of social life. For instance in the 2011 elections, only 9 percent of the members of the House of Representatives in Nigeria were women, unlike South Africa and Uganda with 43 percent and 65 percent respectively.[45]

Despite all efforts made by the Nigerian government to give women a voice through the establishment of gender focal points and desks in various ministries, departments, government agencies and inter-ministerial taskforces for particular programs, and the adoption of the National Policy on Women (2000), the Child Rights Act (2003), the National Gender Policy (2006) and the National Gender Strategic Implementation Framework (2008), gender mainstreaming has been faced by a lot of challenges such as inadequate budgetary allocation, poor perception and trivialization of gender issues by policy makers and the general public, and inadequate number of gender experts, amongst others.

Influence of silence on development in Africa

So long as women continue to have less voice, less power, less control over resources and remain vulnerable to violence in their families and the society at large, efforts made toward reducing inequality and development will remain unfruitful. Silence by women means that women will continue to have minimal access to educational, economic, political and social opportunities.

Women in Africa are still denied easy and equal access to education which is vital in the developmental process. This is due to the general belief that women are inferior to men intellectually as well as the high rate of poverty among women. Without education, is would be impossible for women to meet the other aspects of development. Equal opportunity for girls and boys in education

> has a multi-dimensional advantage and a multiplier effect notably because it will help to reduce poverty, lower mortality rates and promote concern for the environment, aside from the opportunity to learn skills and acquire knowledge that will encourage their participation in the development process through social, economic and political decision-making. On the other hand, blocked or limited access to quality education increases girls' vulnerability to abuse exploitation, disease, poverty and crime. Studies have shown that allowing girls to have full access to education is the single most effective policy of enhancing the overall level of economic productivity.[46]

Women's access to employment in Nigeria has also been limited especially in the areas of trade, industry and governance. Figures from the National Bureau of Statistics (2013) show that labor force participation rate was 64.5 percent for women and 70.3 percent for men. In the State Civil Service, from 2010 to 2013 women occupied 35.5 percent of senior positions compared to 64.5 percent by men.[47] Also at the National Parliament 93.6 percent of the representatives were men with the remaining 6.4 percent only being women.[48]

Women have been silenced even when they have suggestions that can promote the advancement of their homes, communities and nations. Even though the few women in key positions have made meaningful contributions to development, there is still much to be done. This is evident in the national budget which is gender insensitive, and also in poor gender mainstreaming in all political, economic and societal spheres. Health is wealth but the silence by women results in serious health challenges. Female Genital Mutilation results in stillbirth, HIV and other deadly diseases, and death. Fertility rates have been rising in Africa meaning that more women are exposed to risks associated with child birth. In Nigeria, the total fertility rate rose from 4.7 in 1999 to 5.7 in 2008.[49] This implies that a country will one day have more people than it can cater for. This also has a ripple effect on development.

No significant progress has been recorded in the area of female mortality as many women do not have access to quality reproductive and sexual health information, education and services. Child marriage is proof that women are perceived as having no other role except for housekeeping and childbearing. Exposure to domestic violence and rape does not only traumatize women but increases their vulnerability to HIV/AIDS. Health issues will therefore persist as long as government fails to enforce laws which promote gender equality, give women voice, power and control over resources and enable them achieve their full potentials.

Although governments have introduced empowerment programs to enable women have access to health care, employment and education, as well as eliminate discrimination and all forms of violence against women, and change social attitudes and traditional practices, women are still marginalized. Many women, especially those in the rural areas, do not have access to these programs. The few skills acquisition centers are usually situated in the urban areas. The inability of women to secure financial empowerment limits their access to economic stability and independence. According to Reeves and Baden, "empowerment of women does not mean women taking over positions held by men but the need to transform the nature of power relations."[50] Having more women in power will help address some of the issues that affect women especially, resulting in the reduction of poverty, unemployment, conflict and diseases.[51]

Moreover, policies made and institutions set up by the government have not lived up to expectations. They have failed to fulfil the purposes for which they were established. These include the legal system, law enforcement agencies and ministries and other agencies saddled with the responsibility of making sure that the rights of women are guaranteed and protected. The application of laws by the customary courts, for instance, is inconsistent especially when it involves women seeking redress for violations. Women associations have not done much in this regard. Women themselves have also contributed to their situation; some have accepted their plight as a cross which they must carry, while others believe in male headship and therefore will oppose any move made by fellow women to occupy key positions in the society.

Conclusion

Culture of silence has done more harm than good to the female folks and as long as negative traditional practices, beliefs and discriminatory legislations continue to exist, the rights of women will be jeopardized. This does not only deny them of their rights but increases their vulnerability and limits their contribution to national development. African governments therefore need to rise to the challenge and ensure full domestication and implementation of all policies pertaining to gender equality. Perpetrators of these dehumanizing acts should be brought to book.

Community leaders should be re-educated on the dangers of these barbaric traditional practices and beliefs, not just to the women but the society at large. They need to know the important role that women can play in the development of the communities and the nation as a whole. With this done, it is expected that the leaders will initiate dialog with their people on the subject. Women associations should double efforts in educating women on their rights and how to seek redress when they are infringed upon. This is very important as a lot of women do not know their rights. Women need to be enlightened on the dangers that these cultural practices pose to their lives. They should be united and speak with one voice.

Finally, government should strengthen existing empowerment programs and initiate more so that more women will be educationally, socially, economically and politically empowered. By so doing many of them will achieve their full potentials and be able to contribute meaningfully to the development of their societies

Notes

1 The opening arguments of this chapter have previously appeared in a much older version of the paper published as Gift U. Ntiwunka, "Why Women Do Not Benefit from Nigeria: An Assessment of Project Implementation in a Federal Ministry," *International Journal of Innovative Research and Development* 3(1) (May 2014): 735, 736. The full page span of the article is 733–741.

2 Regina Arisi and Patrick Oromareghake, "Cultural Violence and the Nigerian Woman," *African Research Review* 5(4) (July 2011), 370.

3 K. E. Obasala, "Gender Discrimination and Cultural Anachronisms in African Societies: Implication for Girl Child Education," *International Journal of Social Sciences and Education* 3(4) (2013): 1027–1037.

4 Agabus Pwanagba, "70% of Nigerian Women are Living below Poverty Line-Minister," *National*, July 13, 2013, www.dailypost.ng.

5 The World Bank, *World Development Report on Gender Equality and Development* (Washington, DC: International Bank for Reconstruction and Development, 2012), 1–458, https//siteresources.worldbank.orgINTDR2012/Resorces/7778105-129969996 8583/7786210-13159362.

6 Feminist Majority Foundation, "Ratifying CEDAW," Feminist Majority Foundation, March 2014, www.feminist.org; CEDAW, "Women Senators Made the CEDAW Connection to Ending Violence Against Women and Girls," Communication Consortium Media Centre, June 26, 2014, cedaw2015.org.

7 Olusesan Oliyide and Olu Awolowo, *Rights* (Lagos: Throne-of-Grace Limited, 2006), 15.

8   "Federal Ministry of Information Nigeria, FG to Review 2006 National Gender Pol-
    icy—Women Ministry," Press Release December 1, 2011, http://fmi.gov.ng/fg-to-
    review-2006-national-gender-policy-%E2%80%93-women%E2%80%99s-ministry/.
9   The World Bank, *Development Report*, 2012.
10 Arisi and Oromareghake, "Cultural Violence," 370.
11 Channels Television, "Culture of Silence in Nigeria and Rising Gender Based Viol-
    ence," December 14, 2014.
12 Michael Todoro and Stephen Smith, *Economic Development*, 8th edition (India:
    Pearson Education, 2004), 17.
13 Gift U. Ntiwunka, "Gender and National Development: The Role of Ogun State Min-
    istry of Women Affairs and Social Development," *Journal of Research and* Develop-
    ment 1(6): (2013), 2.
14 Hazel Reeves and Sally Baden, "Gender and Development: Concepts and Defini-
    tions," Gender Mainstreaming Internet Resource Report No 55, Department for Inter-
    national Development (DIP) (February, 2000).
15 United Nations International Research and Training Institute for the Advancement of
    Women (United Nations INSTRAW) *Glossary: Related Terms and Concepts* (United
    Nations, March 21, 2011), 2.
16 Patricia Connelly, Tania Murray Li, Martha MacDonald and Jane Parpart, "Feminism
    and Development: Theoretical Perspectives," in *Theoretical Perspectives on Gender
    and Development*, edited by Jane Parpart, M. Patricia Connelly and V. Eudine Barri-
    teau (Canada: International Development Centre, 2000), 51–161.
17 Suzanne Williams, Janet Seed and Adelina Mwau, *The Oxfam Gender Training
    Manual* (Oxfam: UK and Ireland, 1994).
18 Ntiwunka, "Gender," 5.
19 UN General Assembly, "Intensification of Efforts to Eliminate All Forms of Violence
    Against Women: Report of the Secretary General," August 4, 2008, A/63/214; Sharon
    Smee, *Wall of Silence: A Look at Violence Against Women in Northern Zanzibar*
    (Tanzania: ActionAid International 2012), IV.
20 Timothy Okemakinde, "Women Education: Implications for National Development in
    Nigeria," *European Journal of Globalization and Development Research* 9(1)
    (2014), 554.
21 Penal Code (Nigeria). Section 55 (1).
22 Oliyide and Awolowo, *Rights*, 138.
23 *Daily Times*, "Sexual Exploitation of IDPs: Human Right Watch," November 9, 2016;
    Henry Onukwuba, "Human Rights Report: The Girls Deserve a Life Too," *Daily
    Times*, November 3, 2016.
24 Obasala, "Gender Discrimination," 1029.
25 Oliyide and Awolowo, *Rights*, 133; Mary Kimani, "Women Struggle to Secure Land
    Rights: Hard Fight for Access and Decision-making Power," *Africa Renewal*, 2012;
    www.un.org.
26 United Nations Children's Fund, "Ending Child Marriage: Progress and Prospects,"
    UNICEF, New York, 2014, https://unicef.org.
27 United Nations Children's Fund, "Child Right Legislation in Nigeria, UNICEF
    Nigeria—Fact Sheet," 2011, 1–2, www.unicef.org/nigeria/child_legislation_in_
    Nigeria.pdf.
28 Oliyide and Aolowo, *Rights*, 136.
29 International Labour Organization, "More Women Needed at Top Management posi-
    tion in Africa," Press Release, January 12, 2015.
30 British Council of Nigeria, *Gender in Nigeria Report 2012: Improving the Lives of
    Girls and Women in Nigeria, Issues, Policies, Actions*, 2nd edition (British Council
    Nigeria, 2012), v, www.britishcouncil.org/site/default/files/british-council-gender-
    nigeria2012.pdf.

31 International Convention on Civil and Political Rights (ICCPR). Ratified in Nigeria July 29, 1993. Article 2(1).
32 ICCPR, 26.
33 Convention on the Elimination of All Form of Discrimination Against Women, 1981. Article 3.
34 African Charter on Human and Peoples' Rights, 2006, 2.
35 The Constitution of the Federal Republic of Nigeria, 1999. Section 42(1).
36 Ajajemba Uke and Anor V. Alber Iro, 2001. II N. W. L. R. (Pt. 723).
37 Mojekwu V Mojekwu, 1997, N. W. L. R. (Pt. 512) 283.
38 Mojekwu v Ejikeme, 2000, 5 N. W. L. R. (Pt. 657) 402.
39 Federal Ministry of Information, "Gender Policy," 2011; F. Ekong. "Contributions of Women to National Development: Examples from Akwa Ibom State," Stud Home Comm. 2(2).
40 *Voice of America*, "Nigerian Women Lobby for Equal Rights," March 4, 2008, www. voanews.com/content/a-13-2008-03-04-voa26/339914.html; Gift U. Ntiwunka, "Why Women Do Not Benefit from Nigeria: An Assessment of Project Implementation in a Federal Ministry," *International Journal of Innovative Research and Development* 3(1) (May 2014): 735.
41 National Coalition on Affirmative Action (NCAA), *National Gender Policy*, (NCAA: 2006), www.aacoalition.org/National_Policy_Women.htm. Ntiwunka, "Why Women Do Not Benefit from Nigeria," 736.
42 United Nations Educational Scientific and Cultural Organization, *World Atlas on Gender Equality in Education* (France: UNESCO, 2012), 22.
43 United Nations, *Gender Equality in Education*, 75.
44 Ibid., 75.
45 British Council Nigeria, *Gender in Nigeria Report 2012*, 55.
46 Kelly Ejumudo, "Gender Equality and Women Empowerment in Nigeria: The Desirability and Inevitability of Pragmatic Approach," *Developing Country Studies* 3(4) (2013): 61.
47 National Bureau of Statistics, *Statistical Report on Women and Men in Nigeria 2013* (National Bureau of Statistics, December 2014), www.nigerianstat.gov.ng/pdf uploads/2014, 20.
48 National Bureau of Statistics, *Statistical Report*, 23.
49 The World Bank, *Development Report*, 25.
50 Reeves and Baden, "Gender and Development," 35.
51 The World "Chapter 2: What is Empowerment?" http://siteresources.worldbank.org/ INTEMPOWERMENT/Resources/486312-1095094954594/draft2.pdf.

Bibliography

African Union, *African Charter on Human and Peoples' Rights*, 2006.
Ajajemba Uke and Anor v Alber Iro. II N. W. L. R. (Pt. 723), 2000.
Arisi, Regina and Patrick Oeomareghake. "Cultural Violence and the Nigerian Woman," *African Research Review* 5(4) (July 2014): 369–381.
British Council Nigeria, *Gender in Nigeria Report 2012; Improving the Lives of Girls and Women in Nigeria, Issues, Policies, Actions*, 2nd edition. Nigeria: British Council, 2012.
Channels Television, "Culture of Silence in Nigeria and Rising Gender Based Violence," December 14, 2014.
Communication Consortium Media Centre. "Women Senators Made the CEDAW Connection to Ending Violence Against Women and Girls," June 26, 2014.
Connelly, Patricia, Tania Murray, Martha MacDonald and Jane Parpart, "Feminism and Development: Theoretical Perspectives," in *Theoretical Perspectives on Gender and*

Development, edited by Jane Parpart, Patricia Connelly and Eudine Barriteau, 65–189. Canada: International Development Research Centre, 2000.

Daily Times of Nigeria. "Sexual Exploitation in IDPs: Human Rights Watch," November 9, 2016, www.dailytimes.ng/sexual-exploitation-idps/.

Ejumudo, Kelly. "Gender Equality and Women Empowerment in Nigeria: The Desirability and Inevitability of a Pragmatic Approach," *Developing Country Studies* 3(4) (2013): 59–66.

Ekong, F. "Contributions of Women to National Development: Example from Akwa Ibom State," *Studies on Home and Community Science* 2(2) (2008): 113–119.

Federal Government of Nigeria. *Millennium Development Goals Report*, 2010, www. mdgs.gov.ng.

Federal Ministry of Information Nigeria. "FG to Review 2006 National Gender Policy— Women Ministry." Press Release December 1, 2011, http://fmi.gov.ng/fg-to-review-2006-national-gender-policy%E2%80%93-women%E2%80%99s-ministry/.

Federal Republic of Nigeria. *Penal Code* (Northern States) Federal Provisions Act (No. 25 of 1960).

Federal Republic of Nigeria. *Constitution of the Federal Republic of Nigeria*, 1999.

Feminist Majority Foundation. "Ratifying CEDAW," March 2014, www.feminist.org/ news/pdfs/CEDAW_2014FMF.pdf.

International Labour Organization. "More Women Needed at Top Management Position in Africa." Press Release January 12, 2015, www.ilo.org/addisababa/media-centre/pr/ WCMS_335704/lang-en/index.htm.

Kimani, Mary, "Women Struggle to Secure Land Rights: Hard Fight for Access and Decision- Making Power," *African Renewal*, Special Edition No. 37 (2012). Available at www.un.org/africarenewal/magazine/special-edition-women-2012/women-struggle-secure-land-rights.

Mojekwu v. Ejikeme. 5 N. W. L. R. (Pt. 657) 402, 2000.

Mojekwu v. Mojekwu. N.W.L.R. (Pt. 512) 283, 1997.

National Bureau of Statistics, *Statistical Report on Women and Men in Nigeria 2013*, December 2014, www.nigerianstat.gov.ng/pdfuploads/2014.

National Coalition on Affirmative Action (NCAA), *National Gender Policy*. NCAA: 2006, www.aacoalition.org/National_Policy_Women.htm.

Ntiwunka, Gift U. "Gender and National Development: The Role of Ogun State Ministry of Women Affairs and Social Development," *Journal of Research and Development* 1(6) (2013): 1–10.

Ntiwunka, Gift U. "Why Women Do Not Benefit from Nigeria: An Assessment of Project Implementation in a Federal Ministry," *International Journal of Innovative Research and Development* 3(1) (May 2014): 733–741.

Obasola, K. E., "Gender Discrimination and Cultural Anachronisms in African Societies: Implication for Girl Child Education," *International Journal of Social Science and Education* 3(4) (2013): 1027–1037.

Okemakinde, Timothy. "Women Education: Implications for National Development in Nigeria," *European Journal of Globalization and Development Research* 9(1) (2014): 553–565.

Oladoye, Deji. "In Retrospect: 2011 April Polls and Gender Ranking in Nigeria," May 18, 2011, http://agora.nigeriaelections.org/readMore/221/in_retropect_2011_april_polls_ and_gender_ranking_in_nigeria.

Oliyide, Olusola and Olu Awolowo. *Rights.* Lagos: Throne-of-Grace Limited, 2006.

Onukwuba, Henry. "Human Rights Report: The Girls Deserve a Life Too," *Daily Trust*, November 10, 2016.

Pwanagba, Agabus. "70% of Nigerian Women are Living Below Poverty Line—Minister," *Daily Post*, July 13, 2013, http://dailypost.ng/2013/07/13/70-of-nigerian-women-are-living-below-poverty-line-minister/.

Reeves, Hazel, and Sally Baden. "Gender and Development: Concepts and Definitions," Gender Mainstreaming Internet Resource Report No. 55. UK: Department for International Development, 2000.

Smee, Sharon. *Wall of Silence: A Look at Violence Against Women in Zanzibar*. Tanzania: ActionAid International, 2012.

Todaro Michael, and Stephen Smith. *Economic Development*. India: Pearson Education, 2004.

United Nations. *Convention on the Elimination of All Forms of Discrimination Against Women*, 1979.

United Nations. *International Convention on Civil and Political Rights*. 1993.

United Nations Children's Fund. *Ending Child Marriage: Progress and Prospects.* New York: UNICEF, 2014

United Nations Children's Fund. "Child Rights Legislation in Nigeria," UNICEF Nigeria Fact Sheet, 2011, www.unicef.org/nigeria/child_rights_legislation_in_Nigeria.pdf.

United Nations Educational Scientific and Cultural Organization. *World Atlas on Gender Equality in Education*. France: UNESCO, 2012.

United Nations General Assembly. "Intensification of Efforts to Eliminate All Forms of Violence Against Women: Report of the Secretary General," August 4, 2008, A/63/241.

United Nations International Research and Training Institute for the Advancement of Women (United Nations INSRAW). *Glossary: Related Terms and Concepts*, United Nations, March 21, 2011.

Voice of America. "Nigerian Women Lobby for Equal Rights," March 4, 2008, www.voanews.com/content/a-13-2008-03-04-voa26/339914.html.

Williams, Suzanne, Janet Seed and Adelina Mwau. *The Oxfam Gender Training Manual*. UK and Ireland: Oxfam, 1994.

World Bank. "Chapter 2: What is Empowerment?", 2011, http://siteresources.worldbank.org/INTEMPOWERMENT/Resources/486312-1095094954594/draft2.pdf.

World Bank. *World Development Report 2012 on Gender Equality and Development*. Washington, DC: International Bank for Reconstruction and Development, 2012, https//siteresources.worldbank.orgINTDR2012/Resorces/7778105-1299699968583/7786210-13159362.

12 Emasculation, social humiliation and psychological castration in Irene's *More than Dancing*

Mobolanle E. Sotunsa and Francis O. Jegede

Introduction

This chapter examines emasculation as a socio-political condition in which a man is rendered effeminate and castrated in the performance and enactment of sex roles and traits socially constructed for him in a social milieu. It further investigates the reasons and effects of such incapacitation, that results in social humiliation and abuse of identified characters in Irene Isoken-Salami's *More than Dancing*. The analysis was done using a critical and in depth textual analysis of the selected text for the study. Using psychoanalysis and masculinity as theories, the chapter investigates male characters who become victims of emasculation as a result of women's solidarity, conspiracy of silence, male domination and fear of being called weak. The chapter uncovers the fact that emasculation usually results from male domination or fear of domination by the oppressed individual as a defense mechanism. The study also shows that although men have been constructed as breadwinners, or as husbands who are strong, emotionless and rational, there are men who are unable to perform these roles or enact the traits socially constructed for them. Creative writers should therefore focus attention on men's social dynamics beyond women oppression by men, and by so doing men will not be understood from women's perspective only.

Men's portrayal as strong, rational, powerful, aggressive, emotionless and reliable in their roles as father and breadwinner, as compared to women believed to be dependent, weak and emotional puts men under pressure of compliance.[1] No doubt, there are hierarchies among men, especially in the enactment of traits and exhibition of sex roles. Every man, no matter the social status, is expected to meet up with this social construction according to the gender role socialization of a particular cultural setting. However, the inability to meet up with this social construction of roles of course makes the man lose significant self-worth. His incapacitation leads to humiliation and diminishing self-esteem. According to O'Neil and Nadeau humiliation means "to reduce to a lower position in one's eyes or others' eyes; to mortify or abuse; to be extremely destructive to one's self-respect or dignity."[2] This is a function of failure to conform to one's gender-role socialization. Gender-role socialization refers to how a man is socialized in a society to learn masculine attributes that differentiate him from women. Patriarchal society is particularly indicted here as the "spawning ground for men's sexism and violence towards women."[3] According to these authors, "the larger patriarchal society, sexism, and gender-role stereotypes are shown as organizers of our society. Patriarchy instils sexist values and stereotypes that influence how men relate to women, to other men and to themselves."[4]

The individual man whose role has been defined in the society where he socialized from infancy to boyhood and then to adulthood knows what it feels like not to meet up with the specification scripted for him as a male member of the society. This condition increases personal and interpersonal tension and pressure on the male character which may force him to build some self-protective defense mechanism against threats to his gender-role identity. The male character becomes vulnerable and eventually emasculated when the self-protective defense mechanisms break down. All these psychological and gender-role dynamics are explored in Irene Isoken-Salami's play, *More than Dancing*.

This study adopts psychoanalysis and masculinity theory in exploring issues of emasculation, social humiliation and psychological castration in the text. Psychoanalysis was originally used to examine ethical wrongdoing, guilt and the relationship between bottled up emotion or unconscious repressed aggressive feelings and violent outbursts of identified characters. According to Freud, some human behaviors, thoughts and fears considered too bizarre or unacceptable in the social system are said to be repressed into the unconscious state of mind as a form of defense mechanism. The majority of these repressed thoughts or desires are expressed in dreams.[5] As a theory, the psychoanalytic approach has been adopted for use from different perspectives including the Biological, Anthropological, Psychological and Sociological perspectives.

Masculinity, on the other hand, has been used as a tool for the analysis of "ways of being and becoming a man in a given culture."[6] Masculinity, therefore, provides the basis for the understanding of men's lives and experiences as gendered beings "rather than maintaining the patriarchal arrogance that our lives are the lives of generic human beings."[7] Psychoanalysis was adopted in this study to probe into the minds of the emasculated characters and masculinity was used to investigate gender role socialization of the male characters in the text.

More than Dancing: a synopsis

More than Dancing is an exciting political play that opens with women in vigorous dancing on a political campaign ground to entertain spectators and party supporters. Women groups from different regions of Nigeria dance, to the admiration of party supporters and political bigwigs who have already arranged for two bags of rice, a bag of salt, a carton of Maggi cubes seasoning and two fabric rolls for each group.

However, midway into the groups' dancing, Madam Bisi Adigun, the Woman Leader for United People's Liberation Party (UPLP) ordered that the women should stop the dance. She expressed her disapproval of the despicable treatment of women in the party, resulting in a situation in which the only value attached to them came from dancing and entertaining their male compatriots in the party. According to her, UPLP is a "party for men, donated by men, safeguarded by men."[8] Critically appraising the party structure, Madam Bisi reveals that "Men are chairpersons, secretaries, vice chairpersons, treasurers, public relations officers, welfare officers, financial secretaries, publicity secretaries.... They are members of the Board of Trusties,"[9] leaving no significant party positions for women party members.

Madam Bisi's attitude stunned the party executives who, of course, are men. Among them are Alhaji Sani, top male member; Mr Femi, UPLP National Treasurer and Mazi Madu, UPLP National Secretary. With Madam Bisi are other top female members of the party such as Prof Nona Odaro, Hajia Aisha Gambo, Madam Ebele, Madam Omozele, Madam Boma and Madam Alero among others who have resolved to select a female presidential flagbearer for the party. The choice falls on Prof Nona Odaro, who at first declines because of lack of political experience but is later convinced to take up the gauntlet. When the women's move gets to the ears of the party executives, a meeting is called for amicable resolution of the conflict, which both sides agree has the potential to spell doom for the party in the forthcoming polls. However, all efforts to cajole, lure, intimidate and even entice the women, even with a ten million naira bribe, fail. The meeting ends without the women revealing their plans, since the men refused to support women candidacy but rather prefer that Prof Nona becomes the running mate to Alhaji Bala, a male presidential candidate. On the night of the meeting, the women surprise everyone as Nona's posters have adorned every street and mobilization has started in every nook and cranny of the country.

The intra-party election takes place and Nona becomes victorious as the first female presidential flagbearer and subsequently, the first female president of the nation—to the consternation of the male political pundits who vowed that a woman would never be their head. However, when news filters to them—Mazi Madu, Sani, Femi etc.—that celebration was ongoing at the stadium, they swallow their pride to participate. In fact, the most virulent among them, Alhaji Sani, collects the fan from Uyi, president-elect Nona's husband, and starts fanning her. The table, according to Mazi Madu, "turned so fast."[10]

Male characters like Mazi Madu and Alhaji Sani have a gender role socialization that gives them the impression that men are superior to women in all spheres of life, especially in politics. This orientation informs why men practically hijacked all top positions in the United People's Liberation Party and controlled the party structure. According to these men, politics is the exclusive preserve of men who can only be magnanimous by conceding less important political positions to women. Male political stalwarts in the party therefore believe that they are more rational, independent-minded and more qualified to hold sensitive political positions than women. This gender role socialization heightens men's emasculation when Nona, a university professor and woman presidential flagbearer wins a landslide victory by defeating the male candidate foisted on the party by men. For instance, Mazi Madu, Alhaji Sani and Femi who vow never to live in a country ruled by women, have to swallow their pride to join Nona in celebrating her victory at the poll.

Concept of emasculation

Emasculation is a state of being deprived of virility and vigor. It is a form of castration and unmanly weakness. Male Emasculation also results from oppression, either by female or male, that makes a man suffer psychological castration in the performance of roles and exhibition of traits that validate him as a man/boy/male. By male emasculation, we mean a social condition so created to make a man less masculine psychologically, materially, culturally and in terms of social responsibilities.[11]

O'Neil and Nadeau define emasculation as the "fear of losing masculine status and power in the eyes of others."[12] According to them, emasculation is one of the fears associated with gender-role schemas which can be experienced consciously and unconsciously and has the capacity to "play a significant role in males' interpersonal relationships with both men and women." O'Neil and Nadeau posit that:

> One of men's greatest fears is to be emasculated. To be emasculated means to be deprived of virility or procreative powers; to be castrated; to be deprived of masculine energy, vigour, or spirit; to be weakened; to be unnerved by others in terms of your masculine gender-role identity. In short, emasculation means losing one's masculine identity and energy. Being emasculated is part of almost every boy's and man's gender-role identity development. He may feel emasculated by devaluing comments, failures, sexual dysfunctions, and perceived losses of control and power.[13]

Such men are seen in their society as failures, useless and lazy. For instance, in all Buchi Emecheta's novels, her male characters are said to be "irresponsible heads of families who are mostly insensitive to the needs of their wives and children."[14] This statement, true as it sounds, fails to consider social condition(s) that create these characters in those contexts.

The question is, what is the social construction of these male characters in terms of role performance and trait exhibition that make them insensitive and irresponsible? No doubt, certain social conditions have created these men who are products of unrealized ambition and failed aspirations as social lepers, failures and unlucky beings. Jeffrey Hamtover argues that to be masculine is "a cultural construct and adult men need the opportunity to perform normatively appropriate male behaviours."[15] As a social construct, therefore any denial of opportunity to perform the socially constructed roles emasculates the man. He becomes subordinated to the social group behavior regarded as the standard. Such men see themselves as outcasts and social misfits not by any fault of theirs but the way opportunities are structured. Hamtover refers to this as "masculinity anxiety" which arises when adult men know the script and wish to perform according to the directions but are denied the opportunity to act: the fault lies in social structuring of opportunities and not in individual capabilities and motivations.

Masculinity entitlements and castration anxiety in *More than Dancing*

Masculinity entitlements refer to the privileges and rights conferred on the male gender in a sexist society. This, Kimmel refers to as public patriarchy, an "institutional arrangement of a society, the performance of males in all power positions within the economy and polity, both locally and nationally, as well as 'gendering' of those institutions themselves."[16] By this notion of entitlement, men see the spheres of politics and economy as their exclusive preserve in any society such that female participation becomes an aberration. For men, their ability to defend and sustain these privileges prove their manhood but when it breaks down, they become vulnerable and emasculated. This dimension to gender relations plays out significantly in the political struggle between dominant men politicians and the women in United People's Liberation Party (UPLP), in *More than Dancing*. In the same vein, Freud uses his Oedipus project to explain how a "young boy forms an erotic attachment to his mother and unconsciously grows to desire her" while resenting his father.[17] At age five, the boy has to repress his sexual desires and identify with his father due to fear of castration. This is what is referred to as castration anxiety from a psycho-sexual point of view. Scholars however, have developed Freudian castration anxiety to also include deviation from masculinity's social norms where the male child is socialized as breadwinner, rational, aggressive and privileged within the context of Kimmel's public patriarchy. Kaufman says:

> Boys internalize "our culture's definition of 'normal' or 'real' man; ... 'strong' and 'hard' not 'soft,' 'weak,' 'yielding,' 'sentimental,' 'effeminate,' 'passive.' To deviate from this definition is not to be a real man. To deviate is to arouse (what Freud called) 'castration anxiety'."[18]

This anxiety defines the relationship between men and women both at the public and the domestic spheres; both on the political turf and marriage relationship in *More than Dancing*. It must be emphasized here that until these entitlements are understood and foregrounded, the essence of emasculation will not be appreciated. This is because it takes the one in control of power to understand its dynamics and how it feels like to lose it. In Irene's political setting, men see power as their exclusive preserve and its privileges their entitlement.

It is this sense of entitlement to the control and management of the political party—United People's Liberation Party—that makes Madam Bisi's action an affront to men who could not comprehend her audacity to stop women dancing to entertain the spectators and party loyalists. Her speech, like a long manifesto, infuriates the men:

BISI: Stop I say!!! Enough of the dancing! … Year in year out, primaries come and party elections go, all we do is dance…. The men have since stopped dancing, Look at the high table (*points at the top row where the dignitaries are seated*). How many women do you see up there? The seats are filled with men. Where are the women? … Look at us (*points at the lower seats*) applauding the winning team. Look at us (*pointing at the dancers*) dancing and collecting two bags of rice, one bag of salt, one carton of Maggi cubes and two wrappers to be shared among thirty-five women!

(1–2)[19]

Madam Bisi's speech set the tone for the eventual political emasculation of the men in the play. First, the speech is a challenge to men's dominant political role as the prime movers and managers of the party. Madam Bisi, the Woman Leader, stirs the hornets' nest by challenging male political entitlements and rights entrenched and sustained from ages past. This, Mazi Madu, the Party National Secretary, steps out to correct, as he says in anger:

MADU: Madam Bisi, just who do you think you are that you disperse the dance troupes that our party has funded? What do you think you are doing? Mr Chairman sir, Madam Bisi must be called to order.[20]

Part of masculinity entitlements is for the men to dictate how party structures are run and sustained, including who becomes the flagbearer of the party. It must be noted that Irene Isoken's setting in *More than Dancing* is a social environment not ripe enough to tolerate women in political leadership. Political leadership is considered as the entitlement of men and in this lies their pride as "real men." Sani reiterates this when he reminds the women:

SANI: You are not ripe enough to lead. Your time has not come, Wait for your time. Don't jump the gun.[21]

Madam Bisi's pontification about equal representation is seen especially by Alhaji Sani, a top male member of UPLP, as spurning men's traditional hegemonic position in all ramifications. In this play, men do not see domination and control as forms of oppression as Madam Bisi Adigun will want to make people believe, but a natural process of patriarchal subordination of women to men. No wonder, when Bisi warns against perpetuating the traditional role of women as house wives whose place is in the kitchen and not the public arena, Sani is quick to ask rhetorically:

SANI: Is that not true? When you get home this evening where will you end up? In the kitchen, of course! That is the reality.[22]

This sentiment has been so long entrenched that it has become the norm—the unwritten law imbibed and even supported by fellow women. To advocate that men should come down from this political Olympian height is to ask for the impossible because it is the way men have been socialized to act, passed to them from their ancestors. This is vintage masculinity entitlement, and all other perks that accrue to the man as dividends of his gender identity within the social and historical context. Madam Minika, one of the top female members of the party also reminds fellow women about this entitlement and the futility of challenging it. She says:

> MINIKA: I have some reservations about this so called "positive step in the right direction." Which direction are we going? UPLP is a men's party. Men basically started it, they fund it: we cannot displace them in their own party. We have to be content with whatever they offer or drop on us for now. Any contrary move now may lead to disaster.[23]

The notion of the ownership of the political party—as Minika says, "in their own party"—has with it a strong bond and emotional attachment by men to what is theirs. It is therefore natural that they will fight to maintain the *status quo* with all resources within their power. Again, because it is also a form of defense and validation of their manhood, it is unthinkable that they will ever lose it to any one, least of all, women. To contemplate loss of power is to live in perpetual fear of emasculation. Not to sustain and retain power is to deviate and be alienated by castration anxiety which in itself is emasculation. Therefore, the morbid fear of deviating from being masculine, including relinquishing exalted political positions which gender identity has privileged as male, drives their opposition against women flag-bearers for the party. It should be noted that this opposition is not only against Nona, the female presidential flagbearer of the party, but against the thought of losing power and control which her presidential ambition could cost them. The implication to their manhood as "real men," integrity, self-esteem and the possible humiliation from women is better imagined than experienced. "One of men's greatest fears is to be emasculated … to be castrated, to be deprived of masculine energy, vigor or spirit; to be weakened; to be unnerved by others in terms of your masculine gender-role identity."[24]

This fear of emasculation plays itself out at the party secretariat where they hold a meeting to counter the women. Sonsare, an Honourable, and top male member of the party, sees the women's action as a challenge to the men:

> SONSARE: Let them have whatever agenda they want; hidden or open, they will go nowhere with it. They have challenged us. We shall let them know that they are up for a fight.
>
> (30)[25]

To Sani, who represents the repressed emotion of many of the men, they have to stop the women at all costs before the women stop them:

> SANI: *Lai lla ila la!*[26] What is this? Men let it be known to you that the moment women domesticate CEDAW; we will become their domestic

servants. We have to stop them before they stop us. Very soon, they will put their babies on our backs, give us the rattle and ask us to sing for the baby to sleep. Not in this our Nigeria. Let it be known to all that whosoever supports them is our enemy.[27]

With twenty four hours to the election, men already see their defeat staring them in the face. It is an ugly experience. The frustration and humiliation of the men are palpable, and boldly written on their faces. Shame, dejection and anger that usually go with defeat or an impending defeat becomes their lot. They suddenly lose energy, vigor and vitality. They become truly emasculated, down and out. Masculinity entitlement is dismantled and privileges gone. More than anything else, the men become vulnerable and weakened. Sonsare who brings the news of Nona's unstoppable route to victory at the polls in less than twenty four hours says "we are finished:"

> SONSARE: Madu, Sani, Terna, we are finished. The women have mobilized the entire nation. They are on national television, radio, the whole town is booming with "Professor Nona for presidency." All Bawa's posters have been replaced with Nona's posters. Right now, they are at the national stadium celebrating Nona's victory. Imagine.[28]

The loss of this entitlement, and the anxiety of being a "Sissy" or subordinated to women create in the men a psychological sense of rejection and loss. Madu, the National Secretary of the party, like his male colleagues feels empty, politically castrated and belittled. He says:

> MADU: The table turned so fast. Yet, they say I am the party secretary? I never got wind of anything.[29]

Part of the expectations of "real men" is the ability to repress emotion because expression of emotion is a sign of weakness, associated only with women. But this barricade is brought down by Nona's victory as the party's flagbearer which they have vowed will never happen. Terna's expression of frustration is a perfect description of an emasculated male character. He says:

> TERNA: We have been marginalized. We better hurry up and join the others, if we don't, our seats in the house will be endangered also.[30]

Forced to bite the dust, the only option left to men, according to Terna, is to swallow their pride to be subordinated to the women-led government. He counsels again:

> TERNA: Well, if we want to be relevant in Nona's government we better move fast.[31]

Emasculation as a social and psychological condition, occurs when men lose the sense of control and power. Sani, who has been on the forefront of opposition to the women, expresses deep emotion when he asks others, rather rhetorically:

> SANI: Are we dreaming? Please, someone tell me. How did they do it? Even our wives said nothing to us. This is discrimination. This is the real exclusion.[32]

It is demeaning. That men are forced down from their Olympian height to bite the dust in defeat is humiliating. It takes from them their sense of worth, self-esteem and pride, given their highly exalted sense of their manhood and hegemony. Those who have vowed never to ever see or witness a female presidential flagbearer, being the first to swallow their pride "rushing out shouting *Gafara gafara don Allah*"[33] reveals the workings of the mind of a defeated man. Madam Bisi finally rubs salt on the men's injury by further humiliating them in a show of triumph and superiority, when she tells a confused and humbled Madu, "this is politics. Mazi, this is the ideal of politics. Now, you know that we are capable of doing more than dancing. "[34]

Sani's response, *Gaskiya ne*[35] (meaning, it is true, I agree with you), *Sanu de aiki*[36] (Good job) is a final submission to defeat. Sani seems to be saying *so this is life*. He feels a sense of defeat, having been humbled by Nona's victory to swallow his pride—he suffers social humiliation. What has just happened to the men is political castration resulting in social and psychological impotence.

Conclusion

Although men have been constructed to be strong, rational, independent and powerful, the plight of male politicians in *More than Dancing* is a pointer to the fact that not all men are capable of enacting these traits at all times and in all circumstances. The refusal by women to support a male flagbearer for the party and the eventual success of the women in producing, for the first time, a female presidential flagbearer actually emasculated the men. The men were politically castrated. Suffice to say that emasculation as a form of castration is a direct result of hyper-masculinity and masculine mystique. The emasculated characters become victims of their tendencies to dominate and oppress others. Therefore emasculation results from the fear of or actual male domination in which the oppressed reacts by putting the oppressor in check. In *More than Dancing*, men's domination of the political terrain forces women to mobilize and turn the political table against them.

Notes

1 M. Kimmel and M. Messner eds., *Men's Lives* (Boston, MA: Allyn and Bacon, 1995).
2 James M. O'Neil and Rodney A. Nadeau, "Men's Gender-Role Conflict, Defense Mechanisms, and Self-Protective Defense Strategies," in *What Causes Men's Violence?* edited by Minhele Harway and James O'Neil (London: Sage, 1999), 98.

3 Ibid., 92.
4 Ibid., 92–93.
5 As cited in B. A. Dobie, *Theory into Practice: An Introduction to Literary Criticism* (Boston, MA: Wadsworth Centage Learning, 2009).
6 Chris Haywood and Mairtin Mac an Ghail, *Social Practices and Cultural Arenas, Institutional Sites* (Buckingham: Open University Press, 2003), 154.
7 H. Brod and Michael Kaufman, *Theorising Masculinities* (London: Sage, 1994), 4.
8 Irene Isoken-Salami, *More Than Dancing* (Jos: Sanitez, 2004).
9 Ibid., 1–2.
10 Ibid., 103.
11 Michael Kimmel, "Globalisation and Its Mal(e)Contents," in *Handbook of Studies on Men and Masculinities*, edited by M. S. Kimmel, J. Hearn and R. W. Connell (London: Sage, 2005).
12 O'Neil and Nadeau, "Men's Gender-Role Conflict," 98.
13 Ibid., 98–99.
14 Oladele Taiwo, *Female Novelists of Modern Africa* (New York: St Martin's Press, 1984), 19.
15 Jeffrey Hamtover, "The Boy Scouts and the Validation of Masculinity," in *Men's Lives*, edited by M. Kimmel and M. Messner (Boston, MA: Allyn and Bacon, 1995), 74.
16 Kimmel, "Globalisation and Its Mal(e)Contents."
17 Dobie, *Theory into Practice*, 54–55.
18 Kimmel and Messner, *Men's Lives*.
19 Irene Isoken-Salami, *More Than Dancing* (Jos: Sanitez, 2004).
20 Ibid., 2.
21 Ibid., 3.
22 Ibid., 5.
23 Ibid., 7.
24 O'Neil and Nadeau, "Men's Gender-Role Conflict," 98–99.
25 Irene Isoken-Salami, *More Than Dancing*, 30.
26 Ibid., 33. *Lai lla ila la* meaning "There is no God but Allah" in Arabic. This is the Hausa's way of lamenting or expressing surprise.
27 Irene Isoken-Salami, *More Than Dancing*, 33.
28 Ibid., 101.
29 Ibid., 103.
30 Ibid., 102.
31 Ibid., 103.
32 Ibid., 102.
33 Ibid., 103. *Gafara gafara don Allah* means "Give way, give way let me pass through for God's sake" in Hausa language.
34 Ibid., 103.
35 Ibid., 104.
36 Ibid., 104.

Bibliography

Brod, H. and M. Kaufman. *Theorising Masculinities*. London: Sage, 1994.
Dobie, B. A. *Theory into Practice: An Introduction to Literary Criticism*. Boston, MA: Wadsworth Centage Learning, 2009.
Freud, S. "Female Society," in *Complete Psychological Works of Sigmund Freud: Standard Edition*, Vol. 21 (1931): 221ff. London: Hogarth.
Hamtover, J. "The Boy Scouts and the Validation of Masculinity," in *Men's Lives*, edited by M. Kimmel and M. Messner, 74–81. Boston, MA: Allyn and Bacon, 1995.

Haywood, C. and M. Mac an Ghail. *Social Practices and Cultural Arenas, Institutional Sites.* Buckingham: Open University Press, 2003.

Isoken-Salami, Irene. *More Than Dancing.* Jos: Sanitez, 2004.

Kaufman. M. "Men, Feminism, and Men's Contradictory Experiences of Power," in *Theorising Masculinities*, edited by H. Brod and M. Kaufman, 142–164. London: Sage, 1994.

Kaufman, M. "The Construction of Masculinity and the Triad of Men's Violence," in *Men's Lives*, edited by M. Kimmel and M. Messner, 3rd edition, 13–25. London: Allyn and Bacon, 1995.

Kimmel, M. "Globalisation and Its Mal(e)Contents," in *Handbook of Studies on Men and Masculinities*, edited by M. S. Kimmel, J. Hearn and R. W. Connell, 414–431. London: Sage, 2005.

Kimmel, M. S and M. A. Messner, eds. *Men's Lives.* Boston, MA: Allyn and Bacon, 1995.

Marsiglio, W. and J. Pleck. "Fatherhood and Masculinities," in *Handbook of Studies on Men and Masculinities*, edited by M. Kimmel, J. Hearn, and R. W. Connell, 249–269. London: Sage, 2005.

O'Neil, J. M., and R. Nadeau. "Men's Gender-Role Conflict, Defense Mechanisms, and Self-Protective Defense Strategies," in *What Causes Men's Violence?* edited by Minhele Harway and James O'Neil, 89–116. London: Sage, 1999.

O'Neil, J. M., and J. Egan. "Abuses of Power against Women: Sexism, Gender Role Conflict, and Psychological Violence," in *Women, Relationships and Power: Implications for Counselling*, edited by E. P. Cook, 49–78. Alexandra, VA: American Counselling Association Press, 1992.

Pleck, E. "Men's Power with Women, Other Men, and Society: A Men's Movement Analysis," in *Men's Lives*, edited by M. Kimmel and M. Messner, 5–12. Boston, MA: Allyn and Bacon, 1995.

Sotunsa M. E. "Globalising the Gender Discourse: A Synthesis of Indigenous African Women's Theory," in *Women in Africa: Contexts, Rights, Hegemonies*, edited by M. E. Sotunsa and O. Yacob-Haliso, 96–107. Lagos: Jedidiah Publishers, 2012.

Taiwo, Oladele. *Female Novelists of Modern Africa.* New York: St Martin's Press, 1984.

Index

Muslim women 198
Muslims 62, 193–4, 197, 204

Namibia 22, 24, 30, 191
Nandzi 113–16
National Bureau of Statistics 246, 250–1
National Coalition on Affirmative Action
  see NCAA
National Council for Women's Societies
  (NCWS) *see* NCWS
national development 240, 242, 248–51
National Gender Policy 241, 245–6, 249–51
National Institute for Policy and Strategic
  Studies 200–3
National Resources Planning Board
  (NRPB) 218, 233, 235
NC 11–14, 101–2, 104, 106–9, 138–9,
  160, 162, 231, 233–4, 236–8
NCAA (National Coalition on Affirmative
  Action) 250–1
NCWS (National Council for Women
  Societies) 197
negotiation 43–4, 47, 49–50, 97
New African Diasporas 206, 209, 222
New Jim Crow 231, 233, 235
New Media 3, 5–6, 64–77, 79–84; in
  Africa 70; age of 64, 66, 68; and society
  80, 82
Nigeria 4, 8–9, 51–2, 72, 75, 78, 80–1, 83,
  127–8, 138–9, 143–4, 159–62, 193–5,
  197, 200–4, 240–51, 260
Nigerian 61, 81–2, 125, 128, 135, 143–5,
  188, 193, 245, 248
Nigerian women 248, 252
Nigeria's Jos crises 188–9, 191, 193, 195,
  197, 199, 201, 203
Njingti 164, 168–9, 173, 181
nkfu 167, 172, 184
NRPB *see* National Resources Planning
  Board
Ntumbaw Villages 164, 174
nuclear families 56–8

Olaiya, Wunmi 8, 145, 152–5, 158–9,
  161–3; performances 155
Old African Diaspora 206, 209
Operation Ghetto Storm 229, 236
oppression 1, 6–7, 9, 69–72, 76, 79, 84, 87,
  91, 96–7, 111, 115, 121, 206, 228
organizations, governmental 3, 188, 191,
  198–9; social 22–3, 25, 38; women's
  189, 192, 196
owners 44–61; former 47, 49–50, 52; slave
  45, 54

owner's families 46, 48
ownership 194, 259
Oyèrónké Oyěwùmí 11–12

Parpart, Jane 249–51
party 67, 90, 194, 242–3, 255, 258–61
passage 50, 116, 133, 218–19
pastors 169, 181, 184, 198
patriarchy 2, 6–9, 20, 65, 69, 113–14, 116,
  121, 148–9, 158, 193
patrilineal 20–1, 25, 28–33
patrilineal societies 20
patrilineality 20, 29–30, 35
PDP (Peoples Democratic Party) 197
peace 9, 77–8, 83, 91, 97, 156, 188–9,
  191–3, 195, 198–201, 203–4;
  entrenching 188–9, 199, 201; restoration
  of 189, 198–9; sustainable 189, 191,
  195, 198–9
peace activists 196
peace processes 192
peacebuilding 188–9, 191, 193, 196,
  198–204
peacemaking roles, women's 192
performances 8, 143–5, 148–56, 158–61,
  253, 257
petit marronage 44–5, 47–8, 50–3
photographs 6, 8, 73, 156–7, 161
photography 73, 80, 83, 102, 107, 156, 161
photos 156–7, 161
pictures 44, 54–5, 58, 73
Plateau State (Nigeria) 188–9, 193–5, 198,
  200–1, 204
police 98, 158, 205–6, 209, 217, 231, 242
police killings 205–6, 208
policies 10, 221, 227, 233, 242, 247–50
political communication in Africa 78, 80,
  83
politics 2, 7, 10, 21, 62–3, 87, 98, 102,
  108, 144, 224–5, 231–3, 236, 255, 261
politics of difference 12, 14, 230, 233–4,
  239
politics of empowerment 11–12
potters 34–5, 204
poverty 8, 194, 213, 219–20, 223–4, 234,
  237, 241, 246–7
poverty and women empowerment 78, 81
power 1–4, 8, 10–13, 18–21, 28–9, 34–6,
  39–40, 120–1, 147–8, 157–8, 165,
  184–7, 256–7, 259, 263; demonic 182;
  female 174; gendered 4, 35; gendered
  nature of 5, 45; occult 185–6
powerlessness 70, 72; women's 180
Prehistory 36, 40–1

Lightning Source UK Ltd.
Milton Keynes UK
UKHW011500030622
403818UK00013B/251